The Visual C++
Construction Kit

A Programmer's Resource

Keith Bugg
Jack Tackett, Jr.

John Wiley & Sons, Inc.
NEW YORK • CHICHESTER • BRISBANE • TORONTO • SINGAPORE

Publisher: Katherine Schowalter
Editor: Paul Farrell
Associate Managing Editor: Jackie Martin
Editorial Production & Design: Editorial Services of New England, Inc.

Library of Congress Cataloging-in-Publication Data
Bugg, Keith (Keith Edward)
    The visual C++ construction kit : a programmer's resource / by
Keith Bugg and Jack Tackett, Jr.
        p.   cm.
    Includes index.
    ISBN 0-471-00961-X (paper/disk)
    1. C++ (Computer program language)   2. Microsoft Visual C++.
I. Tackett, Jack   II. Title
QA76.73.C15B84   1994
005.265—dc20   94-2366
                                                                   CIP

Printed in the United States of America
10 9 8 7 6 5 4 3 2 1

For my parents, Walter and Sally Bugg.

Keith Edward Bugg

To my wife, Peggy, I love you!

Jack Tackett, Jr.

Contents

Preface

This book deals with the Microsoft Visual C++ software development tool for Microsoft Windows. While we recognize that Visual C++ can also be used to create non-Windows programs, our presentation is strictly for the Windows operating environment. The decision behind this approach is based in no small measure on the exploding growth of the Windows user base. Our target audience includes both developers of Windows programs and programmers with intermediate skills. Experienced C programmers who are just beginning the migration to C++, as well as Windows programmers from the SDK environment, should find the material in this book especially illuminating. Beginners, on the other hand, should be aware that this material is not a primer on C++ or Windows development, except in matters regarding conformance of the user interface to established Windows standards. While the novice may find this book useful as a supplement to other study aids or as a reference, it should be understood that the material is presented in a style and manner more befitting an experienced developer. Our intent is to provide a no-frills, no-fluff approach to mastering the use of Visual C++. The climb up the learning curve is steep, but the view from the top is magnificent. Very few object-oriented concepts (e.g., What is a class? What is an object?) are explained here; it is assumed that the reader is comfortable with such abstractions.

This book was born, as the adage says, of necessity. As seasoned Windows developers, we realized the utility offered by Visual C++. As our experience grew, we came to realize there were no "how to" books on this subject, particularly in regard to sample code for the Foundation Classes. Most programmers learn by example; we felt a book that provided snippets of code demonstrating how to do the mundane things most Windows programmers are called upon to do would be quite useful in traversing the "learning curve hump."

The primary tool that we use in getting you over this hump is quite simple: a plethora of coding examples. As software developers, we have all noticed there seem to be recurring themes in our craft. For example, how do you read a data file into a list box? How do you enable/disable menu items? How can you make use of the serial port for communications? Having faced these challenges, aggravated by the paucity of sample code in the Visual C++ documentation, we have collected a representative sample of most of the coding chores facing most Windows developers. While the coding samples presented here may not be the most efficient or elegant, they do work and should form the basis for further exploration and improvement. This treatment of programming concepts by way of examples is intended to assist you in creating discrete, modular coding units that you can connect to construct your Windows application. As the title of this book implies, we hope you will use these much as, say, a plumber connects various pipes and fittings to complete a utility project. As your experience grows, you should be fully able to exploit the fundamental strength of object-oriented programming—reuseable code. As examples are presented, they will be clarified by explanatory text to help you better understand exactly what the code is doing and why. While we've provided a great number of examples, not every chapter has sample code. Some chapters have information on where to find even more information and/or resources. We also explain the sample programs included with Visual C++ and the Tech Notes that accompany the product.

In addition to presenting coding examples, this book also shows you how to make more efficient use of the Visual Workbench. You'll learn how to configure your workspace for your particular needs, how to include tools, and how to import third-party tools such as Visual Basic controls. And we provide you with tips and point out traps to avoid along the way. For example, Visual C++ is intended for the single user and is difficult to use when more than one person is working on the same application. You'll see how to smooth the integration among multiple developers and synchronize your work.

All the samples in this book are included on the accompanying diskette. Each chapter is devoted to a specific concept, such as file I/O, serial port communications, etc. The diskette contains a generic Visual C++ application that incorporates most of the problems you'll encounter during the developement cycle of most projects. This hypothetical application demonstrates how to read data files into list boxes and VBX controls, access the serial port, select fonts, use dialog boxes, etc. Thus, you can skip around to those areas that interest you the most. As an extra bonus, we've included a Windows Help file that you can install under the **Tools** option of the Visual Workbench. This material is basically a combination "electronic index" and online help file for Visual C++, containing many coding examples that you can cut and paste into your applications.

ACKNOWLEDGMENTS

I would like to express my sincere gratitude to the many friends and colleagues who so graciously provided suggestions, coding examples, and encouragement. Their contributions have greatly added to this book's value. In particular, thanks go to Paul Farrell and Allison Roarty at John Wiley & Sons, for their patience and helpful criticisms; to Beckie Heatherly, Romaine Tenney, and Crystal Sloan, for suggesting topics and resources. Also, to good friends Stacy Nelson, Darwin Johnson, Glen Sizemore, and Paul Combs, for their belief in my abilities at times when I doubted my talents. Lastly, I wish to offer my deepest and most heartfelt thanks to a very special teacher, Mr. J.W. Harrell, for fostering my interest in computing, and for making it possible for these things to come to pass. Thanks for the memories.

KEITH BUGG

I would like to thank the following people, for without their help or encouragement, this project would never have come to pass. For that matter, I would never have gotten to where I am today without their help. First to Keith E. Bugg, for having the dream. Thanks, Skipper! Paul Farrell, our editor at John Wiley, for believing in us. I'm glad I met you at Software Development '93 in Santa Clara. My wife Peggy, who had to put up not only with being an "author's widow," but also with a move across the country when I changed jobs in the midst of preparing this book.

   To my colleagues at the Oak Ridge National Lab, whom I miss dearly. Especially Barb Allen, Randy Haese, Lynn Harder, Beckie Heatherly, Janice Ishee, Larry Lane, Juan Lovin, Phyllis Meredith, Suzanne Pratt, Dianna Smith, Romaine Tenney, Bill Thomas, and, of course, John "goose 'em" Amburgey. To my new colleagues at Wandel and Goltermann Technologies, James Danford, Shankar Lascksman, Tom Jennings, Jim Weis, and Craig Anderson, for putting up with me as a new hire and a writer. To my friends Paul Barrett, Gregg Field, David and Lola Gunter, and Joe Williams, the best bunch of people in the world! To Dr. Joseph Daugherty of The University of North Carolina-Asheville and Myrtice Trent of the Blue Ridge Technical Community College, two teachers who inspired me always to do my best and to believe in myself. Thank you, one and all. To Kathy O'Grady, thanks for everything, kat mamma. Finally, to my combined family, the Tacketts and the Martins, thank you all.

JACK TACKETT, JR.

Microsoft Visual C++

Microsoft's innovative Visual C++ development environment signals a new era in Windows programming. Gone are the giant switch statements of SDK fame, gone is the necessity of rewriting essentially the same initialization code for each application, gone is much of the tedium of writing Windows programs.

This chapter introduces you to Microsoft's Visual C++ environment. We will not try to give you blow-by-blow directions for installing the system, since Microsoft's documentation accomplishes that task. Instead you will learn a few tips and tricks for a smoother installation and then get a glimpse of the various components of the new Visual Workbench, which is the integrated environment surrounding Visual C++.

We have tried to organize the chapters in a cohesive order so that you may read this book from cover to cover, but that is not its primary purpose. Instead we intend this book to act as a "construction kit" that enables you to look up a subject and find an answer to your problem, or at the very least a tip on where to find the answer. To accomplish that goal we have included with the book a sample code disk containing a help file and many of the examples presented in this book. You can use these materials to find quick answers to your questions or sections of source code to cut and paste in your applications.

One way in which this book differs significantly from others of its kind is the absence of a full-length sample program in each chapter. Instead, all example programs appear at the end of the book. You will find that plenty of code snippets exist to illustrate each chapter's points and that these transfer with ease to your own applications. After all, why should you reinvent the wheel when someone else has already written the code?

The new application framework, MFC 2.0, provides the developer with over 100 classes that insulate you from the Windows API, but not from the power of the API calls. Microsoft has finally offered a Windows-hosted development environment that, while having some problems, delivers a multitude of development tools tightly integrated within the environment. Microsoft dubbed this new environment the Visual Workbench.

THE VISUAL WORKBENCH

The Visual Workbench is an integrated environment that contains a myriad of new tools, such as a simple source code editor with color syntax checking, a source level debugger, a class browser, a makefile/project tool, and the ability to compile from within the workbench and still perform other tasks while the compilation proceeds in the background.

Microsoft also provides the developer the ability to add other tools to the workbench through a tools menu, as shown in Figure 1.15. The framework pre-installs several tools, including a new integrated resource editor called App Studio and the Windows and MS-DOS versions of CodeView. App Studio replaces the previous dialog, icon, and font editors included with the Windows Software Development Kit (SDK). App Studio is a standalone application that does not require you to have MSVC (the workbench) up and running, but if you do, the two programs will share information. This allows you to create and edit all your Windows resources from within your development environment.

Another feature of the environment is a set of two case tools, called AppWizard and ClassWizard, that automatically generate source code. AppWizard will generate a complete, working, skeletal Windows application without requiring you to write a single line of code! Of course the program will not perform any custom actions—you still have to write some code—but most Windows actions, like printing, help, MDI, and OLE 1.0 support, can be included in your application before you begin writing a single line of code.

The ClassWizard will allow you to generate and add C++ classes to your source files. The power of C++ in an application framework is the ability to map Windows messages to C++ member functions, and that's what ClassWizard allows you to do. Even though you cannot generate and maintain all the classes you need via the ClassWizard, this tool greatly automates class design and maintenance. We will cover most of these tools in later sections or subsequent chapters, but for now we'll give you an overview of the Visual Workbench and some tips on configuring it.

INSTALLING VISUAL C++

Installing Visual C++ can be a pleasant experience or an outright nightmare. Microsoft provides detailed instructions with their documentation, and you should not consider this chapter a substitute for their directions. However, you will learn a few tips here on how to prevent a nightmare. You will also get a quick overview of which files to install based on what you plan to do with Visual C++. If you have already installed the product, you can skip ahead to the section on customizing the workbench for maximum efficiency. Despite some of MSVC's shortcomings, you will find this new environment will increase your Windows productivity.

SYSTEM REQUIREMENTS

Modern day PC development environments require high-powered equipment, and Visual C++ is no exception. You will need at least a 386 processor, 4 megabytes of memory, MS-DOS 5.0 or higher, and Windows 3.1 or higher, running in Enhanced Mode. If you have this equipment, you can run MSVC, but you will *not* be productive. You should plan on at least a 386-33, but we recommend a 486DX 33 or higher, and while 6 megabytes of RAM will get you up, 8 or more will facilitate productivity and eliminate many frustrations, especially when waiting on long links. As for hard drive space, the more the better. The full development system alone will require over 75 megabytes.

Microsoft has made a version of Visual C++ available for Windows NT and for 32-bit Win32s Windows. MSVC 1.0 will not compile programs from within the framework under IBM's OS/2 2.1, even though the Wizards and tools will function. The compiler will not work because the workbench uses a virtual device driver (VxD), which OS/2 does not support. The command line versions will work providing you apply a patch to the the DOS extender, DOSXNT, used by Windows. You can retrieve this file (OS2FIX.ZIP) from CompuServe's MSLANG Library 1 or from Phar Lap's FTP site (ftp.pharlap.com). (See Chapter 18 for more information on developers' help from sources such as Microsoft, CompuServe, and the Internet.)

PRE-INSTALLATION PREPARATIONS

Before starting, make sure you have increased the size of your FILES and BUFFERS statements in your CONFIG.SYS to at least 30 each. You will be swapping twenty high-density disks containing compressed files, so the more buffers available and the more files that can be open, the quicker the installation will proceed. The setup program will ask for at least BUFFERS = 30.

For the next step, make sure you have a disk caching program such as SMARTDRV loaded and that your installation drives are cached. Once you make these changes to your configuration files, you should back up the files and reboot the system so they will take effect. Depending on your processor and disk drives, if you fail to make these changes, your installation could take as long as 3 hours! (The installation should take no longer than 30 minutes with the proper changes.)

Since a full installation can consume over 70 megabytes, your next consideration is disk space. The amount consumed will depend on which version of MSVC++ you purchased, the Standard or the Professional. You can consider the standard version an entry level product since it only allows you to build Windows applications. To do commercial-quality Windows development, you will need the professional version, which allows you to build the various types of Windows programs listed in Table 1.1.

The professional version also contains the full Windows 3.1 SDK, including the debug version of Windows.

The setup program will present you with a list of options, as shown in Figure 1.1. If you plan to do only Windows development, you can delete all MS-DOS–based choices in the tools and libraries dialog boxes shown in Figures 1.2 and 1.3. To keep

TABLE 1.1
Executables you can build with MSVC 1.0 Professional Edition.

Windows application (.EXE).
Windows dynamic-link library (.DLL).
Visual Basic Custom Control (.VBX).
QuickWin application (.EXE).
Static library (.LIB).
Windows P-code application (.EXE).
MS-DOS application (.EXE).
MS-DOS P-code application (.EXE).
MS-DOS Overlaid application (.EXE).
MS-DOS Com application (.COM).

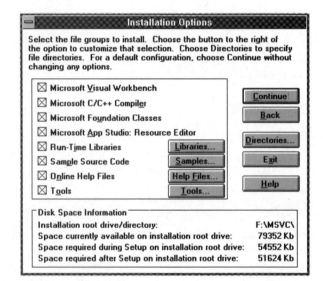

Figure 1.1
Installation Options
screen.

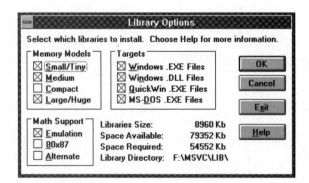

Figure 1.2
Setup Library Options
screen.

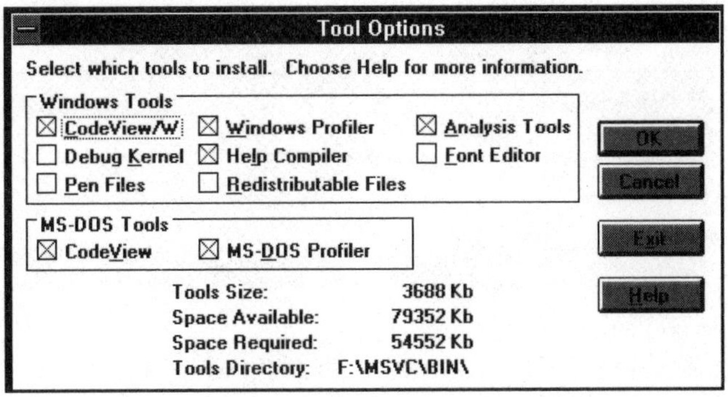

Figure 1.3
Tool Options screen.

MS-DOS files from being copied, simply uncheck the MS-DOS tools and libraries options. With each choice you select or deselect, the screen will update the space required for your options. Since the installation process will also require space, the dialog box will display this value too. You do not need to build all the libraries, either, since the medium and large models should suffice for Windows development. If you find that you need the other libraries later, you can simply build them from the command line using the supplied makefiles.

Once you have made your decisions, you can click OK, answer the prompts, and start swapping disks.

CD-ROM INSTALLATION

If swapping disks is not your forte, you can purchase the MSVC system on CD-ROM and install from your CD drive. With this option you can also choose to leave certain files such as help files and sample code on the CD, rather than copying them to your hard drive. Versions 1.5 and 2.0 of MSVC are available only on CD-ROM.

REINSTALLING VISUAL C++

At a future time you can reinstall files or build libraries that you did not choose during the original installation. To reinstall a file, you should start the setup program as you did previously. When you reach the Options dialog box, uncheck every box except for the category you wish to reinstall. Then press the button to choose which options you wish to install, select only the options you need, and uncheck the rest. This process will not erase any installed files but will overwrite existing files, though that should not cause any problems.

WORKBENCH VS. COMMAND LINE

Microsoft designed the new MSVC system primarily for Windows development from within the workbench and installs the system with this in mind. (Figure 1.4 gives you a view of the Visual Workbench.) In fact, you can only install the system from within Windows; there is no MS-DOS–based setup program. Unfortunately, MSVC 1.0 suffers from the same problem that plagued Visual Basic at first—the workbench hampers multiple developers working on the same project. Fortunately,

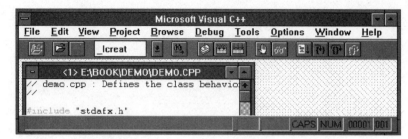

Figure 1.4
The Visual Workbench.

unlike Visual Basic, MSVC allows you to use the various tools—such as the compiler, linker, nmake, and browser—from the command line. This allows you to use your current version control system. To use the tools from the command line, you will need to set various MS-DOS environment variables. You could set these by hand, but the setup program provides a batch file called MSVCVARS.BAT, in the \msvc\bin directory, that will do this for you.

THE VISUAL EDITOR

The editor integrated with the visual workbench is usable for software development, but you may wish to use a different editor. The Visual Editor is a basic text editor with simple formatting features. Macro processing is nonexistent, as are multiple file searching capabilities. Figure 1.5 illustrates the Editor options you can customize.

The View menu item offers other useful features, such as a "Goto" line number choice illustrated in Figure 1.6. You can also set bookmarks in your file to jump back and forth between different sections of your code. Since you cannot jump directly to a named bookmark, you must iterate through all the bookmarks with the next and previous menu options. You may find the integrated browser utility, discussed later, much more useful for hopping around not only your own code, but also the MFC source code.

One double-edged sword feature is the ability to use the C style comment tokens (/* */) to comment out a section of code containing the C++ style line comment characters (//). While this can be useful as a quick debugging technique, it can also cause you to comment out useful code inadvertently. The workbench's color syntax

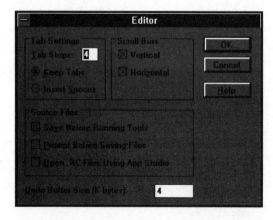

Figure 1.5
Editor options.

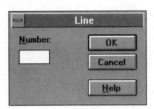

Figure 1.6
Goto Line option.

feature can help prevent this error, since all commented text will appear in the comment color (green by default). You still cannot comment out a section of code containing embedded C style comments.

The editor also gives you the ability to format a selected section of code with the Tab keys. All you need to do is select the text and hit the Tab, or Shift-Tab, key(s) and the editor will position the highlighted text to the same tab stop.

CONTEXT-SENSITIVE HELP

If you can place your cursor on an identifier such as an MFC class name or an SDK API function while in the editor, you can get context-sensitive help by pressing the F1 key. This feature is great for tracking down what type of parameters these functions require. You can also do the same for compiler and linker error messages.

The workbench offers another advantage: It allows you to start a compilation while continuing other activities within the workbench, like editing or reading a help file. One useful technique is to start a compile and then, if there are any errors, jump to the line in the source file and fix the error. You will still have to recompile, but this technique will save time. To jump to the line containing the error, you merely double-click on the offending line in the output window, and the workbench will take you to the corresponding line in the source file while the compiler chugs along. If you wish to stop the compiler and fix the error, you can do so by clicking on the Stop Build menu item under the Project menu. To switch between lines containing errors, step back and forth with the View menu options Next Error and Previous Error.

Finally, note that the Visual Editor has a quirk, which may be more the compiler's fault than the workbench's: If you save a header file without a CR/LF at the end of the file, the compiler will bomb, invoking the message:

```
FATAL ERROR : UNEXPECTED END OF FILE
```

VIEW

The View pull-down menu contains choices relating to how you view the various items in the workbench. The first item, Line, allows you to enter a specific line number in the current source file and jump directly to it. The Mixed/Source choice allows you to see the source code as a mix of text and assembler while you're in the integrated debugger. (See Chapter 16 for more information on the integrated debugger.) The following two items will allow you to step to the next and previous syntax errors recorded in your latest compilation. If you can't bear to look at either the toolbar or the status bar, simply click one of the next two menu items, Toolbar or Status bar. These choices are toggles that control the display of the indicated control bar. The final choice allows you to control the Visual Editor's color syntax feature. This choice allows you to specify which language syntax the workbench will use when highlighting items like keywords and identifiers. Your choices are C, C++, and none.

PROJECT

Under this menu choice you will find a great strength and a weakness of the Visual Workbench (see Figure 1.7). The concept of a project binds the workbench together, since most of the tools work on files associated with a project. A project is simply the collection of files needed to create an application. These include the source files, project and make files, resource files, and database files that the various tools use to do their magic. The first menu item is the AppWizard, the heavy-duty application generator that can create a working Windows program without the developer ever writing a line of code.

The next four menu items allow you to create, open, edit, or close a project file. The workbench will list the last four projects opened in the Most Recently Used (MRU) list at the bottom of the menu. Once you have a project opened, the first toolbar button will become active and will provide a drop-down list of each file in your project. This provides a quick way to edit a project source file without resorting to the File/Open menu item or its toolbar equivalent, the open folder button.

The New menu item will allow you to generate a new project file without running the AppWizard (see Figure 1.8). The workbench will not limit you only to internally

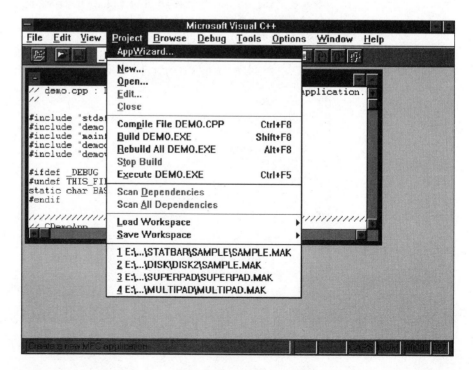

Figure 1.7
The Project menu.

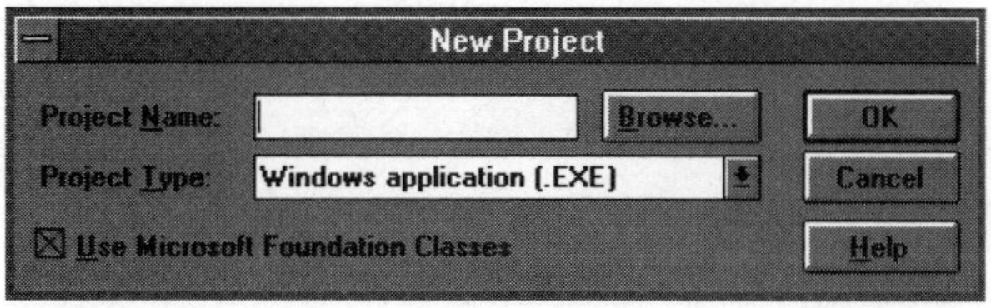

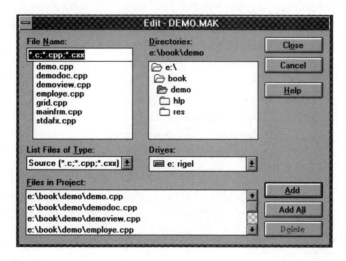

Figure 1.8
The New Project
dialog box.

generated project files. You can use external makefiles, but by doing so you will lose the integration afforded by an internally generated project as the workbench interacts with project files.

If you need to add source files to your project, then you must use the dialog box shown in Figure 1.9 to edit the project file created by AppWizard.

The workbench will not allow you to enter header files, since it automatically adds them to your project's dependencies list. However, just to make sure, you should tell the workbench to regenerate the project file with the Scan All Dependencies menu choice.

The next series of items deals with compiling and executing the executable created with the project, which usually has the same name as the project file. Each choice except Execute has a counterpart on the toolbar as shown in Figure 1.10.

These options allow you, respectively, to compile only the current source file, to recompile the source files that have changed since the last compile, or simply to recompile everything. Sometimes the workbench appears to become confused, and your application may not compile or function properly. In that case, you should try recompiling the entire project to see what happens. More times than not, this may mysteriously solve your problem.

Figure 1.9
The Project-Edit
dialog box.

Figure 1.10
Toolbar compiler
options.

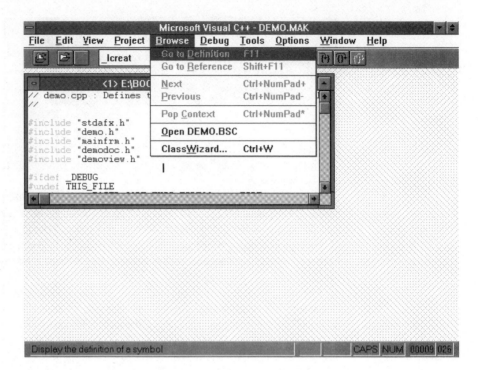

Figure 1.11
The Browse
menu option.

As the application compiles and links, you can continue to do other tasks, such as edit files or gaze through the Tech Notes. The workbench will display all output from the compilation process in an output window called, appropriately, Output. Once your program compiles and links, you can execute the program via the Execute menu item or the Ctrl-F5 accelerator key. Unfortunately, this task has no toolbar counterpart.

BROWSE

MSVC provides a tool called BSCMAKE.EXE, located in the msvc\bin subdirectory, that creates a browser database (see Figure 1.11). A browser database, which has a .BSC extension, lists the name of each identifier contained in the source modules, the location in the file where you defined the name, and then the location of every line that references the name. Once you build this database, you can jump to the location where you defined an identifier either by highlighting or placing your cursor on the identifier and pressing F11. If you then choose the first item in the Browse menu, Goto Definition, the workbench takes you to the line in the appropriate source file where the program defined the identifier. This feature relies on the workbench's ability to share files, so if you do not load the SHARE.EXE program in your AUTOEXEC.BAT file, you will not be able to use the source code browser.

You control the creation of the browser database file via the Options/Project — Listing Files item, shown in Figure 1.12.

If you highlight or place your cursor on a symbol and choose the Goto Reference option, the workbench will take you to the location where the object is first

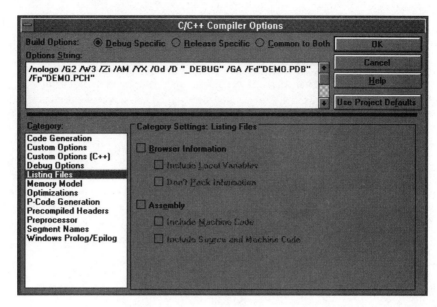

Figure 1.12
Listing Files dialog box.

referenced. You can then use one of the two options, Next and Previous, to step to the next and previous lines in all the source files that reference the symbol. You can use the Pop Context menu item to return to the last symbol you were checking before the current Goto Reference or Goto Definition. The Open menu item allows you to open a browser database file. This can come in handy if you've created a browser database for a library module or even the MFC source files. The final menu choice, ClassWizard, invokes the case tool that allows you to generate C++ classes. (See Chapter 2 for more details on ClassWizard.)

BROWSING THE MFC SOURCE FILES

While the workbench will provide a browser database for your project files, none is available for Microsoft's Foundation Class (MFC) library. If you wish to browse the MFC classes, you will have to build the MFC browser database yourself and then build your browser database in a different way.

First you will have to create the browser database file. BSRMAKE.EXE is an MS-DOS program that the workbench executes. However, for this task you will have to execute the program from an MS-DOS command line. Change to the MFC source file directory, usually \msvc\mfc\src, unless you specified a different directory during installation. Once there, enter the following command line:

```
NMAKE MODEL=M TARGET=W DEBUG=1 "OPT=/FR /Zn"
```

This command will recompile the MFC sources in the medium memory model for Windows, include debug information, and give you the option to place all source file symbols into the .SRB file.

Once nmake has completed the recompilation, you will need to modify how the workbench builds browser information. Begin by disabling the workbench from automatically running BSCMAKE.EXE during each build (compilation). To do this, merely uncheck the browser information check box from the Listing Files options in the categories list box. If you do not disable the workbench from calling BSCMAKE.EXE, then it will only include the symbols from your current project.

Then, dismiss this dialog box and bring up the Custom Options dialog box shown in Figure 1.13. In the Other Options edit box, you will need to add the following command:

```
/Fr.\
```

The final step is to include a new tool option in your Tools menu to execute BSCMAKE.EXE and have it include the symbols from your project and the symbols from the MFC library. You will learn more about the Tools menu and options later in the chapter. For now, simply pull down the Options menu and chose Tools. Click the Add option, which will bring up the Add Tool dialog box in Figure 1.16. Enter the following values into the appropriate fields:

```
E:\msvc\bin\bscmake.exe
```

into the File Name edit box.

```
/o$PROJ /n *.sbr c:\msvc\mfc\src\*.sbr
```

into the Arguments edit box.

The Menu Text field allows you to specify the text appearing in the Tools menu for this particular tool.

Now, after building your program, you can choose this tool to have BSCMAKE.EXE generate a browser information file for your project that includes not only the referenced symbols from your files but also those from the MFC library

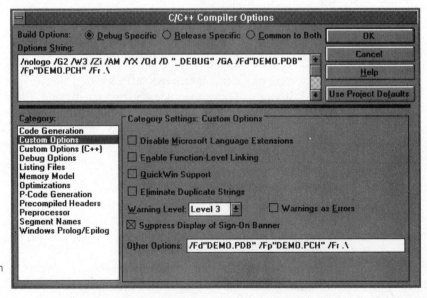

Figure 1.13
Options/Project Custom Options dialog box.

files. Unfortunately, with MSVC++ 1.0 you cannot browse both your source files *and* the MFC files for unreferenced symbols. To create this functionality, you have to exit the workbench to compile your project and then run the BSCMAKE.EXE utility. First you need to edit your project's makefile to include the /Zn and /Fr compiler switches and then compile your project from the command line. Next you need to run the BSCMAKE.EXE utility with the above arguments to create the .BSC data file. Once you create this file, you can reenter the workbench and use the browser options.

DEBUG

This menu (see Figure 1.14) and its associated buttons on the toolbar give you access to the Visual Workbench's integrated debugger, described in detail in Chapter 16.

TOOLS

One of the more utilitarian features of Visual C++ is the next menu bar option, Tools. This menu item, by default, allows you to select App Studio, CodeView for Windows, and CodeView for DOS. However, you can add additional tools to this menu item for a truly versatile, custom configuration. For example, you can install any Windows program (Calculator, Notepad, etc.) or any MS-DOS–based program properly configured with a .PIF file. Incidentally, this is where you will install the "electronic index" found on the accompanying diskette. By including these utilities in your Visual C++ environment, you will save much time because you will not be forced to return to Windows or MS-DOS when you need to run another application.

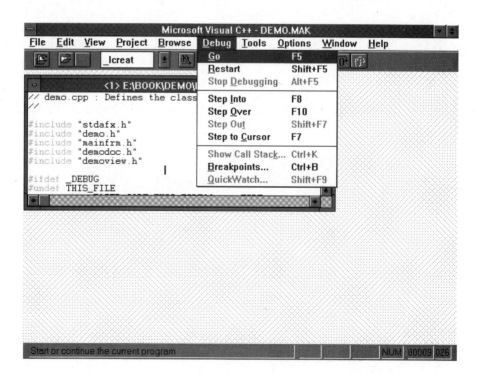

Figure 1.14
Debug menu options.

Installing Tools

To install a program under the Tools option, you first need to know if it is a Windows program or a DOS application. If it's a Windows program, there's no problem. If it's an MS-DOS program, just be sure you have a .PIF file set up that allows the program to work properly—test it in Windows before adding it to the Visual C++ Visual Workbench. To begin, select the Options menu item from the Visual Workbench and then click on the Tools item to open the dialog box in Figure 1.15.

To add a new tool, enter the name of the executable if the tool is a Windows program, or the name of the .PIF file if it is DOS-based, in the edit field labeled Command Line. For example, to install the Windows calculator, enter "CALC.EXE". Press the Tab key to move to the next field, the Menu Text. Here, type in the text that you wish displayed when you select the Tools menu. Continuing with the Calculator example, you might enter "&Calculator." The use of the ampersand allows you to use the accelerator key Alt-C to start the calculator. The workbench will underline the letter "C" in the word "Calculator" in the Tools drop-down menu. Next, tab to the Arguments field and enter the program's command line arguments, if any, in this box. The last field is the Initial Directory field, which is where you want Windows to start the program. With the Calculator, this is most likely your Windows directory (e.g., "C:\WINDOWS"). Finally, if you want Windows to prompt you for arguments, mark the check box Ask for Arguments at the bottom of the dialog box. Now all you need do is click the Add command button, and your application (e.g., Calculator) will be ready to run from inside Visual C++.

Connecting Tools to the Current Project

Sometimes you will want to use a tool in conjunction with the current project. For example, you may have a UNIX-type *grep* command (e.g., Microsoft's MEGREP.EXE) that you wish to use for searching files in the active project. To ensure that the tool runs in the same directory as the project, enter the value "$ProjDir" in the edit field Initial Directory for the tool. This is a macro that establishes whatever directory is associated with the project as the default. Other useful macros that you may find of value appear in Table 1.2.

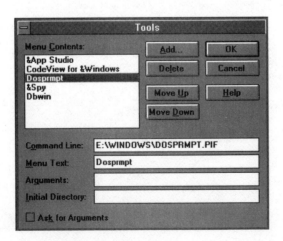

Figure 1.15
Adding Tools
dialog box.

TABLE 1.2
Tool Macros.

1.	$File	Specifies the full path and filename of the current open file. Null means no source file is open.
2.	$Filename	Specifies only the filename and extension.
3.	$FileDir	Specifies the drive and path of the current file.
4.	$Proj	Specifies the current project name, the name you gave to AppWizard to create the current project. (We will discuss the various wizards in later chapters.)
5.	$ProjDir	Specifies the current project drive and path.
6.	$Line	Specifies the line that currently contains the insertion point.
7.	$Col	Specifies the column currently containing the insertion point.
8.	$Dir	Specifies the current working directory.
9.	$Target	Specifies the current target of the project makefiles. This is usually the name of your application, which in turn is usually the name of the project.
10.	$RC	Specifies the resource file of the current project.

OPTIONS

Figure 1.16 shows you the choices available from the Options menu, which allows you to configure most of the workbench's behavior. The first three choices control the compilation process, run-time debugging parameters, and the directory paths the workbench will use during operation.

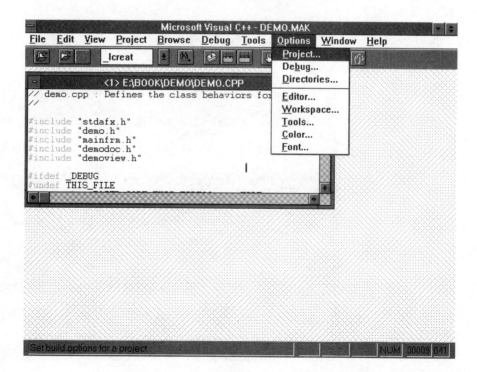

Figure 1.16
The Options
pull-down menu.

Project

Choosing Project will display the dialog box shown in Figure 1.17. This dialog box will allow you to specify what type of executable to build and whether to build a debug or a release version. You use the Use Microsoft Foundation Classes check box to instruct the framework to include the necessary MFC libraries in your project's makefile. This option is set to on by default.

The Custom Options allow you to specify options for compiling, linking, and the resource bindings of your application. The Compiler Options button will display the dialog box shown in Figure 1.18.

The choices you made in the initial dialog box concerning the type of your executable will determine the build options applied throughout the workbench to all of its options, as shown in the Build Options selected on the first line. You can change the options from debug either to release or to options common to both debug and release that are not mutually exclusive. The option string box will display the arguments the workbench passes to the MSVC compiler when you call for a compilation. The list box will reflect the new values as you change options, but you

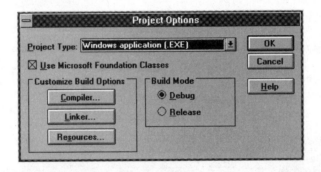

Figure 1.17
Project Options
dialog box.

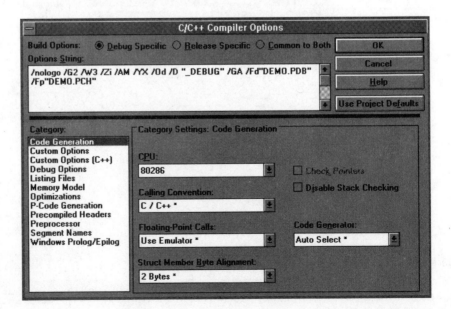

Figure 1.18
Compiler Options
dialog box.

cannot directly edit the arguments via this display. At any time you can cancel your choices with the cancel key, or reset the options to project defaults via the Use Project Defaults key.

The lower part of the dialog will display a list box containing categories of other options you can change, and the right-hand side will display controls to help you set these options. We will not cover every option you can set in these dialogs; instead, we will point out a few useful options. The Custom Options category will allow you to add arguments manually to the argument list and specify the compiler's warning level generation. The higher the warning level, the more warnings the compiler will generate as it compiles your program. You can use this feature as a simple LINT utility. Each category has an associated set of controls from which you can retrieve help about the options from the window's help engine.

The Linker Options button will display the dialog box shown in Figure 1.19. From this dialog you can choose which libraries to include in your program and how to include them. The format of the dialog is the same as the Compiler Options dialog, with each item in the categories list displaying controls on the right to alter the categories' values. The Miscellaneous category will allow you to specify any arguments to the linker that the workbench will not let you specify graphically, just like the Custom Options category above. The Output category will allow you to specify that the linker should create a map file during linking. Because this file will be invaluable during a debugging session, you should activate this choice.

Figure 1.20 displays the dialog box presented when you press the Resource button. This dialog allows you to specify define symbols and custom arguments to the resource compiler.

Debug

The next menu option displays the dialog shown in Figure 1.21, which allows you to specify options for the integrated debugger during a debugging session. The

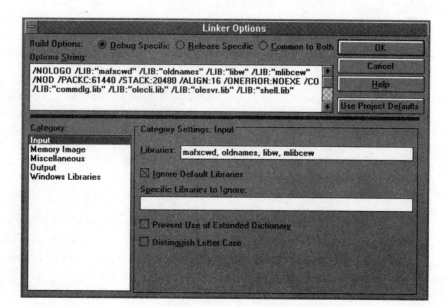

Figure 1.19
Linker Options
dialog box.

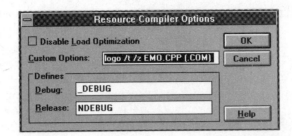

Figure 1.20
Resource Compiler
Options dialog box.

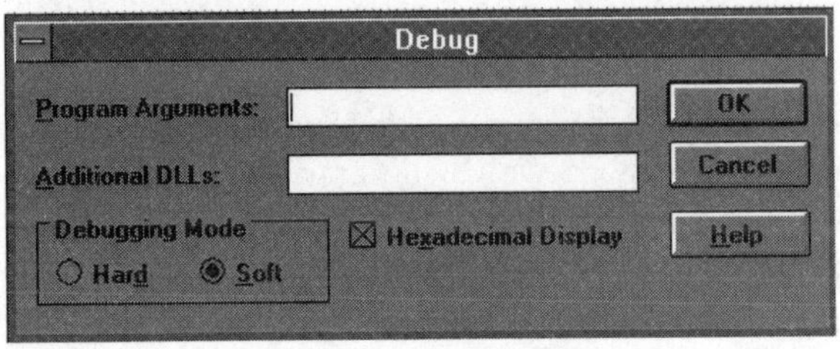

Figure 1.21
Debug options
dialog box.

choices you make here have no effect on the compilation process. Chapter 16 will
provide more information on this screen.

DIRECTORIES

This menu choice will display the dialog screen shown in Figure 1.22, which allows
you to specify the directories the workbench uses during its normal operations. Gone
are the days when you had to set MS-DOS environment variables before invoking
your tools.

WORKSPACE

Since we covered the Visual Editor earlier in this chapter, we will continue with the
next menu choice — Workspace. Once you have configured the workbench, you can
make that setup your default. The Workspace option, shown in Figure 1.23, allows
you to save up to three workspace configurations dealing with the position of the
windows and your current project settings. You can load a workspace via the Project
menu option. However, by default, the Visual Workbench loads the last settings in
effect when you shut down the system. The workbench also maintains a list of the
last four files loaded in an MRU (Most Recently Used) list under the File menu option.

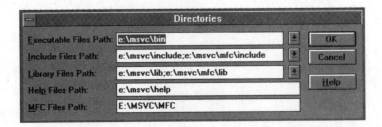

Figure 1.22
Directories options
dialog box.

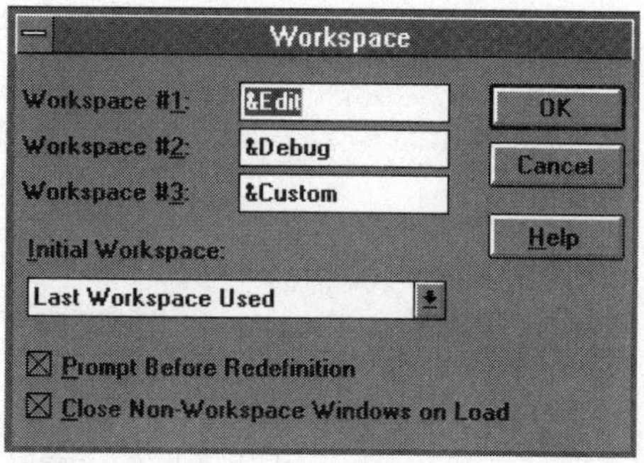

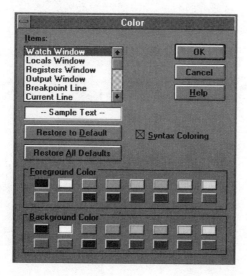

Figure 1.23
Workspace
dialog box.

COLOR AND FONT SELECTION

The Color Options dialog box, illustrated in Figure 1.24, allows you to specify the workbench's foreground and background text colors. You can modify these values to suit your hardware, lighting, and personal tastes. It is here that you can change the default colors used by the Visual Editor for syntax coloring. Syntax coloring will indicate various C and C++ keywords, identifiers, and comments; you can use the Color Options dialog box to specify which colors the workbench will use to identify the various language constructs. If you do not wish to use this feature, you can turn it off by selecting the None option under the View/Syntax Coloring menu item.

Figure 1.25 shows you the font selection dialog box. This dialog allows you to choose the text font and size used by the Visual Editor. This dialog will let you set the selected font as the workbench's default font.

WINDOW

This menu choice provides the workbench with the standard MDI window controls such as cascading, tiling, and closing all open windows. Listed after the MDI controls are the workbench's debug windows, shown in Figure 1.26.

Figure 1.24
Color options
dialog box.

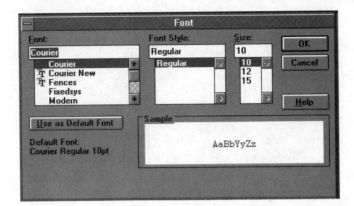

Figure 1.25
Font selection box.

Chapter 16 will cover these windows in greater detail. Until then, you should be aware that the Output window will display all the warnings and errors resulting from a compilation.

HELP

The Help menu option allows you access to Windows help on a variety of subjects, including the Visual Workbench and various Microsoft support services. See Chapter 17 for more information on help for the developer.

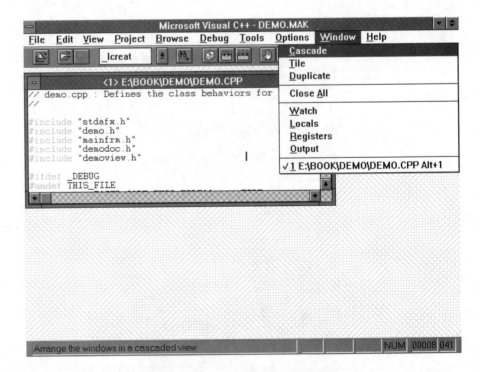

Figure 1.26
The Debug window.

Figure 1.27
Workbench toolbar.

You can also install the help file supplied with this book by adding it to your Tools menu. To do so, specify WINHELP.EXE as the program and the name of the help file on the disk as the argument.

THE TOOLBAR

Below the main menu will reside the framework's toolbar, shown in Figure 1.27. This toolbar provides convenient access to many of the main menu's options with just a single mouse click.

You can open and create files from the File menu option or from the toolbar. To open files associated with your current project, use the first toolbar button. The second button is the same as the File/Open menu choice. Finally, the third button allows you to save the current file. If the file is untitled, the workbench will prompt you for a name. You can mark a file as read-only via the Edit/Read Only menu option, or by checking the Read Only box in the File/Open common dialog box. This is a handy technique to use when cutting and pasting code between source files, especially in a multiple developer project in which you have no automated source code control system.

The next control on the toolbar is a combo box displaying the current search string. The drop-down list provides previous values you have used in the Find and the Find and Replace dialog boxes. The workbench's find-and-replace mechanism will not allow you to search across multiple source files, but it will allow you to use the regular expressions shown in Table 1.3. Figure 1.28 displays the Find and Replace dialog box; the Find dialog is very similar.

TABLE 1.3
Regular expressions supported by the MSVC Visual Workbench.

1.	.	The period will find any single character.
2.	*	The asterisk symbol matches none or more of the preceding characters or expressions.
3.	+	The plus symbol will match one or more of the preceding characters or expressions.
4.	^	This symbol denotes the beginning of a line. It will match the following expression only if it appears at the beginning of a line.
5.	$	The dollar symbol denotes the end of a line. It will match the preceding character or expression only at the end of a line.
6.	[]	This expression will match any one of the characters inside the brackets. You can also specify an ASCII range via a hyphen. For instance, **[a-z]** will match any lower-case character in the alphabet.
7.	\{\}	This expression will match any characters between the braces
8.	\	The escape character will allow you to include the preceding symbols as literal characters in the search.

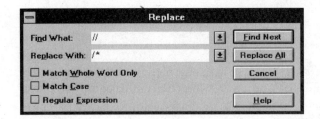

Figure 1.28
Find and Replace
dialog box searching
for all occurrences of
"//" at the beginning
of a line.

To use regular expressions, make sure you check Regular Expression in the dialog box. Otherwise, the workbench will take the string at face value. Once you dismiss the dialog box, you can use the F3 function key or the binocular button on the toolbar to repeat the search.

To use a previous search string, select the string from the combo box on the toolbar and press the binocular button. Alternatively, you may hit Return so long as the selected string appears in the edit part of the combo box. You can also type directly into the box or highlight a word and press Ctrl-F3. This will place the text in the list box and find the next occurrence.

Unfortunately, you cannot configure the toolbar with your own items or rearrange those buttons already provided. The workbench allows you to add tools, as described previously, but not buttons to access those additions. If the editor is not adequate for your situation, then you can take advantage of your favorite editor by adding it to the tools menu.

COMPILATION CONTROL

The next three buttons on the toolbar, shown in Figure 1.29, invoke different build operations. The first button simply compiles the current source file and reports any syntax errors. Note that this option will not invoke the linker to create an executable. The next option will compile only those source files modified since the last time you created the project executable. The framework may also recompile an unmodified source file due to a change in a dependent file, such as an included header file. The workbench generates and maintains these dependencies and will know when to recompile a file. After compiling all the necessary files, the workbench invokes the linker to create the program's executable then the resource compiler to create and bind the project's resources to the programs, and finally the browser, if you've indicated that option. One tip to keep in mind is that sometimes dependencies can get out of sync, and choosing the rebuild all option may take care of any resulting mysterious little problems.

Figure 1.29
The compiler
toolbar buttons.

Figure 1.30
The Integrated
Debugger's buttons.

INTEGRATED DEBUGGER

The next group of buttons, shown in Figure 1.30, deals with the integrated debugger and provides the following functionalities. The first button, which contains the bitmap of a hand, allows you to toggle a breakpoint at the current cursor position. The next button, the eyeglasses, allows you to take a quick look at the value of the currently selected symbol. The next four buttons deal with how you step through a program you are debugging. The first of these buttons starts the debugger and executes the program until termination or until it reaches a breakpoint. If the debugger is already at a breakpoint or stopped while stepping, this button will continue execution to the next breakpoint or to program termination. The next button allows you to step into a function call as you are stepping through a program. The next-to-last button allows you to do the exact opposite—step over a function while still allowing the program to execute the function and return. The final button on the toolbar allows you to step out of a function from any point inside that function. (See Chapter 16 for more information on the integrated debugger.)

MSVC.INI CONFIGURATION FILE

The workbench will save any changes you make to it in the MSVC.INI file. Usually, the workbench creates this file in your Windows directory. Among the items the workbench will save here are all your previous search strings, your replacement strings, your tools additions, your last four project files, and the last four text files you opened. You can edit this file—for instance, to remove the search strings—but you should let the workbench maintain this file itself.

CHAPTER SUMMARY

This chapter has detailed some of the pitfalls you face when installing and using Microsoft Visual C++. While the workbench does have some problems, this environment provides a powerful tool to the Windows Software developer. You will find that you can get applications up and running quicker than with the SDK and straight C. Further down the road, you will find that the object-oriented design will pay off with better maintenance and more reusable code. The remaining chapters provide various tips and tricks and sample code in the form of building blocks and whole routines that you can lift and place into your applications. Enjoy!

CHAPTER 2

The Wizards
and App Studio

In this chapter we will explore the various wizards that come with Visual C++. This material should benefit new users the most, as it provides an overview of the capabilities of the wizards. It is the power of the wizards that truly make Visual C++ a magical workshop. Two wizards come with Visual C++: AppWizard and ClassWizard. Each plays a unique role in greatly relieving the software developer of the mundane and messy chores normally associated with Windows development. Without the features of the wizards, Visual C++ would be just another form of the SDK.

APPWIZARD

AppWizard, short for Application Wizard, is your first port of call when creating a new Windows program under Visual C++. It is this tool that allows you to define the fundamental structure of your program and to include support features such as Help, OLE, etc. AppWizard creates, for all intents and purposes, a skeleton Windows program. You can create a fully functional working Windows program using only AppWizard. (Of course, this program wouldn't *do* anything, but for anyone who cut their programming teeth on the SDK, the AppWizard can virtually eliminate a week's worth of work in a matter of seconds.) AppWizard creates a series of source code and header files, based on options you specify, that form the backbone of all further development. Much consideration needs to go into the selection of these options, as they can have a profound impact on the operability of your program and the support of other features such as context-sensitive help. Later discussions in this chapter will explore these options in greater detail—for now, just understand that it's dangerous to play with the wizard's magic wand . . . .

STARTING APPWIZARD

To start AppWizard, select AppWizard from the menu item labeled Project in the Visual Workbench. This calls up the dialog box shown in Figure 2.1.

In the topmost edit box, Project Name, enter the name of your new Windows application. This can be up to 8 characters long. You can enter more, and AppWizard will even allow you to enter illegal characters such as a period, but AppWizard will reject the invalid project specification when you click the OK button. A pop-up error message box also appears, alerting you to the problem. Perhaps later versions will trap illegal characters and invalid project lengths as they are entered for this field. At any rate, you'll also need to specify a new subdirectory and disk to contain your project. Specify the subdirectory in the edit box at the bottom of the MFC AppWizard dialog box labeled New Subdirectory. The target disk drive is a drop-down list box labeled Drive. The scroll box in the middle of the dialog box, Directory, lets you specify a directory on the target disk. For the sake of disk space and project management, you'll almost always specify your MSVC directory here. Once you have correctly entered your new project name and location, do *not* click the OK button—click the Options button instead in order to specify the additional characteristics of your Windows program.

THE OPTIONS DIALOG BOX

This dialog box is where you *really* have to be careful. This is where AppWizard adds the bones, so to speak, to your skeleton application. Broadly speaking, adding a feature you don't want probably won't hurt you, but failing to add one you need can be near-fatal. The Options dialog box is shown in Figure 2.2.

As you can see, there are eight options from which you can select. Due to their importance and impact on your application, the following discussion explores each of these options in greater detail.

Figure 2.1
The AppWizard
dialog box.

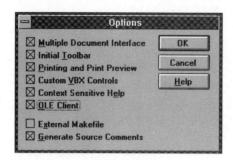

Figure 2.2
ClassWizard Options
dialog box.

Multiple Document Interface

Selecting this option causes AppWizard to create a Multiple Document Interface (MDI). Unchecking the option box results in a Single Document Interface (SDI). An MDI program enables you to have more than one document *type* open; each document has its own window. As an example, you might have an Excel spreadsheet application running in one window to support one type of document (spreadsheets), while another window could be running, say, Word, which is an entirely different type of document. An SDI program, on the other hand, will only allow you to work with one type of document at a time. In situations where you are unsure about the types of documents your project may require, you should choose the MDI option. You can use a single document type with an MDI application, but you can't use multiple documents within an SDI program.

Initial Toolbar

This feature lets you include a toolbar and a status bar in your Windows application. A toolbar is a graphical representation of various menu options. A pair of scissors indicates a Cut operation; a diskette icon means a File Save operation, and so on. The status bar indicates the present status of the keyboard, such as the state of the Caps Lock or Num Lock keys. More importantly, the status bar includes the area that displays the prompt strings associated with a menu item created in App Studio. If you declare this option, you'll see a menu item called View in your main window. This allows you to toggle these features on and off at your discretion. Since the toolbar and status bar add a lot of versatility to your program, you will probably want to include these options in your project.

Printing and Print Preview

Include this option if you plan to support any printing from inside your application. Selecting this option gives you the standard Windows dialog boxes for choosing the printer and the print options (e.g., portrait or landscape mode, etc.). These are invoked under the File option on the main menu bar. Selecting the Print... option, which includes the Windows standard ellipses (...) in the menu text, invokes a dialog box representing about 2500 lines of Windows API coding that you *don't* have to write. If nothing else, this observation should give you an appreciation of the muscle that Visual C++ brings to Windows programming.

Custom VBX Controls

Microsoft's Visual Basic software preceded Visual C++. Thus a lot of third-party vendors out there have written some pretty powerful custom controls, called VBX controls, for this environment. Examples of custom VBX controls include gauges, edit boxes, etc. Visual C++ provides you with an additional VBX control, *grid.vbx*. App Studio, which is the visual design tool for Visual C++, is used for installing the VBX controls. Choosing this option allows you to incorporate these controls into Visual C++ programs. (See Chapter 10 for more information on using VBX controls.) If you're not sure whether or not you'll want to use these controls, you can't do yourself any harm by selecting this option. The proliferation of many low-cost, high-performance VBX controls on the market today makes them generally more cost-effective to use. Should your present or future applications need controls for special processing (e.g., formatted input for dates, currency, etc.), it is better to purchase them than to develop them in-house.

Context-Sensitive Help

You'll definitely want to include this powerful option in most of your applications. This means you must have the help compiler necessary to create Help files for use by the Windows Help engine, WINHELP.EXE. The Visual C++ Professional Edition includes the help compiler; if you are moving up from the SDK or a similar package, you most likely already have the help compiler. If not, it can be downloaded from CompuServe, along with a help authoring tool (you must have Microsoft Word to use this tool). Context-sensitive help, also referred to as "F1" help because pressing the F1 function key invokes it, gives users help based on where they are in your program. Refer to Chapter 15 for more information on writing Help files and using the Microsoft Help engine, WINHELP.EXE.

OLE Client

More powerful than a locomotive, OLE (Object Linking and Embedding) support allows your application to manipulate multiple types of data in the same document. Going back to our example from MDI, suppose you have an Excel spreadsheet running in one window and your program (which you created specifying OLE Client) running in another. OLE lets you "copy" a portion of the spreadsheet to the Clipboard, and then "paste" it into *your* application. Thus OLE goes beyond merely displaying the data—you can actually *change* the data in the original Excel spreadsheet from *your* application. In other words, these two distinct objects are linked. The functionality of OLE instantly provides your application with a great deal of extendibility into the future, as linking is a desirable feature suitable for use in a wide range of programs. If any of your Visual C++ programs will produce tabular results in a grid format, you might want to include OLE when defining your project with AppWizard even if you have no immediate plans to support OLE. This will allow you to add support for OLE in future releases and hopefully extend the shelf life of your Windows application.

External Makefile

This is an option you are not likely to use very often. Visual C++, like other tools for creating Windows-based applications, creates and uses a makefile. The project file created by Visual C++ runs from the Visual Workbench and is also compatible with NMAKE, the utility used by the SDK and others. If you select the External Makefile option, you must use your project as an external project while in Visual C++. When you open a project in Visual C++, there is a check box in which you must specify whether the project is an external makefile. Unless you have some reason for doing so, you are better off not checking this option.

Generate Source Comments

Always, always, always specify this option, which causes AppWizard to insert useful comments into the source files that it creates. Frequently, you will find yourself creating functions in ClassWizard but neglecting to add your application-specific code at that time. Later, when editing your source code, you will notice these comments and realize that you need to add code. Using this option can therefore help you do a better job of managing your project.

BUILDING YOUR APPLICATION WITH APPWIZARD

After you have supplied AppWizard the name of your project, the disk specification, and the application-specific options, all that's left to do is click the OK button on the MFC AppWizard dialog box. AppWizard will create some standard files whose names will be common to all AppWizard derived projects (e.g., MAINFRAM.CPP, MAKEHELP.BAT, etc.). AppWizard will also build your resource file, the project's makefile, and subdirectories, and create files based on the name of the application you supplied. For example, the sample program on the diskette accompanying this book features a program called DEMO. If you look through the source files, you find the word "demo" used conspicuously in filenames such as demo.cpp, demo.h, demo.mak, etc. Also, this program name forms the basis for class names. In the ClassWizard, you'll find a class called CDemo. This convention makes it easy to identify AppWizard files based on your application's name. Another useful by-product of using AppWizard is a file called README.TXT, which lists all the other files in the project. You should probably rename and keep it up to date as you develop; it will save you debugging time as well as provide a general outline for your product's documentation.

CLASSWIZARD

Second in command to AppWizard is ClassWizard. While you'll only use AppWizard once, you'll use ClassWizard many, many times during the development cycle of your application. ClassWizard makes it easy for you to tie together visual objects such as controls with your application's code. Users migrating from Visual Basic should notice the similarity between ClassWizard and Visual Basic's "point-and-click" method of editing code for a control. ClassWizard also creates new classes, directs Windows messages (those messages with the ubiquitous prefix "WM" so familiar to those of you moving up from SDK) to the function responsible for responding, and connects controls to class-member variables. These last two functions are really what ClassWizard is all about and what makes Visual C++ so powerful and easy to use. Every Windows program is born with a mission in life; you accomplish this mission through the use of controls (e.g., a click on a radio button, a keystroke, etc.) and the messages they generate. ClassWizard eliminates most of the tedium associated with the purely mechanical chores of Windows programming and allows you to concentrate on what it is you are trying to do.

Classes and Messages

One of the really nice things ClassWizard does for you is to limit what you see and must address to those messages relevant to your class or control. The ClassWizard dialog box appears in Figure 2.3.

As an example, suppose you have a combo box object in the scroll box labeled Object IDs. The *only* messages that are visible in the Messages window are those that have meaning to a combo box (e.g., CBN_CLOSEUP, CBN_SETFOCUS, etc.). Besides keeping you out of trouble (because you might select a meaningless message), these message options help to keep you focused on what it is your program needs to do. The relevance of this statement will likely become more apparent as you gain experience with ClassWizard.

ClassWizard and Member Variables

Another powerful feature of ClassWizard is its ability to allow you to assign member variables to controls. If the control is an edit box, you can also specify the maximum number of characters permitted. When you choose an object or control in the

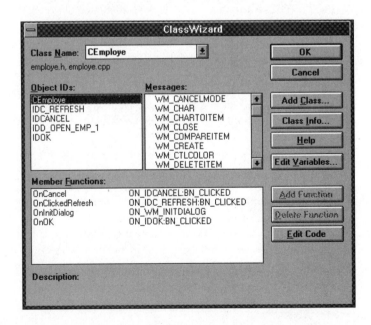

Figure 2.3
The ClassWizard
dialog box.

ClassWizard dialog box and then click the button Edit <u>V</u>ariables..., the dialog box in Figure 2.4 will appear.

Here, you may add variables by selecting an object and clicking on the <u>A</u>dd Variable... button. This action invokes the dialog box in Figure 2.5.

Note the topmost edit box, Member Variable <u>N</u>ame. Visual C++ automatically begins each member variable with "m_," a convention that makes them easier to spot when reviewing your code. The second box, a drop-down list box labeled <u>P</u>roperty, is where you indicate whether the variable you are adding refers to the *control* or the *value* assigned to the control. You can have both. For some objects such as edit boxes, you should go ahead and add one variable referring to the control and another to the value. This will make it easier for you to manipulate the control later in your program (for example, when you want to retrieve the text from the edit box). The last box in this dialog box, Variable <u>T</u>ype, is where you can select the data type for the value (e.g., int, CString, etc.). Click the OK button when you are satisfied with your new variable, and ClassWizard will take care of the rest.

The Project Class File

When you build your application, Visual C++ creates a file with the extension .CLW, containing the information necessary to show you what classes you've created. It sometimes happens that not all your classes are visible—generally, when you've created your own class without going through ClassWizard. The solution is simply

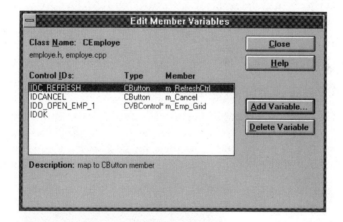

Figure 2.4
The Edit Member
Variables dialog box.

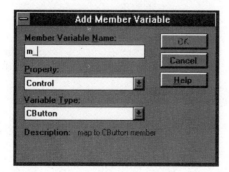

Figure 2.5
The Add Member
Variable dialog box.

to delete your project's .CLW file and then start App Studio. Once inside App Studio, run ClassWizard again. Visual C++ will present a message box informing you that it cannot find the class file and ask if you would like to create it. Responding Yes makes your classes visible in future sessions.

Deleting Functions in ClassWizard

One of the options that ClassWizard allows you to exercise is deleting a function that you previously added. When you select a function from the box labeled Member Functions by clicking on it and then the Delete Function button, Visual C++ comes back with a message box that reads:

```
Deleting this handler will require manually
removing the implementation of Class::Function.
Are you sure you want to continue?

where Class::Function are the class and function you chose
```

The message box has two buttons, Yes and No. If you select Yes, ClassWizard will only remove the handler from the message map; the actual function will still be in your source code. You must then go into the source code file and cut out the function. It is *extremely important* that you do these tasks in the preceding order, always letting ClassWizard remove the handler first. If you delete the function first and then try to delete the handler from ClassWizard, you'll get an error message from Visual C++ stating that it can't find the function. This will make it necessary for you to recreate your .CLW file. To rebuild the file, first delete the existing .CLW file. Then, run App Studio and open your project's resource file. Press Ctrl-W to invoke ClassWizard. Visual C++ will inform you that it can't find the .CLW file and ask if you wish to build it. Respond Yes, and Visual C++ does the rest. This procedure is sometimes necessary when several programmers are all working on the same project—a situation that Version 1.0 of Visual C++ does not handle very well. Periodically, it becomes necessary for the team members to combine their code into a single, composite project, and rebuilding the .CLW file is almost always necessary in this situation. Remember to exercise considerable caution to prevent the contamination of baseline code on such occasions.

Moving and Renaming Classes

It is very important to keep the information about your project's classes up to date, both for your sake and for the compiler's. As your program takes shape, you may find it necessary to rename a class or move it to another file. When making such changes, ClassWizard will prompt you to update the .CLW file the next time you use ClassWizard. Here is a general outline of the steps to follow for renaming classes:

1. Change the name in all files and *all* references, including the comments, which Visual C++ uses to find the new message map.

2. Run ClassWizard. In the Class Name box, choose the name of the class you want to change. ClassWizard will respond with a pop-up box warning that the class is missing. Choose OK to invoke the Repair Class Information dialog box.

3. Enter the class's new name in all the boxes (e.g., Class Name, Header File, etc.), then choose OK.

An additional feature of the Repair Class dialog box is the Browse button. You can use the browsing capabilities of Visual C++ to search for references to classes. This saves you the time required to exit the dialog box and track the information down by other means. This and all the other features of the ClassWizard make it an invaluable asset when it comes to developing Windows applications.

The Browser

An additional feature of the Visual Workbench that is not a wizard, strictly speaking, is the Microsoft Source Browser—a sort of giant "Yellow Pages" for your project. The browser also provides information about your variables, such as their location and type. Something else the Browser can do for you really helps in debugging and in documentation—it generates function call trees and cross-reference tables. Customize the Browser by choosing Options from the Visual Workbench main menu bar, and then clicking on Project. Next, choose Compiler and click on Listing File from the list box. One of the options you'll see is a check box labeled Include Local Variables. If you are debugging and don't need to watch local variables in a function, you can turn this box off and save the build time that would otherwise be needed to build symbol tables for local variables. The name of the Browser database is the name of your project with the file extension .BSC (e.g., YOURAPP.BSC). You will find more information on using the Browser database in Chapter 10 of *The Visual Workbench User's Guide.*

APP STUDIO

App Studio is where you will create the visual aspects of your Windows program's user interface. After AppWizard has created a new project, use the App Studio tool to start designing visual objects such as menus and controls. App Studio, used repeatedly during the life cycle of project development, maintains your project's resource file. Five major components of App Studio are covered in this section: the menu editor, the dialog editor, the accelerator table editor, the string editor, and the graphics editor. Note how all these editors concern themselves in one way or another with the *visual* aspects of your application. App Studio also allows you to install custom controls (i.e., VBX controls) that can greatly extend the functionality of your program. A fuller discussion of VBX controls appears in Chapter 10. For now, just be aware that App Studio is where it all happens. Note that the material in the following discussions concerning these editors is essentially a synopsis of what you can find in the Visual C++ documentation, plus a few suggestions, hints, and cautions thrown in for good measure.

The Menu Editor

The menu editor allows you to create new menus or to modify existing ones. Normally, the menu will be the first resource you'll want to build when you create a new project. Invariably, it is the first resource encountered by the user—other than the actual window—that features command options (e.g., File, Edit, etc.). Also, it is useful to design your main menu first, so as to have it available for subsequent development. The content of the main menu can help to keep you focused on the scope and logical order of your program. The menu editor also creates hierarchical menus; these are virtually always discardable resources, so storing them in your project's resource file is a lot more practical than always keeping them in memory. More information on menus will be forthcoming in Chapter 5, which will explore these operations with closer scrutiny. The menu editor indicates your current cursor position with a gray box; double-click to get the dialog box that allows you to assign ID numbers and the actual text of the menu item. For top-level menu items, you can supply only the main menu bar options (e.g., File, Edit, Help, etc.). Prompt strings—the mini-help messages that appear on the status bar at the bottom of the window— are not allowed at this level. The options under these main items can have prompt strings. In general, it is a good idea to assign your own IDs to the menu items, overriding the defaults suggested by App Studio. This makes it easier for you to recognize what menu option goes where. If one of your main menu items is a pop-up (i.e., drop-down) menu and selecting it results in the appearance of a dialog box, don't forget to indicate this by adding the ellipsis ("...") after the command string. If the menu item invokes another submenu (also referred to as a cascading, hierarchical, or child menu), App Studio will automatically insert a right-pointing triangle to the right of the menu text. These standard visual cues forewarn the user about what to expect prior to selecting the item.

The Dialog Editor

This is probably one of the most frequently used editors, as dialog boxes provide a great deal of control over user interaction. When you create a new dialog box resource, App Studio gives you a default dialog box with a title and two command buttons—OK and Cancel. You can access the properties of a control or object, or even the dialog box itself, simply by double-clicking the mouse on it. Doing so brings up a dialog box that lets you change the properties and styles. This dialog box is represented by an icon of a thumbtack on the menu bar. Clicking this icon attaches the properties box to your workspace, just as if you had taken a thumbtack and placed something on a cork board. The properties dialog box appears in Figure 2.6.

Figure 2.6
The App Studio dialog box Editor Properties box.

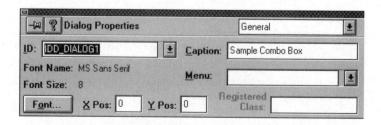

When working with dialog boxes, it is a good idea to click the grid button—the icon that looks like a bunch of dots—on the App Studio toolbar. The grid is a great utility for aligning all your controls and adjusting sizes. The App Studio provides 4 tools for aligning controls—top, bottom, left, and right. To align controls, click an anchor point in the dialog box and drag out a box that encompasses all the controls you wish to align. Then, simply click the appropriate icon on the toolbar to align the controls automatically. These aligning icons, located on the bottom-left toolbar in App Studio, appear in Figure 2.7.

While we are on the subject of aligning your controls, remember to put all your command buttons either vertically along the right side of the dialog box or horizontally along the bottom. Of course, there will be some exceptions to this general rule. For instance, when you have two boxes and you want to allow the user to move items from one box to another, you will naturally want to put the commands between the boxes with the appropriate labels and directional arrows. An example of such a case occurs in App Studio itself, when you choose Install Controls.

Another visual aspect over which you have control is where to place the dialog box within your window. The Properties box has an X and a Y box, which default to 0, whereby you can override the placement of the dialog box. The initial coordinates, 0,0, will cause the upper left-hand corner of your dialog box to appear in the extreme upper-left portion of the window. It is best not to try to adjust these coordinates yourself—there is an easier way. In ClassWizard, you can attach a function to the message WM_INITDIALOG and add the following statement to this function:

```
CenterWindow();   // puts dialog box in center of window
```

This obviates the need to adjust the X, Y coordinates and properly centers your dialog boxes in the middle of the window in which they appear.

Group and Control Ordering

Normally, this subject would appear in the chapter on dialog box controls, but since the controls are so closely associated with App Studio, a brief detour into the subject seems in order. On activating a dialog box in a Windows program, the user can move from a control or control group by pressing the Tab key. A control group might be, say, a group of radio buttons representing communication parameters such as the baud rate. Once the user moves to the first control in such a group, the arrow keys must be used to navigate within the group; pressing the Tab key would take the user to the next *group,* not the next *control.* The order in which you create the controls in App Studio determines the order in which they receive the focus when accessed. This concept is very important, as it can have a profound impact on the way your program operates. Always try to add controls in the order in which you wish the user

Figure 2.7
App Studio
alignment tools.

to access them—in a logical manner. Speaking from experience, this is not often easy to do during development. Should you need to rearrange the visit order, it is fairly easy to fix. Open up your project's resource file, find the dialog box, and rearrange the order of the controls in the dialog box definition. The next time you rebuild your project, the controls will have the modified visit order.

The Accelerator Table Editor

An accelerator, or shortcut key, is a resource that allows the user to go directly either to a control or to a menu item by pressing a certain key combination such as Alt-F or Alt-X. You should include these accelerators to enhance the versatility of your application. The most prevalent accelerator is the Alt-*key* combination, where *key* refers to a regular key on the keyboard. Underlining this key on the control indicates that the *key* is the accelerator. You can specify an accelerator when you assign the text value to a menu item or control by typing an ampersand ("&") before the key of your choice. As an example, specify the familiar File menu option by typing "&File" in the menu editor. App Studio automatically does the underlining for you. You need to exercise some caution when assigning these keys, however, as App Studio will allow you to assign the same accelerator to different controls. It's easy to do this; you can reasonably end up typing in "&Edit" for an edit choice and "&Exit" for an exit button. When your program runs, pressing Alt-E will take you to the first option it finds assigned to Alt-E, which effectively means you have no accelerator key for the other control. Using the accelerator table editor can help you spot these little inconsistencies. To activate the editor, click the icon depicting a finger pressing a button. The properties dialog box lets you assign an ID, a key, and the modifiers (i.e., the Ctrl, Alt, and Shift keys). This procedure is the usual and the easiest way for you to assign and track the keys and modifiers. Refer to Chapter 5 of the *App Studio User's Guide* for more information on using the accelerator editor.

The String Editor

The string editor is an App Studio utility for managing the string resources of your application. Strings can include not only the prompt strings associated with status bar help messages but also those strings that your program will use again and again. For example, your application may be a terminal emulator, and you may wish to display the message "Be sure your modem is properly configured and available" in a window. This is an ideal situation in which to place the message string in your project's resource file instead of letting it take up space in memory. Making this message a member of a string table would allow your program to load the string only when needed and discard it when no longer needed. A much more frequent and practical use of the string editor remains the management of the prompt strings.

Programming and String Tables

A Windows application can only have one string table; Windows logically organizes strings into groups of 16. The group to which a particular string belongs is a function of its identifier. For example, strings having identifiers falling between 0 and 15 belong to one group; those with identifiers 16 through 31 belong to another; and those with identifiers 32–47 to yet a third. Thus the values ranging from 0x0 to 0xFFFF identify strings. Windows uses the first 12 bits for segment allocation. This orderly grouping of strings facilitates reading all related strings at one time and discarding them together. In other words, if you keep all the prompt strings for one menu option in one segment, all the strings for another option in another, etc., this allows Windows to fetch all the prompt strings in a group (up to 16) at once—sort of like catching all the fish with one sweep of the net. When possible, your application should make the table movable and discardable; this is true of tables in general and is the App Studio default setting. The icon with letters [ABC] on the App Studio toolbar corresponds to the string table editor.

The Graphics Editor

The graphics editor is the tool to use for creating and editing graphical objects such as icons, bit maps, special cursors, etc. This editor features a floating tool palette that is very intuitive and easy to use. Every Windows user who has ever used one of the drawing tools in Windows (e.g., Paintbrush) will find the graphics editor quite similar. The editor can handle graphical objects in sizes up to 999×999 pixels and in 2 or 16 different colors. The editor contains the usual tools for drawing lines, flood-filling regions, etc. You should try to keep all special images in your project's \RES directory, as this will reduce clutter in your project directory while making it easier to maintain your resources.

Because of the graphical editor's specialized and intricate nature, a lot of the tools used with it require a mouse. Regardless, even first-time users of Visual C++ should feel comfortable running the graphics editor. The online Help utility or the documentation can probably answer any questions you have about this editor.

CHAPTER SUMMARY

It is the power of the wizards that make Visual C++ so robust and effective. The single most important thing to remember is that you need to know what options you want to include in your program *before* you build your initial framework via AppWizard. Should you need to add an option after this phase, back up all your files to a new area, delete all the old stuff, and rerun AppWizard with the additional options specified. Then salvage what code you can from your earlier version. Believe us, this is painful, as it opens the door to a whole slew of problems.

ClassWizard tends to be well behaved. Your biggest worry here is likely to be deciding the base class from which to derive the classes you create. For things like dialog boxes, this is not likely to be a problem; you would clearly choose CDialog as the base class. Other classes, such as CWnd, Topmost Frame, etc., can be a little intimidating, especially to the new user. The best advice we can offer is to make sure you know the difference between frames, views, etc., and how your class fits in with these.

App Studio is the visual aspect of your program. When creating objects, override the default identifiers assigned by App Studio with more descriptive ones. For example, when you create the first edit box for a dialog box, App Studio assigns it the value IDC_EDIT1. If this edit box is going to be used to enter, say, an employee name, consider using an identifier that more closely indicates the purpose of the control *and* the dialog box to which it belongs (e.g., **ID_EMPNAME_DBOX1**). Later, when you are looking through the resource header file or your project's resource file, you'll be able to associate more quickly where the control belongs and what it does. The same holds true for the Prompt edit box in App Studio for menu items. Even though App Studio will write default prompt strings (the verbiage that appears in the status bar pane), go ahead and write your own strings. They could come in handy later when you are debugging, as you will be more likely to recognize your own prompt strings than App Studio's.

CHAPTER
3

Applications, Frames, Documents, and Views

The document view architecture is probably one of the most confusing features of the new version of the Microsoft Foundation classes, MFC 2.0. Some believe that the architecture only applies to word processors, graphics programs, or spreadsheets, but this cannot be further from the truth. This chapter will give you an overview of Microsoft's Application Framework, as supported by the MFC library, with particular emphasis on this new document view architecture. Chapter 2 introduced you to the Visual C++ Wizards, and this chapter will show you how to use their magic to create applications. Since the document view architecture can appear daunting at first, this chapter will also lead you through the various classes created by AppWizard as you step through the creation, execution, and termination of a sample application.

THE APPLICATION

To begin, we will cover the basic operation of a typical Windows application developed with the SDK. Just as C programs begin execution at the main function, so Windows programs begin at the WinMain( ) function. In WinMain( ) you must indicate whether this is the first instance of the application. If not, initialize a Windows class (not to be confused with a C++ class) and then initialize data for this particular instance. The reason for doing this is that Windows allows multiple copies of an application to run simultaneously. You must initialize the application only once, since Windows loads the code once, and then initialize each *instance* as you start a new copy of the program. After initialization, set up the application's main message pump. The following is a sample of a minimal SDK Windows program.

```
int PASCAL WinMain(    HANDLE hInstance, HANDLE hPrevInstance,
        LPSTR lpszCmdParam, int nCmdShow)
{
  {char   szProgName[] = "Hello World";
  HWND    hWnd;
  MSG     winmsg;
```

```
WNDCLASS WndClass;
 if (!hPrevInstance) // 1st time, register a window's winclass
 {
  WndClass.style          = CS_HREDRAW | CS_VREDRAW ;
  WndClass.lpfnWndProc    = WndProc;
  WndClass.cbClsExtra     = 0;
  WndClass.cbWndExtra     = 0;
  WndClass.hInstance      = hInstance;
  WndClass.hIcon          = LoadIcon( NULL, IDI_APPLICON);
  WndClass.hCursor        = LoadCursor(NULL, IDC_ARROW);
  WndClass.hbrBackground  = GetStockObject(WHITE_BRUSH);
  WndClass.lpszMenuName  = NULL;
  WndClass.lpszClassName = szProgName;
  RegisterClass( &WndClass );
 }
 hWnd = CreateWindow (    szProgName,
    "Hello World Caption",
    WS_OVERLAPPEDWINDOW,
    CW_USEDEFAULT,
    CW_USEDEFAULT,
    CW_USEDEFAULT,
    CW_USEDEFAULT,
    NULL,
    NULL,
    hInstance,
    NULL);
 ShowWindow( hWnd, nCmdShow);
 UpdateWindow( hWnd );
 While ( GetMessage( &winmsg, NULL,0,0) )
 {
  if ( hdlg = NULL || !IsDialogMessage( hdlg, &winmsg) )
  {
    if (!TranslateAccelerator( hwnd,haccel, &winmsg) )
    {
      TranslateMessage( &winmsg);
      DispatchMessage( &winmsg);
    }
  }
 }
 return winmsg.wParam;
}
```

The GetMessage( ) API call retrieves this instance's Windows messages, if any are available. Otherwise the program will return control to the window's Task manager, which will let other tasks execute if they have messages pending. If the message is the WM_QUIT message, then this instance of the application will exit. GetMessage will route each message through the framework to the appropriate handler.

APPLICATION FRAMEWORKS

Sounds simple unless you've done the same thing for countless applications. MFC and most other application frameworks for Windows encapsulate this repetitiveness either into a C library call, or more typically, into a C++ class library. An *application framework* is a library that surrounds an underlying architecture, usually an event-driven GUI. Among the many application frameworks available for Windows are Borland's OWL, Zinc's Zinc Application Framework, and Inmark Development's Zapp.

Not all are C++-based, but most are due to the nature of a framework. Frameworks do not just surround function calls with more calls, but integrate several functions into one function. Most also encapsulate the main message pump with their own and map the event messages to member functions of some "application" class, a paradigm that MFC follows.

An MFC application has a single object representing your program. This object is a CWinApp-based object that encapsulates the window's message pump, maps the various messages to member functions rather than handling them inside a large switch statement as SDK programs do, and performs the application-specific initialization and the instance initialization before processing messages.

CWINAPP

AppWizard will create a class based on the name of your project. For instance, AppWizard generated the demo.cpp and demo.h source files on the disk accompanying this book based on our project's name: Demo.

In demo.h you will find the declaration for our program's CWinApp object, called CDemo, as shown below.

```
/////////////////////////////////////////////////////////////////////////////
// CDemoApp:
// See demo.cpp for the implementation of this class
//

class CDemoApp :: public CWinApp
{
public:
    CDemoApp();
// Overrides
    virtual BOOL InitInstance();
// Implementation
    //{{AFX_MSG(CDemoApp)
    afx_msg void OnAppAbout();
    afx_msg void OnFont();
    afx_msg void OnColor();
    afx_msg void OnHelpIndex();
    //}}AFX_MSG
    DECLARE_MESSAGE_MAP()
};
```

In the sequence of events, WinMain( ) will create this object using code located in the MFC source file, *winmain.cpp*. One thing to note is that many of the MFC variables have the prefix "AFX", which stands for application framework. Inside MFC's *winmain.cpp* you will see several calls to AFX-named functions. These functions set up the internal data structures required by the framework to perform its magic. The framework creates its data variables on the application's global stack— a situation that can cause problems when dealing with DLLs. The function AfxWinInit performs this setup with the arguments the framework sends to the WinMain( ) function. If you wish to replace the framework's WinMain( )—not a recommended procedure but certainly a possible one—and still use the framework, you must call this function to initialize the framework's internal structures. WinMain( ) next calls the MFC AfxGetApp( ) function to get a pointer to the framework's application object. The framework only allows you to have one

TABLE **3.1**
Afx Functions.

```
AfxGetApp.
AfxGetAppName.
AfxGetInstanceHandle.
AfxGetResourceHandle.
AfxRegisterWndClass.
AfxRegisterVBEvent.
AfxSetResourceHandle.
```

application object. Table 3.1 lists the other AFX functions that return the data stored in your application's global stack space.

Using this pointer to your application's object, the WinMain( ) function will then call the member functions InitApplication, InitInstance, and Run, in that order. The WinMain( ) function will return the value returned by Run to Windows, after calling the AfxWinTerm function. This sequence is almost identical to the SDK WinMain( ) procedure described earlier, except that you did not have to write this code. The framework supplies the code for you. You will learn more about the Run member function later in this chapter.

INITAPPLICATION

AfxInitApplication( ) registers the MS Windows WNDCLASS structures listed in Table 3.2 for the framework's use when called by WinMain( ). You do not have to register a WNDCLASS as you did with SDK programs. The problem is that you may need to register your own Windows class.

REGISTERING YOUR OWN WINDOWS WNDCLASS

To register your own Windows class, you can call the SDK function ::RegisterClass or MFC's AfxRegisterWndClass. If you need to know the name of the class you register—for instance to use in a dialog resource file or to find a previous instance of your application—then you must use the SDK API call. AfxRegisterWndClass( ) dynamically generates the class name for the WNDCLASS structure it registers, so this name is not available at compile time. The function ::RegisterClass has the following form:

```
char * classname;
UINT class_style = WS_POPUP | WS_VISIBLE | WS_CAPTION
classname = AfxRegisterWndClass( class_style );
```

TABLE **3.2**
Windows WNDCLASS structure defined by MFC.

```
Child windows.
Control bar windows.
MDI and splitter windows.
SDI and MDI child windows.
```

```
TRACE( "Name of registered winclass is %s\n",classname);
```

Registering your own WNDCLASS might be the only reason you ever have to override the default InitApplication( ) function. AppWizard will not provide a skeleton InitApplication( ) when you generate your program. You will have to manually add the necessary code to your source files.

INITINSTANCE

The next member function you must override, InitInstance( ), allows you to do application-specific processing needed to initialize your application. AppWizard will provide the skeletal body of this function, as shown below.

```
// Demo application's basic initinstance.
BOOL CDemoApp::InitInstance()
{
  // Standard initialization
  // If you are not using these features and wish to reduce the size
  // of your final executable, you should remove from the following
  // the specific initialization routines you do not need.
(1)  SetDialogBkColor();      // set dialog background color to gray
(2)  LoadStdProfileSettings(); // Load standard INI file options
                //(including MRU)
(3)  EnableVBX();          // Initialize VBX support
     // Register the application's document templates. Document
     // templates
     // serve as the connection between documents, frame windows and
     // views.
(4)  AddDocTemplate(new CMultiDocTemplate(IDR_MAINFRAME,
       RUNTIME_CLASS(CDemoDoc),
       RUNTIME_CLASS(CMDIChildWnd), // standard MDI child frame
       RUNTIME_CLASS(CDemoView)));
     // create main MDI Frame window
(5)  CMainFrame* pMainFrame = new CMainFrame;
     if (!pMainFrame->LoadFrame(IDR_MAINFRAME))
       return FALSE;

(6)  pMainFrame->ShowWindow(m_nCmdShow);
(7)  pMainFrame->UpdateWindow();
(8)  m_pMainWnd = pMainFrame;
// create a new (empty) document
(9)  OnFileNew();
(10) if (m_lpCmdLine[0] != '\0')
   {
       // TODO: add command line processing here
   }

(11) return TRUE;
}
>>
```

SECTION I. DIALOG BACKGROUND COLOR

You will now get a glimpse at what happens as the InitInstance function executes. The first function, SetDialogBkColor( ), uses its default parameters to ensure that all your dialogs use the steel gray background color and black text color that have become extremely popular in Windows programs. The function takes two COLOREF RGB parameters: The first specifies the background color, and the second specifies the text color. Thus if you wanted your dialogs to have a black background and red text, you would make the call:

```
SetDialogBkColor( RGB(0,0,0), RGB(255,0,0) );
```

You can remove this function call altogether if you wish to use the system-defined color (usually, white).

SECTION 2. LOADSTDPROFILESETTINGS

Your MFC application will create, by default, an .INI file in your Windows directory. The LoadStdProfileSettings( ) will load various items from this .INI file, which includes the File menu's Most Recently Used (MRU) list and the last print preview state. The following shows our application's default .INI file.

```
Default Demo.cpp .INI file:

[Recent File List]
File1=E:\DEMO\DEMO1.DAT
File2=E:\DEMO\DEMO2.DAT
```

The framework will save these items via a call to SaveStdProfileSettings when it calls the AfxWinTerm function. You can use other CWinApp member functions to access this .INI file, as described in Chapter 11.

SECTION 3. ENABLE VBX

This function call prepares your application to use Visual Basic Custom Controls, or VBXs, and is the only line of code AppWizard adds to your source files when you specify the VBX option during application creation. MFC provides basic support for version 1.0 VBXs, but you are currently unable to use newer versions of VBX controls. See Chapter 10 for more information on using VBX controls in your MFC applications.

SECTION 4. DOCUMENT INTERFACE TYPES

To begin, consider the overview of MFC's document view architecture as presented in Figure 3.1. Before delving further into that "fun stuff," let's take a moment to define the two different types of frame window interfaces found in Windows programs: single document interface (SDI) and multiple document interface (MDI).

In a *single document interface* only one document resides in the client area of the application's main frame window. If the application supports different kinds of data representation such as spreadsheets and graphs, when you choose File/New, the application will ask what type of New document to create. The same applies to File/Open. The File/Open dialog will allow you to specify an extension to search for and open. Thus each different type of data file has a different extension. This feature provides the ability to implement the drag-and-drop feature from the File Manager.

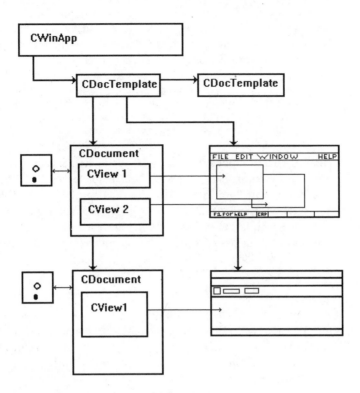

Figure 3.1
Overview of the
document view
architecture.

However, the important thing to remember is that an SDI application can only have a single document open at a time.

The advent of Windows 3.1 and its MDI-specific messages made *multiple document interface* (MDI) programs "easier" for the developer to create. An MDI application allows the user to open multiple documents, each appearing in its own window in the application's client area. As each window receives the focus, the main window displays a different menu bar, depending on the data that particular window models. MDI applications also allow you to open different windows onto the same data file.

DOCUMENTS

The key thing to remember is that a document is simply a storage area—usually a disk file—for your data. From this area your application can retrieve, process, and store information with surprisingly little code. This information can be anything from the content of a spreadsheet to the contents of an editor, the scribble data structures illustrated in Microsoft's sample application, or your own data! You process this information through a portal, or view, into your data that allows you to display information to users and allows them to alter that data. Remember, a *document* holds data, and a *view* allows you to interact with that data, usually through a window.

Holding this document view structure together is a *document template,* an object that glues together the application, a document, the document's views, and the view's windows. Your CWinApp-derived application object maintains a list of document templates associated with your application, thus allowing your application to know what types of files it is dealing with. This allows the application to register the various file types with the File Manager, so that it can launch your application whenever users double-click on your application's data file or drag and drop a data file on your application. The application adds a document template to its list with this function call:

```
AddDocTemplate(  new CMultiDocTemplate (IDR_MAINFRAME,
    RUNTIME_CLASS(CDemoDoc),
    RUNTIME_CLASS(CMDIChildWnd), //standard MDI child frame.
    RUNTIME_CLASS(CDemoView) ) );
```

Since the demo application is an MDI application, it uses the classes associated with MDI applications: namely, CMultiDocTemplate and CMDIChildWnd. If you had told AppWizard to create an SDI application, the classes listed would have been CSingleDocTemplate and the standard CFrameWnd. AppWizard adds only a single document template to InitInstance. If you wish to register other document templates, you will have to construct and add them yourself using the procedure detailed in the following section.

CREATING CDOCTEMPLATES

AppWizard creates the document template as the parameter to the AddDocTemplate function call, as shown in the following sample code. Via the C++ new operator, the framework generates on the heap a new CMultiDocTemplate. The following source code shows the CDocTemplate Constructor:

```
CDocTemplate::CDocTemplate(UINT nIDResource, // string resource id
    CRunTimeClass * pDocClass,
    CRunTimeClass * pWinClass,CRunTimeClass * pViewClass);
```

The variable nIDResource identifies a string in your application's resource file containing the needed information shown in Table 3.3 and illustrated below. The resource string will contain all the items listed in Table 3.3 separated by newline characters. The final "\n" characters are not necessary. The resource string does not

TABLE 3.3
Document template resource string.

```
Window title
Default document name
Default document type
Filename filter for the Common File Open Dialog box
Document's file extension
WIN.INI identifier for this type of document
Registry display name
>>

STRINGTABLE PRELOAD DISCARDABLE
BEGIN
IDR_DEMOTYPE "Demo Program\n demo\n demo doc\nDemo
(*.dmo)\n.dmo\nDemoType\nDemo File Type"
END
```

require an entry for each item, so you can leave out an entry by entering just its newline character.

The next parameters are all pointers to MFC CRunTimeClass structures. These structures provide each MFC class information about itself at run-time. (See Chapter 4 for more information on the CRunTimeClass structure.) You must pass the CDocTemplate constructor a pointer to a CRunTimeClass structure for this template's document type, Windows class, and view class, so that the framework can manage the various activities associated with this document type.

To add a new document template, you first need to add information to your resource file. Since a template binds together several items, you can use the same ID for them, as the sample code illustrates with the identifier IDR_MAINFRAME. Add a unique ID to the resource.h file, such as:

```
#define IDR_SECOND_DOC  100
```

Next, modify the .RC file and add any necessary resources such as the icon for an MDI child window, a Windows menu, and accelerators, as well as the resource string discussed earlier. The resources in this string should all have the same ID so as to have all these resources included with the document template you are defining.

Now, create your document and view classes. You could copy the document, view source files AppWizard created, and rename them. Alternatively, you could use ClassWizard to create the classes and files. Choosing this option will give you skeletal files to start and allow you to return later to add functionality. Regardless, do not forget to add these files to your project file.

ADDING THE NEW DOCUMENT TYPES

You will have to call AddDocTemplate for each document type you intend to add to your application. The following syntax displays the AddDocTemplate's prototype:

```
// AddDocTemplate function prototype.
void CWinApp::AddDocTemplate( CDocTemplate * pTemplate );
pTemplate - a pointer to a CDocTemplate derived template to be inserted into
your applications list of document templates.
```

Your application object will store a list of document templates in the m_templateList, a CPtrLst data member in CWinApp.

DOCUMENTS

Documents provide the ability to manage disk files but not to store data to disks. This makes sense, since each document type may represent its data in a different format: characters for an editor, records for a database, or strokes like those in the MFC sample program scribble. Just as you can store data in different forms in a document, the framework can store data in different file formats. This is why CDocument has the Serialize( ) member function. You must override this function to save and retrieve files by writing the code needed to store and subsequently access your document's data, though CDocument derived classes will handle such chores as opening the Common File dialog box.

Consider what happens when a user chooses the File/Open menu option. This command executes the CWinApp function OnFileOpen or whatever function you have mapped to the ID_FILE_OPEN command in the application's message map (more on message maps later in this chapter). Normally, this designated function will display and process the Common File Open dialog, shown in Figure 3.2, and return with the user's choice. The framework will then call CWinApp's Open-DocumentFile function, which in turn determines what document template to use, based on the file type, to open the document.

If the template is for an SDI document, place your initialization code in the OpenDocumentFile function (which you must override), and the framework will reuse the frame window originally created in InitInstance( ). If your application is an MDI application, the framework will first check to see whether the document associated with the passed file name has a frame window. If so, the framework will reactivate that view. If not, the framework will create a new MDI child window based on the document template and use the various member functions to read in and display the file.

SERIALIZE

To read in a document from disk, you must use the document's Serialize function. If you do not override this function, your application will do nothing, since the base function CDocument inherits from CObject does nothing. AppWizard will provide in your application's document class a skeletal Serialize member function similar to this one, which it generated for the demo program.

```
void CDemoDoc::Serialize(CArchive& ar)
{
   if (ar.IsStoring())
   {
      // TODO: add storing code here
   }
   else
   {
      // TODO: add loading code here
   }
}
```

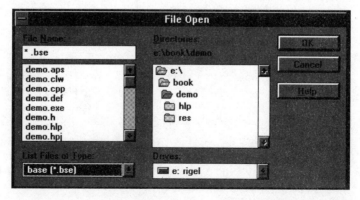

Figure 3.2
The common File Open dialog box.

The passed reference to a CArchive object contains a function, IsStoring( ), that tells the object whether it is writing to or reading from a CFile object. The framework provides this CFile object based on the document template. (See Chapter 4 for more information on the CArchive class and serialization.)

OTHER CDOCUMENT FUNCTIONS

Documents deal with your application's data and its interaction with disk files, and many other member functions facilitate this interaction. The document tracks your data's current state with a member variable called IsModified( ). This function tells you if the user modified the data since reading it in from disk. If the user modified the data, you should give the user the chance to save the changes before shutting down the system. You and the framework can determine the state of the data from any point in the application by first getting a pointer to the current document and then calling the IsModified( ) function. To set this variable, call the CDocument function SetModifiedFlag( ), which has a default TRUE parameter. Your application's view objects will call most of these functions. We will discuss MFC views shortly, but for now understand that users interact with your data through views. The various MFC View classes provide a member function called GetDocument( ) that will return a pointer to the view's document class and thus provide access to the various CDocument methods. The following contrived code illustrates these functions:

```
CDemoView::SomeFunction()
{
  CDemoDoc *doc_ptr = GetDocument();
  if ( doc_ptr->IsModified() )
  {
    // let's mark this data as not modified!
      doc_ptr->SetModifiedFlag(FALSE);
  }
  else
    {
    // data hasn't been modified, but let's mark it as such anyway
      doc_ptr->SetModifiedFlag(); // use default parameter, which = TRUE
    }
}
```

When a user attempts to close a document, the framework will test the flag and prompt the user to decide whether to continue closing or to abort. You can override this functionality by supplying your own version of the CDocument function SaveModified to do any application-specific prompting.

Another disk-related area deals with your document's path and file name. The parameters to OnOpenDocument usually supply this information. The document will allow the developer to set the path name and its frame window title. The framework will supply a title, usually based on the file name, for the frame window. If the user does not specify a file name, the framework will set the window title to the string "untitled." The framework will use "untitled" in response to the OnNewDocument function call, too. Although the framework will supply generic values that for the most part are acceptable, if you wish, you can provide your own using the following syntax:

```
CDemoDoc::SetItems( CString & new_path, CString & new_title )
```

```
{
    CString path = GetPathName();
    CString title = GetTitle();
    // you could now display, or save these values, and then
    // set your own values.
    SetTitle( new_title );
    SetPath( new_path);
}
```

Since the document template governs the document's creation, your document class also provides a member function to retrieve a pointer to the document template. The function CDocument::GetDocTemplate( ) will return a pointer to the document's CDocTemplate class or a NULL if the document is not handled by the template.

The rest of CDocument's functions deal with its interaction with your application's view classes. For example, the document object maintains a list of views and provides you with member functions (GetFirstViewPosition and GetNextView) to iterate through this list. CDocument also provides a member function, appropriately called UpdateAllViews, to tell each view to update itself. We will discuss views in a moment, but for now let's move on to the other item a document template is responsible for creating: your frame window.

SECTION 5. CREATING YOUR FRAME WINDOW

After inserting your document templates into the application object, you must create your main frame window.

```
CMainFrame * pMainFrame = new CMainFrame;
```

This is the window you normally associate with a Windows program, and it can be either a single document window or an MDI frame window. AppWizard creates a basic frame window class, provides a default constructor, and overrides its OnCreate member function, as shown in the CMainFrame class. The constructor creates the MFC frame window object, and the object's Create function creates the MS Windows window. Understanding this concept is very important, as it applies to most of the framework. The class's constructor creates the MFC object, and the object's Create (and sometimes its PreCreate) member function creates the appropriate MS Windows window, whether it be a frame window (as in CMainFrame), a child window (such as an MDI child window), or a control's window (for instance, a button). To alter a window's style, you override the CWnd::PreCreateWindow. This function receives a reference to a CREATESTRUCT, whose fields, shown in Table 3.4, you change to fit your needs. You may need to call the base class implementation of PreCreateWindow if you do not supply all the information needed for the framework to work properly. Never call the PreCreateWindow function directly; instead provide your own override function.

The values of cx and cy specify the height of the new window, and the values of y and x specify the upper left corner of the new window. These values are relative to the parent window if this is a child window or the screen origin if it is not. The lpCreateParams field points to data the framework will use to create the window.

TABLE 3.4
CWnd CREATESTRUCT.

```
typedef struct tagCREATESTRUCT
{
    void FAR *      lpCreateParams;
    HINSTANCE hInstance;
    HMENU   hMenu;
    HWND hwndParent;
    int     cy;
    int     cx;
    int     y;
    int     x;
    LONG    style;
    LPCSTR lpszName;
    LPCSTR lpszClass;
    DWORD   dwExStyle;
} CREATESTRUCT;
```

The hInstance field contains the instance handle of the parent window. The hMenu field contains this window's menu. The hwndParent field contains NULL if the new window is a topmost window; otherwise it identifies the parent window (i.e., the window that owns this new window). The style field contains the new window's style parameters, which can be a series of Windows styles such as WS_VISIBLE, ORed together. The lpszName field holds the new window's name, and the lpszClass field holds the name of the WNDCLASS structure registered with Windows. The latter can be the name returned by the AfxRegisterWndClass function or the name you used in a call to the SDK RegisterClass function. The final field, dwExStyle, specifies extended styles for the new window.

The following function will allow you to get rid of the pesky "-" in your MDI child windows and place your own title there instead:

```
BOOL CMainFrame::PreCreateWindow( CREATESTRUCT & cs )
{
  if ( CMDIChildWnd::PreCreateWindow( cs ) == FALSE )
    return FALSE;.
  // the addtotitle style is the default for MDIChildwindows in MFC, so
  // we must mask out that style
  cs.style &= ~(LONG) FWS_ADDTOTITLE;
  return TRUE;
}
```

SECTION 6. SHOWING THE INITIAL FRAME WINDOW

After you have created your MFC window class and its associated MS Windows window, this section will tell the application how to display itself when it first becomes visible. Set the m_nCmdShow data member to an appropriate value from the list in Table 3.5 if you wish to control how the framework initially displays your application. After calling the ShowWindow function, you must tell the window to update itself via a call to UpdateWindow, as shown in the following sample code:

```
m_nCmdShow = SW_MAXIMIZED; // initially display the program maximized.
m_pMainFrame->ShowWindow( m_nCmdShow);
```

```
m_pMainFrame->UpdateWindow();
```

If you have developed an SDI application, you can set the value of **m_nCmdShow** before calling the OnFileNew function.

TABLE **3.5**
The m_nCmdShow values.

SW_HIDE. Hides the window and passes control to another window.
SW_MINIMIZE. Minimizes the current window and activates the next window in the system's task list.
SW_RESTORE. Restores and activates this window to its original size and position, even if iconized or maximized.
SW_SHOW. Displays and activates this window in its current size and position.
SW_SHOWMAXIMIZED. Activates and displays this window in its maximized state, usually covering the entire screen.
SW_SHOWMINIMIZED. Activates this window and displays it as an icon.
SW_SHOWMINNOACTIVE. Displays this window as an icon and leaves the currently active window active.
SW_SHOWNA. Displays this window in its current size and position and leaves the currently active window active.
SW_SHOWNOACTIVATE. Displays this window in its most recent size and position and leaves the currently active window active.
SW_SHOWNORMAL. Displays this window in its original size and position, even if minimized or maximized.

SECTION 7. ASSIGNING THE VALUE OF THE APPLICATION'S MAIN WINDOW

Every CWinApp object contains a pointer, CWnd * m_pMainWnd, to the application's main frame window. You must supply a pointer for many of the framework's activities to function correctly. Of course, some of your applications may not need a main frame window; instead you can use a dialog box.

There are two approaches to using a dialog box as your application's only frame window: You can derive a view from a CFormView object or use a dialog box to perform all your application's major tasks via the CDialog::DoModal( ) function. Both options require you to create a dialog using App Studio or another dialog editor.

To use the dialog box directly, you would design the dialog in App Studio and then invoke ClassWizard to create the associated class header and implementation files. (See Chapters 9 and 10 for more information on Dialog boxes.) Then you would fill in the needed functionality in the implementation file. After doing these tasks, you would instantiate a variable of this class type in your InitInstance function and call the dialog's DoModal function. This procedure would display the dialog and allow your users to interact with its various controls. After the user closes the dialog, DoModal will return with a status code and you can exit this instance of the application. The following code illustrates this technique, as does the Tracer sample application in the \msvc\mfc\samples\tracer subdirectory of the disk accompanying this book.

```
BOOL CDemo::InitInstance()
{
    if ( m_hPrevInstance ) // only one instance, please
    {
        MessageBeep(0);
```

```
        return FALSE;
    }
    CMyDialog dlg;
    int retv = dlg.DoModal();
    if ( IDOK == retv )
        // do some processing
    ::PostQuitMessage(0);        // Exit application
    return FALSE;
}
```

VIEWS

Views are your users' windows into their data. Invariably, users will interact with your document's data via a class derived from CView. Your frame window will associate an initial view with your document when you open or create a document. AppWizard will create just one view class for your application. If you need other views for your data, you can use ClassWizard to generate them for you.

A view is the child of a frame window, and more than one view can share a frame. Though the framework can only associate one document with a view, it can associate many views with a single document. These views can reside in different child windows in an MDI application or in different parts of a splitter window in an SDI application. The framework mediates the interaction between a view and a document based on the selected document template.

The view function you will use most will probably be OnDraw. This function is a pure virtual function, which means you *must* supply your own version of the function. AppWizard will provide the minimal function shown below:

```
CDemoView::OnDraw( CDC * pDC )
{
    CDemoDoc * pDoc = GetDocument();
    // TODO: add draw code here
}
```

This function allows you to draw anything on anything. You can do TextOut( ) and bitblt procedures to display either screens or printing devices, thanks to the device context pointer, CDC *pDC, supplied by the framework. In fact, you can transfer to a view's OnDraw( ) function any code you have that responds to WM_PAINT messages.

When a user changes a document's data through a view—for instance, by typing some characters into a CEditView object—it is that object's duty to update all the document's views on that data, so that the data will be consistent. The object can do this by calling its document's UpdateAllViews member function. This function, in turn, iterates through the list of attached views and calls each object's OnUpdate function, which by default simply invalidates the view's client area.

The framework supplies several view classes from which to choose and allows you to derive your own unique views from these base classes. Table 3.6 lists the various view classes you can use.

MFC derives each of these view classes from CView, except CFormView, which MFC derives from CScrollView. A CFormView allows you to have a dialog filled with controls as your view window. To accomplish this, you must first create a dialog in App Studio and then create a class to control this new dialog. You must make sure the dialog has the necessary properties: It must

TABLE 3.6
MFC view classes.

CView	Base class.
CScrollView	Provides automatic scrolling.
CFormView	Provides a dialog box as the view.
CEditView	Provides a simple text editor.
CPreviewView	Provides print preview support to framework.

be a child and be visible. To create the new control class, you may opt either to generate a new CView-derived class with ClassWizard and add this class to your existing view file or to code entirely new view class files. If you create new .CPP and header files, you must add them to your project using the Project/Edit menu item. You will then be able to make use of both CView and CDialog functionality from one class.

SECTION SUMMARY

Each member class supporting the document view architecture has particular responsibilities. The application object creates and maintains a list of document templates. The document templates are responsible for creating the documents and the frame window. The frame window is responsible for creating views into the document's data, allowing users to interact with that data. Documents provide file activities affecting their data to the framework, tied together by the document template.

SEQUENCE SUMMARY FOR DOCUMENT/VIEW CREATION

In response to a File/Open command, the framework will send a WM_COMMAND message with the ID_FILE_OPEN ID, which maps to the CWinApp::OnFileOpen function. This action displays the File Open dialog box, which requests a file name from the user. The framework then uses the file's extension to pick the appropriate document template. If the user requests a new document, the framework checks to see whether the application contains multiple document templates. If it does, the framework will ask the user which type of document to create.

After creating the document object specified by the template and constructing the associated frame window, the framework generates the calls to Pre-CreateWindow and OnCreate to generate the MS Windows window. Next, the framework creates the initial view object and the view window. Finally, the framework calls either the document's OnOpenDocument( ) or the OnNewDocument( ) function, depending on whether the user selected the File/Open command or the File/New command.

SECTION 8. ONFILENEW

The OnFileNew command executes the same function the user sets in motion by choosing the File/New menu option, or clicking on the File New button on the toolbar. In response, the framework generates the ID_FILE_OPEN command and

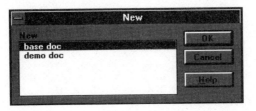

Figure 3.3
Dialog choices for
document types.

dispatches it to the appropriate message map. For an MDI application, the framework also creates a new MDI child window. If you have registered more than one document type, the framework displays a dialog box with the different file types, as shown in Figure 3.3.

When you choose the type of document to create, the framework displays an empty view of that document. This is the basic functionality that you can override with your own OnFileNew command.

SECTION 9. OBJECT LINKING AND EMBEDDING (OLE)

Unlike traditional MS-DOS programs, traditional Windows programs do not usually have a command line. However, since Windows supports DDE, OLE, DRAG and DROP, and application launching by double-clicking on a "document" (AKA data file), current Windows applications do make use of command lines. By default, AppWizard will not generate any code to handle command line arguments; it merely inserts a stub and a comment to the developer. To access drag-and-drop capabilities from File Manager, you must be running Windows 3.1 and call the CWnd function DragAcceptFiles, as shown in the following sample code:

```
m_pMainWnd -> DragAcceptFiles( );
```

This function will post a WM_DROPFILES message to which the framework message map ON_WM_DROPFILES will respond.

The default function called when the File Manager activates your application with this message is CWnd::OnDropFiles. You can instruct the framework to call another function by placing that function in the message map entry for this message. However, at some point in this new function, you should call the base class version. When to call the base class function can be a tricky question during development. This question applies not only to program initialization but to all classes you create or override while building your application. You should call the base class function first if the base class provides information your class will need. If you will supply information needed by the base class function, then you should provide this information and then call the base class function.

After calling DragAcceptFiles, call CWinApp's EnableShellOpen( ). Then you must call CWinApp's RegisterShelFileTypes( ), the function that will iterate through your application's list of document types and register them with the File Manager database, thus freeing you from having to ship a .REG file with your application. Note, however, that Windows will not register the association if one already exists for this file type and another application. The following snippet of code will accomplish the registration and perform any command line processing needed.

```
m_pMainWnd->DragAcceptFiles();
EnableShellOpen();
RegisterShellFileTypes();
if ( m_lpCmdLine[0] == '\0')
{
  // no command line params so create an empty document
  OnFileNew();
}
else if  ( ( m_lpCmdLine[0] == '-' || m_lpCmdLine[0] == '/') &&
    ( m_lpCmdLine[1] == 'e' || m_lpCmdLine[1] == 'E'))
{
  // We've been lauched via an OLE or DDE request

}
else
{
  // Arguments, usually a filename, has been sent on the cmd line
  OpenDocumentFile( m_lpCmdLine);
}
```

SECTION 10. EXITING

If everything has gone well up to this point, then you can return TRUE to the framework's WinMain( ) function to indicate that the application can continue with the run function or FALSE to tell WinMain( ) to exit this instance of the program. One reason for forcing an exit in this manner is to limit the number of active copies of your program to one. You may want to do this to conserve system resources or to protect data files.

You will find reactivating a previous instance difficult when using the default MFC Windows classes. To prevent multiple instances of your application under these circumstances, simply check CWinApp's m_hPrevInstance data member in your InitInstance member function:

```
if( m_hPrevInstance ) // another instance is running
{
  MessageBeep(0);      // Hey, another copy is already running!
  return FALSE;
}
```

However, what happens if your current application and some of its child windows are minimized? The preceding code will leave them in that state, and the user will have to find the icon and double-click to restore them. A more user-friendly process would cause your application to reactivate itself as the current window. If you have registered your own Windows class or know your application's title (i.e., the string appearing in the window's caption area), the following code snippet in InitInstance will reactivate your application.

```
HWND FirstWnd, FirstChildWnd;
if ( FirstWnd = FindWindow( "MyWindows Class Name", NULL) )
{
```

```
FirstChildWnd = GetLastActivePopup(FirstWnd);
BringWindowToTop(FirstWnd); // bring main window to top
if ( FirstWnd != FirstChildWnd)
  BringWindowToTop( FirstChildWnd);//bring child window to top
return FALSE; // don't start this instance!
}
```

Microsoft recommends this method because FindWindow does not rely on aspects of the Windows Operating Environment that might change in future versions. You can also change the second parameter of FindWindow to your application's title, if its title does not change as it executes:

```
if ( FirstWnd = FindWindow( NULL, "Your App's Caption Title") )
```

RUN

The AFX WinMain( ) function will call your application's Run( ) function when your initialization code completes and returns a TRUE value. Run( ) will then call several other CWinApp member functions. Table 3.7 lists the member functions MFC allows you to override.

The Run( ) function will process your program's messages until it receives the message WM_QUIT. Run( ) will then call the termination routine, ExitInstance, and quit this instance of your application.

As long as your application's message queue contains messages, Run( ) will dispatch them through a pretranslate function for special processing and then call a translate method (*method* is the C++ term for a member function) for standard keyboard processing. Finally, the framework will call a dispatch method that allows class member functions to handle many of the Windows messages sent to your application. A default Windows Proc will handle those messages not routed to a member function. MFC handles this magic with message maps, which we will discuss later in this chapter.

The Run( ) function first checks to make sure you have a valid window handle stored in m_pMainWnd; otherwise the framework will call ::PostQuiMessage(0). Next, Run( ) checks for Windows 3.1 compatibility. You can assure this by running under Windows 3.1 or by calling the framework API AfxEnableWin30Compatibility( ) from inside the application's InitInstance member function. To provide Windows 3.0 functionality, you must use the compiler switch /30 to instruct the compiler to generate Windows 3.0 code:

TABLE **3.7**
CWinApp member functions involved with the Run function.

```
virtual int CWinApp::Run().
virtual BOOL CWinApp::OnIdle( LONG lCount);
virtual BOOL CWinApp::PreTranslateMessage( MSG * pMsg );
virtual BOOL CWinApp::ProcessMessageFilter( int nCode, LPMSG lpMsg);
virtual int CWinApp::ExitInstance();
```

```
AfxEnableWin30Compatibility();
```

You must also avoid using any features new to Windows 3.1. The *Class Library Reference* manual marks the beginning of sections referring to such features with the keyword "Windows 3.1 Only " and ends them with a diamond symbol.

The Run function then sets in motion an infinite for loop, checking for messages, calling OnIdle, and pumping the message queue. The function checks the message queue just as any traditionally written SDK program does, with a ::PeekMessage( ) call. If no messages are waiting *and* no OnIdle processing remains to be performed, the function pumps the message queue with a call to PumpMessage( ).

PUMPMESSAGE( )

The CWinApp method PumpMessage function encapsulates the traditional Windows message loop by first calling ::GetMessage( ), then CWinApp's Pre-TranslateMessage, and finally, if necessary, the Windows API functions ::TranslateMessage( ) and ::DispatchMessage( ). PumpMessage( ) calls the same code presented in the beginning of this chapter for an SDK program, except for some framework-specific debugging code. This code allows you to produce applications with background processing ability.

BACKGROUND PROCESSING

While Windows is not multithreaded and does not perform preemptive multitasking, you can simulate this behavior with your own message pump. You can either embed a Windows message loop in a function or override Run to provide your own processing. One thing to keep in mind is that OnIdle performs some framework maintenance, and you should call the base class version of OnIdle to perform these tasks. You can also use the OnIdle function to provide background processing (we will discuss the OnIdle function later in the chapter).

To allow background processing, you need to provide a PeekMessage with calls to GetMessage, PreTranslate, Translate, and Dispatch. The following code snippet illustrates a simple message loop:

```
CWinApp::DoBackgroundTasks( int & i )
{
  BOOL bContinue(TRUE);
  MSG msg;
  while ( bContinue )
  {
    // message loop
    while( ::PeekMessage( &msg, NULL, 0,0,PM_REMOVE) )
    {
      if ( WM_QUIT == msg.message )
      {
        bContinue = FALSE;
        ::PostQuitMessage();
        break;
      }
      if ( !PreTranslateMessage( &msg) )
      {
        ::TranslateMessage( &msg );
```

```
            ::DispatchMessage( &msg);
        }
    } // peekmessage
    // call onidle to free up temporary storage and update user
    // interface items
    OnIdle(0); // UIs
    OnIdle(1); // temp objects
    // Do your background processing here
    // for example, on each iteration, check one gauge and record its
    // value
    m_gauge[i].CheckGauge();
    m_gauge[i].WriteInfo();
    i++;
    i = ( i < NumGauges ) ? 0 : i;
    } // while
}
```

PRETRANSLATE

The PreTranslateMessage function handles special processing for your application object. For instance, the demo application will display a "splash" screen until the user presses either a key or a mouse button, or until a predefined time limit expires, as illustrated here:

```
BOOL CDemo::PreTranslateMessage(MSG* pMsg)
{
    BOOL bResult = CWinApp::PreTranslateMessage(pMsg);
    if (m_splash.m_hWnd != NULL &&
        (pMsg->message == WM_KEYDOWN ||
         pMsg->message == WM_SYSKEYDOWN ||
         pMsg->message == WM_LBUTTONDOWN ||
         pMsg->message == WM_RBUTTONDOWN ||
         pMsg->message == WM_MBUTTONDOWN ||
         pMsg->message == WM_NCLBUTTONDOWN || // NC=non-client area
         pMsg->message == WM_NCRBUTTONDOWN ||
         pMsg->message == WM_NCMBUTTONDOWN))
    {
        m_splash.DestroyWindow(); // get rid of the splash window
        m_pMainWnd->UpdateWindow(); // redraw ourself
    }
    return bResult;
}
```

You might also override this function to provide extra accelerator key handling for your application. If you override any of the base class member functions, such as PreTranslateMessage, you should at some point call the base class function so that the framework can function properly and does not hang. The procedure for this call is very similar to chaining interrupts under MS MS-DOS in such a way that your interrupt handler eventually calls the BIOS/DOS interrupt handler so that the machine does not crash.

ONIDLE

This chapter has already mentioned CWinApp's OnIdle( ) member function several times. This function provides the framework's ability to update user interface items such as menus and the status bar. The framework allocates memory during its processing and must free that memory at some point. The framework also performs some heap management of the safety pool during OnIdle( ) processing. If you override the OnIdle function or provide a default message pump elsewhere in your application, you should use the following code to call the base class version of OnIdle to facilitate the framework's self-regulating system:

```
virtual BOOL OnIdle( LONG lCount );
```

OnIdle( ) takes a LONG parameter, which the framework sets to 0. As long as there is OnIdle processing to do, the function will return TRUE, and Run will continue to call OnIdle until the function returns FALSE. If you override OnIdle to perform background processing, call the base class version in a loop until it returns FALSE, then perform your activities, returning TRUE or FALSE as the case may be. You should not spend much time in an overridden OnIdle function, since doing so can degrade your application's response time. Instead, use the preceding code to process background tasks and provide default processing for the framework's internal system.

Finally, bear in mind that Run( ) will reset the value of lCount to zero at the beginning of its message loop. This allows you to use the value of lCount as a rough estimate of the time your application spends in OnIdle( ) processing. Also remember that if there are no messages waiting for your application *and* no OnIdle( ) tasks to perform, your program will yield itself to the Windows' task manager so that other applications can gain control of the system.

The sample code that follows illustrates the processing done for the demo's splash screen:

```
BOOL CDemo::OnIdle(LONG lCount)
{
  // call base class idle first
  BOOL bResult = CWinApp::OnIdle(lCount);
  // then do our work
  if (m_splash.m_hWnd != NULL)
  {
    if (::GetCurrentTime() - m_dwSplashTime > 2500)
    {
      // timeout expired, destroy the splash window
      m_splash.DestroyWindow();
      m_pMainWnd->UpdateWindow();
      // NOTE: don't set bResult to FALSE,
      // CWinApp::OnIdle may have returned TRUE
    }
    else
    {
      // check again later...
      bResult = TRUE;
    }
  }
  return bResult;
}
```

EXITINSTANCE

PumpMessage( ) returns FALSE to indicate that the application should terminate. Run( ) will then call the ExitInstance( ) function to clean up and shut itself down properly. Clean-up includes updating the application's .INI file. Windows will wipe all traces of this program from memory, barring any memory or resource leaks. You can override the ExitInstance( ) member function to perform application-specific clean-up routines, but make sure you call the base class before exiting your program.

```
int CDemo::ExitInstance()
{
  int retv;
  AfxMessageBox("Put your pre-exit clean up code here");
  retv = CWinApp::ExitInstance();
  AfxMessageBox("Put your post-exit clean up code here");
  return retv;
}
```

Be very careful of the types of actions you perform after calling CWinApp's ExitInstance function, since you no longer have a fully functional Windows program.

MESSAGE MAPS

We will end this chapter with a discussion of how the framework maps messages to the member functions of various CCmdTarget-derived classes.

The mechanism is handled by macros, both in the header file and in the implementation file. You must include the DECLARE_MESSAGE_MAP( ) macro in your class definition to alert the framework that your class will respond to Windows messages. Also, you must use the prefix afx_msg to identify in the class definition each member function that responds to Windows messages. If you use ClassWizard to create the message map entry, it will include those functions between a set of comments and place the corresponding entries in the implementation file. The following sample code illustrates some of ClassWizard's handiwork.

```
// From the AppWizard generated CDemo.h file
  //{{AFX_MSG(CDemoApp)
  afx_msg void OnAppAbout();
  //}}AFX_MSG
  DECLARE_MESSAGE_MAP()
//From the AppWizard generated CDemo.cpp file
BEGIN_MESSAGE_MAP(CDemoApp, CWinApp)
  //{{AFX_MSG_MAP(CDemoApp)
  ON_COMMAND(ID_APP_ABOUT, OnAppAbout)
  //}}AFX_MSG_MAP
  // Standard file based document commands
  ON_COMMAND(ID_FILE_NEW, CWinApp::OnFileNew)
  ON_COMMAND(ID_FILE_OPEN, CWinApp::OnFileOpen)
  // Standard print setup command
  ON_COMMAND(ID_FILE_PRINT_SETUP, CWinApp::OnFilePrintSetup)
  // Global help commands
  ON_COMMAND(ID_HELP_INDEX, CWinApp::OnHelpIndex)
  ON_COMMAND(ID_HELP_USING, CWinApp::OnHelpUsing)
  ON_COMMAND(ID_HELP, CWinApp::OnHelp)
  ON_COMMAND(ID_CONTEXT_HELP, CWinApp::OnContextHelp)
  ON_COMMAND(ID_DEFAULT_HELP, CWinApp::OnHelpIndex)
END_MESSAGE_MAP()
```

TABLE **3.8**
Mapping macros.

```
ON_COMMAND(<command id>, <function name>).
ON_CONTROL(<message>,<control id>,<function>).
ON_MESSAGE(<message id>,<function>).
ON_REGISTERED_MESSAGE(<message id>,<function>).
ON_UPDATE_COMMAND_UI(<command id>,<function>).
ON_VBXEVENT(<notification code>,<message id>,<function>).
```

After declaring the message mapped items, you need to include them in your .CPP file. You begin the message map with the BEGIN_MESSAGE_MAP( ) macro and signal the end of the map with the END_MESSAGE_MAP( ) macro, as shown previously. Between these two macros, place MFC message mapping macros whose parameters identify the member function to call when the framework receives each particular message. Table 3.8 lists the various mapping macros.

The BEGIN_MESSAGE_MAP( ) macro takes two arguments: the current class and the class from which you derived the current class. This information provides a link between the derived class's message map and the parent's message map. The framework will use these links when trying to find which function should handle the current message.

THE MACROS

The ON_COMMAND macro handles the familiar WM_COMMAND message through which each command ID invokes the corresponding member function. For example, the framework will map the command message ID_FILE_OPEN to the CWinApp::OnFileOpen function. If you provide your own OnFileOpen function by overriding the base class version, either replace the CWinApp class name with your class name or simply leave the class name off the function name. This ties the ID_FILE_OPEN command to your function.

The ON_CONTROL macro allows you to tie a function to a control notification message and the control's ID. The ON_VBXEVENT macro ties a function to the VBX control specified by the ID and to the VBX message for response. The ON_UPDATE_COMMAND_UI macro ties a function to a command ID. This function determines whether to enable or disable the given command's menu, toolbar, or status bar user interface items. (See Chapter 7 for more information on this macro.)

The ON_REGISTERED_MESSAGE macro ties a window's message, registered with Windows through the ::RegisterWindowMessage function, to a member function. Note that the registered message may come from an external application of the types the SDK function registers. For messages internal to your application, you can use the ON_MESSAGE macro. The ON_MESSAGE macro ties a message you define to the member function specified in the message map. The developer usually defines this message ID by a symbol in the range of WM_USER to 0x7FFF. Besides these macros, the framework has mapped many Windows messages to CWnd class member functions and made them available to you through the ClassWizard.

ROUTING MESSAGES

The framework routes the messages to the indicated member functions via macros for efficiency. If a C++ application framework were to provide virtual functions for every possible event, the system would require huge pointer tables and be slow in searching those tables for the correct function to call. The MFC application framework only keeps track of those functions you specify in the message map, passing the rest to the familiar SDK-type DefWindowProc that the framework provides. The framework also follows a predetermined path in routing messages by first routing the message to the target's children, then to the target class itself, and finally to other target objects. Thus a view class will try to find a message mapping in its own message map first and then in its document's message map. A document will search its map first and then its document template's message map. A frame window will first search its currently active child window or view class, then its message map, and finally the application's message map. The framework constructs this sequence from the parameters you pass to the BEGIN_MESSAGE_MAP( ) macro. The MFC CCmdTarget class provides these mapping and searching capabilities.

CCMDTARGET

MFC uses the CCmdTarget base class for its message map architecture. Only CCmdTarget and its derived classes can handle message maps, but these parameters include all CWnd classes, CWinApp, CDocTemplate, and CDocument classes. The framework takes advantage of the OnCmdMsg member function to route and dispatch the various Windows messages. This function dispatches the command to other objects or handles the message itself by calling the base class version of this command. MFC Tech Note #21 provides information on overriding this member function to alter the framework's default command routing.

CHAPTER SUMMARY

This chapter has covered much of the material surrounding the MFC framework. You have stepped through the creation and execution of a simple MFC application. We have briefly touched on the document view architecture, a paradigm suitable for all types of applications. The litany goes something like this—the application object creates a document template, which binds the document, its views, and its frame window to the application and to the framework. The template knows how to create the document and its frame window and guides the framework through this process. The document houses your application's data and facilitates its storage to and accessibility from a file. A frame window creates and mediates the interaction between a document's view and its data. A view allows the user to interact with the document's data. It also allows the framework to display data to a screen device or a printing device, thus providing printing capability with minimal effort from the developer instead of the typical thousands of lines of SDK code normally required for printing and print preview. By following the document view architecture, the framework provides a vast amount of functionality with very little coding on your part. All you have to do is fill in application-specific parts. Finally, we lead you through the MFC message loop and how it dispatches messages from the MS Windows system to your classes' member function via the message map architecture.

CHAPTER
4

The Microsoft Foundation Classes

An application framework is a wrapper around MS Windows that makes programming easier. There are several commercially available frameworks, such as OWL, Zapp, and Zinc. Some make Windows programming easier, while others offer cross-platform development. Various authors' home-grown frameworks and others from sources like the Internet are also available. This book covers the framework developed by the creators of Windows, Microsoft. The Microsoft Foundation Classes provide a close mapping from the class library to the Windows SDK API's. This compatibility allows you to switch freely from one mode to the other, calling the SDK calls when appropriate or when no counterpart exists in MFC. In this chapter we will touch briefly upon the various MFC classes, adding to the material in Chapter 3 and indicating where we will cover other classes. This chapter is not intended to be a "bible"; covering the MFC classes would require an entire book. Instead, this chapter will supplement Microsoft's *Class Library Reference: Volume 1*.

The mother of all objects, from the Small Talk point of view, is the CObject Class. MFC derives many of its classes, directly and indirectly, from CObject and provides several useful services via CObject without much processing overhead to bog down your programs.

COBJECT

The CObject base class provides your application with several useful services, such as object persistence from one invocation to the next, diagnostics as to the validity of your class's current state (e.g., "Is this data member valid?"), and run-time information (e.g., "What am I?").

PERSISTENCE

A class is simply a structure created in memory and manipulated there during your program's execution. Your program will lose this structure and its data when the

TABLE 4.1
Persistence macros prototypes.

```
DECLARE_SERIAL( class_name )
IMPLEMENT_SERIAL( class_name, base_classname, Schema )
DECLARE_DYNACREATE( class name)
DECLARE_DYNAMIC()
```

program stops. You could save this data to a file, but classes contain much more than simple data members. Classes also include items such as function pointers and the data pointed to by data pointers. CObject handles this diverse information with the help of the CArchive Class. Thus you can store an object from memory, exit the application, return later, and reconstruct the object back into memory as if you'd never left.

In order for your CObject-derived function to offer such persistence, you must place the DECLARE_SERIAL macro in the class declaration, usually contained in the class header file, and include this header file in every module using this class. The DECLARE_SERIAL macro provides all the functionality of the DECLARE_DYNCREATE and DECLARE_DYNAMIC macros. Next, you must include the IMPLEMENT_SERIAL macro in the class's implementation file, usually a .CPP source file.

These two macros inform the framework that this class is capable of reading and writing itself to a disk file or a memory file via a CArchive object. Table 4.1 displays the prototypes of both macros, and the following code corresponds to our demo program's header files.

The second parameter in the IMPLEMENT_SERIAL macro is the name of the base class and is not necessarily a CObject. The final parameter is an unsigned integer that represents the current version of the object being written. CObject will include this number in the object to identify it, thus allowing a future program to identify prior, perhaps now incompatible, persistent objects and provide some exception handling or maybe even conversion to the new format. Never set this Schema number to −1, since the framework uses that value to indicate the inability to serialize a class.

CARCHIVE

After invoking these macros, CObjects can write themselves to and from a CFile object with the help of a CArchive object. A CArchive object can either write CObjects to a CFile object or read CObjects from a CFile object, but it can never do both simultaneously. You can test this state with two CArchive member functions, IsLoading and IsStoring. As you write information, the archive will accumulate the data into its buffer and then write the buffer to the CFile object, thus reducing the number of physical accesses to the hardware. If you explicitly wish to force a write, you can call the Flush member function, as shown in the following code sample:

```
//Header file for example function.
class employee : public CObject
{
```

```
public:
  DECLARE_SERIAL( employee )
  employee() { };
  int m_NumEmployees;
  char m_FirstName[20];
  char m_LastName[20];
  void Serialize( CArchive & archive );
};
// example code for a serialize member function.
IMPLEMENT_SERIAL( employee, CObject, 1 )
void employee::Serialize( CArchive& archive)
{
  CObject::Serialize( archive );
  if( archive.IsStoring() )
  {
    for ( i = 0; i < m_NumEmployees;i++)
    {
        archive << m_FirstName[i] << m_LastName[i]; //write
        archive.Flush();// force to the disk, aka CFile object.
    }
  }
  else // we're reading data into a class
  {
    archive >> m_NumEmployers;
    for( int i=0; i < m_NumEmployers; i++)
    {
      archive >> m_FirstName[i] >> m_LastName[i];
      archive.Flush();
    }
  }
}
```

This example covers a hypothetical class containing an array of first names and last names. The class maintains the number of names defined in the m_NumEmployees variable. The function illustrated in this example represents an override of CObject's base Serialize function. If possible, you should let the framework handle its part for you, as in the case of Serialize. The framework will make this function part of your document class, since it is responsible for the program's data. You should first call the base class's Serialize function to serialize the base class's data properly. You can then write out your object's data. The preceding function uses the CArchive's overloaded >> and << operators to perform the reads and writes, but you could have used the function calls just as well. After writing the data to the archive, the Flush( ) function forces the object to write its buffer to the CFile object now instead of when the buffer becomes full. The archive accomplishes reading in a similar way, by forcing the archive object to write its buffer to the various member functions of the object rather than waiting for the buffer to fill.

Note the empty constructor in the sample's header file. The framework requires this empty constructor to facilitate serialization. On reading data into an archive, the framework creates an object based on this empty constructor and then fills this object with the data read. One thing to remember is that the archive object uses a CFile object, but you do not need to create the object explicitly if you are using the framework. If you create an archive object yourself, you need to provide a file.

MFC Technical Note #2 provides details on the information written by the archive object. (See Chapter 17 for more information on the MFC Tech Notes.) Another interesting item to note is the schema number referred to earlier. The archive will throw a CArchiveException if it finds a number stored in the serialized data that differs from the one contained in the current memory object. The CArchiveException::m_cause data member will equal CArchiveException::badSchema. (See Chapter 16 for more information on exception handling.) You can catch this exception to report an error or try to reconstruct the archive within a valid object by converting the stored object into one of the current objects. You can get the valid schema number from the CRuntimeClass structure for your object.

CRUNTIMECLASS STRUCTURE

This structure is a Microsoft extension to the C++ language that allows a CObject-derived class to know certain things about itself at run time. Table 4.2 shows the parameters this structure can contain.

The m_lpszClassName, the first parameter in the macro, identifies the name of the class (e.g., employee). The m_nObjectSize field holds the size, in bytes, of the class unless the class contains pointers to data. If the class contains pointers to data, the m_nObjectSize field will only contain the size of the pointers, and not the data these pointers reference. The next field is the schema number indicating the object's current version. You can query this value in an exception to see which version of an object caused the exception. The following sample code illustrates that sequence. The next field contains a function pointer to the class default constructor. The m_pBaseClass field contains the name of the base class, another value supplied to the macros. Finally, the framework uses the last field of the CRuntimeClass structure, CreateObject, to support dynamic creation of a class at run time.

```
// employee class ...
TRY()
{
   archive << m_item;
}
CATCH( CArchiveException, e )
{
   switch ( e->m_cause)
   {
     case CArchiveException::none :
       TRACE(" no exception");
     break;
     case CArchiveException::generic:
       TRACE(" Unspecified Error");
     break;
     case CArchiveException::readOnly:
```

TABLE **4.2**
CRuntimeClass structure.

```
LPCSTR m_lpszClassName.
int m_nObjectSize.
WORD m_wSchema.
void (*m_pfnConstruct)(void *).
CRuntimeClass * m_pBaseClass.
CObject * CreateObject().
```

```
               TRACE("Cannot write to archive, opened for reading only");
               break;
               case CArchiveException::endOfFile:
                 TRACE("End of File reached while reading an object.");
               break;
               case CArchiveException::writeOnly:
               TRACE("Can not read from archive, opened for writing.");
               break;
               case CArchiveException::badIndex:
                 TRACE("Invalid File Format encountered in archive.");
               break;
               case CArchiveException::badClass:
               TRACE("Tried to read one object into a different type of object.");
               break;
               case CArchiveException::badSchema:
               {
                CRuntimeClass * ptr = RUNTIME_CLASS( employee );
                switch ( ptr-> m_wSchema )
                {
                  case : -1:
                    // mega error, dudes/dudettes!
                  break;
                  case 1 :
                    // version, so is this object newer? handle it
                  break;
                  default :
                    // cannot handle the number encountered.
                } // switch on schema #
               }
               break;
           }
         }
         END_CATCH()
```

DIAGNOSTICS

CObject classes provide you with the ability to dump out the state of the object to a debugging device, usually a window. CObjects provide two methods for dumping information: through a CDumpContext class and via the AssertValid member function. The CDumpContext functions will print formatted listings of your internal data members to the file associated with the dump context. This dump context is usually STDERR in MS-DOS or the debug window in Windows. The dump will print the name of your class if you use the IMPLEMENT_DYNAMIC or IMPLE-MENT_SERIAL macros. Otherwise, the dump will simply print "CObject."

CDumpContext

The MFC framework creates a standalone CDumpContext object called afxDump. This object is only available in the debug version of the library, but the CDumpContext objects you create are available in both the debug and the retail versions. (See Chapter 16 for more information on debugging MFC programs.) Note that MFC samples will place Dump code between preprocessor macros for conditional compilation, as shown in the following example.

```
// example of CDumpContext conditional compilation.
```

```
/////////////////////////////////////////////////////////////////////////
// CDemoDoc diagnostics
#ifdef _DEBUG
void CDemoDoc::AssertValid() const
{
   CDocument::AssertValid();
}
void CDemoDoc::Dump(CDumpContext& dc) const
{
   CDocument::Dump(dc);
}
#endif //_DEBUG
```

CDumpContext will allow you to output formatted information in a variety of ways, including HEX. The Class overloads the << operator for CObject classes as well as for most other MFC classes and data types. Table 4.3 lists the items you can dump to a CDumpContext.

You can dump the contents of a memory address in HEX by using the HexDump function, which has the following prototype:

```
void CDumpContext::HexDump ( const char * hdrline, BYTE * data, int
   numdump, int numperline);
```

where *hdrline* indicates a string printed at the beginning of each line, *data* is a pointer to the buffer containing the bytes to display, *numdump* indicates the total number of bytes to dump from the buffer, and *numperline* indicates the number of hex digits to print per line.

If your CObject-derived object contains pointers to data, by default the dump will not print the contents of that data, just its pointer. You recurse and display each data item by specifying a *depth* value, a number that instructs the dump context to recurse the indicated number of references down into the object. Thus, if you had a collection class of structures, you could tell the dump to display each element in your list. Use the CDumpContext::SetDepth function to indicate how many levels to display. You must be careful not to allow any loops—one object pointing to another object, which in turn points back to the first object—in your data structure. If one is present, your dump may wind up in an infinite loop.

TABLE 4.3
Dump items overloaded for << operator.

Pointer to a CObject	CObject *p_obj
Pointer to a FAR string	char FAR * lpsz
Pointer to a void FAR *	void FAR * lpvoid
Pointer to a void NEAR *	void NEAR * lpnear
A BYTE	BYTE ch
A WORD	WORD wd
A DWORD	DWORD dwd
An int	int num
A LONG	LONG ld
An unsigned int	UINT unum
Be aware that each output operation can throw a CFileException.	

AssertValidValidation

Another support service from CObjects is the ability to verify that your objects are indeed valid and ready for use. The AssertValid member function enables your classes to check their internal consistency, providing you override the base class version to add your class specific checks. For instance, you could use several ASSERT macros to check on the value ranges of data members and the contents of data pointers. The following code illustrates such an overloaded function:

```
//AssertValid function.
CEmployee::AssertValid()
{
  CObject::AssertValid(); // call base class first
  ASSERT ( !m_LastName.IsEmpty() ); // hey, they need a name!
  ASSERT (!m_SSNum.IsEmpty() ); // need an SS num too.
  ASSERT_VALID( m_Employed ); // is this a valid employment code ?
}
```

The last macro in this sample invokes the AssertValid member function of m_Employed.

NON-COBJECT CLASSES

Table 4.4 lists the MFC classes derived from CObject. Short discussions of each class constitute the remaining sections of this chapter.

TABLE **4.4**
Non-CObject classes and structures.

```
Run-Time Object Support
        CArchive
        CDumpContext
        CRunTimeClass
Simple Values
        CString
        CTime
        CTimeSpan
        CRect
        CPoint
        CSize
Structures
        CFileStatus
        CCreateContext
        CPrintInfo
        CMemoryState
Support Classes
        CDataExchange
        CCmdUI
```

Simple Values

This group of classes provides simple value types to your programs.

CPoint, CRect, and CSize

These three classes refer to Windows objects and are class representations of the SDK POINT, RECT, and SIZE structures. You can use these classes interchangeably with their SDK counterparts, especially as parameters to API functions. These classes provide data members to hold their respective data structure and overload arithmetic and logical operators such as +, −, and ==, for easier object manipulation.

CTime and CTimeSpan

You cannot use the CTime class or the CTimeSpan class to derive a new class. The CTime class represents a time and date via an encapsulated time_t data member. Furthermore, you cannot use the CTime class in a Windows DLL because of its ties to an unsupported Windows function, strftime. CTime encapsulates most of the C Run-Time Library time functions in a very rigid way, and since these classes contain no virtual member functions, they will always occupy 4 bytes (MFC 2.0). You will find most of their functionality maps directly to low-level DOS calls via inline functions.

The CTime objects represent Gregorian dates, and the times are based on Greenwich Mean Time (GMT). You can compensate for local time by setting the DOS environment variable TZ in your AUTOEXEC.BAT file as follows:

```
SET TZ=EST5EDT
```

This sets the TZ variable to Eastern Standard Time. (See your DOS manual for more information.) To get the current time and date, you do not need to make DOS calls—at least not directly. You can simply use the CTime static member function GetCurrentTime and the various member functions to extract the needed components and display them. The MFC class also overrides several operators so that you can compare time components and test them against each other. The following sample code illustrates several CTime functions:

```
#include "time.h" // for time_t definition
void CDemo::TimeTest()
{
    CTime cur_time = CTime::GetCurrentTime() // note how to call static
                          //functions
    CTime made_time( 1994, 4,1,17,30,0); // 5:30 pm, April 1st, 1994
    time_t crtl_time; // a c run time library time_t variable
    // format a string
    CString curstr = cur_time.Format( "Current date/time is %A, %B, d, %Y");
    AfxMessageBox( str );
    // Extract the various date/time components
    int day = cur_time.GetDay(); // range 1-31, no checking is done
    int hour = cur_time.GetHour(); // range 0-23
    int minute = cur_time.GetMinute(); // range 0-59
    int second = cur_time.GetSecond(); // range 0-59
    int year = cur_time.GetYear();  // 1970 to 2038
```

```
    int month = cur_time.GetMonth() // 1 through 12 (Jan. thru Dec.)
    int dow = cur_time.GetDayOfWeek(); // day of week, 1 = Sunday etc.
    char MonthArr[12][4] = { "Jan", "Feb", "Mar", "Apr", "May", "Jun",
            "Jul", "Aug", "Sep", "Oct", "Nov", "Dec" };
    char WeekDay[7][4] = {"Sun", "Mon","Tue","Wed","Thu","Fri","Sat" };
    char charstr[32];
    sprintf( charstr,"Month = %s and DOW = %s", MonthArr[month-1],
    WeekDay[dow-1]);
    AfxMessageBox( charstr );
    // you could also have used the Format functions' formatting strings
    // See Table 4.4 for details
    // CTime gives you access to time_t and struct tm
    crtl_time = cur_time.GetTime(); // time_t item
    // struct tm, defined in time.h
    struct tm * rtltm = cur_time.GetGmTm(); // using default NULL parameter
    // or you could use GetLocalTm for local times rather than GMT times
    int tmsec = rtltm-> tm_sec; // 0-59
    int tmmin = rtltm-> tm_min;// 0-59
    int tmhr = rtltm-> tm_hour; // 0-23
    int tmday = rtltm-> tm_mday; //day 1-31
    int tmmonth = rtltm-> tm_mon; //month 0-11
    int tmyr = rtltm-> tm_year; // actual year—1900 ( 70-138)
    int tmdow = rtltm-> tm_wday; // day of week 1-7, Sunday = 1
    int tmyday = rtltm-> tm_yday; // day of the year, Jan 1 = 0 to 365
    int tmisdst = rtltm-> tm_isdst; // daylight savings time, always 0
}
```

The MFC library does not provide a way to change the system time or date; for that you will have to resort to MS-DOS–specific calls, which could prevent your application from being ported to future versions of MS-Windows.

The CTimeSpan class represents the difference between two CTime variables. This function keeps track of time in seconds and provides member functions to convert seconds into the required time entity, hour or minutes. The CTime and CTimeSpan classes hold this value in a signed, 4-byte (time_t) variable and thus can represent a time span of plus or minus 68 years. These classes provide several operators as inline functions for setting and testing CTimeSpan objects, plus a formatting function to display the time. The CTimeSpan::Format function uses the formatting codes shown in Table 4.5 and specified for the C Run-Time Library to display time values.

The percent sign (%%) is common to both CTime and CTimeSpan, as are the formatting symbols %D, %M, and %H.

The following sample code illustrates the use of a CTimeSpan object:

```
void CDemo::TimeSpan()
{
    CTime t = CTime::GetCurrentTime();
    CString str = t.Format("Current time is %A, %B, %d, %Y");
    AfxMessageBox( str );
    CTime t2(1993, 8,1,12,0,0);  // aug 1 1993, 12:00pm noon

    CTimeSpan diff = t - t2;

    str = diff.Format("Total time elapsed = %D days, %H hours, %M \
            "minutes, and %S seconds");
    AfxMessageBox( str );
}
```

TABLE **4.5**
CTime and CTimeSpan formatting codes.

CTime-specific formatting codes

%a	Displays an abbreviated weekday name, "Mon."
%A	Displays the full weekday name, "Monday"
%b	Displays the abbreviated month's name, "Sept."
%B	Displays the full month's name, "September"
%c	Displays the date and time representation according to the [intl] section of the WIN.INI file
%d	Displays the day of the month as a number (01–31)
%H	Displays the hour in 24-hour format (00–23)
%I	Displays the hour in 12-hour format (01–12)
%j	Displays the day of the year as a number (001–366)
%m	Displays the month as a number (01–12)
%M	Displays the minute as a number (00–59)
%p	Displays the AM/PM indicator
%S	Displays the seconds as a number (00–59)
%U	Displays the week of the year as a number (00–51), with Sunday as the first day of the week
%w	Displays the weekday as a number (0–6), with Sunday = 0
%W	Displays the week of the year as a number (00–51), with Monday as the first day of the week
%x	Displays the date representation as specified in the WIN.INI file
%X	Displays the date representation as specified in the WIN.INI file
%y	Displays the year of the current century as a number (00–99)
%Y	Displays the year as a number, including the century
%Z	Displays the system's time zone name or abbreviation, providing it has been set in the DOS environment table
%%	Displays the percent sign

CTimeSpan-specific formatting codes

%D	Displays the total number of days represented in this CTimeSpan object
%H	Displays the number of hours in the current day
%M	Displays the number of minutes in the current hour
%S	Displays the number of seconds in the current minute
%%	Displays the percent sign

CString

The final simple value class deals with strings. Strings form the heart of most C++ class libraries. In fact, most beginning texts illustrate C++ techniques by building a string class. This string class usually hides the representation of the string (array, pointer, null terminated, length, and string, etc.) from the system but provides the user with a standard interface for using the string contents. The MFC CString class offers many of these same versatile features but also presents a few pitfalls to avoid. Many of the member functions allow the string to grow dynamically, thus forcing a reallocation of memory. The framework will throw an allocation exception if the allocation fails, but this exception will not cause a fatal error. Instead, the failure causes unpredictable program behavior. The *Class Library Reference* manual details those functions and operations that can cause problems.

If you look at the reference material , you will find the class has many overloaded conversion operations, and the other MFC classes that operate on "normal" C-strings will operate on CString strings. The exception will occur when you need to pass a pointer to a non-const pointer to char * (a string). You will then need to access the buffer inside the CString Object. Fortunately, MFC supplies a function to do just that, as shown below:

```
CString string = "This is a test";
....
char *ptr;
int len;
len = string.GetLength(); // get the current length of the string
ptr = string.GetBuffer( len ); // return to ptr a pointer to a string of
'len' bytes
// use the string pointer
string.ReleaseBuffer(-1);
...
```

The CString function GetBuffer will return a buffer containing the encapsulated string up to *n* characters. You can request more space than the string currently uses, but doing so may cause a memory exception if your system does not have the memory resources to satisfy the request. A good value to use is the current length of the string returned by the CString function GetLength. While you have this pointer, you cannot perform any other related CString operations until you release the buffer with a call to ReleaseBuffer. The CString function will restore the string to the size returned in GetLength( ) if you pass ReleaseBuffer a −1. Note that the pointer returned by GetBuffer will be invalid after the call to ReleaseBuffer.

CString and the C Run-Time Library

You will find many of the familiar string functions from the run-time library encapsulated in the CString class, plus a few extras. String copies and concatenation have overloaded operators (= and +=) to provide the functionality of the strcpy( ) and strcat( ) functions. And while you should think of a CString object as a string object, and not as a pointer to a null-terminated character array, you can still access the internal buffer as an array with the GetAt and SetAt functions, as illustrated in the following example:

```
CString str = "Hello World";
char ch = str.GetAt(4);  // ch =
"o"
// you also could have used the "[]" operator
ch = str[4]; // gives the same result.
ch = 'p';
str.SetAt( 4, ch ); // str now = "Hellp World"
```

CString also overloads the [] operator to provide the GetAt functionality, as shown in the preceding example. Unfortunately, because of a limitation in the C++ language, you cannot use the [] operator to overload the SetAt function (i.e., to perform str[4] = 'p').

Since you should not think of a CString as a null-terminated character array, you should neither test for an empty string via the null terminator nor create an empty string with a null terminator. To help you with this concept, CString provides two functions: IsEmpty( ) and Empty, and the following code details their use:

```
CString str = "Hello World";
if ( str.IsEmpty() )
  AfxMessageBox( "The string is empty");
else
  AfxMessageBox("The string is NOT empty");
str.Empty(); // str is now empty!
```

CString and Windows

You can use CStrings in both Windows programs and MS-DOS programs. However, the class does have three member functions you can only access from within a Windows program: AnsiToOem, LoadString, and OemToAnsi. The first and last functions deal with converting the characters in a CString object from the ANSI character set to the character set supported by the current hardware manufacturer. In the United States most PCs follow the IBM PC extended character set, whereas in Japan many machines support the Kanji character set. Windows provides facilities to make programs portable across machines and across cultures.

The CString::LoadString function lends support to this portability paradigm by allowing you to load a string from the resource table by ID, rather than hard coding the string into your source code. Thus in the future you can replace the string with a translated version and simply recompile and rebind the resource, rather than changing the source code and recreating the entire executable. For example, if you had defined the string table entry

```
IDS_MEM_FMT_STR   "Memory available = %ld"
```

you could load this resource into your program with the following code:

```
CString str, fmtstr;
fmtstr.LoadString(IDS_MEM_FMT_STR);
sprintf(str.GetBuffer(80), fmtstr, GetFreeSpace(0) / 1024L);
str.ReleaseBuffer();
SetDlgItemText(IDC_AVAIL_MEM, str);
```

Memory Leaks with CStrings

Memory leaks occur when a program allocates memory but never releases that memory back to the operating system. This typically occurs when you allocate an object on the heap (for instance, using the new operator) and an exception occurs in which the framework does not call the object's destructor or delete operator. To prevent this with CStrings, wrap those member functions that allocate memory with a TRY/CATCH exception handling macro block. Chapter 16 gives plenty of examples using MFC's exception handling macros.

```
CString str;
TRY()
{
  str = "Hello";
  str += "World"; // may not be enough memory
}
CATCH( CMemoryException, e )
{
  str.Empty(); // release any memory
  THROW_LAST();
}
END_CATCH
```

Structures

MFC supplies the developer with four support structures for the application frame-work: CFileStatus, CCreateContext, CPrintInfo, and CMemoryState. The CFileStatus structure holds various fields containing information about a CFile object. This structure, which we discuss in Chapter 11, is not specific to Windows programs. You can use these classes and the CMemoryState structure, which helps to detect memory leaks, in MS-DOS applications. The other two functions, CCreateContext and CPrintInfo, are specific to the framework and support its operation during window frame creation and printing.

CMemoryState

This structure allows you to detect memory leaks in your program by comparing its memory state at various points during execution and allowing you to dump infor-mation about its memory state at any point of execution. This structure helps with those C++ objects created with the new and delete operators; it does not function with objects allocated with the RTL malloc and free functions or the SDK Local(Global) Alloc and Free functions. In fact, Microsoft recommends not mixing these memory allocation functions together in a Windows program.

The CMemoryState structure contains various member functions to support run-time diagnostics. You can place functions inside C++ structures, just as you can in classes. The biggest difference between a structure and a class is that the members of a structure are public by default, and those of a class are private by default. You should bracket the member functions of CMemoryState structures by the conditional preprocessor commands #ifdef _DEBUG and #endif, so that you only include them in the debug builds of your program. Table 4.6 lists the CMemoryState functions.

TABLE **4.6**
CMemoryState member functions.

```
CMemoryState
CheckPoint
Difference
DumpAllObjectsSince
DumpStatistics
```

The CMemoryState::CheckPoint function obtains a snapshot of your application's current memory state. You can take multiple snapshots at various points in your application and then compare these states with the CMemoryState::Difference function, whose prototype is shown below:

```
BOOL Difference( const CMemoryState& oldstate, const CMemoryState& newstate);
```

You must initialize the old and new state parameters by calling their checkpoint member functions. The Difference member function stores the result in itself so that you can dump the statistics via the DumpStatistics memory function.

```
CMemoryState first, second, diff; // constructs 3 empty structures
first.CheckPoint();
CEmployee *emp1 = new CEmployee("Jack",' ',"Tackett","123-45-6789");
CEmployee *emp2 = new CEmployee("Keith",'E',"Bugg","987-65-4321");
second.CheckPoint();
diff.Difference( first, second);
diff.DumpStatistics();
```

The member function DumpAllObjectsSince will dump all the CObject-derived objects that the framework allocated since the last call to the structure's CheckPoint function. If you call the DumpAllObjectsSince member function of an uninitialized structure (i.e., without first calling the CheckPoint function), the object will dump all objects currently in memory. Note that DumpAllObjectsSince dumps objects via their particular defined Dump member function, so be sure to include an override for this function in your CObject-derived classes.

The CMemoryState::DumpStatistics function displays the results obtained by the Difference function to the standard debug output window (the afxDump device), which can be the DBWIN program, the framework's output window, or an auxiliary device on your AUX port. Table 4.7 shows the format of this function's report.

The first line of this report describes the number of memory blocks whose deallocation is currently being delayed because of the value of the afxMemDF variable. You can set this variable in your program or from within your debugger to control how your application allocates and deallocates memory. The afxMemDF variable can have the values enumerated in Table 4.8 or any ORed combination of them. To set the value in your program, you could use the following syntax:

```
afxMemDF = allocMemDF | delayFreeMemDF | checkAlwaysMemDF;
```

TABLE 4.7
Format of memory state diagnostics.

```
0 bytes in 0 Free Blocks
16 bytes in 2 Object Blocks
0 bytes in 0 Non-Object Blocks
Largest Number used: 16 bytes
Total Allocations: 16 bytes.
```

TABLE **4.8**
Possible afxMemDF values.

```
allocMemDF
delayFreeMemDF                          .
checkAlwaysMemDF
```

The allocMemDF is the default value in a debug build and turns on the debugging allocator. The delayFreeMemDF value delays the return of a freed block of memory to the operating system. You can use this value to put maximum resource stress on your application during testing. The final value forces your application to call the AFX function AfxCheckMemory after every memory allocation, which can significantly impair your application's performance. The AfxCheckMemory function marches through the list of allocated objects, checks their consistency, and reports any errors it discovers as follows:

```
if ( AfxCheckMemory() ) // memory errors reported to developer
{
    AfxAbort();  // Abandon ship! No need to recover now; go and fix the
    // problem first and then recompile and retest!
}
```

The second line in the DumpStatistics report displays the number of object blocks allocated with the new operator that still reside on your application's heap. The next line contains the number of memory blocks still on the heap that were not allocated by an object's new operator. The fourth line indicates in bytes the total amount of memory that your application uses at any one time. The last line reports the total amount of memory your program uses.

CCreateContext

The framework uses this structure during the creation of the frame windows and views associated with a document. You should not have to use this structure unless you plan to override parts of this creation process. The structure contains the fields listed in Table 4.9.

As can be seen in this table, the structure contains pointers to the document, the view, the frame window, the template, and the CRuntimeClass of the item to be created. The m_pCurrentDoc contains the pointer to the current document to which a new view is to be attached. The m_pNewDocTemplate contains the document template if the

TABLE **4.9**
CCreateContext member fields.

```
CRuntimeClass* m_pNewViewClass
CDocument* m_pCurrentDoc
CDocTemplate* m_pNewDocTemplate
CView* m_pLastView
CFrameWnd* m_pCurrentFrame
CCreateContext() // constructor
```

TABLE **4.**10
MFC classes requiring a CCreateContext object.

```
CFrameWnd::Create
CSplitterWnd::Create
CWnd::Create
CFrameWnd::LoadFrame
CFrameWnd::OnCreateClient
CSplitterWnd::CreateView
```

frame window to be created is an MDI frame window. The m_pLastView field contains the original view upon which the framework will base additional views, as in the case of a second view on the same document. Finally, the m_pCurrentFrame field holds a pointer to the frame window upon which the framework will base additional windows. The preceding fields are optional, and the framework may set them to NULL. In fact, unless you try advance functionality as shown in the MFC VIEWEX sample program's SPLITTER.CPP file OnCreateClient function, you can ignore this structure and simply pass a NULL pointer in its place to the routines listed in Table 4.10, which require a CCreateContext.

CPrintInfo

One of the greatest advantages of the framework supported by MFC is the printing and print preview functionality. The CPrintInfo structure, shown in Table 4.11, plays a support role in this functionality by storing information about the current print job—whether directed to the printer or to the screen during a print preview. The framework creates a CPrintInfo structure each time it responds to the Print or PrintPreview command and destroys the structure when it completes the commands.

TABLE **4.**11
The CPrintInfo structure.

```
Data Members:
        BOOL m_bContinuePrinting
        BOOL m_bPreview
        LPVOID m_lpUserData
        UINT m_nCurPage
        UINT m_nNumPreviewPages
        CPrintDialog * m_pPD
        CRect m_rectDraw
        CString m_strPageDesc
Functions:
        UINT GetFromPage()
        UINT GetMaxPage()
        UINT GetMinPage()
        UINT GetToPage()
        void SetMaxPage( UINT max_page )
        void SetMinPage( UINT min_page)
```

TABLE 4.12
CView class member functions that use CPrintInfo.

```
DoPreparePrinting
OnBeginPrinting
OnEndPrinting
OnPreparePrinting
OnEndPrintPreview
OnPrepareDC
OnPrint
```

The framework passes a CPrintInfo structure between itself and your application's view class to pass information back and forth regarding the current process. Table 4.12 lists the CView member functions that use a CPrintInfo structure.

Printing

Windows does not care if it prints to a display, a printer, or another output device, since it represents everything in a device-independent context. To change output media, you merely change the device context, and not your code. Thanks to Windows' GDI interface routines and to various device drivers, your code will not know it is printing on one device rather than another. This insulates the developer from having to support a multitude of hardware devices but pressures hardware vendors to supply device drivers for their machines that enable them to operate with Windows.

Your application has certain duties to perform during printing, as does the framework. The framework first creates a CPrintInfo structure and passes its pointer to the view's OnPreparePrinting function, which calls the view's DoPreparePrinting function. The DoPreparePrinting function is responsible for displaying the Windows Common Dialog Printer box and for creating the device context for the printer.

In the AppWizard-generated OnPreparePrinting, set the values of the CPrintInfo structure to the values you have available, such as the number of pages in your document. You can then pass the structure to the DoPreparePrinting function. When this function returns, CPrintInfo will contain various pieces of information supplied by the user via the Print Dialog box. In our demo application, the process looks like the following:

```
///////////////////////////////////////////////////////////////////////
// CDemoView printing
BOOL CDemoView::OnPreparePrinting(CPrintInfo* pInfo)
{
  // default preparation
  pInfo->SetMaxPage(1); // only one page.
  return DoPreparePrinting(pInfo);
}
```

The framework then calls two of your view's member functions: OnPrepareDC and OnPrint, and passes them a pointer to a CDC and a pointer to a CPrintInfo structure, repeating this process for each document page to be printed. Each time the framework calls this pair of functions, it will change the m_nCurPage data member of CPrintInfo to tell the view which page to print. Now, if the view is to render the document page on a screen context rather than a printer context, the framework will set the CPrintInfo pointer to NULL.

The view's OnPrint member function is responsible for printing the current page, including headers and footers. If you change the size of a printable page (for instance, to make room for a header or a footer), you should then resize the m_rectDraw data member of the CPrintInfo structure to compensate for the reduction in usable space.

The framework will continue printing as long as the CPrintInfo data member m_bContinuePrinting is TRUE. The default framework activity is to set this variable to TRUE for the first page and the rest of the document's pages, provided you have set that value in the view's OnPreparePrinting function. If you have not set this value, and m_nCurPage is greater than one, the framework will set the m_bContinuePrinting field to FALSE and stop printing. The reason why this occurs is that the base class version of OnPrepareDC will set the m_bContinuePrinting variable to FALSE if the current page is greater than one.

Print Preview

The framework also supports Print Preview capabilities with the same code used for display and printer imaging by sending a CPreviewDC device context to the routines. The biggest difference with Print Preview is that it simulates printing to a printer by "printing" to the display. Also, Print Preview prints only a selected number of pages at a time and then pauses for user input.

The framework calls the view's OnPreparePrinting function with a CPreviewDC device that you can modify through the CPrintInfo structure before calling the base class version. The one item you can change is the number of pages to display in the print preview. The framework will support displaying one or two pages at a time, depending on the value stored in the CPrintInfo m_nNumPreviewPages field. You can also tell your routines their current mode (printing or print preview) by testing the CPrintInfo m_bPreview field, which the framework sets to TRUE when invoked by Print Preview.

```
/////////////////////////////////////////////////////////////////////
// CDemoView printing
BOOL CDemoView::OnPreparePrinting(CPrintInfo* pInfo)
{
   // default preparation
   if ( pInfo->m_bPreview )
   {
      // perform print preview specific initialization
      pInfo->m_nNumPreviewPages = 2;
      pInfo->m_strPageDesc = "Chapter 1: Page %u\nPages %u-%u\n";
   }
   return DoPreparePrinting(pInfo);
}
```

The Print Preview architecture will display a description at the bottom of the screen. The CPrintInfo member variable m_strPageDesc controls this description, which contains a formatting string for page numbers. This variable provides, by default, the following formats for both single- and double-page displays:

```
"Page %u\nPages %u-%u\n".
```

The framework combines both formats into one string, separating them with a newline (\n).

Support Classes

The final group of nonderived CObject classes includes the CDataExchange and CCmdUI classes. The CCmdUI class provides a mechanism for allowing the framework to tie together command user interface objects and menu items. (See Chapter 8 for more details on this class.) The CDataExchange class supports the framework's dialog data exchange and validation routines (DDX/DDV). You would use this class to create DDX/DDV routines for custom dialog controls or data types not currently supported by the framework. Chapters 9 and 10 contain more information on the DDX/DDV process, as does MFC Tech Note #26.

Collection Classes

The current (3.1) C++ language definition specifies a language feature called templates. Templates allow you to create a new version of a function or class that has the same functionality (e.g., accessing a data element) but a different data type based on a code template you supply. All that changes in the code you write for a template is the data type on which you operate—a data type you specify in the function definition—not the code that manipulates the data type. This feature provides a powerful tool to the C++ developer, by allowing for development of a generic link list class that can operate on any data type. Unfortunately, the current Microsoft compiler does not support C++ templates. What Microsoft does supply is a group of *collection classes* that operate on a variety of data types such as CObjects, CStrings, WORDs, and a variety of data structures such as lists, arrays, and maps. Microsoft built these collection classes with a tool they supply to you, TEMPLDEF, in the \msvc\mfc\sample\templdef subdirectory. With this tool you can create classes in which the only item that will change is the data type, just as with a real C++ template, and you can quit it more easily, too.

The MFC derives its collection classes from CObject. These collections fall into three categories: arrays, lists, and maps. Maps may not be intuitive, but they do represent, in a fairly simple form, a collection of objects that associate a key with the object value, much like a compiler's symbol table. The array collection classes provide a zero-based array of the indicated object, while the list collections provide a variety of linked lists for the specified object.

Lists

The list collections provide a double-linked list data type for CObject pointers, void pointers, and CString objects. The list collections allow you to insert or remove an object at the head or tail of a list. You can also insert or remove a specified element

TABLE **4.13**
MFC list collection classes.

CPtrList	A list of void pointers
CObList	A list of CObject pointers
CStringList	A list of CString objects

at any other point in the list. Since the collection is a double-linked list, you can travel the list in either direction. The list collections provide fast insertion speeds but slow search capabilities, since the class does not index the lists. Table 4.13 details the list collection classes supplied by MFC.

The CPtrList collection class supports the framework's dump context, so you can get a diagnostic dump of your list. However, it does not support the framework's serialization mechanism, so you cannot save a CPtrList list to a file. Since the CObjects and CString Objects know how to serialize themselves (i.e., save themselves to and read themselves from a file), you can save these types of lists. All the list collections have a distinct constructor, but their member functions perform the same action on each data type.

Arrays

The array collections provide the familiar C/C++ array data structure for various data types, but with a few twists. These arrays can grow or shrink on demand; they all have the same member functions (except for their constructors) and perform the same operation, but each operates on a different data type. Array collections store the various data elements contiguously and also provide a zero-based index. They are therefore slow when searching for a specific element, unless you know and provide its index. Table 4.14 lists the array collection classes supported by MFC.

The number of elements in a CObArray will depend on which memory model is used to compile the program, since all the elements (not the objects they reference) must reside in a 64K segment, along with 100 bytes containing framework overhead. If you use a memory model where pointers are 16 bits, as they are in the small and medium memory models, your arrays will hold approximately 32,000 elements. If the pointers are 32 bits, as they are in the compact and large memory models, then MFC will limit your arrays to approximately 16,000 elements.

TABLE **4.14**
Array collection classes.

CByteArray	Array of bytes
CWordArray	Array of words
CDWordArray	Array of double words
CPtrArray	Array of void pointers (cannot be serialized)
CObArray	Array of pointers to CObjects
CStringArray	Array of CStrings
CUintArray	Array of unsigned ints

Up to these limits, the array collection classes will add items to the array, even if doing so exceeds the original size of the array. The framework increases the number of items the array can hold by a default value of one. This can cause a performance bottleneck in your program. To increase efficiency, you should have the array allocate a block of items at once, rather than one at a time. Use the SetSize member function to accomplish this feat. Note that this function can increase the size of an empty array as well as an array currently in use. The function's prototype is:

```
void SetSize( int nNewSize, int nGrowBy = -1);
```

The *nGrowBy* parameter tells the framework how many empty items to add every time the array allocates more space. This extra space will not interfere with the size of the array reported by the GetSize member function. If the framework cannot allocate the needed space, it will throw a CMemoryException.

Maps

The map collection classes allow you to map a key in the given data type to the specified value data type. For example, the CMapWordToOb map collection allows you to map a pointer to a CObject-derived data item to a key contained in a 16-bit word. You insert items into the collection class by passing both the key and the element to the class's SetAt function or its overloaded operator, [ ], as illustrated here:

```
CMapWordToOb map;
WORD index;
CEmployee *emp;
index = CEmployee.GetNewNumber();
map.SetAt( index, new CEmployee("Jack"," ","Tackett","919 555 1212" );
map.Lookup( index , emp); // emp contains the newly inserted record.
map[index] = new CEmployee("Keith","E","Bugg","615-555-1212");
delete emp; // to prevent a memory leak.
```

For the map collection classes listed in Table 4.15, you should realize you that the framework can delete the map and the individual elements within the map. However, if you have mapped a key to a pointer value, e.g., by using CMapStringToPtr, then the framework will delete the pointer, but NOT the object reference by the pointer, thus causing a memory leak. It is the programmer's responsibility to explicitly delete the object in order to prevent a memory leak.

TABLE **4.15**
List of Map collection classes.

CMapWordToPtr
CMapPtrToWord
CMapPtrToPtr
CMapWordToOb
CMapStringToOb
CMapStringToPtr

Creating Your Own Collections

The MFC library provides many useful collection classes, but if your needs require a different data type from the ones supported, you should create a new one derived from one of those supplied. On the other hand, if you have a function or class in which the only item that changes is the data type, rather than the code, then you should use the TEMPLDEF tool supplied by Microsoft. MFC Tech Note #4 provides information on using this tool.

CHAPTER SUMMARY

This chapter introduced several MFC classes, including the mother of all classes, CObject. It does not, however, present the entire MFC Class library, which contains over 100 different classes. While most of the MFC library code concentrates on Windows APIs, some MFC classes, such as CString and CTime, fall outside the derivation path of CObject, and others, including CFileStatus and CMemoryState, are not dependent on Windows.

This chapter also covered the framework's printing process, as well as some of its diagnostic capabilities. Finally, the chapter showed you the various container classes supplied by MFC to provide the developer with a variety of ready-to-use collection classes.

CHAPTER 5

Of Mice and Menus

This chapter explores one of the fundamental aspects of the Windows application—the menu bar and how you attach code to the various options presented on screen. Much of the chapter's focus will be on the Microsoft Foundation Class CMenu and the member functions for manipulating the menu. Along the way, you'll learn about the messages generated by the mouse and how you can process them. Additional topics of discussion include interaction with the keyboard and the use of accelerator keys. Although you'll find an abundance of sample code for menus in this chapter, coverage is limited to those topics considered most important to general programming needs. You should therefore find that the examples provided cover most of the tasks you will face in routine application development. For good measure, we will also cover the "standards" that apply to menus, as suggested by Microsoft.

DESIGN CRITERIA AND CONSIDERATIONS

Menus define the available options and the directions in which a user can proceed at any given point in a Windows application. While the mouse is the most expedient way to invoke a menu option, you must provide a mechanism to allow the user to access a menu item via the keyboard; the familiar accelerator key and the direction arrow keys accomplish this task.

Menus come in three flavors:

1. Drop-down or pull-down menus. An example is the classical menu bar with the standard items: File, Edit, etc.

2. Pop-up menus. These are like the drop-down variety, except that they do *not* have a title (e.g., File) and they are intended for context-sensitive commands. Hence, pop-up menus should not have a short-cut key, nor should they use multilevel (i.e., cascading) menus. Likewise, they should contain as few options as possible.

3. Cascading, or hierarchical menus. These are menu options that, when selected, activate another menu. These should have a right-pointing triangle after the menu item text. Visual C++ automatically adds the right-pointing triangle when necessary. See the example later in this chapter under ModifyMenu( ).

If a menu choice requires the user to supply additional information via a dialog box, an ellipsis (i.e., "...") should follow the text of the menu choice. As an example, the familiar "$\underline{S}$ave As..." option under $\underline{F}$ile requires more input before it can take effect—you must provide a new filename and path. Since Visual C++ has no way of knowing if a choice requires additional information, it's up to you to add the ellipsis where appropriate (do this in App Studio under "Caption"). When laying out a menu, you should group logical operations together and separate them with a horizontal line (i.e., the MF_SEPARATOR flag). For example, if your application allows the user to specify font characteristics such as size, bold, italic, etc., you should place these together in the menu.

CREATING MENUS IN APP STUDIO

One of the things that makes working with Visual C++ so pleasant is that you can create your application *visually*. This is especially true when using App Studio to create or edit menus, as you can see them just as they will appear in your program. This really helps you to see the logic flow of your program and helps to keep track of what options are completed as well as what options are still under development. There are several hints and guidelines for working with menus inside App Studio that warrant consideration. First, lay out the main menu bar. Insert as many of the options that your program uses as you can, such as "File" and "Help." This will keep you focused on the hierarchy of your program and help you spot little errors such as assigning the same accelerator key to multiple options. The App Studio tool will let you disable menu items; go ahead and use it for options that are still under development. It is a good alternative if you are working in a rapid prototyping environment. Likewise, assign all the Help strings (using the edit box labeled "Pro$\underline{m}$pt:" in the Properties dialog box) for the menu options. At the very least, change the default string written by App Studio to something unique, if for no other reason than the fact that it comes in handy when debugging. Moving the mouse over the menu options updates the Help message in the status bar, and seeing your unique strings there should tell you the menu is working, at least in some sense.

MANAGING THE MENU

There are some general guidelines to follow when it comes to managing your application's menus. For related menu items, use the check mark to signal the user that a choice has been previously selected. In our example using fonts, it is possible to select a font that is *both* bold and italic. Should the user specify both, be sure a check mark appears to the left of the both to remind the user that he or she has enabled both characteristics. You'll see how to enact these features later in this chapter. During the design process, you should strive to keep your menu options terse, complete, and flexible. This prevents the confusion confronting users forced to wade through screen after screen of options and allows them to navigate through the program at their discretion. Of course, the logical flow of your application will dictate what options are available at what times; but you can avoid or at least minimize confusion by disabling and enabling menu items in relation to the general flow of the program. For example, if you disable Option B because Option A has not yet been selected, it is your responsibility as the programmer to ensure that Option B is enabled after Option A has been selected. The sample program on the enclosed disk provides a member function for graying out (and reasserting) a menu item independent of the actual number of menu items presented. In this manner, you do not have to hard code the number of menu items to process. If another programmer adds or deletes menu items at a later date, the member function provided for disabling and enabling a menu's option(s) does not require modification. Jumping ahead somewhat, this holds true for the MFC member functions InsertMenu( ) and AppendMenu( )—if you find it necessary to add an option to your menu bar dynamically, the code will automatically "see" and process the option. You can accomplish this functionality by using the member function GetMenuItemCount( ), which returns the number of options, or items, in a menu. You will find this information most useful when displaying a modal dialog box. Since a modal dialog box stays on the screen until the user gives a response (i.e., it "captures the focus"), you should disable *all* menu items on the main menu bar before displaying a modal dialog box, and enable them *after* the user has given you a valid response. Doing this helps shift the user's attention to the dialog box, which "demands" a response. Also, it helps to position the dialog box *below* the main menu bar, so that users can see it grayed out; novice users may not realize that they can drag a dialog box around the screen. Such visual cues go a long way toward giving new users a level of comfort when using your application.

DIALOG BOXES WITH MENUS

While on the subject of dialog boxes, be aware that it is possible to give a dialog box a menu. While implementing this option is not recommended, as it is not part of the Microsoft design standard, there may be times when it is advantageous to do so. It is actually quite easy to assign menus to dialog boxes in VC++. Should you require this feature, here are the steps to follow:

1. Create the menu (e.g., MY_MENU) in App Studio.

2. Create the modal dialog box in App Studio.

3. In the dialog box definition inside the resource file, add the line:

    ```
    MENU MY_MENU
    ```

    before the BEGIN statement (usually, after the CAPTION statement).

Now, when you display the dialog box, it will have a menu across the top automatically. For example, here is a sample definition of a dialog box as it might appear in your project's resource file; the line you will add to include a menu is emphasized here in italic:

```
IDD_MY_SAMPLE DIALOG DISCARDABLE 10, 30, 350, 210
STYLE WS_POPUP | WS_VISIBLE | WS_CAPTION | WS_SYSMENU
CAPTION "SAMPLE MODAL DIALOG BOX"
MENU MY_MENU
FONT 8, "MS Sans Serif"
BEGIN
 DEFPUSHBUTTON "&OK", IDOK ,235,180,50,14
 PUSHBUTTON  "&Cancel", IDCANCEL,295,180,50,14
END
```

CHILD WINDOWS AND MENUS

In addition to the fact that child windows do not use menus with dialog boxes, observe that a child window *cannot* have a menu (you can try to attach them, but Windows will go haywire). The reason we point this out here is that it is very easy to overlook this fact when deriving classes or designing your application, and it can be one of those really stupid bugs that bite you. Likewise, don't forget this fact if you override the creation of a window using the PreCreateWindow( ) function to customize your windows using your own definition of the CREATESTRUCT structure member, *cs.style*.

KEYBOARD ACCELERATORS

Now is a good time to point out something about the keyboard accelerators, the so-called "shortcut" keys that allow the user to access an onscreen object such as a menu item, radio button, or other control. In the sample dialog box described earlier, pressing the key combination Alt + O would be the same as clicking the mouse on the OK button. Accelerators are always recognized by the presence of the ampersand (&) *prior* to their hot key. The preceding sample has two accelerators, Alt-O and Alt-C. Be advised that in VC++, you can get away with assigning the *same* accelerator to more than one control. While you clearly would not want to do this deliberately, it is easy to do on menus having many pull-down options. VC++ will not alert you to this error; using the accelerator will cause the program to execute the first accelerator defined in the resource file that it encounters. So be careful, and visually inspect your work before testing.

APPENDING TO A MENU

The first member function to examine is AppendMenu( ). Use this function to add new options to an existing menu. AppendMenu( ) works with any menu resource, regardless of whether or not the menu is in a window or a dialog box. Incidentally, this is the case because class CDialog is derived from class CWnd, but there are distinctly different functions for each class. To append a new option to a menu, you must first instantiate a variable of the target class, or a pointer to it. Then call AppendMenu( ), passing it the three parameters required. The following sample demonstrates how to append the option "Salary" to a menu bar associated with a dialog box:

```
CMenu *pMenu = CDialog::GetMenu();
pMenu->AppendMenu(MF_STRING, MF_ENABLED, "Salary");
CDialog::DrawMenuBar();
```

This adds the option "Salary" to the menu and enables it. Other flags are available for this parameter and can be ORed together if necessary. (See the documentation for a full explanation.) In this case, "Salary" has no drop-down option under it. But suppose you have a Windows program that allows the user to access an employee data file. You could add a password feature that updates the menu option "Salary" and thus avoid having to have two dialog boxes, one for regular users and one for "privileged" users. You would simply modify the menu so that only users with authorization (i.e., the password) could access salary information. This provides an additional level of security far superior to simply graying out an option. A grayed-out string still tells a potential hacker that there is something else out there, whereas "out of sight is out of mind."

UPDATING MENU CHANGES

The previous example also illustrates something else you must provide for when dynamically changing a menu—it *must* be updated (i.e., redrawn) by Windows. That is the purpose of the statement

```
CDialog::DrawMenuBar()
```

in the example. Neglecting to call DrawMenuBar( ) can cause you to think mistakenly that your program is not working, when in fact, it is; you just can't see the results. Also, be aware that you *must* call DrawMenuBar( ) after modifying a menu, even if the window or dialog box to which the menu belongs is currently not visible. The preceding example simply added the word "Salary" to our hypothetical menu bar—no drop-down options are available if the user clicks on it. The obvious extension to this is to add additional choices that appear when the user selects "Salary." The pseudocode to construct this modification is as follows:

1. Get a CMenu handle to the window's main menu bar.

2. Create an empty pop-up menu using the CreatePopupMenu( ) function.

3. Use the AppendMenu( ) function to add the additional choices to the newly created, empty pop-up menu.

4. Use AppendMenu( ) to add the new, nonempty pop-up menu.

Note that it is not necessary to use AppendMenu( ); you could instead use InsertMenu( ). This allows you to install the "Salary" option at some point on the main menu bar other than at the end. The only serious pitfall to avoid in using dynamic menus in this manner comes in the assignment of the numerical values corresponding to the menu choices. Recall that when you create menus in the App Studio, you assign each item an ID, and these IDs end up in your resource header file as #defines. Here, you do not have the luxury of having the tool (i.e., the Menu

Editor) monitor your work to prevent duplication and conflict. In the upcoming example, we will use AppendMenu( ) to add three new menu options under a main menu option called "Salary." For this demonstration's purposes, these options have the values 100, 200, and 300, respectively:

```
CMenu *pMenu = CDialog::GetMenu(); // get the main menu bar...
HMENU hmenuPopup = CreatePopupMenu(); // create empty, pop-up menu
AppendMenu(hmenuPopup, MF_STRING, 100, "&Hourly");
AppendMenu(hmenuPopup, MF_STRING, 200, "&Salaried");
AppendMenu(hmenuPopup, MF_STRING, 300, "&Both");
   // Add the pop-up menu to the main menu bar
AppendMenu(pMenu->GetSafeHmenu(), MF_ENABLED | MF_POPUP, (UINT)
   hmenuPopup, "&Salary");
CDialog::DrawMenuBar();    // always redraw the menu
```

There is a lot of horsepower packed into this example, so take a moment and study it carefully. The first three calls to AppendMenu( ) create the new option that has the three new choices. The last call to AppendMenu( ) actually appends the new menu to another menu, the main menu bar.

COUNTING MENU ITEMS DYNAMICALLY

Another useful member function is GetMenuItemCount( ). This function returns, as an integer, the number of items, or choices, in a menu. This information comes in really handy when you want to gray out (and/or ungray out) an entire menu bar. Instead of hard coding in the number of menu items, use the return value from GetMenuItemCount( ); this easily allows future changes to a menu resource *without* changing the source code elsewhere. GetMenuItemCount( ) returns a -1 if an error occurs, so make sure any error traps you build allow for a return value of zero (since it is possible, though not likely, to have a menu with no items). Here is an example using GetMenuItemCount( ) to simultaneously gray out and disable all the items in a menu:

```
CMenu* ptr = CWnd::GetMenu();// get the window's menu
for( int i=0;                 i < ptr->GetMenuItemCount(); i++ )
                              // loop thru all items
{                             // gray out and disable the items
   ptr->EnableMenuItem( i,    MF_BYPOSITION | MF_GRAYED )
}
CWnd::DrawMenuBar();          // always redraw the menu
```

This example also demonstrates the member function EnableMenuItem( ). This function is also used to *disable* a menu item, contrary to the functionality suggested by its name. As you can see, the difference is in the second parameter. This function takes two parameters, both of type UINT; the return value is also UINT. As a bonus, the return value is the bitwise representation of the previous state of the menu items (or -1 if an error occurs). This information is useful when you want to restore the menu to its original state; simply supply the return value as the second parameter. This example also illustrates the fact that graying out an item also disables the corresponding menu option, as opposed to simply disabling it via the flag MF_DISABLE. In virtually all cases, you will want to use the MF_GRAYED flag to avoid confusing the user.

RETRIEVING A MENU'S STATE

A helpful member function of CMenu to assist in the management process is GetMenuState( ). This function is nearly identical to EnableMenuItem( ), in the sense that it has identical parameters and can also change the state of a menu. However, GetMenuState( ) is different in that you can use it strictly to *read* the status of a menu item. You could use this information to determine if you need to change the menu. Here is an example illustrating the use of GetMenuState( ):

```
CMenu* ptr = CWnd::GetMenu();// get the window's menu
UINT ret_value;
ret_value = ptr->GetMenuState(0,MF_BYPOSITION);
```

The variable ret_value will now contain the status of the first option on the menu bar fetched by the call to GetMenu( ). Note that you can use the parameter MF_BYPOSITION in place of MF_BYPOSITION. Actually, there can be a certain advantage to using the MF_BYCOMMAND parameter. It might happen that a menu item's position could change, but its command value would not. So, for those cases where your application might modify the position of certain items, you would probably want to use the MF_BYCOMMAND operator. Using the previous example, the following code segment demonstrates how to use the command value as a parameter:

```
CMenu* ptr = CWnd::GetMenu();        // get the window's menu
UINT ret_value;
ret_value = ptr->GetMenuState(nCommandIDvalue,MF_BYCOMMAND);
```

Here, nCommandIDvalue is the numerical value (e.g., 100, 200, 300, etc.) associated with the menu item in question.

CHECK MARKS AND MENUS

A first cousin to the EnableMenuItem( ) function is the CheckMenuItem( ) function, which is applicable *only* to pop-up menus (i.e., drop-down or submenus). You cannot place a check mark next to an item on your window's main menu bar. As in a lot of the functions we've already examined, you can specify either MF_BYPOSITION or MF_BYCOMMAND, with one exception: If one of the items causes another pop-up menu to appear, you *must* use MF_BYPOSITION, since the item does not have a numerical identifier associated with it. To place a check mark next to an item in a pop-up menu, follow this example:

```
CMenu *pMenu = CWnd::GetMenu();// get the main menu;
                   // assume Item 2 has a
                   // submenu
CMenu* pSubmenu;          // pointer to the submenu
//
// Next line assumes item 2 has a submenu under it...
//
pSubmenu = pMenu->GetSubMenu(2);
//
// next line puts check mark beside item 0 in the submenu
//
pSubmenu->CheckMenuItem(0,MF_BYPOSITION | MF_CHECKED);
CWnd::DrawMenuBar();      // always redraw the menu
```

As you may suspect, you can use this function to remove the check mark. To do so, use the preceding example, but replace MF_CHECKED with MF_UNCHECKED.

Bitmapped Check Marks

If you like, you can change the default check mark used by Windows with a custom-made bitmap. There is a little bit of work involved, but nothing overwhelming. The main chores are to manage memory (i.e., delete any bitmaps you load) and to scale the bitmapped check mark to the size of the window. To use a special check mark in your Visual C++ application, follow these steps:

1. Create the bitmap in App Studio.

2. Load the bitmap using CBitmap::LoadBitmap( ).

3. Get the size of the check mark using GetMenuCheckMarkDimensions( ).

4. Use StretchBlt( ) to resize the bitmap, if necessary.

5. Use CMenu::SetMenuItemBitmaps( ) to assign the new check mark.

6. Delete the bitmap before your program terminates, to free memory.

Bitmaps and other special objects that consume memory, such as brushes, should be loaded in your class constructor and deleted in the class destructor. That gives you one way in and one way out, so to speak. Besides using bitmapped check marks, you can go another step further and draw menu items with different pens and/or colors. Avoid using such practices except for special applications, because they consume considerable amounts of memory.

THE GETSAFEHMENU( ) FUNCTION

The CMenu class includes a member function that returns a "safe" handle to a menu. This is a handle that Windows "knows about" (or thinks it does), and it can be very useful for debugging purposes, as well as for increasing the level of error trapping in your program. If you experience difficulty with any of the CMenu functions, you might try using the GetSafeHmenu( ) function in conjunction with the API call IsMenu(HMENU hMenu). The function IsMenu( ) returns a Boolean value. If the return value is 0, the CMenu object is definitely unrecognizable by Windows as a menu. However, a nonzero return value does not guarantee that it is a safe menu, so further checking may be necessary. The following example uses these functions and assumes that the application has a menu bar with at least six options, and that the sixth option has a drop-down menu of at least two options:

```
CMenu *pMenu = CWnd::GetMenu();      // get the window's menu
CMenu* pSubMenu;                     // pointer to the submenu
pSubMenu = pMenu->GetSubMenu(5);     // under item 5
HMENU hMenu;                         // declare variable type HMENU
hMenu = pSubMenu->GetSafeHmenu();    // get handle to menu
```

```
if( IsMenu(hMenu) == 0)              // check for validity
    AfxMessageBox("Not a safe MENU!!",MB_OK);// *** ERROR ***
```

Naturally, your program will likely handle the error condition differently from this. Should you encounter an invalid menu in this manner, debugging and trace procedures should be used to isolate the cause of the problem. This function call can be very useful when you're sure you've done everything right and your program still doesn't work properly.

INSERTING MENU ITEMS DYNAMICALLY

The next CMenu member function that we'll cover is the InsertMenu( ), which is a lot like AppendMenu( ), except that it allows you to specify a location for the new item at a position other than the end of the menu bar, as with AppendMenu( ). The function prototype for InsertMenu( ) is as follows:

```
InsertMenu(UINT nPosition,UINT nFlags,UINT nIDNewItem,LPCSTR lpNewItem);
```

nPosition	declares the menu item that the new option is to be inserted *in front of.*
nFlags	how item is referenced: MF_BYPOSITION or MF_BYCOMMAND.
	MF_POPUP is ORed with MF_BYPOSITION if the item to be inserted is a submenu.
nIDNewItem	numerical value of the item or of the submenu handle if a pop-up menu.
lpNewItem	The text of the item (e.g., File, Edit, etc.) or a bitmap representing the image of the option. In the latter case *lpNewItem* is of type CBitmap.

Two examples follow. The first simply adds a new choice to the main menu bar and does not have a pop-up menu under it. The second demonstrates the more typical case of using a submenu:

```
CMenu* pMenu;
pMenu->InsertMenu(0,MF_BYPOSITION,400,"MyNew");
CDialog::DrawMenuBar();
```

This example adds a new menu item, "MyNew," at the beginning of the menu attached to a dialog box. The first parameter, *nPosition,* is a zero, which InsertMenu( ) interprets to mean "Insert this in front of item zero of the menu." The second example, based on the previous example using AppendMenu( ), inserts the new submenu as the third item in the menu bar. Please note that this example assumes there are initially at least three items on our fictitious menu bar: To make your application more bulletproof, you would use some of the CMenu functions already discussed (e.g., GetMenuItemCount( ), to ensure that you are inserting at a valid position, etc.).

```
CMenu *pMenu = CDialog::GetMenu();    // get the main menu bar...
HMENU hmenuPopup = CreatePopupMenu();// create an empty, pop-up menu
AppendMenu(hmenuPopup, MF_STRING, 100, "&Hourly");
AppendMenu(hmenuPopup, MF_STRING, 200, "&Salaried");
AppendMenu(hmenuPopup, MF_STRING, 300, "&Both");
//
// Insert the pop-up menu as the 3rd item (i.e., nPosition = 2) on the main
menu bar
//
pMenu->InsertMenu(2,MF_BYPOSITION | MF_POPUP, (UINT) hmenuPopup,
  "&Salary");
CDialog::DrawMenuBar();  // always redraw the menu
```

MODIFYING A MENU DYNAMICALLY

The next example is for the member function ModifyMenu( ). As you may suspect, this function allows you to make a change to an existing menu. One of its more useful aspects is that you can use it to add a submenu to a submenu (i.e., a cascading or hierarchical menu). As part of the Microsoft recommended design guidelines for Windows, a cascading menu should have a right-pointing triangle to the right of the menu text. Happily, ModifyMenu( ) recognizes the creation of a cascading menu and places this graphical object there for you. The following example creates a dummy submenu labeled "Test," which is placed under the first menu item of a hypothetical window; the right-pointing triangle is to the right of the word "Test" in the menu list:

```
CMenu *pMenu = CWnd::GetMenu();     // get the window's menu
HMENU hmenuPopup;                   // new menu object
CMenu* pSubMenu;                    // pointer to the submenu
pSubMenu = pMenu->GetSubMenu(0);    // under item 0 — File
hmenuPopup = CreatePopupMenu();     // create a new menu
AppendMenu(hmenuPopup,MF_ENABLED | MF_STRING,100,"Text1");
AppendMenu(hmenuPopup,MF_ENABLED | MF_STRING,200,"Text2");
AppendMenu(hmenuPopup,MF_ENABLED | MF_STRING,300,"Text3");
//
// add the new pop-up with 3 options to the main menu bar
//
pSubMenu->ModifyMenu(0, MF_BYPOSITION | MF_POPUP,
  (UINT) hmenuPopup,"Test");
CDialog::DrawMenuBar();  // always redraw the menu
```

DELETING A MENU OR SUBMENU

There may be occasions when you will want to delete a menu item altogether, usually as a result of some option exercised by the user in a different portion of your application. It is much more efficient to use the InsertMenu( ) and DeleteMenu( ) functions to simply adjust the menu in these situations than to load in an entirely new menu. To delete a menu item, call the function DeleteMenu(UINT *nItemPosition*, UINT *nFlags*). As in many of the previous examples, the argument *nItemPosition* is determined by *nFlags*. Argument *nItemPosition* specifies the item to be deleted and represents either the positional index into the menu or the command value assigned in App Studio when the menu was created. If *nFlags* is MF_BYPOSITION, then *nItemPosition* takes the index; if it is MF_BYCOMMAND, then it takes the command string (e.g., IDC_SALARY_INFO). If the menu item being deleted is itself a pop-up menu, the entire pop-up is deleted, too, and the memory it consumed is released. Here is an example using DeleteMenu( ):

```
Menu *pMenu = CWnd::GetMenu(); // get the window's menu
pMenu->DeleteMenu(1,MF_BYPOSITION); // delete second menu item
CWnd::DrawMenuBar();       // must always redraw after changing
```

The last line could also have read CDialog::DrawMenuBar( ) if the menu was attached to a dialog box and not a window. A note of caution: If the menu item being deleted is a pop-up menu, DeleteMenu( ) will destroy the handle to the pop-up, rendering it unusable in the future. Should this not be what you intend, use the member function RemoveMenu( ) instead. The arguments to RemoveMenu( ) are identical to those for DeleteMenu( ), and should be used in the same manner. Should you elect to use RemoveMenu( ) for this purpose, be sure and call GetSubMenu( ) *before* calling RemoveMenu( ) in order to fetch the pop-up menu object. Both functions, DeleteMenu( ) and RemoveMenu( ), return a nonzero value if the call completes successfully, or zero if it does not. Remember, when the documentation says nonzero, this means a negative return value is OK. It's very easy to forget that and thus write a test like this:

```
if(pMenu->RemoveMenu(0,MF_BYPOSITION) > 0) // WRONG !!
   AfxMessageBox("Removed menu item 0",MB_OK);
else     // does not catch negative return values
   AfxMessageBox("Failed to remove menu item 0",MB_OK);
```

Since the test condition only checks for values greater than zero, an erroneous message could be displayed. A proper test might be:

```
if(pMenu->RemoveMenu(0,MF_BYPOSITION) == 0) // RIGHT !!
   AfxMessageBox("Failed to remove menu item 0",MB_OK);
else        // catches negative return values too
   AfxMessageBox("Removed menu item 0",MB_OK);
```

RETRIEVING MENU ITEM IDENTIFIERS

Another member function of CMenu is GetMenuItemID(int *nPosition*). This is one of those functions that you're not likely to use too often, but which can be quite useful. It returns the menu-item identifier (e.g., IDC_SALARY_INFO) assigned to a menu item by App Studio. You supply the index, or position, into the menu. The return value from this function is helpful in other useful ways, too. If the return value is a –1, then the index to which *nPosition* points is a pop-up menu. If it is 0, then it is referring to a menu item SEPARATOR line. These return values can be used to walk through a menu to see what's there—maybe another function modified the menu, and you need to determine the current state of the menu. Here is an example using GetMenuItemID( ) in a nested configuration. It begins by checking the main menu bar of the window; when it encounters a submenu, it starts another loop to walk through it. This example merely counts the number of SEPARATOR bars:

```
Menu *pMenu = CWnd::GetMenu(); // get the window's menu
CMenu* pSubmenu;              // pointer to any submenu
int num_sep_bars = 0;        // counter for SEPARATOR bars
for(int k= 0; k < pMenu->GetMenuItemCount(); k++)
{
   if(pMenu->GetMenuItemID(k)== -1)// found a submenu
   {
     pSubmenu = pMenu->GetSubMenu(k);
     for(int j= 0; k < pSubmenu->GetMenuItemCount(); j++)
     {
        if(pSubmenu->GetMenuItemID(j) == 0)
          ++num_sep_bars; // increment counter
   }  // end for loop through submenu items
   }    // end if found a submenu
}       // end for-loop through menu items
```

SLUGGISH MENU BEHAVIOR IN VISUAL C++

From time to time during the development and testing phase of building a Visual C++ application, you may notice that some menu options seem to act very sluggish. For instance, it may take a noticeable amount of time to highlight a command when the mouse cursor is dragged over the option. You'll only experience these phenomena when running a debug version of your application, and the problem only occurs when the cursor is passed over an item to which you have not yet assigned a prompt string. A prompt string refers to the text that appears in the status bar at the bottom of the screen (assuming you specified this feature in AppWizard). Similarly, this time delay will only manifest itself when you do *not* have the debug window (DebugWin) active while using the Afx TRACE feature. Don't be fooled into thinking you have a bug, or have written bad code. What is actually happening is that TRACE is attempting to give you a diagnostic message, but it can't find the debug window. To really confound you, since TRACE can't find the debug window, it defaults to the AUX device, which very few Windows programmers have defined. So behind your back, so to speak, Windows is running around looking for a place to put this TRACE message. You can see this in action very easily. Enable TRACE, but not the debug window, from the Visual C++ group in Windows. Then run a debug version of your application and move the mouse through a menu option for which you do not have a prompt string defined (from App Studio). You'll see the time delay quite clearly. Then go back and enable the debug window and repeat. This time, your menu will behave as expected.

MENU BAR IN WINDOWS HELP

If you include a Help file with your application (highly recommended), there may be occasions when you would like to make changes to it. The entire subject of Help files is covered in more thorough detail later, in Chapter 15. For the moment, at least as far as menus are concerned, note that you can include special *macros* inside the project file used to build your application's Help file (i.e., "yourapp.HPJ"). These macros provide you with a lot of the functionality you've encountered in this chapter: for example, the ability to add new menus or menu items, to enable and disable menus, etc. To whet your appetite, the customization of your Help file menus adds a lot of horsepower to your program. From the Help menu, you can have your custom bitmaps on buttons comprising the toolbar and even start other Windows applications (e.g., Clock, Calc, etc.). A detailed discussion of these techniques is deferred until Chapter 15 for purposes of continuity.

CHAPTER SUMMARY

This chapter has presented a rudimentary introduction to the functions related to manipulating the menus of a Windows program. The mechanics of these functions are pretty straightforward. The challenge lies in eliminating the ambiguity and inconsistencies of managing your menu resources. These include, for example, when to disable certain menu items based on the presence or absence of external events or data. Menus are an excellent way to organize logically the direction(s) that a user can follow and supply a certain underlying level of comfort. This can and should be substantiated by drawing upon the daily experiences faced by the general public. Banking machines guide us with menus, as do appliances such as VCRs and microwave ovens. Remember to keep your menu options succinct, complete, and consistent. Also, sit back and reflect on your windows and dialog boxes that have menus—do they allow the user to abort an activity gracefully and to retreat from a previously selected direction? Are the menu choices clearly named, without ambiguity or subtle errors like duplicate keyboard accelerator keys? Can a menu option be replaced by a command button? Attention to details such as these are part of the ingredients that go into a successful design that makes your application a pleasure to use.

CHAPTER 6

Keyboards, Cursors, and Mice

In this chapter, we'll explore some of the basic messaging apparatuses needed for interacting with the user in a Windows program, such as the keyboard and the mouse. In addition, you'll see how to change the shape of the cursor and when it is appropriate to do so. An overview of the different coordinate systems used by Windows will be given, since different member functions use and return different value types. Functions related to manipulating the cursor or caret will also be covered, since they generally go hand-in-hand with operations involving the keyboard and/or mouse. Finally, at the end of this chapter is a brief discussion of special cursors. But for starters, let's begin by taking a look at one of the main input devices, the keyboard.

THE KEYBOARD

The keyboard is an area that is often overlooked by budding Windows programmers. This oversight can perhaps best be explained by the fact that Windows is more than somewhat skewed toward the use of the mouse as the primary input device. Nevertheless, your application should allow for keyboard input under all circumstances and never assume the user will use the mouse exclusively. Indeed, in some instances, such as when supplying information via an edit box, interaction with the keyboard is unavoidable. These cases are covered in greater detail in Chapter 9. For now, our focus will be on understanding how a Windows program interacts with the keyboard. The primary concept underlying this interaction is that of the virtual key.

Keyboard Basics

The keyboards furnished with today's PC-compatibles are really sophisticated pieces of equipment. Bear in mind that there are different styles of keyboards (some have 81 keys, others 101, etc.), and that the arrangement of keys can change for use in foreign markets. Notwithstanding, here is an overview of what happens when you press a key: The keyboard's microprocessor generates a hardware interrupt, which passes a scan code to the ISR (interrupt service routine). This scan code is an 8-bit number that identifies only the *physical* key; for example, the same code is sent for a lowercase "a" or an uppercase "A." The keyboard driver traps the interrupt and calls a Windows API to place the keystroke in the system queue. For every scan code generated, there is a matching virtual key code. Here is where it gets a little complicated, because the converse of this statement is *not* true. For example, most keyboards have two Shift keys (a left and a right), and each of these generates a different scan code, since they are *physically* different keys. However, the Windows keyboard driver always translates either of these scan codes to the same virtual key (in this case, VK_SHIFT). It is the virtual key codes that we are most interested in, and they are the next subject of discussion.

Virtual Keys

Since the original IBM PC was released, the keyboard has undergone some changes. New keys, such as additional function keys and the arrow keys, have dramatically changed the original QWERTY-style keyboard. The Windows developers foresaw that changes that they could not anticipate would be forthcoming and subsequently came up with the idea of *virtual keys*. A virtual key is really nothing more than the assignment of a numerical code to a key. Thus the F1 function key corresponds to the same numerical code regardless of the keyboard on which it is found. Similarly, new keys that may be added in the future will merely be given new codes. By the way, you can see these numerical codes by looking in *windows.h;* all virtual keys have the prefix "VK_" (e.g., function key F1 is VK_F1, F2 is VK_F2, etc.). As a programmer, there are a couple of things you need to watch out for when dealing with virtual keys. First, don't assume that your target platform will have all the virtual keys—some keyboards have only 10 function keys, for example. Also, the values of the numerical operator keys (e.g., "*", "+", etc.) on the numeric keypad are different from those on the regular keypad.

Caps Lock and Num Lock Key States

The standard Windows API calls can and often must be used to determine such things as the type of keyboard installed, etc. One of the things you may need to have your application do is find out if the Caps Lock key, the Num Lock key, and/or the Scroll Lock key are set. The state of these keys can be determined by calling GetKeyState(int *vKey*), where *vKey* is the code of the virtual key in question—in the case of the following example, the Caps Lock. This function returns an integer whose bit pattern reflects the state of the key. If the high-order bit is 1, the key is set. If the bit is 0, the key is not set. If the low-order bit is 1, the key is *toggled*. A toggle key, such as the Caps Lock or Num Lock, is considered to be toggled if it has been pressed an odd number of times since the last system boot. Here is an example to show you how to test for these conditions:

```
if(0x0001 & GetKeyState(VK_CAPITAL))// check the Caps Lock key
    AfxMessageBox("Caps Lock key is ON.",MB_OK);
else
    AfxMessageBox("Caps Lock key is OFF",MB_OK);
```

Substitute the values VK_NUMLOCK or VK_SCROLL for VK_CAPITAL to test for the Num Lock and Scroll Lock keys, respectively. Please remember that, while these examples aren't that spectacular by themselves, they will come in very handy when combined with other aspects of Visual C++ (e.g., when you want to use the keyboard as a communications terminal emulator).

The Messages

Ostensibly, only three types of keyboard messages interest the average applications developer. You want to know when a key is *down*, when it is *up*, and whether any ancillary keys (e.g., the Control, Alt, or Shift keys) were used in conjunction with it. Use ClassWizard to create the message handlers for trapping these key events: the WM_KEYDOWN, WM_KEYUP, and WM_CHAR messages. Generally speaking, you'll probably use the WM_CHAR message most of the time, since it can be used to ascertain *all* of the other key states that we're interested in.

WM_CHAR

When you add a function in ClassWizard to trap a WM_CHAR message, Visual C++ builds the following prototype:

```
void CYourClass::OnChar(UINT nChar, UINT nRepCnt, UINT nFlags)
{
    // TODO: Add your message handler code here

    CYourClass::OnChar(nChar, nRepCnt, nFlags);
}
```

This function is called after a key is pressed. It gets called *after* the WM_KEYDOWN message is processed, but *before* the WM_KEYUP. Here is an explanation of each of the arguments:

nChar	The virtual-key code value of the key being pressed.
nRepCnt	This is the number of times the keystroke is repeated when the user holds the key down.
nFlags	This has the scan code, key-transition code, previous key state, and context code.

The bit positions in the following list describe nFlags:

BIT POSITION	DESCRIPTION
0–7	Scan code (OEM-dependent value).
8	If a 1, key is an extended key (function key numeric keypad key)
11–12	Used internally by Windows.
13	1 if Alt key also pressed, 0 if not.
14	1 if the key was down before the call, 0 if it was up before the call.
15	Transition state; 0 if key being pressed, or 1 if it is being released.

When using IBM Enhanced 101- and 102-key keyboards, enhanced keys are the right Alt and Ctrl keys on the main portion of the keyboard; the Insert, Delete, Home, End, Page Up, Page Down, and arrow keys in the group to the left of the numeric keypad; and the slash (/) and Enter keys on the numeric keypad. Other keyboards may also make special use of bit 8 in the nFlags argument, so try to minimize any reliance on the extended key bit of nFlags.

Keyboard Summary

Most of the things you'll ever need to process keyboard messages are handled quite nicely by ClassWizard. One way in which you can use these messages is allowing the user to move the cursor with the arrow keys. For instance, you can trap WM_KEYDOWN messages to find out the current position of the cursor and to update the cursor position when or while an arrow key is depressed. The rate of travel of the cursor can be increased by adding an arbitrary value to the cursor's position whenever an arrow key is pressed. Use GetCursorPos( ) to fetch the cursor position and convert it to client coordinates using the ScreenToClient( ) function. You can use GetClientRect( ) to find out how big the client area is and thus always keep the cursor "in bounds." Reset the value of the "speed-up" variable for the cursor's movement to readjust it when the arrow key is released. This use of the arrow keys for purposes of navigation should be included in your Windows programs to allow the user to operate them without a mouse. Using the "speed-up" variable is likewise very important, as it can take a long time to move the cursor from one end of a line to another. Should you decide to include these features, don't forget that you'll need some way to toggle and/or select an object, such as a radio button. The spacebar and Enter keys are usually reserved for these operations, respectively.

COORDINATE SYSTEMS

Windows uses several different coordinate systems in conjunction with various mapping modes in order to draw text and graphics on the screen. The ones we are interested in the most are screen coordinates and client coordinates. In either case, the standard unit of measure is the pixel for both the horizontal (x) and vertical (y) axis. The x-coordinate value increases from left to right, and the y-coordinate value increases from top to bottom.

Logical Units

In order to take full advantage of the various MFC functions affecting cursors and how they are drawn and used, it is prudent to review briefly the coordinate systems in Windows and how they relate to mapping modes. Since Windows is a complete GUI, everything you see on the screen is the result of a pixel being set to a certain color. Now, there are many different video displays out there, all of different resolutions. Windows must therefore have a way of adjusting to these different devices. To do so, it makes use of 6 mapping modes and 2 coordinate systems. The coordinate systems are based on either *logical* units or *client* units, which provide a scaling factor between what Windows wants to draw and the physical device on which it wants to draw it. The 6 mapping modes are summarized in Table 6.1.

TABLE 6.1
Mapping modes and their respective units.

MAPPING MODE	LOGICAL UNITS	PHYSICAL UNIT
MM_HIENGLISH	1000	
MM_HIMETRIC	100	1 millimeter
MM_LOENGLISH	100	1 inch
MM_LOMETRIC	10	1 millimeter
MM_TEXT	1	1 pixel
MM_TWIPS	1440	1 inch

All modes except MM_TEXT map the logical units to the device units in a manner that sometimes deviates from the conversion factors given in the table. This deviation is necessary so that the object displayed will appear with the same clarity regardless of the resolution of the monitor. Your application can make use of the CDC member function GetDeviceCaps( ) to ascertain how these units are scaled by your user's video display device. In simpler terms, your program specifies logical units whenever you want something drawn—Windows uses the mapping mode to translate these units into something that will look "right" when displayed.

Screen Coordinates

Screen coordinates are used when dealing with the entire video display area, not just the active window. Thus, they are generally used with functions that either do not have a window (e.g., cursor functions) or that move a window in reference to some point on the screen. With a little experience, you should be able to recognize when to call the various conversion functions based on the type of message (e.g., WM_MOVE) you are processing.

Client Coordinates

The next system of coordinates we'll look at are called *client coordinates*. While screen coordinates are based on the entire screen as a whole, client coordinates are confined strictly to the client area of the window. This area is *always* measured in pixels; thus, the value in screen coordinates for any given point will be greater than its value in client coordinates. The important thing here, from a practical point of view, is knowing how to convert from one type of coordinates to the other when that is called for by a function. Luckily, this conversion is made easy by the following functions:

```
CWnd::ClientToScreen (LPOINT lpoint);
CWnd::ScreenToClient(LPOINT lpoint);
```

For both of these routines, you pass in the coordinate to be converted in the argument lpoint. The converted values are returned in the lpoint structure. When passing the argument lpoint, it is important that you pay close attention to the type of coordinate expected by the function you are calling; it is easy to make a mistake in this regard.

When using client coordinates, take advantage of the function GetClientRect(&rRect). This function has many useful purposes, some of which you've already seen. Recall that a rectangle structure has 4 members:

```
rRect.top
rRect.left
rRect.bottom
rRect.right
```

These values can be put to good use. For example, if you are displaying text, you can do some simple calculations to determine how many lines and how many characters you can display in a given window, as follows:

```
RECT rRect;        // size of client area
int nRows;         // number of lines that can fit on screen
int nHeight        // average height of a character of current font
TEXTMETRIC tm;     // for getting size of characters

  GetTextMetric(&tm);     // get size of text, etc.
nHeight = tm.tmHeight;    // get height of character
  GetClientRect(&rRect);  // get size of client area
nRows = ((rRect.bottom - rRect.top)+1)/nHeight;
```

The number of characters that will fit on a line (e.g., the number of columns) can be similarly determined using:

```
int nCols = ((rRect.right - rRect.left)+1)/tm.tmAveCharWidth;
```

Combining the different function calls in this way can give you a pretty good handle on most programming tasks involving the keyboard, cursor, and screen coordinate system.

CURSORS

Changing the Cursor

Most of the time, Windows will change the shape of the cursor for you into something relative to the context of your position. For example, in a Help file the cursor will change automatically into a pointing finger when moved over a hypertext topic or term definition. But for those times when you want to use a different cursor, it's pretty easy to do so. First, you'll need to create the new cursor in App Studio by creating a new resource (choose Icon). When creating new icons, follow a few common-sense guidelines to produce a useful tool. Color selection should allow for a high degree of contrast, so that the icon is plainly visible when your application is minimized. Consider also the background color of any window or dialog box where you may wish to display the icon. These should blend harmoniously. The graphical content of the icon should convey as much universal, or at least cultural, meaning as possible to enhance the appeal and ease of use of your program. To change a cursor, you must first load and then set it. These steps can be combined in a single statement, as shown in this example:

```
CURSOR oldcur = SetCursor(myApp.LoadCursor(IDC_NEWCURSOR));
```

The Hourglass Cursor

If some aspect of your program is going to be time-consuming (e.g., format a floppy disk, download a large file from a server, etc.), you should change the shape of the cursor to an hourglass (you won't have to draw one—Windows provides several cursors as stock objects) to convey to the user the fact that a lengthy operation is in progress. Another design feature you may wish to create is some sort of progress gauge that is updated periodically to reassure the user that the system has not somehow "locked up." For flexibility, you may want to add a Cancel button to this progress gauge, so that the user has the option of aborting the operation. Should you go this route, *don't* change the cursor's shape beforehand. It should remain as a pointer so that the Cancel button may be clicked. The hourglass cursor has the resource ID of IDC_WAIT. In order to use this or any other cursor, you must load and then set it. If you use the SDK form of LoadCursor( ), you must supply the instance handle of your application as the first argument in the call. If you use the MFC flavor, you must instantiate an object of your application. For example, if you called your application DEMO in AppWizard, you should perform the instantiation a global variable in your DEMO.CPP file, as in this example:

```
CDemoApp myApp;   // create global variable for use anywhere
```

CDemoApp is the name assigned by AppWizard to your application's constructor. Here are examples of both ways to load and set a cursor:

SDK:
```
HCURSOR oldcur = SetCursor(LoadCursor(NULL, IDC_WAIT));
//
//do time-consuming operation here
//
SetCursor(oldcur);  // reset the cursor to its previous shape
```

MFC:
```
HCURSOR oldcur = SetCursor(myApp.LoadCursor(IDC_WAIT));
//
//do time-consuming operation here
//
SetCursor(oldcur);  // reset the cursor to its previous shape
```

While you're obviously free to choose whichever method you prefer, we suggest the latter, as it has the subtle advantage of weaning you off the SDK nomenclature—which is, after all, why you are moving to OOP and Visual C++.

Creating a Caret Cursor

In Windows, you have basically two types of cursors: a graphical cursor (e.g., the familiar arrow, or pointing finger) used for dealing with purely graphical objects such as buttons, window frames, etc., and a text cursor, or caret, used for dealing with text. The caret indicates where the next letter will appear in applications such as word processing programs. Incidentally, carets that appear inside edit box controls have their own built-in control logic, so you will not have to be concerned with these.

In some situations, you may wish to override the default caret with one that is slightly more visible and proportional to the current font and point size. This modification is easily done with the MFC call CreateSolidCaret(*width*, *height*), where *width* is the width of the caret in logical units, and *height* is the height of the caret, also in logical units. To create a sense of scale with the current text characteristics, set these values to the average character width and character height, respectively. These can be ascertained by a call to GetTextMetrics( ). Here is an example that creates a caret proportional to the text size and sets it to the upper left-hand corner of the window:

```
TEXTMETRIC tm;          // need the text structure TEXTMETRIC
CClientDC dc(this);     // get the display context for current window
dc.GetTextMetrics(&tm); // get the text characteristics
CreateSolidCaret(tm.tmAveCharWidth, tm.tmHeight);      //create caret
CPoint caret_location;  // declare a CPoint object
caret_location.x = caret_location.y = 0;  // initialize x,y to 0,0
SetCaretPos(caret_location);              // move the caret to 0,0
```

Hiding and Showing the Caret

Another little item related to good screen management involves temporarily removing the caret and restoring it at a later time. This practice is particularly useful when you are drawing text on the screen and want the caret to move along with the text as it is displayed. If you do not hide the caret, your screen will have "trails" from the point where new characters were written on top of the caret, and as a result those characters will be displayed with a reverse video effect. To obviate this little annoyance, call the functions HideCaret( ) to remove the caret and ShowCaret( ) to display it again. Normally, you will also want to provide some sort of routine to update the cursor position between the calls to HideCaret( ) and ShowCaret( ). There is one other detail you'll need to watch out for—the number of calls to Show Caret( ) *must* match the number of calls to HideCaret( ). These functions do not take a parameter as illustrated below:

```
HideCaret();          // to remove the caret
ShowCaret();          // to display the caret
```

Before we get further into the mechanical aspects of cursors, keep in mind that some cursor functions are dependent on where they are used. For example, the calls to manipulate a cursor inside an edit box are different from those for a cursor in a regular window. The calls for cursors in edit boxes will be covered in detail in Chapter 9. For now, just be advised that special MFC functions exist for processing certain situations.

SETTING THE CARET'S POSITION

For those occasions when you need to reposition the cursor or caret to a new location, use the CWnd member function SetCaretPos(CPOINT *point*). The *x* and *y* coordinates of *point* must be supplied as client coordinates. This function only works in the window that owns the caret—remember, in Windows you can have several applications running simultaneously, all of which can have a caret (but, the caret can be *visible* only in one window at a time, the window that has the input focus). On the other hand, this function will move the caret location regardless of whether or not the caret is visible. Thus, you can hide, move, and redisplay the caret as shown in this example:

```
CPoint new_loc;          // new location of caret
HideCaret();             // hide the caret
new_loc.x= 0;
new_loc.y= 0;            // set new coordinates
SetCaretPos(new_loc);    // now move the caret
ShowCaret();             // and redisplay the caret
```

GETTING THE CARET'S POSITION

Just as there are times when you want to move the caret to a certain location, there are also times when you need to find out where it is. For example, the user may have moved the mouse into a line of text and clicked the mouse button in preparation for a text insertion operation. To determine exactly where the caret is, use the CWnd function GetCaretPos( ), which returns a CPoint object containing the *x,y* coordinates of the caret's location. The CPoint value is given in client coordinates. Observe that no error condition is ever returned by this call, as the caret will always be somewhere in the current window. Here is a simple example using GetCaretPos( ):

```
CPoint cur_pos;          // declare an object of type CPoint
cur_pos = GetCaretPos(); // get the current caret position
```

That's all there is to it; cur_pos.x now contains the horizontal coordinate, and cur_pos.y the vertical.

The Cursor's Hotspot

The *hotspot* is a point used by Windows to track the cursor's location. This is, by default, the upperleft-hand corner of the cursor's bitmap (0,0). Should you desire to change this default position for a special cursor, a tool is available in App Studio's Graphics Editor for setting a new pixel as the hotspot. This hotspot should not be confused with the hotspots set by the Hotspot Editor in your Visual C++ group. This editor is used to designate regions on a bitmap for *hypergraphic* operations, such as Help. These hotspots are linked to Help topics or Help macros that are executed when the user clicks the mouse in their respective hotspots. In such cases, the cursor's appearance also changes (e.g., from an arrow to a pointing finger, etc.).

SPECIAL CURSORS

We'll conclude this overview of cursors by saying a few words about special cursors. The most visible member of this club is the cursor used in Visual Basic Controls (.VBX), especially with the grid, or spreadsheet, control. This control comes bundled with Visual C++ and will serve as our model. In this capacity, the cursor is actually nothing more than a highlight box surrounding whichever cell in the grid has the current *focus*. Operations here become an exercise in tracking the cursor, and not modifying its appearance (although this, too, can be done). In such circumstances, the particular VBX control you use will provide access to member functions to handle such needs. Examples of other special cursors include Windows-based games and special applications. These cursors are usually garden-variety icons that are loaded as shown earlier in this chapter in the Changing Cursors section.

MOUSE ACTIVITY

As far as sources of input go, the mouse is your program's biggest contributor. Despite how often the mouse is used, the developer can generally get by with just a few mouse message handlers. These handlers use member functions similar to those discussed earlier for getting the cursor, converting coordinates, etc. Once again, ClassWizard takes most of the work out of these tasks. But as you learned in the discussion on "Key States," with the mouse you also need to track two similar items: the *location* of the mouse cursor and the *state* of any button. A button's state is similar to a key's: Is the mouse button being pressed (WM_KEYDOWN) or released (WM_KEYUP)? Fortunately, the MFC class CWnd provides a member function that actually allows you to track both the mouse's location *and* the button states. This function is called OnMouseMove( ).

The OnMouseMove( ) Function

This CWnd member function is prototyped as follows:

```
afx_msg void OnMouseMove(UINT nFlags, CPOINT cur_pos);
```

The first argument indicates whether or not the Ctrl and Shift keys are down, or if any one of three mouse buttons is being pressed. The second argument is the location of the cursor, in *device coordinates*. For a good example using OnMouseMove( ), take a look at the function CScribView::OnMouseMove( ) in the "Scribble" sample provided with Visual C++. When you're just interested in the position, use the CWnd member function OnNcHitTest, which is prototyped as follows:

```
afx_msg UINT OnNcHitTest(CPOINT cur_pos);
```

The cursor position (e.g., *cur_pos*) in this function is returned in *screen* coordinates, so be sure to call any appropriate functions needed to convert these values for use in another function. The return values are listed in the documentation, but suffice it to say that every possible place on the screen is covered. One of the return values, HTNOWHERE, even indicates if the mouse is in a "no-man's-land" between adjacent windows. Contrast this return value with HTERROR, which can produce a system beep.

Button Events and States

The mouse button event most often monitored is the click, which is used by many other Windows objects (e.g., check boxes, radio buttons, command buttons, etc.). Just as you can determine if a key is being pressed or released, you can do the same with mouse buttons. In ClassWizard, you can trap the messages WM_LBUTTON-DBLCLK, WM_LBUTTONDOWN, and WM_LBUTTONUP for the left mouse button (nearly identical messages are available for the right mouse button). To keep the user in control, you only want an event to start *after* the mouse button has been released. This fine-tuning pays off whenever you want the user to be able to "drag" something with the mouse. When the WM_LBUTTONUP message is selected in ClassWizard, it automatically builds the prototype:

```
void CYourClass::OnLButtonUp(UINT nFlags, CPoint point)
{
   // TODO: Add your message handler code here and/or call default

   CYourClass::OnLButtonUp(nFlags, point);
}
```

You can insert your own special code within this prototype to process a left mouse button click on a particular object. One of the uses to which you can put the mouse functions discussed in this chapter is to create your own command buttons, or spin controls. For example, you could place a bitmap on a window to represent the face of your button. For spin controls, you can use any of several up/down arrow bitmaps supplied with Visual C++. (See LoadOEMBitmap( ) in class CBitmap in the Class Library Reference, Reference Volume 1.) By trapping a mouse click, your program could test whether the click occurred while the mouse was inside the bitmap. Or, you might wish to track the mouse's position constantly. This would enable you to change the prompt string in the window's status bar each time the mouse moves over a different object on the screen and thus allow the user to read what a control or object does *before* clicking it. To accomplish all of these tasks, the only other values you really need to know are the coordinates of the area where you placed a bitmap. The size of the Windows bitmaps for the up and down arrows can be mapped into a rectangle by using CRect::SetRect( ). In the function for WM_LBUTTONUP shown in the preceding example, you could use the CRect member function PtInRect(POINT pt) to find out whether the mouse click occurred within your bitmap. If it did, you can execute the code associated with a click. If the click was not within the bitmap, you simply return from the function without executing any code. If you decide to experiment with creating your own spin control, consider adding the option of slewing. *Slewing* means traversing the range of the spin control by holding a mouse button down while over one of the spin control's arrows. You could use the preceding example to allow the user to single-step the spin control, and perhaps trap the WM_RBUTTONDOWN message to support slewing. Spin controls are very useful in Windows programs that let the user select values from a range.

CHAPTER SUMMARY

You can add a lot of versatility to your program via the judicious use of cursors, mice, and keyboard messages. By combining ClassWizard message handlers with your code, you can deftly allow others to use your program without a mouse. Special processing needs, such as real-time updating of the prompt string in the status bar, are made possible by building in reactions to commands at certain locations. Likewise, such reactions allow you to build an unsophisticated but workable spin control. Regarding cursors, the name of the game is consistency. Use the same cursor for each class of operation (e.g., time-consuming operations, error reporting, and resolution, etc.). As for the keyboard, be consistent, and take care not to collide with de facto standards such as F1 (Help), Ctrl-X (Cut to Clipboard), and so on. You should be able to combine the information in this chapter later with that given in Chapter 9, which deals with dialog box controls, to come up with some pretty snappy applications.

CHAPTER 7

Belly up to the Bar: Using Toolbars, Status Bars, and Dialog Bars

Take a look at most contemporary Windows applications and you will see examples of toolbars, status bars, and dialog bars. Toolbars are rows of bitmaps below the main menu allowing users to push a button rather than pull down a menu to make a choice. Status bars are a row of text panes, usually at the bottom of a frame window, providing users with current information about the application. Dialog bars are modeless dialog boxes containing a group of dialog controls, such as combo boxes, edit fields, and buttons, which you can place anywhere in a frame window's client area. Control bars afford users added functionality, but providing them used to require a lot of code and processing. Now, with MFC 2.0, you can provide these features to your users with a single mouse click!

AUTOMATIC GENERATION OF CONTROL BARS

You can provide your application with initial toolbar and status bar support by clicking the Toolbar check box in AppWizard as shown in Figure 7.1. This action generates code to display and process the default MFC toolbar and status bar.

AppWizard will include the needed bitmaps in your resource file (.RC) and place the bitmap files in your \res subdirectory. AppWizard will also include toolbar and status bar objects as protected members in your application's main frame object.

```
//Mainfram.h relevant section of class definition :
protected: // control bar embedded members
CStatusBar  m_wndStatusBar;
CToolBar    m_wndToolBar;
```

If other objects in your program need access to these member variables, you can either provide access functions that return references to the members or simply make them public member functions.

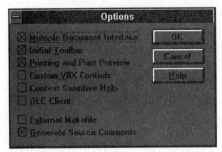

Figure 7.1
AppWizard with Toolbar
creation selected.

ADDING CONTROL BARS TO EXISTING MFC PROJECTS

AppWizard will generate all the code needed to construct and process an application's basic toolbar and status bar. However, you can only run AppWizard once, so if at first you decide not to add toolbar and status bar support to your application, are you done for? Nope! Just use the AppWizard to create another, temporary application with toolbar support and cut and paste the necessary components from that application to your other application. In fact, you may wish to generate and save a "temporary" application that includes every conceivable option for future transfers of components to your other applications as needed.

THE TOOLBAR AND MESSAGE COMMANDS

Toolbar buttons are shortcuts for menu commands and are processed the same way. (See Chapter 6 for more information on menus.) Fortunately for developers, MFC takes care of this processing via the handler function for menu commands. The application framework calls the function for each toolbar button using the same command ID assigned to the corresponding menu item. Thus you only need one message map entry to handle both the menu and the toolbar. You assign the command IDs in the buttons array AppWizard generates in your CMainFrame class as illustrated below:

```
// Toolbar button ID Array.
// toolbar buttons - IDs are command buttons
static UINT BASED_CODE buttons[] =
{
  // same order as in the bitmap 'toolbar.bmp'
  ID_FILE_NEW,  // 1st bitmap
  ID_FILE_OPEN, // 2nd bitmap
  ID_FILE_SAVE, // 3rd bitmap
  ID_SEPARATOR,
  ID_EDIT_CUT,  // 4th bitmap
  ID_EDIT_COPY,
  ID_EDIT_PASTE,
  ID_SEPARATOR,
  ID_FILE_PRINT,
  ID_APP_ABOUT,
  ID_CONTEXT_HELP,
};
```

The framework usually associates the control bars with your application's frame window. The controls themselves are windows positioned around the frame. The framework creates and initializes the control bars in the frame window's OnCreate function, as illustrated here:

```
//Creating the control bars.
int CMainFrame::OnCreate(LPCREATESTRUCT lpCreateStruct)
{
  if (CMDIFrameWnd::OnCreate(lpCreateStruct) == -1)
    return -1;

  if (!m_wndToolBar.Create(this) ||
    !m_wndToolBar.LoadBitmap(IDR_MAINFRAME) ||
    !m_wndToolBar.SetButtons(buttons,
     sizeof(buttons)/sizeof(UINT)))
  {
    TRACE("Failed to create toolbar\n");
    return -1;          // fail to create
  }

  if (!m_wndStatusBar.Create(this) ||
    !m_wndStatusBar.SetIndicators(indicators,
     sizeof(indicators)/sizeof(UINT)))
  {
    TRACE("Failed to create status bar\n");
    return -1;          // fail to create
  }

  return 0;
}
```

ADDING ITEMS TO THE TOOLBAR

Each time you add a menu item to your resource file and wish to have a corresponding toolbar button, you must add the item's ID to the button array. You must also remember to edit the toolbar bitmap to include your new button. Use App Studio or any other resource editor to change your toolbar. (See Chapter 5 in the *Class Library User's Guide* for details on adding toolbar buttons.)

MESSAGE MAP ENTRIES

The message map in your main application's implementation file will resemble that for our demo application:

```
BEGIN_MESSAGE_MAP(CDemoApp, CWinApp)
  //{{AFX_MSG_MAP(CDemoApp)
  ON_COMMAND(ID_APP_ABOUT, OnAppAbout)
  //}}AFX_MSG_MAP
  // Standard file based document commands
  ON_COMMAND(ID_FILE_NEW, CWinApp::OnFileNew)
  ON_COMMAND(ID_FILE_OPEN, CWinApp::OnFileOpen)
  // Standard print setup command
  ON_COMMAND(ID_FILE_PRINT_SETUP, CWinApp::OnFilePrintSetup)
  // Global help commands
  ON_COMMAND(ID_HELP_INDEX, CWinApp::OnHelpIndex)
  ON_COMMAND(ID_HELP_USING, CWinApp::OnHelpUsing)
  ON_COMMAND(ID_HELP, CWinApp::OnHelp)
  ON_COMMAND(ID_CONTEXT_HELP, CWinApp::OnContextHelp)
```

```
            ON_COMMAND( ID_DEFAULT_HELP, CWinApp::OnHelpIndex)
        END_MESSAGE_MAP( )
```

As you can see, adding new **ON_COMMAND** macros to handle the toolbar was not necessary. The framework will handle all the toolbar processing if you assign the same IDs to the buttons in the button array as to the menu items.

THE CTOOLBAR CLASS

Here are some of the CToolBar's member functions:

```
CToolBar::Create( CWnd* pParentWnd, DWORD dwstyle = WS_CHILD | WS_VISIBLE |
CBRS_TOP , UINT nID = AFX_IDW_TOOLBAR ).
```

In the preceding snippet of code, we created a toolbar object like so:

```
m_wndToolBar.Create(this).
```

We passed the function the C++ *this* pointer (a pointer to the current object, a CFrameWnd-derived class in our case) as the first parameter, the parent window, and used the default values for the rest of the parameters.

The library derives all control bar objects from CWnd objects, so control bar objects require window styles. The default values are: Make the window enclosing the toolbar a child window and make it visible. To the default values generated by the framework you should bitwise OR any additional control bar styles your application requires. Table 7.1 explains these values.

The final parameter, *nID,* is the child window ID. The prototype of the next member function called in the OnCreate function, LoadBitmap, appears below:

```
CToolBar::LoadBitmap( UINT nIDResource)
```

This function loads the indicated bitmap resource, which you should specify using a unique resource ID number defined in your program's resource.h and .RC files. In addition, this function sets default values for the toolbar's height. If you wish to override these default values, you will have to call SetHeight( ). The framework overloads this function to take a LPCSTR string that contains the name of a bitmap file to be loaded.

The prototype for the next function is:

```
CToolBar::SetButtons( const UINT FAR* lpIDArray, int nIDCount)
```

TABLE 7.1
Position IDs.

CBRS_TOP	Indicates the control bar will be positioned at the top of the parent window. (toolbars)
CBRS_BOTTOM	Indicates the control bar will be positioned at the bottom of the parent window. (status bars)
CBRS_NOALIGN	Flag indicating that the control bar will *not* be repositioned when the frame window is resized.

This function sets each button to the command ID specified in the array named in *lpIDArray*. The first parameter is a pointer to this array of command IDs. The second parameter indicates the number of items in the passed array. In the toolbar button array shown in the Toolbars and Message Commands section, note that for any element with the value ID_SEPARATOR, the framework will create a separator at that position on the toolbar; you do not need to worry about supplying a bitmap, since the framework will take care of that for you. The framework will also assign your command IDs to the appropriate bitmap buttons. If you pass a NULL as the first parameter, this function allocates enough space for *nIDCount* buttons, and you must call the SetButtonInfo( ) function to initialize each button in your toolbar. Both SetButton( ) and SetButtonInfo( ) return FALSE to indicate an error.

Most of the other CToolBar member functions listed in Table 7.2 deal with creating your own toolbar. The framework will maintain a one-to-one correspondence between the items in the button array and the pictures in the bitmap.

Use the SetSizes(Size *sizeButton*, Size *sizeImage*) function to change the toolbar to a different size from those specified in *The Windows Interface: An Application Design Guide*. The value of *sizeButton* specifies in pixels the size of the button image plus 6 pixels (3 on each side). If you do not provide the 3-pixel border, the function will fire an ASSERT in debug mode. The *sizeImage* parameter specifies the size of the image in pixels. Call this function to set the default sizes, including the height of the toolbar, as illustrated in this example:

```
Size image = 12;  // set size of a button image to 12
Size button = 20; // each button will have a 12-pixel image, plus a 4-pixel
  border
m_wndToolBar.SetSizes(button, image);
```

Use the SetHeight( ) function to set the height of the toolbar in pixels to the size specified by *cyHeight*. Call this function after SetSizes( ) to override the default height of the toolbar. If you do not allow enough room, this function will clip the bottoms of the images.

The CommandToIndex( ) function searches the toolbar array for the command ID specified in *nIDFind*. The function will return −1 if it cannot find the given command ID. If it finds the command ID, this function returns its zero-based index into the array.

```
Example:
int fFound = m_wndToolBar.CommandToIndex( ID_EDIT_CUT);
if ( fFound != -1)
```

TABLE **7.2**

The CToolBar member functions.

```
void SetSizes(Size sizeButton, Size sizeImage)
void SetHeight(int cyHeight)
int CommandToIndex(UINT nIDFind)
UINT GetItemID(int nIdex) const
void GetItemRect(int nIndex, LPRECT lpRect)
void GetButtonInfo(int nIndex, UINT & nID, UINT & nStlye, int & iImage) const
void SetButtonInfo(int nIndex, UINT nID, UINT nStyle, int iImage)
```

```
{
  if( fFound == 4)
  {
    AfxMessageBox("Found at index 4 (fifth item) )");
  }
  else
  {
    char str[80];
    sprintf(str,"ID %d Found at index %d",ID_EDIT_CUT,fFound);
    AfxMessageBox(str);
  }
}
else
{
  AfxMessageBox("Command ID_EDIT_CUT not found in toolbar indicator array");
}
```

The GetItemID( ) function is the reverse of CommandToIndex. If you pass the index into the toolbar array, GetItemID( )will return the value of the ID stored there. You could use the base class function CControlBar::GetCount to find out how many items are in the toolbar array, iterate through the array, and get each command ID stored there. If the item is a separator, the function will return the value of ID_SEPARATOR rather than an index, since the framework does not assign index values to separators. The following provides an example.

```
int index(4); // C++ initialization.
int nID;
int count, numsep(0);
count = m_wndToolBar.GetCount();
for ( int i = 0; i < count; i++)
{
  nID = m_wndToolBar.GetItemID( i );
  if ( nID == ID_SEPARATOR )
  numsep++;
  // now do whatever you wish with the command ID.
}
```

The GetItemRect( ) function will return, in the rectangle buffer provided, the rectangle containing the image specified by *nIndex*. These rectangle coordinates will be relative to the upper left of the toolbar and specified in pixels.

The GetButtonInfo( ) function retrieves the command ID, style values, and position in the bitmap of the toolbar image at *nIndex*.

You can use the SetButtonInfo( ) function to change the default order of the items in the toolbar. You can also use this function to change the styles of the individual buttons. The framework supports the styles summarized in Table 7.3.

If the item is a separator, you can change its width by specifying a value in the *iImage* parameter.

```
Example:
UINT nID, nStyle, int iImage;
int index = 3; // information on buttons[3].
m_wndToolBar.GetButtonInfo( index, nID, nStyle, iImage);
// change the style to a check box
nStyle = TBBS_CHECKBOX;
m_wndToolBar.SetButtonInfo( index, nID, nStyle, iImage);
```

TABLE 7.3
Toolbar button styles.

TBBS_BUTTON	Standard pushbutton and the default value
TBBS_SEPARATOR	Separator between button groups
TBBS_CHECKBOX	Creates an auto check box button. You can also use the CCmdUI::SetCheck function to turn a pushbutton into a check button.

THE TOOLBAR AND THE MAIN MENU

In Chapter 5 you saw how to call EnableMenuItem( ) to gray out menu items that are not intended to be available to users. For static menu items—those created at compile time instead of run time—the framework provides an easier method for graying out and activating menu and toolbar options. You can accomplish this action with the ON_UPDATE_COMMAND_UI macro. When you add a menu and toolbar item, its ID will appear in the ClassWizard's Object ID's list box, as shown in Figure 7.2, and the two messages it responds to will appear in the Messages list box. Those messages are COMMAND and UPDATE_COMMAND_UI.

MESSAGES

The command message is the familiar Windows' **WM_COMMAND**, while the UPDATE_COMMAND_UI message is a private message registered by the framework,

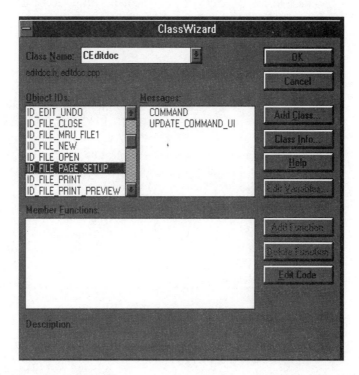

Figure 7.2
ClassWizard showing
IDs and
COMMAND UIs.

with the value WM_IDLEUPDATECMDUI. (MFC documents all internal framework messages in Technical Note #24.) Before the framework displays a menu, it will check each menu item for an ON_COMMAND handler and gray out any option that does not possess such a handler. If the framework finds an ON_COMMAND handler, it will execute the ON_COMMAND function, which enables the user to select the menu option. The framework processes each ON_COMMAND handler found by creating and passing a CCmdUI object to the ON_UPDATE_COMMAND_UI function defined in your message map. Your message map entry might look like this:

```
ON_COMMAND( ID_TESTFLAG,OnTest)
ON_UPDATE_COMMAND_UI( ID_TESTFLAG, OnUpdateTest)
```

and the function prototype in your header file like this:

```
afx_msg void OnTest();
afx_msg void OnUpdateTest( CCmdUI *pCCmdUI);
```

Your responsibility inside this function is to determine if the item should or should not be grayed out. The function will then call the Enable( ) member function of the CCmdUI object passed.

```
void CMyTest::OnUpdateTest( CCmdUI* pCCmdUI )
{
   pCCmdUI->Enable( m_bTestFlag);
}
```

If the value of m_bTestFlag is FALSE, the framework will gray out the menu item and its associated toolbar button. The item will be accessible if its value is TRUE, the default value.

CCMDUI CLASS

You will seldom directly instantiate a CCmdUI variable, since the framework handles most of the processing dealing with this class. To see how the framework does its job, look in the AFX source file BARCORE.CPP. The MSVC setup program will place this file, along with the other AFX source code files, in the msvc\mfc\src subdirectory. During your application's OnIdle( ) and menu processing, the framework will create CCmdUI objects and dispatch their messages.

The CCmdUI class has several member functions you can use in your user interface update handlers (see Table 7.4). One is the CCmdUI::Enable(BOOL bflag = TRUE) described in the section on "Messages."

TABLE 7.4
CCmdUI member functions.

```
Enable( BOOL bflag = TRUE)
SetCheck( int nCheckState = 1)
SetRadio( BOOL flag = TRUE)
SetText( LPCSTR str)
```

The SetCheck( ) function will, depending on the value of the parameter *nCheckState*, place or remove a check mark from the menu item. For a toolbar button, a check means the button was depressed, and the absence of a check means the opposite. The values are: 1 = checked, 0 = unchecked, and 2 = indeterminate.

```
void CMyTest::OnUpdateTest( CCmdUI* pCCmdUI )
{
   pCCmdUI->SetCheck( m_nTestState);
}
```

The SetRadio( ) function activates and deactivates the other items in its group, thus implementing the familiar behavior of the mutually exclusive radio buttons, allowing the user to choose only one item in the group. If *flag* is FALSE, the framework will deactivate the item. This action is not automatic, so either the items must maintain this behavior themselves (recommended), or else you must handle the toggle activity yourself in your code (not recommended).

The SetText( ) member function will set the pane's text to the value passed in *str*.

```
void CMyTest::OnUpdateTest( CCmdUI* pCCmdUI )
{
   if ( 1 == m_nCheckState )
   pCCmdUI->SetText( "ON" );
   else if ( 0 == m_nCheckState )
     pCCmdUI->SetText("OFF");
   else
     pCCmdUI->SetText(" ? ");
}
```

You will not be able to pass a CString object directly, since the function takes a LPCSTR parameter. Therefore, you will have to extract the buffer from the CString object, as demonstrated in Chapter 4, and pass that buffer to the SetText( ) function.

FLOATING TOOLBARS

Not all toolbars reside statically attached to an application's frame window. You can provide some toolbars that can still be active though the user may move them to any location on the screen. App Studio's Dialog Editor has an example of a floating toolbar, the control bar, which contains the various controls that you can drag and drop on a dialog box under construction.

You will find a full implementation of such a tool "palette" in the MSVC sample program CTRLBARS, located in the \msvc\mfc\samples subdirectory (see Figure 7.3). You will need to create a bitmap containing the tool images you wish to place in your palette. Fortunately, in the COMMON.RES resource file, located in the \mfc\samples\apstudio directory, MSVC provides several stock bitmaps that you can add to your application. (See Tech Note #23 for directions on how to transfer the bitmaps from the common resource file to your resource file.) The code to process such a toolbar is too lengthy to include here, but the MFC sample program CTRLBARS provides a detailed example.

Figure 7.3
A floating toolbar.

STATUS BARS

Status bars display information at the bottom of an application's window. This information can include such items as mnemonics for menu commands and the status of toggle keys like Caps Lock. The framework displays this information in windows, called panes, in the style specified by The Windows Application Design Guide. In the framework you can provide an initial status bar just by including a toolbar. If you wish just a status bar, you can cut the toolbar initialization code from your MAINFRM.CPP OnCreate( ) function and cut out the m_toolbar data member from the MAINFRM.H header file.

STATUS BAR PROCESSING

The AFX source file BARCORE.CPP contains the code that handles most status bar processing. Processing occurs when your application enters its OnIdle( ) function and the framework sends the WM_IDLEUPDATECMDUI message to all the descendants of the status bar, which are Windows windows. The framework will do this processing each time it enters OnIdle( ), before releasing control back to the Windows task manager. If you have no OnIdle( ) processing to do or no messages in your queue, the framework will not perform OnIdle( ) processing nor control bar updating. You will see later how to bypass this default behavior and update the status bar yourself.

INITIAL STATUS BAR GENERATED BY APPWIZARD

The initial status bar consists of four panes plus a separator, as shown in Figure 7.4. The first pane displays the default message assigned to the resource ID AFX_IDS_IDLE-

Figure 7.4
Initial status bar
generated
by AppWizard.

MESSAGE in the application's .RC file string table. However, when the cursor is over a menu item, the first pane will display a prompt reminding the user about the purpose of the command. The framework provides default prompts for standard message IDs defined in your application's string tables. Also, as you add menu items, App Studio allows you to enter prompt strings in the Properties box. These strings appear in a string table associated with the command IDs you gave your menu choices. (See Chapter 5 for more information on adding menu items.) The framework displays such prompts automatically. You need write no code to get this functionality.

ADDING YOUR OWN PROMPT

Sometimes you may wish to provide your own prompt strings, for instance when you dynamically create a menu item (see Figure 7.5). In such cases, the framework uses an internal message, WM_SETMESSAGESTRING, which it sends to the frame window to update the prompt message. You can specify either a resource string ID or a string itself, but not both, for this parameter. To send a resource ID, place the ID in the wParam parameter and NULL in the lParam. To send the string itself, set wParam to 0 and place a pointer to the string in lParam. You could then either post or send the message to the framework as follows:

```
m_pMainWnd->SendMessage( WM_SETMESSAGESTRING, (WPARAM) IDS_STRING, 0L);
```

or

```
char str[] = "HELP !!!!!"
m_pMainWnd->SendMessage( WM_SETMESSAGESTRING, 0L,str);
```

STATUS PANES

The next three panes in the initial status bar are indicators for the toggle keys Caps Lock, Num Lock, and Scrl Lock. The framework provides their string values in the .RC file, in a string table whose identifiers begin with ID_INDICATOR_*, and defines these values in the file AFXRES.H in the mfc\include subdirectory. AppWizard then includes them in your resource file.

DEFAULT INDICATORS

MFC defines the six default indicators shown in Table 7.5 with their values and the default strings assigned to them. The framework provides default processing for three: CAPS for Caps Lock, NUM for Num Lock, and SCRL for Scroll Lock. While your application is executing, if a user presses any one of those keys, the framework will reflect its current state in the status bar. For the three other

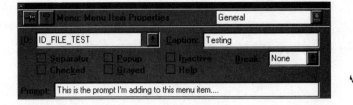

Figure 7.5
Adding prompts to
Menu items.

indicators, EXT for extended selection, OVR for overstrike, and REC for record, you must provide the processing yourself.

The framework constructs the initial status bar with the following code:

```
if (!m_wndStatusBar.Create(this) ||
   !m_wndStatusBar.SetIndicators(indicators,
    sizeof(indicators)/sizeof(UINT)))
{
   TRACE("Failed to create status bar\n");
   return -1;            // fail to create
}
```

The indicators are defined in an array, such as:

```
static UINT BASED_CODE indicators[] =
{
   ID_SEPARATOR,             // status line indicator
   ID_INDICATOR_CAPS,
   ID_INDICATOR_NUM,
   ID_INDICATOR_SCRL,
};
```

The item's order in this array indicates its position in the status bar, and all items and panes are zero-based.

MODIFYING THE STATUS BAR

It's relatively easy to add status indicators to the default status bar. Most of your modifications will be in the resource file and in your application's CMainFrame class implementation file.

To add a pane, first add a new ID to your resource file, RESOURCE.H, and then map this ID to a string resource in the *.RC file. You could edit both the RESOURCE.H and the .RC file manually or use App Studio to define an ID and its

TABLE **7.5**
PreDefined indicators.

ID_INDICATOR_EXT	0xE700	"EXT"
ID_INDICATOR_CAPS	0xE701	"CAPS"
ID_INDICATOR_NUM	0xE702	"NUM"
ID_INDICATOR_SCRL	0xE703	"SCRL"
ID_INDICATOR_OVR	0xE704	"OVL"
ID_INDICATOR_REC	0xE705	"REC"

associate string. Be sure to give the indicator a default value as a place holder, so the initialization code will provide a default width for the text pane. You can later use CStatusBar member functions to change this default value. Since this is an ID and not a class, you will not be able to use the ClassWizard to create the message maps and the function bodies. You will have to add these items yourself to the string table in the resource (*.RC) file:

```
ID_INDICATOR_COL    "000"
ID_INDICATOR_READONLY  "READ "
```

Indicator ID Array

Next, you must modify the indicator array located in MAINFRM.CPP. Add your indicator IDs in the positions where you want them to appear. In the status bar represented in the array below, our new identifiers will appear in the second and sixth panes, and their indices will be one and five, respectively.

```
static UINT BASED_CODE indicators[] =
{
   ID_SEPARATOR,          // status line indicator
   ID_INDICATOR_COL,      // current column number
   ID_INDICATOR_CAPS,
   ID_INDICATOR_NUM,
   ID_INDICATOR_OVR,
   ID_INDICATOR_READ      // read only
};
```

The framework will create the status bar in your application's main frame window's OnCreate( ) function. After the framework successfully creates the status bar, you may wish to use the CStatusBar member functions to change some of the default settings. The following code shows you how to make the first pane appear inset, i.e., a sculpted 3-D appearance, like the others shown in Figure 7.4.

```
UINT style,ID;
int width;

// pane 0 - need ID and width
m_wndStatusBar.GetPaneInfo(0,ID,style,width);
m_wndStatusBar.SetPaneInfo(0,ID,SBPS_STRETCH,width);
```

We will go into the various CStatusBar member functions later.

UPDATING THE STATUS BAR PANES

The framework will update your panes during OnIdle( ), so you need to provide the framework with an entry in your class's message map to allow it to receive the WM_IDLEUPDATECMDUI message. To do so, add the function's definition to the header file, place the implementation in the class's .CPP file, and add the ON_UPDATE_COMMAND_UI macro to the class's message map. In the example that follows, we assume this pane's definition is local to the CMainFrame object, but you can place this information in any CCmdTarget-derived class. Note, however, that if you place the message map entry in a class other than the one in which you declare the pane, you need to add a global scope operator to the function name in the message map entry.

```
// header file implementation
afx_msg void UpdateCol( CCmdUI* pCCmdUI );
// Message Map
ON_UPDATE_COMMAND_UI( ID_INDICATOR_COL, UpdateCol ) or
ON_UPDATE_COMMAND_UI( ID_INDICATOR_COL, CMyClass::UpdateCol)
```

When implementing your UI handler, you can add a member variable with access functions to provide the information you need to display in the status bar. For example, add a member variable to your application class to keep track of the current cursor position and provide an access function to return the current position to any function that needs that information, such as your status bar pane:

```
void CMainFrame::UpdateCol( CCmdUI *pCCmdUI)
{
  char text[8];
  sprintf(text,"%3d", theApp.GetCurrentCol() );
  pCCmdUI->SetText(text);
  pCCmdUI->Enable();
}
```

SETTING THE PANE'S TEXT

You can also set the pane's text after initialization with a call to CStatusBar::SetPaneText( ). The prototype is :

```
CStatusBar::SetPaneText(int nIndex, LPCSTR lpszNewText, BOOL bUpdate =
TRUE);
```

The parameter *nIndex* is the index in the indicators array. The framework displays the string contained in LPCSTR *lpszNewText* when your program enables its pane. The *bUpdate* flag, if TRUE, tells the framework to invalidate the pane after setting the text. The example below illustrates the use of this function.

```
m_wndStatusBar.SetPaneText( 5,"WRITE");
```

The framework will truncate the text if it is too wide, but you can call SetPaneInfo to increase the pane's size. Remember, once you register the ON_UPDATE_-COMMAND_UI function in your message map, you need do nothing. MFC will update this function during OnIdle processing.

UPDATING THE STATUS BAR YOURSELF

There may be times when you wish to update the status bar immediately. To do so, send the AFX message WM_IDLEUPDATECMDUI to the status bar, and then tell the window to update itself (see Figure 7.6). MFC Tech Note #24 describes this message as a private MFC message, and thus it is subject to change in future versions of the framework. (See Chapter 17 for more information on Tech Notes.) Given that caveat, here's a sample function to perform on-demand updates.

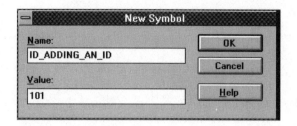

Figure 7.6
Adding new IDs with
App Studio.

```
void CMainFrame::UpdateStatusBar()
{
   m_wndStatusBar.SendMessage(WM_IDLEUPDATECMDUI);
   m_wndStatusBar.UpdateWindow();
}
```

There may also be times when you need to override the framework's default message process. You will then need to update the UI objects, such as menu items and status bar panes, and allow the framework to perform the resulting necessary cleanup activities. When taking over the translate/dispatch run cycle, make sure you call the application's OnIdle member function with something resembling the following code:

```
theApp.OnIdle(0); // update user interface objects
theApp.OnIdle(1); // clean up this mess
```

THE CSTATUSBAR CLASS

If you look at CStatusBar's derivation path, you will notice that one of its parents is CWnd. Thus you may use functions defined in CWnd within CStatusBar, as you saw in the preceding code segment. For another example of the utility of this relationship, you could use it to detect whether the status bar (or any CControlBar-derived class) is currently visible:

```
if ( m_wndStatusBar. IsWindowVisible() );
   ; // status bar is visible
else
   ; // status bar is not visible
```

CSTATUSBAR FUNCTIONS

Table 7.6 lists some of the CStatusBar functions. The Create( ) function, which is similar to CToolBar's Create( ) function, sets the default values. Note the use of the CBRS_BOTTOM style and the ID of AFX_IDW_STATUS_BAR.

The GetPaneInfo( ) function returns the information about the indicator specified by *nIndex .nID,* which holds the ID of the indicated pane, as in ID_INDICATOR_CAPS.

The variable *nStyle* holds the style of the pane. Table 7.7 shows the possible values of *nStyle,* which you can OR together for greater functionality. The variable *cxWidth* returns the width of the pane.

The SetPaneInfo( ) function parallels the GetPaneInfo( ) function, setting the pane's parameters to those passed to the function. With this function you can change the pane's style, its width, or the ID_INDICATOR that it represents.

TABLE 7.6
CStatusBar member functions.

```
BOOL CStatusBar::Create( CWnd* pParent, DWORD dwstyle = WS_CHILD | WS_VISIBLE
| CBRS_BOTTOM, UINT nID = AFX_IDW_STATUS_BAR);
   void CStatusBar::GetPaneInfo( int nIndex, UINT& nID, UINT& nStyle, int&
cxWidth) const;
   BOOL CStatusBar::SetPaneInfo( int nIndex, UINT nID, UINT nStyle, int
cxWidth);
   BOOL CStatusBar::SetIndicators( const UINT FAR* lpIDArray, int nIDCount);
```

The SetIndicators( ) function sets each indicator's ID to the value in the corresponding *lpIDArray* array. It loads the string resource identified by that value and sets the indicator's text to that string. This function uses the *nIDCount* parameter to know how many IDs are stored in the array.

INSERT/OVERSTRIKE MODE

Most On/Off indicators have a string for the "ON" condition, as evidenced in the insert/overstrike mode of text editors. In most programs you will only see "OVR" to indicate overstrike mode. The following code allows you to add insert/overstrike indicators to your code, giving an "INS" indicator as well as the usual "OVR."

The framework provides default processing for the CAPS, NUM, and SCRL indicators, but not for insert/overstrike. To add this capability to your code, you must add an ID in your indicator array; you should then go ahead and use the predefined ID_INDICATOR_OVR, and your function prototype will be:

```
afx_msg void OnUpdateIns( CCmdUI *pCCmdUI );
```

This will provide your application with the pane and the framework with the needed message map. To make your program more portable, enter the string "INS" into your application's string table, giving it the identifier ID_INDICATOR_INS. You can then set the pane's text, based on the current state of the insert key:

```
void CMainFrame::OnUpdateIns( CCmdUI *pCCmdUI )
{
   BOOL flag = ::GetKeyState(VK_INSERT);
```

TABLE 7.7
Status bar pane styles.

SBPS_NOBORDERS	No third border around the pane.
SBPS_POPOUT	The pane's text will "pop out."
SBPS_DISABLED	Tells the system not to draw the pane's text.
SBPS_STRETCH	Causes the pane's width to stretch to fill unused space. The first pane (index 0) usually has this style. The documentation states that only one pane can have this style, but try placing an extra ID_SEPARATOR in the status bar indicator array and see what happens.
SBPS_NORMAL	The default value. No stretch, no borders, no popping out.

```
    if ( flag )
      pCCmdUI->SetText("INS");
    else
      pCCmdUI->SetText("OVR");
    pCCmdUI->Enable();
}
```

This code will allow you to show your users the application's exact state at any given moment—the ultimate purpose of the status bar.

DIALOG BOXES AND STATUS BARS

Since MFC now encapsulates status bars in their own class, you can add them to any interface object, including dialog boxes. *The Windows Application Design Guide* frowns upon this practice, but not every one of your customers' applications will fit this standard. One thing to remember when adding a status bar to a dialog is that the framework will no longer automatically perform the updates. You will have to do that on your own with the functions shown previously.

To include a status bar, you will first have to provide in your dialog class an object (a data member) of type CStatusBar, such as m_dlgStatBar. Then, following the procedures detailed earlier, add a string resource for your IDs and an indicator array for your panes. You will need this array in a call to the SetIndicators function later. Another item you will need is the client rect area of the dialog, so that you properly position the status bar in the dialog's client area. The application usually handles this for frame windows, but not for other types of windows such as dialog boxes. You can get the client rect of the dialog with the following function call:

```
CRect dlgClientRect;
GetClientRect( dlgClientRect);
```

After you have the size of the dialog box, you will need to move the status bar to the bottom of the dialog's window and initialize the status bar with the following code:

```
m_dlgStatBar.MoveWindow( 0,
dlgClientRect.Height() - GetSystemMetrics(SM_CYCAPTION),
dlgClientRect.Width() - GetSystemMetrics(SM_CYCAPTION) );
m_dlgStatBar.SetIndicators(m_wndStatusBar.SetIndicators(indicators,
      sizeof(indicators)/sizeof(UINT)));
```

You can now update your new status bar by setting the pane text and calling the Invalidate( ) member function to force a redraw:

```
m_wndStatusBar.Invalidate();
```

BITMAPS AND STATUS BARS

Simple text strings are not the only items you can display in a status bar. You can also display bitmaps. To do this you need to derive a new class from CStatusBar and override the DoPaint member function. At the same time, you may also decide that it would be beneficial to display the status bar text in different fonts and colors. Note that the CStatusBar functions handling this functionality are static functions to the BARCORE.CPP file. To accomplish this feat, you must therefore derive a new class and then cut and paste the functions to your class implementation.

The following code illustrates a new status bar class and its implementation of the DoPaint function.

```
The header file:
class CBitmapStatusBar : public CStatusBar
{
public:
   void DoPaint( CDC * pDC);
   void set_bitmap( CBitmap * bitmap ) { m_pBitmap = bitmap };
   void set_pane( int pane ) { m_pane = pane };
private:
   int m_pane; // data member to hold the pane to put the bitmap
   CBitmap * m_pBitmap; // bitmap you wish to display
};
```

The preceding class inherits publicly from CStatusBar and overrides the DoPaint function. The class also provides two data members, m_pane and m_pBitmap, to provide a means of specifying which status bar pane you wish to paint with the specified bitmap. The framework provides two set functions to set these values.

```
The Implementation File:
void CBitmapStatusBar::DoPaint( CDC * pDC)
{
   ASSERT( pDC == NULL);
   CBitmap * pOldBitmap;
   CRgn paneRegion;
   CDC srcDC;
   CRect rect;

// Fill in m_pane's rect structure.
   GetItemRect( m_pane, &rect);

// Paint the rect with the base class's function. Make sure to exclude
// the rectangle that we will be painting in a moment.
   pDC->ExcludeClippedRect( &rect);
   CStatusBar::DoPaint( pDC);

// Set the clipping region for the bitmap to our rectangle.
   paneRegion.CreateRectRgnIndirect(rect);
   pDC->SelectClipRgn( &paneRegion);

// Now we will save the bitmap pointed to by m_pBitmap into a compatible
// DC and bitblt it into the pane.
   srcDC.CreateCompatibleDC(NULL);
   pOldbitmap = srcDC.SelectObject(m_pBitmap);
   pDC->BitBlt(    rect.left, rect.top, rect.Width(),
           rect.Height(),&srcDC, 0,0,SRCCOPY);

// Now restore our DC.
   srcDC.SelectObject( pOldBitmap);
```

```
// Tell the window to update itself.
  InvalidateRect( rect, FALSE);
}
```

DIALOG BARS

Dialog bars are toolbars with an assortment of dialog controls, such as combo boxes and pushbuttons. Examples of dialog bars exist in such applications as Microsoft Word, the Windows' Help engine WINHELP.EXE, and the MSVC visual framework. You can align dialog bars to any edge of the frame window, just like toolbars and status bars. Users of dialog bars can tab from one control to another. To create dialog bars, you must first design a dialog template in App Studio.

DIALOG PROPERTIES

You must set your dialog's properties to WS_VISIBLE OFF and its style to WS_CHILD. Since the controls in your dialog will become commands, you must make sure their resource IDs are in the range of MFC command IDs. These values must be greater than or equal to 0x8000 because they will become part of the message map. To set these values, add an = sign to the ID and then the value, as shown in Figure 7.7.

Next, connect this template to a CDialogBar class or a class derived from CDialogBar. Since the ClassWizard does not recognize such classes, you must manually create a class and incorporate the template. You can also derive a class from CFormView and change all CFormView references to CDialogBar with a global search and replace. (See Chapter 3 for more information on CFormViews.)

CDIALOGBAR CREATE

Now, add an instance of this CDialogBar object to your mainframe class, just as you did for your CToolBar and CStatusBar objects. Then call CDialogBar::Create( ) in your mainframe's OnCreate( ) function, just as you call CStatusBar's Create function. This will attach the dialog bar to your frame window. The order in which you create your control bars will affect how your application will display them on the screen. The first one created will appear first, followed by the second, etc. Thus if you create your CToolBar first and your CDialogBar second, giving both a style of CBRS_TOP, the toolbar will appear under the main menu, and the dialog bar will appear under the toolbar.

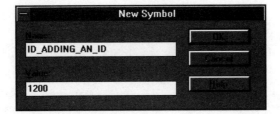

Figure 7.7
Initializing IDs
with a value.

CDIALOGBAR CREATE( )

Since CDialogBar does not provide default parameters for the Create function, you will have to provide them. CDialogBar provides two versions of Create (overloaded for your convenience). This allows you to create a CDialogBar with either the dialog template name or its ID.

The function's prototypes are:

```
BOOL CDialogBar::Create( CWnd* pParentWnd, LPCSTR lpszTemplateName,
   UINT nStyle, UINT nID);
BOOL CDialogBar::Create( CWnd* pParentWnd, UINT nIDTemplate, UINT
nStyle,UINT nID);
```

where *pParentWnd* is a pointer to the parent CWnd object. The *lpszTemplateName* points to the name of the CDialogBar object's dialog box resource template. The *nStyle* parameter indicates the alignment style of the dialog bar. Along with the defined styles documented earlier, there are two other positions on the frame window to which you can align a dialog bar. Table 7.8 lists the styles.

MFC Tech Note #24 states that *nID* must be between AFX_IDW_CONTROL-BAR_FIRST and AFX_IDW_CONTROLBAR_LAST, and that it should be AFX_IDW_CONTROLBAR_FIRST + 32, since MFC's print preview dialog bar makes use of the first few numbers. However, *nID* and *nIDTemplate* can be the same number, as long as the number itself is unique in RESOURCE.H. You can assure yourself of a unique number by using the dialog's resource ID number.

Your sample call may look like this :

```
if ( !m_dialogbar.Create( this, IDD_DBAR, CBRS_TOP, IDD_DBAR) )
   return FALSE;
```

MESSAGE MAPS FOR DIALOG BARS

Once you add an ON_COMMAND macro, the framework will map the resulting messages to your handler functions, just as it does with the menu and toolbar commands. And just as with menu and toolbar items, the framework will disable those controls without a message map entry. You should place the handler functions in your frame class, since that is where your control bars usually reside. They take the same form as all ON_COMMAND message map entries:

```
ON_COMMAND( IDD_PREVIEW_NEXT_PAGE, OnNextPage )
```

TABLE 7.8
Control bar alignment IDs.

CBRS_LEFT	Control bar is at the left of the frame window.
CBRS_RIGHT	Control bar is at the right of the frame window.
nID	The control ID of the dialog bar.
nIDTemplate	The resource ID of the CDialogBar object's dialog box template.

CHAPTER SUMMARY

Solving problems and getting the job done with minimal work and training are the goals of every Windows developer. Toolbars, status bars, and dialog bars provide ease of use and much-needed information to users and make their jobs easier. But the bane of all developers is that the easier we make a program for a user, the more difficult a job it is for us to write the code. MFC gives the Windows developer an edge in providing users with better, easier-to-use applications. This chapter demonstrated how easy MFC makes adding control bars to applications. Check out the MFC source file BARCORE.CPP and the sample program CTRLBAR.CPP for more information on control bars. You should also check out the MSDN CD or CompuServe area. (See Chapter 17, Help for the Developer, for more information.)

Dialog Boxes

Dialog boxes are resources that are easily created and maintained for a Windows-based application. The App Studio provides an easy-to-use tool kit for operations associated with these boxes. In this chapter, you'll get a broad-based introduction to the Microsoft Foundation Class functions that handle dialog boxes and learn the fundamentals of designing dialog boxes and including them in your applications. In other words, this chapter will focus on general concepts related to dialog boxes. The specifics and the mechanics of generating dialog box controls and messages are found in Chapter 9. Dialog boxes provide an easy way to get input from and send messages to the user in cases such as error conditions encountered during the normal flow of your program. As an example, your program may allow the user to transfer a file from one device to another, but there may be insufficient space on the target device chosen by the user for the selected file. Now, your program has no way of knowing the file won't fit until after the device is selected by the user. Here, then, the error condition interrupts normal program flow (i.e., performing the file transfer) in order to inform the user of the problem and request new instructions. Dialog boxes are excellent mechanisms for handling these sorts of situations. Essentially, dialog boxes are child windows that have designated styles and controls. The availability and functionality of those controls are what make dialog boxes so useful.

CDIALOG BOX FUNCTIONS

In addition to the controls, the Microsoft Foundation Class libraries include a rich set of member functions for working with dialog boxes. Some of these are in Class CWnd, and not in CDialog as you would expect. This is not really surprising, since CDialog is derived from class CWnd. Among these functions for dialog boxes are public functions for filling in a list box with file and/or directory listings, for setting radio buttons, and so on. Using these features as basic construction blocks, you can exploit dialog boxes for their maximum utility. For example, you could produce a "home-brewed" progress gauge to update users during time-intensive operations; it could be something as stripped-down as a text box that you update periodically or something snappy using graphics. A familiar case in point is the "Percentage Done" status bar used when you install Windows (and other software packages). Naturally, you would encapsulate these dialog boxes into their own class, complete with data members and functions. As a design feature, when implementing objects such as progress gauges or other time-oriented instruments, you might also consider changing the shape of the cursor to an hourglass and restoring it to its previous shape on completion of the task.

MODAL AND MODELESS DIALOG BOXES

Dialog boxes fall into two categories: modal and modeless. A *modal* dialog box retains the focus until the user initiates a course of action such as clicking an Ok or Cancel button. *Modeless* dialog boxes do just the opposite, in that the user can close the box without responding or otherwise move the input focus to another window. Because of this subtle difference, you'll probably find yourself using modal dialog boxes more often than not. So, before going into a discussion of how to create and interact with dialog boxes, it is prudent to take a few moments to review Microsoft's design recommendations for incorporating dialog boxes into the user interface.

DESIGNING DIALOGS

It is sometimes difficult to know when it is advisable to use a dialog box in your application. Failure to allow for the nature of the application can lead to some nasty impacts on project development. As an example, your application may specify some sort of "visual object" help information, such as updating a status bar with help for an object under the mouse cursor whenever the cursor passes over that object (e.g., a control) on the screen. Since modal dialog boxes have their own message queue, the programmer in this situation faces the choice of either changing the design specs or writing some very tricky code. While we are on the subject of using Help, realize that you cannot use Shift-F1 to access Help from inside a modal dialog box. If your product specifications require this feature, use a modeless box so you can still incorporate it. Another consideration, covered in Chapter 5, concerns the use of menus. While assigning menus to dialog boxes is permissible, it is better to use command buttons instead. Also, when displaying a modal dialog box, be sure to disable the parent window's menu bar, even though users cannot select anything from the parent's menu while the dialog box is displayed. Remember that disabling a menu grays out its text, thus providing a visual cue that helps to focus users' attention on the dialog box.

Dialog Box Positions

Dialog boxes can be either movable or nonmovable. A movable dialog box is distinguishable from a nonmovable one by the presence of a title bar and a control menu in the upper left-hand corner with the options Move and Close. It is usually best to use a movable dialog box, as this allows the user to exert greater control over the application and to access any information obscured by the dialog box. When presenting dialog boxes, make them clearly visible by placing them in the center of the screen. This may be done by adding the statement

```
CenterWindow();
```

in your message handler for WM_INITDIALOG.

The Visit Order of Controls

Regardless of any considerations discussed up to this point and of whether you use a modal or a modeless box, all dialog boxes start by placing the focus on a control, allow users to move to other objects within the box, and ultimately permit them to exit the box. It is important to know that the order in which users can visit the objects in a dialog box is determined by the order in which the objects were created in App Studio (or, essentially, the order of the controls in the application's resource file). For example, suppose you were to build a dialog box in App Studio that had five simple controls: three buttons (End, Cancel, Help) and two edit boxes (Name, Ph#). If you create these controls in the order Help-Cancel-End-Ph#-Name, this will be the order in which the cursor moves when the user presses the Tab key. This may not be what you intended, and it would certainly be poor programming. Fortunately, it is easy to correct this situation. Should you find yourself needing to rearrange the visit order, simply edit your project's resource file and cut and paste the controls into the desired order.

KEYBOARD NAVIGATION

The next design criterion to enforce is how the user may move using the keyboard. Obviously, a mouse allows a full range of motion with respect to screen navigation. App Studio assigns accelerator keys, too. Be careful not to assign the same key to multiple controls (e.g., &Edit, &Exit). Pressing Alt-E in this example would cause Windows to move the focus to whichever control, Edit or Exit, appeared first in the application's resource file. Likewise, bear in mind that a dialog box must have a default control. When you run App Studio and create a dialog box, you automatically get two command buttons, Cancel and Ok, with Ok as the default. You can change this in App Studio by checking the "Default button" check box on the styles palette. If the dialog box under consideration is capable of deleting data or files, don't forget to make the Cancel button the default. This gives users an extra margin of safety by preventing them from inadvertently destroying data.

The Tab Key

The Tab key is the usual way to navigate the box. When users tab to a control group (e.g., radio buttons depicting baud rate options), you need to allow them to select one of the controls in the group by using the arrow keys and to change that control's state. Once you are inside the group, the arrow keys should allow you to move from control to control. In the case of exclusive radio buttons, as in our baud rate example, the act of moving to each option should also enable it. When you wish to leave the group, pressing Tab should take you to the next group or control in the visit order. Pressing Enter normally enables the control with the focus, but also closes the dialog box.

As you will see in the upcoming material on controls, it is the responsibility of the developer to enforce the logic rules concerning the controls in a group. In the earlier example about a group of radio buttons representing baud rates, you clearly do not want to allow the user to set two or more buttons to ON. You'll see code later in this chapter to allow for exclusivity.

CONTROLS AND LABELS

The controls and groups of a dialog box must have labels. If a label is two or more words, you should capitalize the first and last words (e.g., Baud Rate). Also, disable (i.e., gray out) the labels of unavailable controls. In general, always use a bold font for labels, so that even the dimmed labels can still be easily read.

Microsoft recommends positioning labels relative to the control as set forth in Table 8.1.

Besides disabling a control by dimming its label, you can also change the label at run-time. This is necessary, for example, whenever the user has passed the "point of no return" in response to an operation (e.g., "Delete Employee?", "Copy File?", etc.). If one or more options become meaningless or unavailable as a result of a previous choice exercised by the user, you should change their labels in the box. For example, a button labeled Cancel should be renamed to, say, Close, after the action has been irreversibly committed. Also, when the dialog box closes, be sure to return the label to its original value. A private data member could serve as a flag to specify the label should the user's action be such that the original default label does not make sense.

DATA VALIDATION

When using dialog boxes to receive information from the user, there is no clear standard on the issue of validating the data. However, we suggest that you enforce validation when users leave the *control*, not when they exit the dialog box. This makes it clearer to the user not only *what* is wrong, but *where* the problem lies. You may wish to reserve the use of sound, such as a beep, for error conditions only. Also keep in mind that validating upon receipt is not always practical, as in the case where two separate data fields are mutually dependent. For example, you might have a

TABLE 8.1
Positions of labels relative to controls.

CONTROL	INSIDE THE BUTTON
Command button	Inside the button
Check box or option button	To right of the box or button
Text box, spin box, list, combo box, slider, read-only, pop-up, text field	Above or to left of control, followed by a colon, and left-aligned with the section of the dialog box in which it appears
Group box	On top of (and replacing) part of top frame line, starting just after upper left corner

dialog box that lets the user provide address information. Here, the values for the state relate to another field, the zip code. As it is customary to supply the state before the zip code, in the event of a discrepancy, validation becomes a question of ascertaining which piece of information is correct, the state or the zip code. The main thing is, no matter where or when you validate, to be consistent whenever possible.

GENERAL DESIGN

When you create a new dialog box in App Studio, Visual C++ assigns an identifier to each of its controls. With ClassWizard, you connect the code to message handlers for those events that interest you. The identifiers assigned in App Studio are your means of referring to the controls and the events and responses associated with them. OnInitDialog( ) is an example of such an event. This is the module where you'll want to set up the general characteristics of your dialog box. For example, you could add the API call CenterWindow( ) to have Windows always display your dialog box in the center of the user's screen. This saves you the trouble of calculating and converting coordinates. Also, as a general design consideration, it is a good idea to assign member variables to controls while you are in App Studio. Member variables make it a lot easier to refer to controls. For example, compare the following code samples for two identical dialog boxes. Each dialog box has an edit box and Ok and Cancel buttons; we wish to write the string "Hello World" in the edit boxes. The edit boxes have the identifier IDC_MY_EDIT in App Studio and the member variable *m_myeditbox*:

```
CWnd *ptr;        // pointer to edit box
ptr = GetDlgItem(IDC_MY_EDIT);
ptr->SetWindowText("Hello World");// write the string
```

Compare this to the following code, which is clearly a lot simpler:

```
m_myeditbox.SetWindowText("Hello World");
```

As you can see, the prudent use of member variables takes a lot of work out of dialog box operations.

Modal Dialog Boxes and Menus

Before activating a modal dialog box, it's a good idea to disable the menu on the active window. Conversely, you must reenable the menu when the dialog box disappears. See the examples in Chapter 5 for information about these kinds of coding requirements. The point here is that disabling the menu bar sends a visual signal to users that helps to redirect their attention to the dialog box. This is particularly helpful to new users, who will quickly realize they cannot click on the background menu bar, but must instead concentrate on the requests of the dialog box.

Dialog Box Color

The Windows setup determines the background color of the dialog box. You can change this default when you call InitInstance( ) for your application, but you should exercise caution when using this option, as it can invite trouble. Setting the system color(s) in one Windows program also changes them in others, which violates the basic idea behind Windows—multitasking. If you had two or more Windows tasks active and both changed the background color, the unexpected crash of one of them could affect the other(s). Clearly, you could include some code to monitor these settings whenever your application is running, but this inevitably leads to a larger program with more moving parts, so to speak. For something like a dialog box, you're better off sticking with the user's defaults. Again, overall design considerations should influence your decisions regarding default modifications.

When designing your dialog box, you should have at least one button that acts as the default when the Enter key is pressed. Usually, this will be the first control to get the focus when the dialog box appears initially, and it should be a nonvolatile control (e.g., Cancel). This helps keep users from causing damage by initiating an action that they did not intend.

Control Arrangement

How you lay out the controls in a dialog box is very important, as this affects both the user's perception of the quality of your application and the application's usability. Controls should be neatly aligned, using the grid tool in App Studio, and logically ordered in terms of their purpose. Also, arrange buttons in either a vertical tier on the right side of the box or horizontally across the bottom. Using the grid in App Studio allows you to insert the same amount of space (consistency, consistency, consistency!) between each control across dialog boxes.

You may find it easier simply to design your dialog box visually without worrying about the visit order of its controls. This approach is a simple way to arrange controls initially within a group; then, after you have the box looking the way you want it, you can establish the visit order simply by editing the application's resource file. Just cut and paste the controls so that they will receive the focus in the order you want.

MESSAGE BOXES

A special type of dialog box is the message box, which you get "for free." This is a pop-up box that you can use for warnings, error reporting, and so on. You can assign these boxes a level of severity, so to speak, by associating an icon with the message for emphasis. A message box has the form:

```
int AfxMessageBox(LPCSTR lpszText, UINT nType, UINT nIDHelp);
```

where *lpszText* is the text that appears in the box, *nType* specifies the number and type of buttons in the box, and *nIDHelp* is the Help-Context ID for the message (0 indicates none). Generally, you'll just use the first two arguments. The *nType* argument can be ORed with other parameters to change the buttons and the icon that appear in the box. For example, to invoke a message box that displays an exclamation mark, the message "File not found," and the buttons "Retry" and "Cancel," the call would look like this:

```
AfxMessageBox("File not found", MB_RETRYCANCEL |
MB_ICONEXCLAMATION);
```

The return value is an integer that reflects which button the user selected. Possible values are given in Table 8.2.

The message box styles, which can display different icons (e.g., a stop sign, exclamation point, question mark, etc.), should be used appropriately and consistently. Table 8.3 lists the various styles and their values; this material is taken directly from the *windows.h* file. The symbols displayed are evident from their names.

The message box gets to be somewhat expensive, in terms of memory demands. For the sake of efficiency, consider placing all the text messages in your resource file's string table. When you need to display a message, simply use the appropriate string. This will reduce the overall size of your data segment, since the string containing the text of the message is now a discardable resource. See the *Class Library Reference, Volume I,* for more information about message box styles, icons, and usage.

CHAPTER SUMMARY

Dialog boxes are powerful weapons in your arsenal for interacting with the user. Exercise discretion as to when and where they should be used vis-à-vis the overall nature of your application. Remember that the order in which you add controls to a dialog box in App Studio has a big impact on the operation of the dialog box. This order can be changed by editing your project's resource file and placing the dialog box controls in the order desired. Also, keep in mind that the styles associated with a control can be used to support customization, such as allowing only numerical

TABLE **8.2**
Return values of AfxMessageBox().

IDABORT	The Abort button was selected.
IDCANCEL	The Cancel button was selected.
IDYES	The Yes button was selected.
IDNO	The No button was selected.
IDIGNORE	The Ignore button was selected.
IDRETRY	The Retry button was selected.
IDOK	The OK button was selected.

TABLE **8.3**
Message box styles.

#define MB_ICONHAND	0x0010
#define MB_ICONQUESTION	0x0020
#define MB_ICONEXCLAMATION	0x0030
#define MB_ICONASTERISK	0x0040
#define MB_ICONMASK	0x00F0
#define MB_ICONINFORMATION	MB_ICONASTERISK
#define MB_ICONSTOP	MB_ICONHAND

values for an edit box, dates, etc. These possibilities are covered in greater detail in Chapter 9. Be sure to enforce, as far as possible, the standards suggested by Microsoft for keyboard navigation, labels, etc. And finally, remember that consistency is the watchword for a well-behaved user interface, in which dialog boxes can play an important role.

Dialog Box
Controls

In Chapter 8 we discussed general concepts related to dialog boxes, which showed you what to do with them. This chapter will show you how to accomplish those things. Think of the dialog box as a song and its controls as the individual musical notes. In this chapter, we'll explore in greater detail the mechanics of manipulating the controls and provide you with sample code that you can use to accomplish a lot of routine programming tasks. This chapter will not discuss custom controls (e.g., Visual Basic add-ons, etc.) per se, though we mention them here as a suggested alternative to in-house development. Consult Chapter 10 for more information on issues and considerations dealing with VBXs. In addition to purely mechanical information regarding controls, this chapter explores how grouping controls together makes it easy to produce unique, or special process-ing, dialog boxes. Our example involves an application using a dialog box that allows the user to select a date.

BUTTONS

These controls come in three flavors: radio buttons, check boxes, and pushbuttons (also referred to as command buttons), all from class CButton. You can replace the text that appears on a pushbutton with a bitmap, if desired. Bitmaps are a handy alternative to use when building an interface for children, games, or the visually impaired; they are from the class CBitmapButton, and will not be covered. To return to the subject of command button text, be sure to display it and any other dialog box item that you can disable using a bold font. Disabled items are difficult to read, and using a bold font enables your users to read these strings easily when they are in this mode. Novice Windows programmers need to remember that command buttons are nothing more than child windows. In order to disable the text on a button, use the CWnd member function EnableWindow( ). An example of this member function appears later in this chapter.

RADIO BUTTONS

For each button in your dialog box, create a member variable from App Studio. These variables always have the "m_" prefix assigned by ClassWizard; for example, you might assign variables m_9600, m_4800, m_2400, and m_1200 to buttons reflecting baud rates in a group. Since radio buttons in a group such as this must be mutually exclusive, your biggest programming chore is to manage the state of the buttons. Upon activation, your code must initialize these states. In many cases, such as communications parameters, an .INI file stores these initial states. When the user clicks the mouse on a button different from the one currently enabled, Windows clears the previous button and then sets the state of the one just clicked (assuming, of course, that the buttons are part of the same group). For those times when you need to manipulate the state of a button directly, two member functions allow you to do just that: GetState( ), which returns the status of a button, and SetState( ), which sets or clears the button. These two functions return a more "verbose" amount of information concerning the buttons. The return value can be checked using a bit mask to ascertain whether a button is checked or highlighted or has the focus. Related functions for testing simply whether or not the button is checked are: GetCheck( ) and SetCheck(int flag). Using the baud rate example and a hypothetical MY_APP.INI file in which the *baud* rate is assigned to a string called baud stored in the section labeled *[comm],* the following code illustrates how to initialize one of three radio buttons associated with the baud rate:

```
CWinApp theApp;          // an instance of your application (need for
GetProfileString)
CString pStringVal;      // return value from GetProfileString()...
//
// as part of initialization, set all baud rate radio buttons OFF
//
m_9600.SetCheck(0);      // turn off the 9600 baud button
m_4800.SetCheck(0);      // turn off the 4800 baud button
m_2400.SetCheck(0);      // turn off the 2400 baud button
//
pStringVal = theApp.GetProfileString("comm","baud",NULL);
if (pStringVal == "9600")// test for rates of 9600, 4800, and 2400
   m_9600.SetCheck(1);   // file had 9600 baud, so set radio button
else if(pStringVal == "4800")
   m_4800.SetCheck(1);   // file had 4800 baud, so set radio button
else
   m_2400.SetCheck(1);   // as default, set 2400 radio button to ON
```

The good news is, since you built these variables as a group, you don't have to write any code for handling the arrow keys or mouse clicks. Pressing the arrow keys sequentially through this group would cause each radio button to turn ON as it received the focus and OFF when the next radio button gained the focus. If you clicked on, say, the 2400-baud button while the 9600-baud button was ON, the 2400-baud button would turn ON and the 9600-baud button OFF. Of course, you'll still have to write code to make sure your .INI file gets updated with the new baud rate selected, etc.

Member Variables and Radio Buttons

We'll close our discussion of radio button controls by pointing out a bug in App Studio that concerns radio buttons. If you try to attach a member variable to a radio button from inside App Studio, you'll discover it can't be done. The command button labeled "Add Variables" remains grayed out, preventing you from adding variables, *unless* the radio button is part of a group. There is at least one solution to this problem with which we are familiar—here are the steps to follow to get around it:

1. In App Studio, make the radio button(s) part of a group by checking the Group check box.

2. Start ClassWizard, and add the member variables.

3. Go back into App Studio, and uncheck the Group property.

CHECK BOXES

Check boxes are virtually identical to radio buttons with one exception: when check boxes are part of a group, more than one check box can be ON (i.e., contain an "X"). For example, your group may have check boxes related to font characteristics: style, bold, italic, size, etc. Since these options are not mutually exclusive (e.g., you could have a font displayed in both bold and italic), you must allow users to so specify their preferences. Also, as a design consideration, you may find it convenient to have a check box that allows the user simply to select "all of the above" (i.e., to enable all choices in the group). The functions discussed in the previous section on radio buttons (e.g., GetCheck( ), etc.) are applicable to check boxes, too. The main thing you need to watch out for is managing the logic behind your application: When a check box that disables other options is selected, be sure to gray out these options and thus not allow the user to specify them.

COMMAND BUTTONS

Command buttons are controls that initiate a certain action or response; the text displayed on the button (e.g., Ok, Cancel, etc.) indicates what the command does. Always designate a command button as the default button—the action that occurs when the user presses the Enter key. Usually, this should be the Cancel button, as it is the most innocuous choice. Command buttons are ostensibly the mechanism by which you can create toolbars, which are nothing more than bitmapped command buttons and are handy when you need to avoid cluttering up the dialog box with a lot of text. Again, ClassWizard lets you trap the events associated with the command button, such as single and double mouse clicks, quite easily. The real work is adding your application-specific processing and associating it with the button.

Disabling a Command Button

There are times in your program when you wish to disable a command button temporarily. For example, if you have a dialog box that allows the user to select a file from a list of choices and a command button marked "Compress" that will compress the selected file, you will not want the "Compress" button to be available until *after* a file has been selected. You will also wish to convey this fact to the user by graying out, or dimming, the word "Compress" until such time as the user selects a file. It's quite easy to do this; we'll show you two ways.

The first way is simply to assign a variable—call it "m_Compress" in keeping with our current example—to the button in ClassWizard. A command button is derived from class CButton automatically by ClassWizard, and a button of any type is derived from class CWnd. Thus you can use the CWnd member function EnableWindow(BOOL bFlag), where bFlag is either TRUE or FALSE, with TRUE enabling the button and FALSE disabling it. So, to gray out the word "Compress" on our imaginary button, the following call suffices:

```
m_Compress.EnableWindow(FALSE);// gray string and disable option
```

Whenever you wish to enable the command again, just repeat this call changing the argument to TRUE. The second method is rarely used, given the fact that ClassWizard does all the work for you. Nevertheless, this alternative is just to get a pointer to the button (which is really nothing more than a window itself), and call EnableWindow( ). So, for example, if we had created the button "Compress" in App Studio and given it the identifier IDC_COMP_BUTTON, the following code would disable the dialog box button:

```
CWnd *ptr;          // need a pointer to the button
ptr = GetDlgItem(IDC_COMP_BUTTON); // get pointer to button
ptr->EnableWindow(FALSE);// disable the button
```

LIST BOXES

List boxes provide a visually appealing way to display a list of choices to the user. For example, a dialog box related to setting text characteristics may contain a list box that presents the names of all available fonts. From a design standpoint, you should simply omit options that are not available from the list box. The one exception to this rule is in the case where you need to let users know that a certain option exists, even though they may not access it. In this situation, go ahead and add the option to the list box, but make the text dim and nonselectable.

To populate a list box with values from a data file, follow this example:

```
CStdioFile datafile;              // the data file
char bufr[81];    // buffer to hold 80 char. string + NULL terminator
//
//   open file for reading; report any errors if open failed
//
if(!datafile.Open("YOURFILE.DAT",CFile::modeRead,NULL))
  AfxMessageBox("Could not open file YOURFILE.DAT",MB_OK,0);
else
{
  while(datafile.ReadString(bufr,80))  // read in a line from file
  {
    if(bufr != NULL)
      m_Listbox.AddString(bufr);   // add to list box
  }
```

```
}
datafile.Close();        // close the file
```

In this example, the fictitious data file YOURFILE.DAT, assumed here to be an 80-character-per-line ASCII file, is opened for reading. As each line is read, it is added to a list box with which a variable has been associated via ClassWizard—in this case, the list box variable *m_Listbox* was defined as type CListBox in ClassWizard. If the data turns out to be less than 80 characters, then only those characters on the line are read into the list box.

Retrieving the User's Selection

After you have populated a single-selection list box with options, you can use GetCurSel( ) to fetch the zero-based index (or item) into the list box. This function returns LB_ERR if no item is selected or if the control is a multiple-selection list box. Using terminology from the previous example, the following demonstrates how you retrieve the user's selection:

```
CString buf;  // variable to hold user's selection
m_Listbox.GetText(m_Listbox.GetCurSel(),buf);
```

Insert this code in a function created by ClassWizard in response to a click or double-click on an item in the list box.

Counting List Box Items

Another useful function for list boxes is GetCount( ), which returns an integer value representing the number of items in a list box. You may want to use this function instead of simply relying on a static value that you "know" is right. For example, you may read into a list box a file containing information on the 50 U.S. states. Don't assume the list box gets read accurately; always use GetCount( ) to find how many items are in your list box. A simple error trap here can save you a lot of debugging headaches later.

Searching a List Box for an Entry

It is sometimes necessary to search a list box to determine whether an entry is present. The member function used for this purpose is FindString(int *nStartAfter*, LPCSTR *lpszItem*), which returns an integer representing the location in the list box of the string you are searching for. Again, this value is zero-based. If the string is not found, the return value is LB_ERR. This search for a string is, incidentally, case-independent, so you don't have to worry about converting all the characters in the strings to uppercase or lowercase. The argument *nStartAfter* specifies the zero-based index from which you wish to begin the search. Set this to –1 to search the entire list box. The second argument is the string in the list box for which you want to search. For example,

```
int found = LB_ERR;      // in case string is item 0 in list box
found = m_Listbox.FindString(-1, "Courier New");
if(found == LB_ERR)      // LB_ERR is defined as -1 in windows.h
```

```
    {
        // string not found, process error condition
        AfxMessageBox("Font Courier New not found.",MB_OK);
    }
```

This function only lets you know whether a particular string is in the list box; it does not select it (i.e., highlight the string, etc.). To find *and* select a string, use the member function SelectString(int *nStartAfter*, LPCSTR *lpszItem*). This function also scrolls the list box for you, bringing the string *lpszItem* into view. The argument *nStartAfter* is identical in content and functionality to *nStartAfter* in FindString( ).

Clearing a List Box

Sometimes you need to remove all the entries in a list box and replace them with something else, perhaps as the result of a menu selection or a command button response. Regardless, it usually turns out to be easier simply to clear the entire list box and fill it back up with the new values than to find and delete each item individually. The function to clear a list box is ResetContent( ), which returns void and takes no arguments. As an example, using our previous nomenclature, the following code would clear and redraw the list box *m_Listbox*:

```
    m_Listbox.ResetContent();
```

PUTTING IT ALL TOGETHER

The functions discussed in the previous sections can be combined to create some pretty useful and powerful software components. An example of one such application is the familiar "To-From" dialog box. This is a dialog box that has two list boxes. The first one contains a list of items (e.g., files, data items, etc.) that the user can select and move into the second list box. A typical view of such a dialog box appears in Figure 9.1.

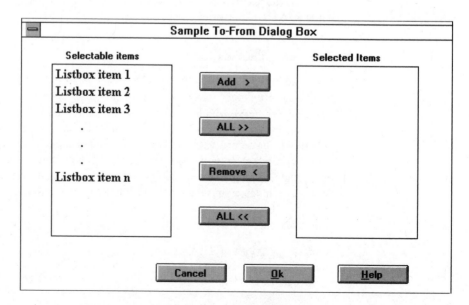

Figure 9.1
A To-From dialog box.

If you have installed any Visual Basic custom controls, you have already used a dialog box incorporating these features. Because this type of dialog box uses list boxes and is frequently implemented, the following discussion focuses on the essential design features to consider. Coding examples supplement the explanations where applicable.

The minimum controls for this type of dialog box are two list boxes and six buttons. Your program may require other controls, but our focus here is strictly on what you need to select items from one list box and move them to another. By way of nomenclature, the left-hand list box will be called the "From box" and the right-hand list box the "To box." The button to allow the selection of just one item in the From box will be called the "Single add" button. The button to allow selecting all the items is the "Add all" button. The button to allow deselecting a single item (i.e., moving it back from the To box to the From box) is the "Single remove" button. The button to remove all the items is the "Remove all" button. The last two buttons that will be considered are the "Ok" and the "Cancel" buttons.

Why All the Buttons?

There are good reasons why you should plan to include command buttons that allow both single selection and mass selection. Mainly, these allow users to exercise greater control over the operation and can greatly speed up their work. For example, it may be simpler for users to add all options and then remove one by one those options that they do not want. If the From box has 100 entries and the user wants 99 of them, it would be very time-consuming indeed to have to select all 99 individually; it is much easier to select all 100 and then remove the one not desired. Secondly, while you will obviously want to allow the user to select an item in the From box by double-clicking the mouse, you must allow for the potential situation in which the user does not have a mouse. For these cases, the user should be able to select an item via the space bar (which would highlight it), use the Tab key (or an accelerator key) to go to the Add single button and activate it, and carry out the move operation by pressing the Enter key. Alternatively, you could dispense with the Single add and Single remove buttons and allow the Enter key to perform the move directly. However, a potential problem with this approach arises when there is only one item in the From box. Pressing Enter in this case would move the item to the To box, but leave the focus remains in a now-empty From box.

As a general guideline, you should remove any item from a list box when it is moved to another box. Doing this helps keep users from selecting the same item twice and provides a sort of visual "countdown" mechanism that allows users to monitor their prior activities. This procedure is demonstrated in the following coding example, which assumes the user has double-clicked the mouse on an item in the From box. This function could also be used in the case described above, where the user presses the Enter key to move the item. For our purposes, we have added some member variables in ClassWizard to refer to all the controls. These have the familiar "m_" prefix attached to a descriptive label (e.g., *m_From* is assigned to the From box, *m_Ok* to the OK button, etc.).

```
void CSomeClass::OnDblClickFromBox()
{
  //
  //get index into the "From" box
  //
```

```
CString buf;                          // variable to hold item text
int index= m_From.GetCurSel();  // index into From box
//
if(index != LB_ERR)                   // no error in selection
{
   m_From.GetText(index,buf);     // get From item as text
   m_To.AddString(buf);           // Put in the To list box
   m_From.DeleteString(index);    // remove from the "From" box
}
}
```

To remove an item from the To box after it has been moved back to the From box, simply create another function identical to this one (call it OnDblClickToBox( )) and reverse the names of the "m_" variables; for example, change *m_From to m_To* and vice versa.

Combo Boxes

A combo box, also called a drop-down list box, is a combination edit control and list box. In some situations, it can be a combination static text control and list box. Refer to the *Class Library Reference, Volume I*, for a description of the three possible styles of combo boxes and their configurations. The combo box has a down arrow on the right side of a text window; clicking this arrow causes a window to drop down from under the text window, displaying more choices. Clicking on an entry in the list selects the text and moves it into the text window. The user can also enter text directly into the text window as part of a search; this is useful for adding new options to the combo box. A familiar example of a combo box is the Search option in a Windows Help system. As you begin typing in characters, the drop-down list jumps immediately to those entries matching your input. For this reason, among others, you should specify that all entries be sorted when added or inserted into a combo box. To do this, use the CBS_SORT style on the combo box definition in your application's resource file.

Code Examples

Since combo boxes are so similar to list boxes, refer to the previous sections on list boxes for examples of member functions such as AddString( ), FindString( ), GetCount( ), etc. The coding examples presented in the following sections focus on those frequently used functions *not* shared with list boxes. Again, we'll assume you have created a combo box in App Studio and assigned it a variable such as *m_Combo*, which is used in the examples.

Clearing a Combo Box's Text Window

The Clear( ) function removes any selection displayed in the edit control portion of the combo box. The entry remains present in the drop-down list box, however. To use Clear( ), follow this example:

```
m_Combo.Clear();          // clears the combo box's text window
```

A similar function is Cut( ). Cut( ) not only clears the edit box but puts the selection onto the Clipboard. The format is:

```
m_Combo.Cut();            // clears text window, copies to Clipboard
```

To move the current combo box selection to the Clipboard *without* deleting it from the edit control, use the Copy( ) function:

```
m_Combo.Copy();           // Copies to Clipboard, does not clear
                          // the edit control text window
```

Clearing the Entire Combo Box

The member function ResetContent( ) clears the entire combo box, including both the edit control and the drop-down portion. Most of the time, you'll want to use this function when you initialize a dialog box, etc. The format of the command is simply:

```
m_Combo.ResetContent();   // clear entire combo box
```

File and Directory Operations Using Combo Boxes

Combo boxes provide an elegant way to allow the user to specify files by disk and directory. This is the presentation method used by Visual C++ itself; choose File/Open, and you'll get a dialog box with several combo boxes: One allows you to specify a disk, another a directory on the disk, and yet another the file type (e.g., *.cpp, *.h, etc.). You can construct similar entities in your applications using the combo box member function Dir(UINT *attr*, LPCSTR *lpszWildCard*). The arguments passed to this function work in tandem, so to speak. Consult the documentation for more information. Basically, the first argument can have up to 8 values ORed together and supplements the argument *lpszWildCard,* which indicates the file type requested (e.g., *.txt, etc.). The first argument indicates whether the second argument includes a directory specification, for example. An example of the use of Dir( ) will be presented shortly. First, a quick study in using the Dir( ) function to get a file specification is in order. To use the Dir( ) function effectively, you must allow users to specify not only what type of file they wish to list, but where it may be found. That is the reason for the three combo boxes. You *could* use just one, but this limits your range to the current directory (of course, there may be times when that is perfectly acceptable). To use Dir( ) to access a file as in Visual C++, follow these basic steps:

1. Create the dialog box with three combo boxes: one for the disk device, one for the directories on the disk, and the last one for the file type.

2. Use ClassWizard to create functions that respond to the user's selection in each box.

3. Pass each selection made to the next combo box (e.g., after the user selects a disk and the focus moves to the directory box, you'll need the disk drive in order to build lpszWildCard).

Here is an example using these principles. We have created a dialog box as described above and assigned the variables *m_Drive, m_Directory,* and *m_FileBox* to each of the combo boxes. The variables for the directory and file combo boxes are initially set to zero via a call to ResetContent( ) in our dialog box initialization routine. The disk drive box is filled with a listing of all the disk drives on the system via this call:

```
m_Drive.Dir(DDL_DRIVES,"*");
```

Once the user has given us a disk drive, we need to get all the directories on that drive. By responding to the message CBN_SELCHANGE on the disk drive box, we know the user has picked a disk, and it is time to list the directories, as follows:

```
int select;                           // index into disk drive box
select = m_Drive.GetCurSel();         // get index into disk drive box
CString drive;                        // the text pointed to by "select"
m_Drive.GetLBText(select,drive);      // get drive as string
char tmp[64];                         // a working buffer
char *p = drive.GetBuffer(6);         // drive in format "[-n-]"
drive.ReleaseBuffer();                // ALWAYS release after a get
tmp[0]= p[2];                         // format is [-d-]
tmp[1]= 0;                            // add NULL terminator for strcat()
strcat(tmp,":\\*.");                  // request all directories on drive
m_Directory.ResetContent();           // start with an empty box
m_Directory.Dir(DDL_DIRECTORY, tmp);  // fill up the box
```

There are a couple of pitfalls to look out for in this example. First, the drives are returned in the format [-*n*-], where *n* indicates the disk drive (e.g., a, b, c, d, etc.). We're only interested in the letter, so the rest must be stripped out. The statement tmp[0]= p[2]; does this for us. The other thing to remember is the use of the backslash (\). Since this character is an escape sequence prefix (e.g., \n, \t, etc.) in C and C++, you have to use two backslashes in the following statement of the previous example to print one. What we have done is build a string that looks to the compiler something like:

```
c:\*.
```

assuming the user selected the C disk drive in the first combo box. So at this point in our program, we have two of the three combo boxes populated with data. Assuming that the user now selects a directory, we again write a function in ClassWizard to respond to a CBN_SELCHANGE message on the second (i.e., the directory) combo box. Note in the following coding example how we keep going back to get what the user selected in the preceding combo boxes—this is what we meant when we said you need to pass each combo box selection to the next. This keeps you from actually having to change directories in order to see what directories and files are on the disk. Returning to our example, we now need to build a string that has the disk *and* the directory, along with a mask that specifies what kinds of file we want listed. In our example, this mask is all files, or "*.*".

```
m_FileBox.ResetContent();             // start with an empty file box
har tmp[64];                          // a working buffer
char spec[64];                        // the full file specification
int select;                           // index into a combo box
select = m_Drive.GetCurSel();         // get index into disk drive box
```

```
CString drive;                          // the disk drive user selected
m_Drive.GetLBText(select,drive);        // get drive as string
char *str = drive.GetBuffer(3);
drive.ReleaseBuffer();
spec[0]= str[2];                        // strip out the disk drive letter
spec[1]= 0;
strcat(spec,":\\");
int index;
index = m_Directory.GetCurSel();        // get index into dir. box
CString directory;
m_Directory.GetLBText(index,directory);// get dir. as string
char *p = directory.GetBuffer(63);
directory.ReleaseBuffer();
//
// format is "[directory]", e.g., [windows], [dos], etc.
// so strip away the brackets to get the directory...
//
int len = strlen(p);                    // get length of directory
strncpy(tmp,p+1,len-2);                 // discount the [, and the ]
tmp[len-2]= 0;                          // need NULL terminator for strcat()
strcat(tmp,"\\*.*");
strcat(spec,tmp);                       // finish building arg. lpszWildCard
m_FileBox.Dir(DDL_READWRITE | DDL_DIRECTORY, spec);
```

This code could be modified to include multiple levels of directories.

Displaying the Combo Box

Combo boxes are unlike list boxes in that the programmer has the option of displaying the combo box either in its drop-down state or as a single line with the down arrow. There are times when you will wish to present the combo box to the user in one state or the other. The function to use for these situations is ShowDropDown(BOOL bState), where the argument *bState* indicates whether to show the drop-down portion or to keep it hidden. The format is as follows:

```
m_Combo.ShowDropDown(TRUE);             // show the drop-down portion
m_Combo.ShowDropDown(FALSE);            // show as a box with down arrow
```

EDIT BOXES

The edit box is a versatile control in that you can use it to get input from the user, to send information to the user, or both. Visual C++ allows you to stipulate formatting rules, an option that facilitates data validation when used as an input control. Coupled with the messages you can trap, edit boxes give you a good deal of control over what, where, and how the user may respond. Also, as was the case with some of the other controls presented in the preceding sections, you can use edit boxes to access the Windows Clipboard.

Creating Edit Boxes

For the sake of convenience, create edit boxes in App Studio. By jumping into ClassWizard from App Studio, you can incorporate the features and trap the messages of interest that your application requires. For example, you can limit the number of characters than can be entered or displayed or determine whether the edit box is to be used as an "Enter Password" control. The latter is a convenient feature that causes keystrokes to be displayed as asterisks (i.e., "******") for security purposes. Convenience of this sort is another case for using edit boxes as input/output controls: Doing so is much simpler than getting a device context, painting to the screen, etc. When you are running ClassWizard, create and associate two variables with the edit box—one of type Control (e.g., *m_EditCtrl*) and one of type Value (e.g., *m_EditVal*). Thus you'll already have the variables available for manipulating either the edit box itself or the text that you want to get or set in the edit window. Our next examples will use the variable names *m_EditCtrl* and *m_EditVal* in their respective contexts.

Retrieving Text from an Edit Box

There are several ways to fetch the text that is in the window of an edit box. The first method uses the member function GetWindowText(CString &rString); this is also the easiest technique. The syntax of the command is:

```
m_EditCtrl.GetWindowText(m_EditVal);// get text from edit control
```

The variable *m_EditVal* now contains whatever text is present in the edit box text window after the statement executes. Another way to accomplish this is to declare a pointer to the edit box of class CWnd; this approach is possible since edit boxes are ostensibly child windows. Thus, if you assigned an edit box the ID value IDC_MY_BOX in App Studio, the following code would retrieve the contents of this edit box:

```
CWnd* pEditbox;                      // declare pointer for edit box
CString my_string;                   // variable to hold edit box contents
pEditbox = GetDlgItem(IDC_MY_BOX);   // get pointer
GotoDlgCtrl(pEditbox);               // now go to it (i.e., set focus)
pEditbox->GetWindowText(my_string);  // get contents
```

This method may be preferable in those situations when you're going to do something else to the control that requires a CWnd pointer. A third method is to use the CWnd member function GetDlgItemText( ), which is prototyped as follows:

```
int GetDlgItemText(int nIDCtrl, LPSTR lpBuffer, int nMaxLength);
```

where:

nIDCtrl is the integer identifier of the edit box
lpBuffer is the buffer to hold the text
nMaxLength is the maximum number of bytes to be copied

The return value is the number of bytes copied, or 0 if nothing is copied. An example of this function's use follows:

```
CWnd* pEditbox;                      // declare pointer for edit box
LPSTR my_string;                     // variable to hold edit box contents
pEditbox = GetDlgItem(IDC_MY_BOX);   // get pointer
```

```
GotoDlgCtrl(pEditbox);                    // now go to it (i.e., set focus)
int maxlen;
maxlen = pEditbox->LineLength(-1); // gets length of text in edit box
pEditbox->GetDlgItemText(IDC_MY_BOX, my_string, maxlen );
```

Writing Text to an Edit Box

The member functions for writing text to an edit box are a lot like those for reading text from the box. The first technique is quite simple:

```
m_EditCtrl.SetWindowText("Put this into the edit box");
```

The string "Put this into the edit box" will now appear in the edit box's text window. The alternate way to do this is to use a pointer to the edit box:

```
CWnd* pEditbox;                       // declare pointer for edit box
pEditbox = GetDlgItem(IDC_MY_BOX); // get pointer
GotoDlgCtrl(pEditbox);                // now go to it (i.e., set focus)
pEditbox->SetWindowText("Put this into the edit box");// set contents
```

Edit Boxes and Formatted Input

There are times when you want an edit box to accept formatted input only (e.g., only numbers). This requirement is fairly easy to implement, as you will see in a later demonstration. If you're serious about Windows development, we suggest you purchase a collection of custom controls. Custom controls are so inexpensive and offer so much utility that you will come out ahead by going this route. These VBX edit boxes already have a plethora of formatting capabilities built in, including formats for numerical fields, dates, currency, etc. Nonetheless, an overview of the programming requirements for scenarios requiring special formatting begs consideration. From a design or user interface perspective, the problem of error trapping is most apparent. As long as the user gives you data in the type, quantity, and format you expect, everything works just fine. As the programmer, you must anticipate both what the user might do and where and when he/she may do it. Let's consider the example of an edit box that accepts only numbers along with a decimal point. What if the user accidentally presses the "O" key instead of the zero key? For optimum performance, you don't even want the "O" character to appear in the edit box—it should be detected and removed *before* it gets to the screen. This capability can be enabled by using the EN_UPDATE message from ClassWizard, which allows you to intercept a keystroke before it makes its way to the edit box. (Incidentally, the message EN_CHANGE is similar to EN_UPDATE, except that EN_CHANGE puts the character into the edit box.) The second part of our problem is to manage the user's input. In this example, we're going to allow the user to enter decimal points. What happens if the user enters more than one? Clearly, a number like "14...65.33" is meaningless; we need to ensure that the user only gives us one decimal point. That's the bad news. The good news is that we get paid back for all our labors downstream. By isolating all our formatting checks in this one location, we know that any value entered into the edit field will, if accepted, be acceptable elsewhere in our program. This knowledge can have a significant impact on the overall program in terms of data verification and validation; likewise, the final size of the executable will tend to be smaller, since it becomes unnecessary to check a variable constantly for validity. By the way, don't be hypnotized by our strictly numerical example—the same conditions can arise when dealing with text fields. A handy example is that of getting a directory specification from the user; when the user enters a slash (e.g., "\"), you'll need to insert an additional slash into your working buffer (e.g., the entry "C:\DOS" becomes "C:\\DOS").

Example

As promised, we'll present an example here that shows how you can set up an edit box to accept only numbers. Our example is very simple—it accepts only numbers and does not check or permit other numerical formatting characters such as the decimal point, plus or minus signs, etc. You should be able to add these features yourself fairly easily by modifying our example. Also, note that this example does not check for error conditions; you'll see that we allow up to 30 characters to be entered into the edit box, and no enforcement of this condition is installed. Also, we only check the last character typed. There is nothing to prevent the user from moving the cursor inside the string and inserting an illegal character. As usual, we're trying to focus on the task at hand and let you add any extra rules and checking as needed. Our edit box was called IDC_CX_EDIT in App Studio, which is reflected in the title of the function:

```
void CBoxes::OnUpdateCxEdit()
{
  //
  m_EditCtrl.GetWindowText(m_EditVal);  // get text in edit box
  char p[30];                            // string to hold the text
  p[29] = 0;                             // ensures that we have a NULL term
  _fstrcpy(p,m_EditVal.GetBuffer(20));   // go from CString to char[]
  m_EditVal.ReleaseBuffer();             // always release buffer!
  int c;                                 // the last character user typed
  int len;                               // length of string in box
  len = _fstrlen(p);                     // _f for LARGE memory model
  c = p[len-1];                          // isolate last character typed
  if(isdigit(c) != 0)                    // user gave me a number
  {
    m_EditVal = p;                       // everything OK
  }
  else                                   // user typed nondigit
  {
    m_EditCtrl.SetSel(len-1,len,FALSE);// hilight illegal character
    m_EditCtrl.ReplaceSel("");           // replace with a NULL
  }
}         // end function
```

One thing you need to notice is that this function responds to an EN_UPDATE message. This fact is important, because an EN_UPDATE message is trapped *before* the keystroke is echoed back to the screen. By using EN_UPDATE instead of EN_CHANGE, we avoid introducing a brief but discernible flickering of the screen as the offending character is highlighted and then removed.

Enforcing String Lengths in Edit Boxes

As we implied in the previous example, there may be times when you want to monitor the number of characters that the user has entered into an edit box and enforce a limit on that number. For example, suppose you have an employee record database, such that a 4-character badge number uniquely identifies each person. When a new employee is hired, the employee's record is entered into the system, and an employee badge number is assigned. (Observe that a truly robust system would automatically assign this value; our system is for demonstration purposes only.) In this case, you want *exactly* four digits or characters to be entered for the badge number. There are two places where this parameter must be checked. The first is the point where the user enters the badge number (if, say, five characters are entered, we want to alert the user at the point of entry, not when all the other fields on the screen have been supplied and the user is exiting the screen). The second point is the moment when the user presses Tab or Return to move to the next field (this traps the case when fewer than four characters have been entered). For the first case, you will want a function to trap the message EN_UPDATE; for the second case, the function must trap EN_KILLFOCUS. The code to enforce these conditions is presented here for a hypothetical edit box in a dialog box; the names of the class and controls have been invented for the sake of clarity:

```
void CYourCls::OnUpdateYourEdit()
{
    // This function checks each keystroke as it is entered into the
    // edit box but before it goes to the screen. If the key is a number,
    // we allow it to be displayed. If not, we complain and remove it.
    // Also, we want exactly 4 numbers to be entered. Another
    // function will check the string's length when the edit box loses the
    // focus (i.e., the user could enter 3 numbers and press Tab).
    //
    int nChars= 0;            // number of characters/digits in edit box
    int maxChars = 4;         // maximum characters/digits we will allow
    char str[5];              // string to hold it; 4 chars + NULL term
    memset(str,0,5);          // start with a clean, empty string
    //
    //** NOTE:    In this example, we have also added the variables
    //m_EditCtrl (of class CEdit) and m_EditVal (of class CString)
    //in ClassWizard to make things simpler; that is why you do not
    //see them defined here...
    //
    nChars = m_EditCtrl.GetWindowTextLength();  // get length of text
                                                // in edit box
    m_EditCtrl.GetWindowText(m_EditVal);        // get text in edit box
    strcpy(str,m_EditVal.GetBuffer(5));    // go from CString to char[]
    m_EditVal.ReleaseBuffer();             // always release after
                                           // calling GetBuffer()
    int c;                                 // the last character the user typed;
    //
    // make sure it's a numerical digit
    //
    c = str[nChars-1];
    if((c==0) || (c == VK_BACK))           // nothing in box or backspace OK
       return;
    if(isdigit(c) == 0 )                   // user did not give me a number
    {
        AfxMessageBox("Must give me a number",MB_OK);
        m_EditCtrl.GetWindowText(str,maxChars);
        str[nChars-1]= 0;
        m_EditCtrl.SetSel(0,-1);
        m_EditCtrl.ReplaceSel(str);
```

```
                    return;
            }
            //
            //
            if(nChars > maxChars)  // make sure string doesn't exceede length
            {
                    AfxMessageBox("Cannot exceed 4 digits",MB_OK);
                    m_EditCtrl.GetWindowText(str,maxChars+1);
                    m_EditCtrl.SetSel(0,-1);
                    m_EditCtrl.ReplaceSel(str);
            }
    }
```

The following function responds to an EN_KILLFOCUS message. Whereas the preceding code handled all the checking for overflow, this example checks for "underflow." When responding to the EN_KILLFOCUS, the user cannot use the Tab key to go to the next field before entering exactly four numbers. Observe, however, that this rule is also enforced for mouse clicks on other buttons and it could have a deleterious effect on your program; for example, if you have a command button for Help, Cancel, etc., this code still expects four numbers to be present in the employee badge number field before the user can move to another button. One solution to this little potential problem is to check where the focus is going (i.e., what button event occurred) *before* you check the length of the text. If the change in focus is something your program will allow, you can return immediately and bypass the usual checking of the length. This option has been added to the following example, which allows the user to click on a Cancel button that was given the identifier IDCANCEL in App Studio:

```
void CYourCls::OnKillfocusYourEdit()
{
    // This function "demands" the user supply exactly 4 numbers in
    // an edit box before allowing the user to leave the field. The
    // user can, however, click the Cancel button in violation of
    // this rule...
    //
    CWnd* ptr;                // let's see where the focus is going...
    ptr = GetFocus();         // ...by getting the focus
    if(ptr == GetDlgItem(IDCANCEL))   // user clicked Cancel button
            return;
    int len = m_EditCtrl.GetWindowTextLength();  // check length
    if(len != 4)   // trouble - not 4 characters in field
    {
            AfxMessageBox("Must give me exactly 4 numbers.",MB_OK);
            m_EditCtrl.SetFocus();
    }
}
```

To modify the preceding routine to include floating point numbers, you'll have to add in some more smarts. Namely, you'll need to control the decimal point *and* the sign. This presents two problems: first, you can only have one decimal point and one sign, and secondly, the sign must be in the first position. You can easily trap these conditions by including some static BOOL flags to track whether the user has already given you the necessary parameters and whether those parameters are in the right position. As you can see, as the number of specific formatting needs grows for your program, you may be better off just to buy some Visual Basic controls that have these features. The time you spend writing and testing code for something as simple as this example adds up quickly—imagine how much more work there is to do for something like dates and currency! The bottom line is, buy this sort of thing off-the-shelf when you can (but if you really want to do it yourself, the preceding routines should get you started).

Edit Boxes and the Clipboard

Edit boxes are really nothing more than miniature word processors. As a bonus, you get access to the Windows clipboard, which allows you to support the familiar Cut, Copy, Paste, and Undo commands. The user selects the text to be manipulated by dragging the mouse over it, which simultaneously highlights it. You can easily connect the menu options (e.g., Cut, Copy, etc.) to code in ClassWizard; your member functions should "remember" which control has the focus and return to it at the completion of the menu option (e.g., Paste). All the calls are simple and require no arguments. Here is an overview of the clipboard-related functions:

```
m_EditCtrl.Cut();      // cut the current selection from the edit box
m_EditCtrl.Copy();     // copy the current selection to the clipboard
m_EditCtrl.Paste();    // insert the clipboard contents into edit box
m_EditCtrl.Undo();     // undo the last edit operation
```

Special Controls

Another common chore in writing an application involves creating some sort of special control or interface feature that is generally dedicated to a specific task. Examples of these include formatted numerical input (discussed earlier) or something weird, such as dates. These can cause a lot of heartburn, since dates can be supplied in a variety of formats and can thus cause ambiguity when the user provides them. In this section we'll show you how to combine the various controls in a dialog box to create a date-input interface that is pretty darn bulletproof. Eliminating ambiguity from the user's input results directly in increased data integrity. Take a look at the following ways to display a date:

```
6/7/95
07-Jun-1995
```

In the first case, it takes a moment to "translate" the date—is it the 6th day of the 7th month, or the 7th day of the 6th month? The second format eliminates all ambiguity, and our example will use this format. In this example we will present sample code only as it relates to the fundamentals of our date processor, which consists of the dialog box and its controls, as shown in Figure 9.2.

As you can see, the controls consist of 2 edit boxes, 1 combo box, 2 spin controls, and 2 buttons. We lead off our discussion with a couple of things you need to do in App Studio. The edit boxes *must* be marked READ_ONLY; also, their sizes must be set (allow 2 characters for the Day, 3 for the Month, and 4 for the Year) in ClassWizard when you assign variables. By marking these READ_ONLY, you deny the user keyboard access to the edit box. This establishes the spin controls as the sole mechanism for selecting or changing the values. Secondly, the combo box *must*

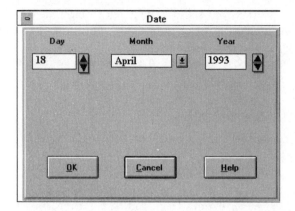

Figure 9.2
A date processing
dialog box.

not be marked SORTED, which is the default. For our purposes, we want the combo box to maintain the order that we establish when we populate it (i.e., the actual sequence of the months of the year: Jan, Feb, Mar, etc.). In App Studio, you can enter the strings for the months directly into the combo box, which is the reason why the box is not sorted—we are going to use the index into the combo box for its numerical properties. To accomplish this, just remember to press Ctrl-Enter when you are ready to add a new month. This command accepts your string and moves to the next position in the box. After you've built this dialog box, assigned its control variables, and so on, all that's left is to throw in your own logic. For illustration purposes, we've set an artificial range of acceptable years from A.D. 1900 to 2050. However, this example also calculates all leap years in that range and automatically changes the number of days allowed for February to 29. In effect, the user can always select a valid date, though that date may not be what is desired. Also, exercise caution if you plan to use these routines to read data that was entered elsewhere. For example, if you read in birth dates from some personnel file, you can't be sure those dates are valid. By modifying these routines, you could include some form of validation. Another feature this sample code demonstrates is using the Microsoft Foundation Classes 2.0's CTime class. Our example uses the current system date as the default and obtains the system date via a call to a CTime member function. Your program could, of course, change this protocol quite easily. To initialize the date processor when the dialog box is activated, use code similar to:

```
BOOL CMyClass::OnInitDialog()
{
        CDialog::OnInitDialog();
        //
        // Define variables for dealing with date dialog box.
        //
        CTime t;                        create instance of CTime
        int day= 0;                     // day of the month
        int month= 0;                   // month of the year
        int year = 0;                   // the current year
        //
        // Now get the current system time.
        //
        t = CTime::GetCurrentTime(); // gets hours, mins, secs, too
    //
```

```
        day = t.GetDay();                   // get the day as an integer
        month= t.GetMonth();                // get the month as an integer
        year = t.GetYear();                 // get the year as an integer
        //
        // Now initialize the edit boxes with the current date...
        //
        char tmp[5];                        // for string-to-integer conversion
        memset(tmp,0,5);                    // initialize for safety's sake
        sprintf(tmp,"%d",year);             // convert year to a string
        m_Year_Box.SetWindowText(tmp);// display the current system year
        //   Get the month here, make it a string, and display it.
        // First, use variable "month" as index into unsorted combo box.
        //
        m_Month_Box.SetCurSel(month-1);   // show current month as string
        sprintf(tmp,"%d",day);              // now convert day to string..
        m_Day_Box.SetWindowText(tmp);       // ...show it here
        CenterWindow();                     // align the dialog box
        return TRUE; // return TRUE unless you set the focus to a control
        //
    } // end of hypothetical initialization routine for date processor
```

The date processor is now ready to go to work. Our example uses spin controls (the up and down arrows on the right side of an edit box). The user clicks the up arrow to increase the value in the edit box and the down arrow to decrease the value. This example does not scroll around when limiting values are encountered (e.g., clicking to increase on Day 31 would not roll over to Day 1). As for the actual spin controls, these are readily available as VBX controls (see Chapter 10 for more information). You can even make your own spin controls by bitmapping the arrows and assigning them hotspots (see Chapter 6). Here is an example of how to process a click on the up arrow for the year:

```
    void CMyClass::OnSpinupYearSpin(UINT, int, CWnd*, LPVOID)
    {
      //
      // Increase the year for each click of the spin up control
      //
      int year;                              // integer variable for the year
      m_Year_Box.GetWindowText(m_Year_Val); // get year from editbox
      char* p = m_Year_Val.GetBuffer(5);    // CString->text buffer
      m_Year_Val.ReleaseBuffer();           // always release after GetBuffer
      *(p+4) = 0;                           // stick on NULL terminator
      //
      year = atoi(p);                       // convert string to integer here...
      if((year < 1900) || (year > 2050))    // safety check...
      {
        MessageBeep(0);                     // alert user, show message
        AfxMessageBox("The year is NOT VALID (1900-2050). Please
        correct.",MB_OK | MB_ICONSTOP);
        return;
      }
      if(year < 2050)           // never lets us increment past 2050
        sprintf(p,"%d",++year);// increment and convert
      m_Year_Box.SetWindowText(p);// display updated year
    } // end routine for user clicking spin-up on year field...
      //
```

The routines for clicking down are logically the same, except for the obvious differences in parameters such as the range checks. By making the edit boxes READ_ONLY in App Studio, you keep the user from entering an invalid year such as "199n," by mistake or otherwise. This validation feature extends to include the month field. For instance, we obviously wish to limit the number of days that a given month can have in order to prevent the user from ever giving us an invalid date like 31-Apr-1994. In our next example, we'll show how to enforce these limits and how to check for a leap year (based on the year). Here, we'll use a spin up message handler, since a spin down always has a bottom limit of 1.

```
void CMyClass::OnSpinupDaySpin(UINT, int, CWnd*, LPVOID)
{
    //
    // First thing to do is get the month. Limit the number of days
    // to 30 or 31 for all months except February. For February, we
    // need to get the year, too, and see if we can allow 29 days...
    //
    char err_msg[80];      // for showing user valid day ranges
    int maxdays = 0;       // maximum number of days a month can have
    int year;              // need year for leap year calculations
    //
    // Next array has the maximum number of days a month can have. //
    int days[12]= {31,28,31,30,31,30,31,31,30,31,30,31};
    int month= 0;          // month in combo box, as numerical value
    //
    month= m_Month_Box.GetCurSel();// get the month in combo box
    maxdays = days[month]; // get limit of days month has
    //
    // Check 2nd month, Feb., for leap year. Remember, the index
    // into combo box is zero-based, so Jan. is 0, Feb. is 1, etc.
    //
    if(month == 1)         // Check for a leap year
    {
        m_Year_Box.GetWindowText(m_Year_Val);// get year string
        char* p = m_Year_Val.GetBuffer(5);
        m_Year_Val.ReleaseBuffer();
        *(p+4)= 0;         // add NULL terminator
        //
        year = atoi(p);    // year as an integer
        if((year % 4 == 0 && year % 100 != 0) || year % 400 = 0)
            maxdays= 29;   // It's a leap year!!
    }
    //
    // Now it's safe to check, and possibly increment, the day.
    //
    int day;
    m_Day_Box.GetWindowText(m_Day_Val);
    char* p = m_Day_Val.GetBuffer(5);
    m_Day_Val.ReleaseBuffer();
    *(p+2) = 0;            // Day is 2 bytes wide; add NULL term.
    //
    day = atoi(p);
    if((day < 1) || (day > maxdays))    // safety check
    {
        MessageBeep(0);
        wsprintf(err_msg,"Day must be from 1 to %d. Please
            correct.",maxdays);
        AfxMessageBox(err_msg,MB_OK | MB_ICONSTOP);
```

```
        m_Day_Box.SetFocus();
        return;
}
//
if(day < maxdays)
        sprintf(p,"%d",++day);
m_Day_Box.SetWindowText(p);

} // end of routine to process click of day spin up arrow
```

Although these routines work pretty well for data input, be cognizant of the fact that should you wish to use them in applications where they can receive dates from external sources such as files (or whatever), you'll need to do a little bit more coding. As a side note, observe that if your application needs to compare dates or to calculate the number of days between two calendar dates, the advantages of having access to a date as a numerical quantity become apparent. This information facilitates, for example, conversions from the Gregorian to the Julian calendar, which is more computationally friendly. We hope that these sample routines have given you some insight into special controls as well as enlarged your thinking on how to apply them. Clearly, these examples hardly reflect the coding necessary to cover all bases, but they do demonstrate the fundamentals. What to do with the date when the user clicks the Ok or Cancel buttons will be up to your code. But if you follow this model, allowing your users to select only valid data, you'll save a lot of error checking elsewhere, which more than pays for itself. Should you utilitize special dialog boxes and controls as has been discussed herein, remember to do the little things (especially if you change fonts or colors) such as setting the background mode for drawing colored text, processing all WM_CTLCOLOR messages, etc. (This message and the handling function associated with it, which change the background color of a dialog box, are discussed more fully in Chapter 14.) The judicious use of special controls should weigh heavily in your design considerations; these and other related factors are discussed again in Chapter 14.

CHAPTER SUMMARY

The dialog box controls pack quite a punch—the challenge is to combine them in an effective and consistent manner. Keep related controls together using a group box, and as much as possible, use the same alignment scheme from one dialog box to another (e.g., all buttons along the right side of the dialog box or the bottom of the screen). Remember to define one command button as the default, and make sure no damage can result should this button be pressed by mistake. In the event that pressing a default command button *can* damage the integrity of your application's output, due to some strange quirk in the nature of your program, consider using a confirmation message box that appears after the default button is pressed. For an extra margin of safety, make the default command of your dialog boxes either a NO or a CANCEL. Better to have the user repeat the action than to delete an entire file or directory. Also, avoid changing any Windows or system defaults, such as the background color, simply for the sake of appearance. Should the user, particularly a new user, switch to another Windows application while running your program, the background colors and any other Windows or system defaults will also be changed in these applications.

This breeds inconsistencies and can result in a general lack of comfort among users working with your program.

Lastly, if you're going to do any serious Windows work (e.g., commercial applications), you'll be way ahead of the game if you simply purchase a set of custom controls for use with your dialog boxes. For a modest fee you can purchase a package of ready-made custom controls that will provide you with all the versatility that you need. This is far cheaper than writing them yourself. Serious developers, especially those wishing to write their own VBX controls, should consider opting for a bit more muscle, however. So, for more information on custom controls, refer to Chapter 10.

CHAPTER
10

Visual Basic
Controls

OVERVIEW OF VBX CONTROLS

In Visual C++, you can use controls originally written for use with Visual Basic. These controls are an extension of the Control Palette used in the App Studio; indeed, after you install Visual Basic Controls in Visual C++, their icons are added to the Control Palette automatically. A *custom control* is nothing more than a special type of dynamic-link library (DLL) that contains functions that you can call, for example, to read or write the control's properties.

Visual Basic controls are useful for a variety of reasons. They can dramatically change the visual impact of your Windows program by adding such amenities as 3-D fonts, beveled panels, and custom frames. Besides changing the perceived quality of your program, Visual Basic custom controls save you a lot of time and work. You can simply purchase a control package from a third-party vendor, add its functionality to your program, and ship the control with your finished product (almost always without any licensing hassles). To illustrate, most custom controls include some sort of gauge, generally presented as a speedometer or some other like familiar object. For those activities inside your program that may take some time (e.g., downloading data from a host or server, periods of intense disk activity, etc.), you can simply display this gauge and move its indicator at periodic time intervals to mark the routine's progress. Using a custom control for this purpose is a lot easier than writing your own. However, the real power of VBX controls is far greater than simply giving your application the "look and feel of rich Corinthian leather." Managing the *properties* of VBX controls has been made relatively easy by their producers; VBXs come shipped from the factory with a lot of "smarts" built in to save you a great deal of programming costs. Among the features included are special edit boxes that accept only formatted input such as currency or calendar dates. Graphical objects, command buttons, and communication functions are further examples of the types of VBX controls generally sold as a group. Some vendors provide VBX controls that perform only one function, such as spreadsheet grids, edit boxes for large files, or other specialized formatting needs.

Initializing VBX Run-time Support

In order to use VBX controls in your program, you need to initialize the VBX support within the Microsoft Foundation Class Library. To accomplish this, add the following statement anywhere within your application's InitInstance function:

```
EnableVBX();
```

If you use AppWizard to create your application and check the box for adding the VBX support option, this line gets added automatically to your application's InitInstance( ) function. Note that if you are unsure as to whether or not your application will need VBX controls, you can't do any harm by specifying this option in AppWizard.

GRID.VBX

Visual C++ provides you with one Visual Basic custom control, GRID.VBX, a matrix or spreadsheet-style control of columns and rows. In this chapter we will use this control as the basis of our examples for a couple of reasons: first, because all Visual C++ users have access to it, and secondly, because it is a very powerful tool that lets you change how the user interacts with your application's data. Our examples will demonstrate two features of all custom controls: They have *properties* and they generate *events.* Examples of properties include data type, size, and format. Events include mouse messages, keyboard messages, and so on.

INSTALLING A VISUAL BASIC CUSTOM CONTROL

The steps for installing a custom control are very simple. In this example we assume that you are installing GRID.VBX for the first time.

1. Run App Studio and select the option "Install Controls..." under the "File" option on the main menu bar.

2. A dialog box appears showing you what controls are available for installation and which are presently installed. For a first-time installation of GRID.VBX, the dialog box will resemble the one shown in Figure 10.1.

3. Click on GRID.VBX in the list box on the left and add it to the list box on the right. Then click the button labeled "Install." The grid control will now be installed for use in App Studio, and its icon will appear on the floating control palette.

During the visual design phase of creating resources (e.g., while running App Studio), you'll use custom controls like any other option on the control (i.e., tool) palette. For example, if you're adding the grid to a dialog box resource, click on the

Figure 10.1
App Studio dialog box for installing VBX controls.

grid icon and then on the dialog box at the location where you want the grid to appear; you can resize or otherwise modify the grid after pasting it onto the dialog box.

While working in App Studio you must also establish the default properties of the custom control. You do this by double-clicking the mouse on the control; a pop-up dialog box like the example shown in Figure 10.2 for the grid will then appear.

Note that the upper right-hand corner has a drop-down box that reads "General" when the dialog first appears. Click the drop-down arrow to see the option "Styles." If you click this option, a scroll window appears with all the properties of the selected custom control that you can modify. Remember, you may also change these at run-time. Examples of these activities will be presented later in this chapter.

One last suggestion about custom controls and the App Studio: Go ahead and assign a class to your resource while in App Studio. Do this either by clicking on the ClassWizard icon or by pressing Ctrl-W. After assigning the class, click on the button labeled "Edit variables..." to bring up the dialog box for assigning variables to the custom control (and any other variables desired). Choosing "Add Variables..." invokes the dialog box shown in Figure 10.3.

These variables, which as you can see always begin with "m_", are very important, because they provide the mechanism for referring to the control(s) from inside your Windows program.

THE MFC AND CUSTOM CONTROLS

Once again, Visual C++ and the Microsoft Foundation Classes supply you with a lot of firepower when it comes to Windows programming and VBX controls. The MFC class for these controls is called CVBControl and is derived from class CWnd. This

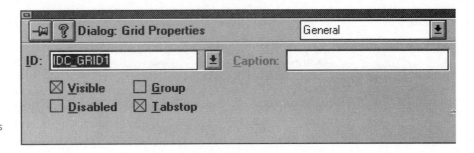

Figure 10.2
App Studio Properties dialog box.

comes as no surprise, since controls are ostensibly nothing more than child windows. The CVBControl class has a lot of member functions that you can use to interrogate the VBX control. You can, for example, find out the number of events associated with a control, their names (e.g., "click," "lost focus," etc.), and their properties. The snippet of code in the following section demonstrates many of these functions. You may want to modify these statements and put them in your own programs whenever you use a VBX. You can then work backwards from the control and learn more about it. Again, sticking with our previous example, we'll use the grid as our model.

Using CVBControl Functions

This sample assumes that you have a dialog box containing a grid and that you've called the grid's variable *m_MyGrid* in ClassWizard. To retrieve all the event names and properties associated with grid.vbx, run this example:

```
//
// Demonstrates member functions in class CVBControl
//
LPCSTR lpszPropName;      // property name as a string
LPCSTR lpszName;          // event name as a string
int nProp= 0;             // number of properties
nProp = m_Emp_Grid->GetNumProps(); // gets number of properties here
int nEvents= 0;           // number of events in grid.vbx
nEvents = m_MyGrid->GetNumEvents();// gets count of events in grid.vbx
for(int k= 0; k < nEvents; k++)// loops through all events
{
   lpszName = m_MyGrid->GetEventName(k); // get event
}
//
// do another loop for the properties
//
for(k= 0; k < nProp; k++)
{
   lpszPropName = m_Emp_Grid->GetPropName(k);// get property
}
```

For your edification, the grid has 14 events and 48 properties. The first event is "click," the second "dblclick," the third "drag drop," and so on. The first property is "Caption," the second "Index," the third "BackColor," etc. You can use the CVBControl class functions in combination with each other to form your own C++ class for working with the VBX control. It just takes a little planning. The next member functions we will examine are GetPropIndex( ) and GetPropName( ). They are the converse of each other and could be used together to build a table of property values, for example:

```
int index = m_MyGrid->GetPropIndex("ROWS");  // get index from string
//
//next line gets string from index
//
LPCSTR lpszPropName = m_MyGrid->GetPropName(index);
```

Another useful function, Refresh( ), serves to update the grid's cells after their data values have changed. As an example of such a case, you might have incoming real-time data such as stock quotes and need to do a portfolio recalculation. Call Refresh( ) as in this example:

```
m_MyGrid->Refresh();      // update grid
```

After this call, the cells would be updated with the new values that your application calculates.

Retrieving Properties

Of all the CVBControl class functions, you will probably end up using GetNumProperty( ) and GetStrProperty( ) often. As their names suggest, these functions retrieve a numerical property such as the cursor's location and a string property such as the contents of a grid cell, respectively. Please refer to the section on "Grid Properties" later in this chapter for a look at the prototypes for these functions and some related code.

The Move Function

The member function CVBControl::Move(RECT& rRect) may be used to move a VBX control to a rectangle defined by parameter *rRect*. The origin (i.e., the upper left-hand corner) of the control moves to *rRect.left* and *rRect.top*; resizing of the control takes place automatically inside *rRect*.

Constructing and Creating a VBX Control

When you call a VBX control from inside a dialog box or form view created using App Studio, the dialog template (which is the base class from which you derived the dialog box), contains the information necessary to create the VBX control. This is not true when the control is in a window that is *not* a dialog box or form view. In such cases, you'll need to use the Create( ) function of the CVBControl class. This is demonstrated in one of the samples shipped with Visual C++; see \MSVC\MFC\SAMPLES\VBCIRCLE\frame.cpp for an example of Create( ).

CREATING CUSTOM MEMBER FUNCTIONS

Another tip you'll find useful when working with custom controls is that you should encapsulate in a single class all the functions that manipulate the properties. In the sample program that accompanies this book, the grid has class CGrid, with member functions for sizing the cells and other similar purposes. This program really doesn't do anything powerful; its purpose is to illustrate some of the more salient and frequently used features of the grid. For example, the sample program simply reads a list of fictitious employees into the grid; no editing capability has been incorporated. However, you may wish to play around with adding more functionality. For instance, try superimposing an edit box on top of the cell you wish to edit. All the information you need to do so (e.g., the cell location, size, etc.) may be obtained by writing member functions to retrieve these parameters, which in turn may be used to establish the size and position of the edit box. This sort of "floating" editor would insulate users from the inner workings of your program without distracting them by resorting to some other alternative, such as a dialog box, for editing. Should you wish to try this tactic, here are a few hints to get you started:

1. Create an edit box in App Studio and place it on the dialog box with the grid. Set the *Visible* and *BorderStyle* properties of this edit box to FALSE. These settings give you an invisible edit box with no border.

2. Designate some event as the signal to allow editing. This might be a single right-button click, or a left double-click, or whatever. Also, you'll need some event such as pressing the Enter key to signal the end of editing.

3. In the function that responds to the event listed in step 2, determine the size of the cell (based on a common coordinate system or reference, such as pixels) and resize the invisible edit box.

4. Save the contents of the cell (remember, the user may wish to cancel the editing, and your program should be capable of restoring the previous value). Now move the edit box over the cell and set its Visible property to TRUE.

5. Upon receipt of an "end edit" or "cancel edit" event, update the cell and make the edit box invisible again.

Don't be afraid to try combining different controls in this fashion. Remember, all the user sees is what is on the screen. Make the experience of using your application as pleasant and consistent as possible.

VBX COLOR PROPERTIES

Another consideration from the realm of human factors is the use of color. Visual Basic custom controls allow you to install, for example, command buttons (e.g., Ok, Cancel, Help, etc.) that use colored fonts. Our practice is to draw the command text using colors that convey a certain meaning in Western culture. For example, most all of us are familiar with traffic lights: Red means stop, green means go, and yellow signals caution. Thus consider making a Cancel button with red (stop) text; use green (go) for Ok and yellow (caution) for Help. Don't go overboard with color and select your color schemes judiciously. Studies have shown that the use of bright (e.g., "neon") colors instills in users a sense that the program is "cheap," while flat, gray tones evoke confidence in the professionalism of the product. Consider Visual C++ and other Windows-based tools from Microsoft: They all use gray for the toolbars, status bars, and other features as well.

VISUAL C++ AND GRID.VBX

As promised, the focus in this chapter remains on GRID.VBX; we'll now begin to take a closer look at this control and its properties and events. At this point in our discussion, we assume that you have installed the grid in App Studio and have included it in your application. Refer to the sample program, DEMO, on the accompanying diskette as an example (or for review) of how to use the grid. This control is not as fancy as some others on the market, but it does work. However, if you're going to need a lot of cells or some special feature, consider purchasing a grid from a commercial vendor.

GRID PROPERTIES

You can retrieve and set the properties of GRID.VBX. Functions exist that allow you to manipulate properties based on their *type*, which is either a numerical attribute or a text (i.e., string) attribute. The functions for retrieving (i.e., reading) properties take the following forms:

Numerical :   int value = *m_Grid*->GetNumProperty("*property*", int column);

Text: CString value = *m_Grid*->GetStrProperty("TEXT", int column);

Functions for setting properties are very similar:

Numerical: *m_Grid*->SetNumProperty("*property*", int value);

Text: *m_Grid*->SetStrProperty("TEXT", CString value);

where *m_Grid* is the variable assigned to the grid with ClassWizard from inside App Studio, and *column* is the index into the cell's column. As a rule, you will generally have to use two functions to retrieve or set a cell property: one call to get/set the cell's row and another to get/set the property, specifying the column.

Depending on the property to be retrieved, these functions may require only one argument. For example, to get the maximum number of rows and columns assigned to a grid at design time, use the following code:

```
int maxrow, maxcol;
maxcol = (int)(m_grid->GetNumProperty("COLS")); // get maximum columns
maxrow = (int)(m_grid->GetNumProperty("ROWS")); // get maximum rows
```

You can use these values in a function that clears *all* the entries in a grid, for example, when the application first starts or when the user selects a "Clear All" or "Reset Grid" command. Using *maxrow* and *maxcol* from the previous coding example, just set up a nested loop in which the outer loop runs through all the columns and the inner loop runs through all the rows. Inside the inner loop, simply index each cell's position and call SetStrProperty( ) to set the TEXT property there as a space. For example:

```
int i,j;
for(i= 1; i < maxcol; i++)// loop through all the columns
{
  m_grid->SetNumProperty("COL",i); // move grid cursor to column
  for(j=0; j < maxrow; j++)// loop through all rows with this column
  {
    m_grid->SetNumProperty("ROW",j); // index each row
    m_grid->SetStrProperty("TEXT"," "); // set cell to a space
  }
}
```

Note carefully in this example the fact that the starting index for the outer for loop is 1, not 0. The reason for this is that you'll almost always reserve the top row for labels such as "Employee Name," "Department," "Salary," or whatever. If you copied this code inside the Reset function described earlier, you'd wipe out your column labels along with the cell values.

THE CURSOR AND THE GRID

The preceding example illustrates a problem with using the grid that may not be readily apparent—you, the programmer, are responsible for tracking and maintaining the location of the "cursor." The cursor for GRID.VBX is simply a narrow rectangle around the cell boundary. If you ran the preceding, unmodified sample code, you would find the cursor in the *last* cell of your grid, at *maxrow, maxcol.* In other words, the cursor always stays where you leave it last. Bear this in mind when you write the code to populate the cells with data, perhaps by reading in values from a file. You'll need to keep track of the present cursor location *and* the next cell to visit. Here, then, is where you must coordinate the values of *maxrow* and *maxcol* with such additional information as the total number of fixed columns and rows. The sample Demo program on the accompanying disk demonstrates all these factors in their entirety in the *EMPLOYE.CPP* file, which reads in a list of fictitious employees from a formatted text file and populates a grid with the employee data that file contains.

ERROR REPORTING

Every object in class CVBControl, including GRID.VBX, has a public data member for reporting whatever errors result from a call to a member function (e.g., trying to read or write to a cell outside the range of *maxrow, maxcol*). This public data member is:

```
int m_nError
```

You can access this data member by using your instantiation of the grid object. Here is an example in which it is assumed that you have previously established a grid class, a member variable that points to it, etc. This example illustrates what happens when the user attempts to move the cursor to an invalid column:

```
m_Grid->SetNumProperty("COL",-1); // -1 is not a valid column
if(m_Grid->m_nError != 0) // check for error
  AfxMessageBox("Error, invalid column",MB_OK); // alert user
```

THE VBX ERROR CODES

The error codes for m_nError are listed in Technical Note 27 of the Visual C++ group icon window and repeated in Table 10.1 for the sake of convenience. Included in this table are the general errors for any .VBX control as well as those specific to the grid. All codes related to the grid have values of 300xx:

VIRTUAL SPREADSHEETS

In the preceding material, we've covered the basics of installing and using the grid. You can clearly see that the grid is nothing more than a mathematical matrix that has all the trappings of a classic spreadsheet. Now we'd like to introduce to you a novel software construct that we call the *virtual spreadsheet*. The virtual spreadsheet is, for all intents and purposes, identical to a regular spreadsheet with

Table 10.1
The VBX error codes.

M_NERROR CODE	MEANING
7	Out of memory
61	Disk full
62	Input past the end of the file
380	Invalid property value
420	Invalid object reference
422	Property item not found
30000	Cannot use RemoveItem on a fixed row
30001	Cannot use AddItem on a fixed row
30002	Grid does not contain that row
30004	Invalid column number for alignment
30005	Invalid alignment value
30006	Unable to allocate memory for grid
30008	Not a valid picture type
30009	Invalid row value
30010	Invalid column value
30011	Unable to register the memory manager
30013	Invalid row height value
30014	Invalid column width value
30015	Cannot remove last nonfixed row
30016	FixedRows must be one less than Rows value
30017	FixedCols must be one less than Cols value
30018	Rows must be one more than FixedRows value
30019	Cols must be one more than FixedCols value

one difference—the user *selects* data, rather than entering it. In a larger sense, a virtual spreadsheet is actually a paradigm allowing the developer to integrate the *logical* structure of the application easily with its *physical* structure. Thus virtual spreadsheets offer the advantages of rapid data entry and edition while minimizing the possibilities of human error. By their nature, virtual spreadsheets are generally intended to be used in Windows applications whose data requirements tend to be static and redundant. For our example, we'll use a model bill-of-materials spreadsheet, since their data requirements tend to be quite simple (e.g., 100 2 × 4s @ $1.90 each).

Elements of a Virtual Spreadsheet

The fundamental elements of a virtual spreadsheet are: one or more data file(s) and combo or list box(es) and the grid itself. In our hypothetical bill-of-materials spreadsheet, we wish to produce a summary of all the materials needed—the type, quantities, unit cost, item subtotal costs, and total job materials cost. To do so, we first read into a combo box a data file containing all the different materials (e.g., 2 × 4 studs, #8 nails, roofing, paint, etc.) and their unit costs. When the user clicks on an item in this box, the item goes into a column in the grid, along with its unit cost. Next, the user must enter the quantity of that item needed, using a floating numerical pad. Once the user enters the amount needed, a third column is updated with a subtotal cost for that particular item (e.g., if the user specifies 100 2 × 4s at $1.90 each, the subtotal cost will be 100 * 1.90, or $190.00). There are a couple of reasons why we use a combo box to contain the various materials. First, this type of box allows keyboard entry for searching. Since the materials listed in the box are sorted, pressing the letter "S" would take the user to the first entry beginning with this letter faster than scrolling with the mouse. Secondly, the combo box provides a mechanism whereby you can allow the user to enter new data. If no item in the box matches the user's string, a pop-up dialog box gives the user the chance to enter a new material type.

Sample Code for Virtual Spreadsheets

This section breezes over some of the code you'll need to implement a virtual spreadsheet. Here you'll see how to load up the combo box from the bill-of-materials data file and move a selection from the combo box into the grid. All the other details are left for you to devise. Note that we're using some dummy class names and member functions created in ClassWizard. The significance of this example is that it illustrates not only how to use some of the file and string functions, but also how to add items to a combo box. Variables assigned to controls via ClassWizard are indicated by the use of the prefix "m_":

```
CStdioFile datafile;                    // the materials data file
char bufr[80];                          // read entire line
char type[51];                          // holds the material ONLY, not units/cost
if(!datafile.Open("MATERIAL.DAT",CFile::modeRead,NULL))
   AfxMessageBox("Could not open MATERIALS file.",MB_OK,0);
else
{
   while(datafile.ReadString(bufr,80))
```

```
    {
      if(bufr != NULL)
      {
        bufr[strlen(bufr)]= '\0';     // ensure NULL terminator
        //
        // extract only the material description here
          // assume material is in columns 1-50 of file
        strncpy(type,bufr,50);
        type[50]= '\0';               // add NULL
        m_Material.AddString(type);   // add to combo box
      }
    }
  }
  datafile.Close();                                // close material data file
```

Now we need something to move the combo box selection into the grid. This action is accomplished in ClassWizard, where we specify a function to respond to an EN_CHANGE message as follows:

```
void CVirtSpr::OnSelchangeMaterial()
{
  CString buf;    // buffer to hold combo box selection
  int row, col;          // these managed "globally"
  m_Material.GetText(m_Material.GetCurSel(),buf); // get material
  m_grid->SetNumProperty("ROW",row);// move to proper row
  m_grid->SetNumProperty("COL",col); // move to proper column
  m_grid->SetStrProperty("TEXT",buf); // insert the material
  //
  // next you would add in the units and unit costs in the
  // appropriate columns, and call up a number pad to allow
  // the user to enter the quantity.
  //
}
```

We've obviously left out a lot of details here, such as getting the units, the unit cost, and managing the current row and column, because most involve just basic programming that you should already know how to do. These examples strive to capture the essentials of coordinating activities among the different controls, rather than show you how to extract substrings from strings or test whether it's time to move to another row.

Design Considerations for Virtual Spreadsheets

While using a virtual spreadsheet makes life easier for the user, it does impose on the developer some additional duties, to which we've alluded in the previous examples. Probably the main concern is keeping track of the cursor. For example, you don't want the user to be able to edit directly a cell containing a material item—that would defeat the virtual spreadsheet's whole purpose. Should users need to change a material item in a cell, they should first have to click on the item to set the focus to the cell, and then reselect an item from the combo box. Of course, users should be able to edit the quantity of an item directly at any time. The problem of cursor management is not so bad, since you have to do it anyway; just add some extra code to check for conditions such as those described here.

Another concern is mathematical accuracy. If your spreadsheet deals with large numbers and lots of them, you'll want to be sure to use the proper data types for the appropriate variables (e.g., *grand_total* might need to be of type double, etc.).

WRITING VBXs FOR VISUAL C++

The software requirements for writing your own VBXs are pretty simple—all you need is a compiler that can create DLLs (Dynamic Link Library) for Windows, which is a feature of Visual C++. While you don't actually need Visual Basic to write a VBX, you will need it for testing (and running!) your program. Also, you may want to consider purchasing a third-party tool for simplifying custom control development. If you intend to write custom controls that will be supported in Visual C++, there are certain things you need to consider. Most of these things can be found in Visual C++'s Technical Note 27. There are a few quirks in the way Microsoft Foundation Classes 2.0 implements the emulation layer with Visual Basic. The primary two to watch out for are the VBGetMode and VBSetErrorMessage functions. VBGetMode returns the state of the debugging mode in Visual Basic, defined as MODE_BREAK. Since no similar mode exists in MFC 2.0, this value never returns, which could cause problems for your debugger, something everyone wants to avoid. The second potentially problematic function, VBSetErrorMessage, ignores the incoming string argument; as a result, you can't retrieve the error string associated with an error, though the error can, of course, still be trapped.

DYNAMIC DATA EXCHANGE AND VBXs

Dynamic Data Exchange (DDE) is a messaging protocol that lets one Windows application exchange data with another. An example of an application that might use DDE is a program that monitors stock market quotations in real-time. One Windows program could be responsible for retrieving the price of a stock and then using the DDE protocol to update that value for use by a second program. If the application you are developing needs to use DDE features and support a VBX, there is a small caveat concerning the HSZ data type. The HSZ is essentially a string, the length of which is determined by the location of the first NULL character. This Visual Basic data type is different from the corresponding data type in the Dynamic Data Exchange Management Library (DDEML). In order to use them both together in the same program, you'll need to do one of the following:

1. Place your code for the VBX and the code for the DDEML into different modules. You'll need to define the preprocessor symbol NO_VBX_SUPPORT in the module containing the DDEML code.

2. If you can't follow step 1, define the HSZ data type where needed with the #undef and #define preprocessor directives.

Whenever you have both the AFXEXT.H and DDEML.H include files in the same source file, you'll receive the error message: *error C2371: 'HSZ' : redefinition; different basic types*. This error is due to a naming conflict between DDEML and VBX controls involving the HSZ data type—both have the data type (HSZ), but each assigns a different meaning to that data type.

For now, developers need to remember that DDE is dependent on Windows messages and that this dependency may cause difficulties. We believe that future versions of the OLE libraries will use the DDEML.

CHAPTER SUMMARY

The VBX controls provide an impressive performance boost to Visual C++ at very modest prices. No serious Windows development site can afford to do without them. VBX controls can greatly enhance the appearance and acceptability of your Windows application and significantly reduce its size, complexity, and maintenance requirements. Their usefulness becomes even more apparent when they are applied to special processing situations such as validating formatted input for dates, currency, etc. By using the properties and error trapping capacities of the VBX control, you can eliminate redundant checking of data for validity and logical ambiguities. While it would be difficult to quantify the overall contributions made by custom controls, the ability to trap errors *at their source* is a very important consideration because it directly contributes to the overall quality and reliability of both your data and your program. Foremost among the generic VBXs is probably the grid, since it allows data to be managed in a manner that is both easy to use and easy to program. It allows the user to see his or her data in clear, tabular fashion and lets the programmer think about the control as a giant, two-dimensional array. The GRID.VBX can provide a considerable performance boost to an application under the right circumstances, and that is probably one of the main reasons why it is shipped with Visual C++. For example, because you can place pictures as well as text inside the cells of the grid, you can conceivably use this feature to make a scrolling toolbar for your application by placing in each cell an icon representing a certain tool or feature of the program. Such an application might be particularly useful in programs designed for the visually impaired—operations could be performed by clicking on relatively larger pictures, instead of the more customary small controls.

For more information on using Visual Basic custom controls from inside Visual C++, take a look at Tech Note 27; this Help file contains a lot of esoteric information and other goodies (as do the Help files for the other Tech Notes). Should you elect to include Visual Basic controls in your Windows-based application, be mindful that your program's installation procedure should copy the VBX controls required into the target platform's WINDOWS\SYSTEM subdirectory. See Chapter 19 for more details on setting up an automatic install program. Also, be sure that you have the legal right to ship a third-party control with your application and that you have included the control on your installation disk. Finally, be mindful of the version of Visual Basic that may (or may not!) be found on the target platform. It is essential that you allow for variances in this regard or at least specify the appropriate requirements should your VBXs work properly only with a certain version of Visual Basic.

File I/O

CHAPTER
II

If it did not give you the ability to save and restore data, programming would be pointless. As a Foundation Class programmer, you will find the framework does not limit you to the file I/O operations provided by the CFile class and its derived classes. You also have access to the Windows API functions and the standard C run-time library calls, most of which MFC conveniently encapsulates in the CFile class. This chapter does not deal with storing CObject-derived data, a topic we covered in Chapter 4.

Since you have access to the standard C run-time calls and the underlying MS-DOS calls, we will show you how to manipulate the file status information. The CFile class has several static member functions that mimic the run-time library calls. One of these static functions, SetStatus( ), allows you to check a file's status without opening the file. Be forewarned that some of our examples involving this function may not be directly portable to your operating system because they are so closely tied to MS-DOS.

Next, you will see how to get a directory listing, both on your own and with MFC. The MFC Common File Dialog gives your application a consistent look and feel across many Windows applications and also plays an important part in the MFC document and view architecture described in Chapter 3.

Finally, Microsoft has given Visual C++ users the ability to customize the environment through initialization files, usually called INI files because they end in the extension .INI. Several short examples will show you how to read and write to your application's INI file, as well as to the Windows system files.

CFILE

CFile provides the base class for file I/O in the framework. The framework derives this class from CObject and provides a helper structure called CFileStatus that allows you access to information about a file and also defines an exception handling class,

CFileException. Another class the framework derives from CFile is the CStdioFile class for text-only file operations.

In C, especially when opening files, you test for error conditions by testing for NULL return values. In MFC, you have this option as well as wrapping the calls in TRY/CATCH logic. Most operations will throw an associated exception that you can catch and allow better error recovery.

Open

The first step for file I/O is to create a CFile object and associate it with the file (e.g., MYFILE.TXT) that you wish to open. If the resulting object is an automatic variable, which is allocated on the function's stack, the C++ run-time environment will destroy the object when the function loses scope. The default constructor simply sets the *m_hFile* member variable to CFile::hFileNull to indicate no file is currently associated with this object. The *m_hFile* variable usually contains the OS specific file handle.

```
CFile temp; // calls the default constructor
```

To open the file you would call the Open member function and test for a NULL condition in the traditional C way. This function will not throw a CFileException per se, but you can pass a pointer to a CFileException object, setting the default value for its address as NULL; if the function returns FALSE, the CFileException object's *m_cause* variable will contain the reason for the failure.

CFileExceptions

```
if ( !temp.Open("temp.txt",CFile::modeRead) )
{
  AfxMessageBox("Could not open temp.txt for reading)";
}
```

To see what caused the error, instantiate a CFileException object and pass the address of the object as the third parameter to the CFile Open( ) member function. You can then test the m_cause value of the exception object against the values listed in the *Class Library Reference, Volume 1,* and shown in the code snippet below:

```
CFileException except;
char fname[32] = "temp.txt";

if ( !temp.Open(fname,CFile::modeRead, &e) )
{
  char errmsg[80];
  sprintf(errmsg,"Could not open %s for reading",fname);
  AfxMessageBox( errmsg );
  switch( except.m_cause)
  {
    case CFileException::none : // no error occurred
      break;
    case CFileException::generic :
      break;
    case CFileException:: fileNotFound :
```

```
        break;
      case CFileException::badPath :
        break;
      case CFileException::tooManyOpenFiles :
/* This may require you to increase the number of file handles available to
your system.*/
        break;
      case CFileException::accessDenied :
        break;
      case CFileException::invalidFile :
        break;
      case CFileException:: removeCurrentDir :
        break;
      case CFileException:: directoryFull :
        break;
      case CFileException:: badSeek :
        break;
      case CFileException::hardIO:
        break;
      case CFileException::sharingViolation :
        break;
      case CFileException::lockViolation:
        break;
      case CFileException::diskFull:
        break;
      case CFileException:: endOfFile:
        break;
    } // end switch
  } // if !temp
```

This process bypasses the traditional TRY/CATCH macro exception handling performed by other MFC classes.

File Handles

You may need to make some adjustments to your system if you receive the CFileException::tooManyOpenFiles exception. By default, every Windows program receives enough memory to hold 20 file handles, including the traditional 5 MS-DOS preallocated file handles, stdin, stdout, stderr, aux, prn. To increase the number of free handles available to a number greater than 15 and less than 255, use the SetHandleCount API call:

```
case CFileException::tooManyOpenFiles :
  SetHandleCount( 50 );
  // Try again!
  break;
```

Note, however, that you will only be able to use the Windows functions _lopen, _lclose, _lread, _lcreat, _lseek, and _lwrite if you use this SDK call. Unfortunately, the MFC library file, *filecore.cpp,* uses the low-level MS-DOS calls to perform file I/O, so you will not really be able to use the preceding solution unless you do not use CFile operations in your application (almost an impossibility, considering the CDocument class makes extensive use of CFile member functions). If your application requires you to use the CFile class, you must modify the C startup code to increase the number of available file handles. Better yet, merely download the previously built startup code files that Microsoft provides on CompuServe in the MSLANG forum. (Chapter 17 contains information on accessing Microsoft Support on CompuServe.)

Openflags

The *openflags* parameters are similar to C run-time values such as "w" and "r+". In fact, if you search through the MFC source code, you will see the *openflags* mapped to the C run-time values! Table 11.1 illustrates the *openflags* values used most often. The *Class Library Reference Manual* illustrates the rest. All of these values begin with CFile::<some enum value>. These values can be ORed together with the logical or symbol "|" to combine functionalities. Other values for this parameter control how files are shared, providing you have loaded the MS-DOS program SHARE.EXE.

Openflags for Derived Classes

The derived classes use two *openflag* parameters: CFile::typeText and CFile::type-Binary. The first flag handles the carriage return/linefeed translation found in ASCII text files, while CFile::typeBinary indicates CR/LF are to be treated as separate characters. These flags are necessary because of the way MS-DOS and C/C++ treat the newline ("\n") character. C/C++ treats this as one character, while MS-DOS treats the newline as two characters (CR and LF). The CFile::typeText instructs the program to translate the character pairs CR/LF to and from the newline character.

CMEMFILE

The derived class CMemFile provides the framework a mechanism to create RAM-based files rather than disk-based files. The advantages are very quick access time and the ability to share memory between applications by treating the memory as a disk-based file.These objects do not use the member variable *m_hFile,* since there is not a physical hardware device attached to the file. You can pass the default constructor a parameter to indicate how much memory to allocate for those objects that need more memory than the default, which is 1K.

```
CMemFile temp;
CMemFile temp(512); // allocate 512 byte chunks of memory.
```

If this function is unable to allocate the memory requested, it throws a CFileException and a CMemoryException. The framework does not support the Duplicate, LockRange, and UnlockRange functions and will throw a CNotSupportedException if you try to use those functions. In addition, if you try to set the length of a CMemFile object, either to truncate or expand the file, the result may be a CMemoryException.

TABLE 11.1
CFile openflags.

CFile::modeCreate	Creates a file by overwriting an existing file
CFile::modeRead	Reads only
CFile::modeWrite	Writes only
CFile::modeReadWrite	Reads or writes

```
TRY()
{
temp.SetLength( 50 );      // set the memfile length to 50 bytes,
// throwing an exception if there is an
// allocation error.
}
CATCH(CMemoryException,e)
{
  AfxMessageBox("Memory Exception");
}
END_CATCH()
```

CSTDIOFILE

CStdioFile is another derived class that does not support the Duplicate, LockRange, and UnlockRange functions and will throw a CFileException if you attempt to invoke them. Objects of this class allow for both text and binary buffered file I/O and will translate a newline (\n) character into a 2-byte sequence (0xA,0xD) if you open a CStdioFile file with the CFile::typeText parameter. Conversely, the objects of this class will also translate this pair of characters in a file into a single newline character.

STANDARD FILES

You can also construct a CStdioFile object for files that are already opened, such as the standard system files: stdin, stderr, and stdout.

```
CStdioFile file(stdout); // write to standard output
file.WriteString("hello world\n");
```

CStdioFile::WriteString( ) will not write the buffer's null character to the stream and will throw one of the exceptions mentioned in the section on CFileExceptions if an error occurs.

CFile Reading

Reading buffered data is similar to using the fgets C run-time function. In fact, if you inspect the MFC source files, you will see calls to the trusty RTL functions buried inside the member function definitions! For an example check out the *mfc* source file *filetxt.cpp* in \msvc\mfc\src.

The following snippet of code illustrates opening a file named *temp.txt* for both reading and writing :

```
CStdioFile ifile("temp.txt",CFile::modeRead | CFile::modeWrite );
char buffer[80];
ifile.ReadString( buffer, sizeof(buffer) );
```

The CStdioFile::ReadString( ) function will read a maximum of *sizeof (buffer)* −1 characters into the buffer, or all characters that precede a newline, whichever is less. This function appends a NULL (\0) to the string and returns a NULL if it encounters EOF. Since this function also reads the newline character into the buffer, you may wish to eliminate the newline character before using the buffer. The following code snippet illustrates a quick technique to eliminate the newline character from a string buffer.

```
char *loc = strrchr(buffer,'\n');
if ( loc )
  *loc = 0;
```

The base class CFile object also allows you to write and read bytes to the file. You must specify the number of bytes to read or write as follows:

```
char buffer[80];
temp.Write( buffer, sizeof(buffer) );

CFile input("data.dat",CFile::modeRead);
int numread = input.Read(buffer,sizeof(buffer) );
```

Thus CFile provides the functionality of the C run-time functions fread( ) and fwrite( ), while CStdioFile provides the functionality of fgets( ) and fprintf( ).

Reading/Writing Huge Amounts of Data

The routines presented in the previous sections will work for most of your needs, as long as you do not wish to read or write data items larger than 65,535 bytes. If you try to pass a buffer of this size or larger to your routine, the result will be an ASSERT failure. The reason? Such buffers require HUGE pointer manipulation and the MFC library does not contain functions to handle huge pointers that cross segment boundaries. Or does it?

The MFC library provides two undocumented functions, prototyped in the AFX.H header file and used in the DIBLOOK.CPP sample program. (See Chapter 17 for more information on the sample programs.) These functions have the following prototypes:

```
DWORD CFile::ReadHuge(void FAR* lpBuffer, DWORD dwCount);
void CFile::WriteHuge(const void FAR* lpBuffer, DWORD dwCount);
```

You can use an SDK API call to ::GlobalAlloc( ) to create a huge buffer and then fill this buffer and write, or else fill the buffer from a file and process the data.

Closing a File

Of course, if you open a file, eventually you will want to close it. All of the classes discussed in the preceding sections provide a Close member function. An assertion failure will result if you try to close a closed file. The framework will throw an exception if an error occurs. Closing a file will set the *m_hFile* (except for CMemFile objects) to CFile::hFileNull and make the file unavailable for I/O. Note that if the object loses scope, the destructor will close the file before deleting the object. If you allocate the object off the heap, then you must explicitly delete it after closing the file.

```
CFile *file = new CFile("test.txt",CFile::modeWrite);
file->Write( buffer, sizeof( buffer) );
```

```
file->Close();
delete file;
```

FILE PROCESSING

PC file processing used to be simple, but with data files exceeding OS limits and the explosive growth of networks, that's no longer true. The MS-DOS SHARE.EXE program permits several applications to access the same file simultaneously. This allows multiple access to data files in such products as FoxPro or Paradox. CFile provides member functions to control file sharing, beginning with the open function and the share options specified. Most of the open parameters defined by the framework restrict access by other processes to the file opened by the framework.

CFile File Processing Example

One example of CFile file processing involves a simple database of fixed-length records. You may want to open the file for reading by several people, but lock the current record you are accessing to prevent anything from being done to it. The following example illustrates several CFile member functions used to open a file, move to a given record, lock and read the record, and then close the file.

```
typedef {
char fname[32];
char lname[32];
char mi;
int status;
} RECORD;

// We will seek to record 5, lock the record, read it, unlock it,
// then exit. No exception handling is shown.

BOOL COurApp::ReadDB()
{
    char fname[] = "DB.dat";
    RECORD data;
    CFile DB;

    if ( !DB.Open(fname,CFile::modeRead | CFile::shareCompat) )
    {
      AfxMessageBox("Error opening file");
      return FALSE;
    }

    // Calculate offset into datafile
    LONG pos = sizeof( RECORD) * 5; // Use sizeof because of
    // possible byte padding in the structure.
    LONG newpos;

    // Seek starts at the position specified in the second parameter.
    //This can have the value of : CFile::begin, CFile::end, or
    // CFile::current. It will throw a CFileException on error.
    // CFile also provides the member functions CFile::SeekToBegin and
    // CFile::SeekToEnd to go directly to the
    // beginning or end of a file.
    newpos = DB.Seek( pos, CFile::begin);
```

```
        // Lock this record.
        DB.LockRange( pos, sizeof(RECORD) );

        // Read the record. Note that we could also write a new record at this
        // point, if we had specified the correct settings in the
        // open parameters.
        DB.Read( &data, sizeof(data) );

        // Unlock the record.
        DB.UnlockRange(pos,sizeof(RECORD));

        DB.Close();

        return TRUE;
}
```

FILE STATISTICS

A file contains several pieces of information useful to both the developer and the user: statistics such as the file's size, its creation date, and its name. MFC provides a helper structure, CFileStatus, that contains this information in the following fields:

```
CTime m_ctime;      // creation date/time
CTime m_mtime;      // last modification date/time
CTime m_atime;      // last date/time accessed for reading
LONG m_size;        // file size as reported in the DIR command

// the file's attributes, shown by the ATTRIB command
BYTE m_attribute;

// the filename in the windows character set
char m_szFullName[_MAX_PATH];
```

Under MS-DOS, the three time and date fields hold the same value. To change the time stamp, simply set the *m_mtime* field to the desired value.

GetStatus

The MFC source file *filest.cpp* contains the GetStatus functions that make use of underlying MS-DOS calls. For the *m_attribute field*, the MFC provides the following enumerated values:

```
enum Attribute={normal, readOnly, hidden, system, volume, directory,
    archive};
```

Under MS-DOS, you must specifically open a file, usually with a low-level OS call, to check or change its status. The overloaded function GetStatus allows you to check the status of an opened file. The static version of this function allows you to check the status of any file, regardless of whether or not it is open. Unfortunately, these functions do not support network names.

```
    void teststats()
    {
```

```
CFile ifile;
CFileStatus fstats;
ifile.Open("temp.txt",CFile::modeRead);
ifile.GetStatus( fstat );
// You could now display the information.
ifile.Close( );

char fname[16] = "data.dat";
// Call to the static member function. note the "::".
CFile::GetStatus(fname,fstat);
// You could now display the information.
// Change to the current time.
fstats.m_mtime = CTime::GetCurrentTime;
CFile::SetStatus( fname,fstat);
// You could now display the information.
}
```

CFile::SetStatus will throw a CFileException if the user marked the file as ReadOnly.

FILE SIZE

You may at times need to find out the size of a file or resize a file on the fly. CFile provides you this functionality through various member functions. To get the size of the file, you could query a CFileStatus structure or call:

```
CFile myfile;
DWORD fsize;

fsize = myfile.GetLength( );
```

To change the size of a file, you would call:

```
// shrink the file by 200 bytes
fsize = ( fsize - 200 > 0) ? fsize - 200 : 0;
myfile.SetLength( fsize);
```

Both functions will throw exceptions on errors. The framework will throw a CMemoryException if an allocation fails while you are trying to increase the size of a CMemFile.

Static Functions

CFile contains other static functions that mimic the C run-time functions for renaming and removing files and are as simple to use as their C RTL counterparts. These static functions are:

```
CFile::rename( pfoldname, pfnewname);
CFile::remove( fname);
```

Both will throw a CFileException on error. Neither will work on network names or with directories. Note also that you cannot rename a file across drives (i.e., from drive C: to drive E:).

FILE LISTINGS

Traditionally, you prompt a user for a filename and allow the user to type in a response, and then check to ensure that the filename given includes a valid path and extension or otherwise ensure that the file exists before trying to open it. While this approach is acceptable in a text-mode world, GUIs demand a graphical approach to prompts and validation. Microsoft provides developers with a set of common dialogs to accomplish certain actions such as prompting for a file. These give users a consistent interface across all Windows applications and make learning to use these applications much easier.

COMMON FILE SAVE/SAVE AS... DIALOG

An application usually prompts for a filename in response to the *File/Open* and the *File/Save As* menu selections (see Figure 11.1). The program then presents the Common File Open Dialog so that the user can choose a filename and path, including the file extension and the drive where the file is located. The MFC class CFileDialog encapsulates this functionality. If you need additional functionalities, you may derive a new, custom dialog.

To use the common file dialog, instantiate an instance of the class and pass values to the constructor. Before calling the DoModal member function, set the values of the member variables according to how you intend to use the dialog (i.e., either as an Open File or as a Save File As). DoModal will return either IDOK or IDCANCEL, which instructs you to either process the information gathered by the file dialog, or to ignore the information. You can gather the information from the file dialog by using various member functions (described later in the chapter). To create the file dialog you call the constructor with the values:

```
CFileDialog Prompt(     BOOL bOpenFileDialog,
        LPCSTR lpszDefExt,
        LPCSTR lpszFileName,
        DWORD dwFlags,
        LPCSTR lpszFilter,
        CWnd* pParentWnd );
```

You must set *bOpenFileDialog* to TRUE to create a File Open dialog. The constructor will create a File Save As dialog if you set the flag to FALSE.

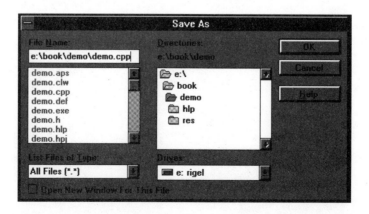

Figure 11.1
The Common File Save As dialog box.

The value *lpszDefExt* contains the default extension supplied to a filename if the user does not supply one. You can enter from one to three characters, without the dot ".", or give the extension the NULL, or empty string, value.

Default Filename

The value *lpszFileName* will appear in the Filename edit control. For the *File/Open* functionality, this will be a wild card value with a default extension (supplied by you, not by the *lpszDefExt* parameter). In the case of *File/Save As*, this parameter will contain the current document's name.

File Flags

The *dwFlags* parameter allows you to customize the dialog. This flag's values, created by bitwise ORing #defined constants, initialize the *m_ofn.Flags* member variable. This member variable is of type OPENFILENAME as defined in the commdlg.h header file and in Windows 3.1 SDK online help.

```
typedef struct tagOPENFILENAME
{
  DWORD  lStructSize;
  HWND hwndOwner;
  HINSTANCE hInstance;
  LPCSTR lpstrFilter;
  LPSTR  lpstrCustomFilter;
  DWORD  nMaxCustFilter;
  DWORD  nFilterIndex;
  LPSTR  lpstrFile;
  DWORD  nMaxFile;
  LPSTR  lpstrFileTitle;
  DWORD  nMaxFileTitle;
  LPCSTR lpstrInitialDir;
  LPCSTR lpstrTitle;
  DWORD  Flags;
  UINT   nFileOffset;
  UINT   nFileExtension;
  LPCSTR lpstrDefExt;
  LPARM  lCustData;
  UINT   (CALLBACK* lpfnHook)(HWND,UINT,WPARAM,LPARAM);
  LPCSTR lpTemplateName;
} OPENFILENAME;
```

- The DWORD Flags field contains OFN_HIDEREADONLY | OFN_OVER-WRITEPROMPT as its default setting. To modify the dialog, you may either OR your choices together with these defaults or change the defaults. Some of the most useful alternative values are discussed in the following paragraphs. You can find a complete list in the SDK Online Help.

- The OFN_ALLOWMULTISELECT value allows the user to choose multiple files instead of just one. Use this functionality to allow a single operation on multiple files. The CFileDialog member functions GetFileName( ), GetFileExt( ), GetFileTitle( ), and GetPathName( ) apply only to the first file found when you set this flag. If you set this flag, you should also set *m_ofn.lpstrFile* to a buffer that you supply to hold all the filenames.

- The OFN_CREATEPROMPT value allows the user to create a file of the given name if it does not already exist. Setting this flag will also set the OFN_FILEMUSTEXIST and OFN_PATHMUSTEXIST flags.

- The OFN_FILEMUSTEXIST flag indicates that the user may only enter a valid file name. Otherwise the framework will display a warning message. If the OFN_CREATEPROMPT flag is also set, then the user is allowed to create the named file. Setting the OFN_FILEMUSTEXIST flag will also set the OFN_PATHMUSTEXIST flag.

- The OFN_HIDEREADONLY value is part of the default settings for the flag field. Set this value to indicate that the Read Only check box must not appear in the dialog.

- The OFN_NOCHANGEDIR flag forces the application to reset the current directory to the directory where the application resided on the dialog box's creation. This allows the user to change directories to get a file and forces the application to return automatically to the default directory after that operation.

- The OFN_NOREADONLYRETURN value prevents the user from choosing a file with a ReadOnly attribute or a file located in a ReadOnly directory.

- The OFN_OVERWRITEPROMPT flag prevents the user from accidentally overwriting a file by asking permission to overwrite the file. This flag will let the user cancel that action and enter another filename.

- The OFN_PATHMUSTEXIST flag indicates that the user must enter a valid path for the filename.

- The OFN_READONLY flag checks the Read Only check box. Also, on an exit caused by the OK button, the framework will reflect the state of this check box via this flag. Thus you can set this flag on creating the dialog so that the framework will check this box when it displays the dialog. Note, however, that if the user toggles this check box during processing, you can check its state after closing with this simple test:

```
CFileDialog    CmyFileDlg;
...
...
if ( CMyFileDlg.m_ofn.Flags & OFN_READONLY )
{
   // The flag is set!! Don't modify.
}
else
{
   // Have at it.
}
```

File Filter

The next parameter you pass to the Create function (remember the Create function?) is *lpszFilter*. This value defines a list of files displayed in the combo box labeled "List Files of Type" in File/Open, or in "Save File as Type" in the File/Save As dialog boxes. An MFC 2.0 application will base the default values on the document templates your application registers. The framework places the strings in the resource file. An example of this parameter's usage is the case in which the user may save data in or convert it from a variety of formats.

The filter string contains the following items:

1. The text displayed in the list box, ending with the binary OR operator "|".

2. The text displayed in the filename edit box, which usually contains a wild card expression. This item also ends with the "|" symbol.

Repeat these two steps for every data file type you wish to list. End the list with a final "|" symbol in the string as illustrated in the following code snippet:

```
char filter[] = "Source Files (*.cpp)|*.cpp|Include files|*.h, *.hpp||";
```

USER HELP

The parameter *pParentWnd* provides custom help and is set to NULL by default, but you should set it to the parent window in order to call the WINHELP.EXE engine. The Common File Dialog will use either of the MFC-defined values, AFX_HIDD_FILEOPEN or AFX_HIDD_FILESAVE, as the context ID for the help system. (See Chapter 15 for details on providing user help.)

On an IDOK return value, you can use various member functions to get the filename the user wishes to process. Here's a snippet of code showing how to use this parameter:

```
CString path, ext, fname;
char *p_ext, *p_fname, *p_path;
char message[80];

ext = "txt"; fname = "*.txt";
// Create an open file dialog.
p_ext = ext.GetBuffer(32);
p_fname = fname.GetBuffer(32);
CFileDialog MyFileDlg( TRUE,p_ext ,p_fname, OFN_NOCHANGEDIR, filter,
        OurApp.m_hWnd);
ext.ReleaseBuffer(-1);
fname.ReleaseBuffer(-1);

int retv = MyFileDlg.DoModal();

if ( IDOK == IDOK)
{
  // Get the path.
  path  = MyFileDlg.GetPathName();
  p_path = path.GetBuffer(32);
  fname = MyFileDlg.GetFileTitle();
  p_fname = fname.GetBuffer(32);
  sprintf(message,"path = %s, title = %s",path,fname);
  fname.ReleaseBuffer(-1);
  path.ReleasBuffer(-1);
  AfxMessageBox(message);
}
return retv;
```

MFC Common Dialog Support

The preceding code sample may look like a lot of work to get something as simple as a filename. Luckily for you, the MFC 2.0 Document classes provide default behavior for File/Open and File/Save As. The resource file (.RC) lists the default extensions for all your data files, and the filters will depend on the document templates you registered with your application.

If you wish to change this default behavior, you will have to call the common dialog routines yourself as shown in the preceding examples instead of using the default document member functions.

INI FILES

When you run AppWizard, it creates an INI file in the Windows subdirectory with the same name as your project. This file allows your application's users to save preferences from session to session. These INI files have the following layout:

```
[section name] or for the API functions: [application name]
entry = string                          keyname=string
or
entry = integer
```

The CWinApp member functions GetProfileString and GetProfileInt will look for the INI files in the Windows subdirectory. If you place them in a different subdirectory from this default location, you can use the Windows API functions **::GetPrivateProfileString** and ::GetPrivateProfileInt to retrieve the settings. These SDK and MFC functions allow you to request information and update the information contained in the INI files.

You can also explicitly set your application's INI filename. The CWinApp data member *m_pszProfileName* contains the name of the application's INI file. To rename the INI file in your application's InitInstance, use this prototype:

```
m_pszProfileName = "C:\\myapp\\data";
```

If user preferences affect more than one program, you should consider writing that information to the WIN.INI file. Its default location is also the Windows subdirectory, but the Windows API functions **::GetProfileString** and **::GetProfileInt** will allow you to specify the file's full path in any event.

CWINAPP AND WINDOWS SDK INI FILE PROCESSING FUNCTIONS

The CWinApp member function WriteProfileInt allows you to write integers to the INI file. Unfortunately, the Windows API has no corresponding function, so you must use the SDK **::WriteProfileString** and **::WritePrivateProfileString** functions to write the integer as a string (e.g., "100").

If the requested information, whether a string value or a numeric value, is not in the INI file, then the SDK and MFC functions allow you to specify default values that are returned. You can test and use these default values rather than causing the program to become unstable, or worse, crash. The framework and API allows you to write entries into the INI files, and if the file, section, or entry does not exist, the functions will create them for you.

```
// Handle ini files
void COurApp::IniExamp()
{
// the default section in our INI file
// [defaults]
// defdir = c:\project\files
// defint = 23

CString FileDir COurApp::GetProfileString("defaults","defdir",NULL);
if ( FileDir.Empty() )
{
 AfxMessageBox("entry defdir not found");
}

// Provide a default.
CString FileDir = COurApp::GetProfileString("defaults","defdir","C:\DOS");
//Set the defdir directory.
BOOL bResult = COurApp::WriteProfileString("defaults","defdir","d:\newdir");

// Get the default integer.
UINT uInt = COurApp::GetProfileInt("DEFAULTS","defint",-1);
char temp[32];
sprintf(temp,"Default int is %d",uInt);
AfxMessageBox(temp);

// Set the default integer.
bResult = COurApp::WriteProfileInt("Defaults","defint",4);

// Let's internationalize our application and retrieve the thousands
// separator from the WIN.INI file. It is in the [intl] section with
// the entry sThousands=, (for English separator).

bResult = ::GetProfileString("intl","sThousands",",",temp, sizeof (temp) );

}
```

Changing the WIN.INI File

When the user or another program changes the WIN.INI file, your application will receive a message to that effect. If your application changes the WIN.INI file, then you should send a message to all top-level windows. The message indicates that applications should check the relevant sections of the WIN.INI file (supplied in the *lParam* parameter) to see whether they need to reinitialize themselves. To receive this message, invoke ClassWizard for your mainframe object and add a function to respond to the WM_WININICHANGE message, as shown in Figure 11.2.

You will receive a message, in the form of a string naming the section to check in the WIN.INI file, for which you may write an appropriate message handler. The resulting code would look like this:

```
void CMainFrame::OnWinIniChange(LPCSTR lpszSection)
{
    // Call base class first.
```

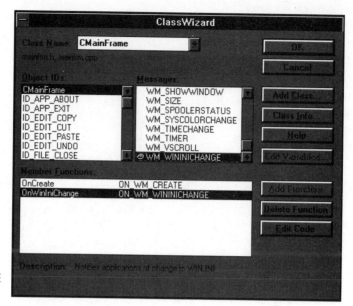

Figure 11.2
Adding the
WM_WININICHANGE
message handler.

```
CMDIFrameWnd::OnWinIniChange(lpszSection);

// TODO: Add your message handler code here.

}
```

If *lpszSection* equals NULL, you must check each section of the WIN.INI file on which your program depends. If your application changes the WIN.INI file, send the following message:

```
char lpszSection[16] = "intl"; // not "[intl]" - Do not add the "[" or "]"
to the string.
::SendMessage( HWND_BROADCAST, WM_WININICHANGE,0, lpszSection);
```

Do not add the the brackets around your search string; otherwise the function will assume you're looking for the following section: "[[intl]]."

CHAPTER SUMMARY

Whereas previous chapters showed you the file archiving capabilities of the framework's CDocument class, this chapter has shown you how to manipulate files outside that paradigm using the file manipulation classes provided with MFC 2.0. With this information you can read and write large blocks of data exceeding 64K bytes. You have also learned how to query and modify your application's INI files, detect and respond to a change in the WIN.INI file, and alert other Windows programs when you change the WIN.INI file. This information allows you to coexist and dynamically respond to the ever-present changes in the Windows environment.

CHAPTER 12

Serial Port
Programming

The bad news about serial port programming is that the amount of material on this subject in the documentation accompanying Visual C++ is pretty sparse. The good news is that serial port programming is not difficult if you understand a few fundamentals and stick to the straight and narrow when processing Windows messages. In this chapter we restrict our discussion to Windows 3.1 unless otherwise noted because this version has a really handy feature that we'll get to shortly.

Before we get started, note that this chapter will not cover the details of the basic operation of the serial port and general communications. Plenty of other books are available in the market for you to consult if you feel deficient in this subject matter. Don't expect more than a cursory overview of the most salient points of serial port communications under Windows; you won't find any long-winded explanations of concepts like DTE, DSR, handshaking, etc. This book deals with writing software that exploits these techniques, not explaining them.

WINDOWS AND SERIAL COMMUNICATIONS

Serial port programming is somewhat more complicated under Windows than in good old vanilla DOS. What makes it so is the fact that Windows uses messages that cause control to branch to different portions of the code segment, which may or may not be related to interacting with the serial port. Two simple examples are the user's movement of the mouse and the resizing of the active window. Clearly, Windows must respond to these sorts of user requests as soon as possible—forgetting all about anything coming into or going out of the serial port. In a DOS program, you would probably call a function that writes something out through the serial port, and when you were satisfied that everything was copacetic, your program would continue to its next logical operation. Under Windows, the order of the universe changes, and one must be capable of operating more or less asynchronously. Happily, Visual C++ accommodates asynchronous operations in an easy fashion and extends the utilitarian aspect of your user interface. For example, if you are writing a terminal emulator or similar tool, you can make your screen scrollable along both the x and y axis by deriving your view from class CScrollView, which includes these features automatically. You can simply write all terminal I/O to your document and attach a scrollable view. This is just one of the many extensions that Visual C++ and the Foundation Classes provide for your exploitation.

The fundamental issues to address in programming for the serial port follow these basic steps:

1. Select, configure, and open a port. The IBM PC has four ports, COM1 through COM4, capable of baud rates up to 256,000, 8 data bits, etc. For serious programming you'll probably want to create a class with member variables that reflect the preferred configuration. You'll also write member functions that allow you to set and edit the communication parameters, such as CMyConfig::SetPort*(int nPortnum),* CMyConfig::SetBaud*(int nBaudrate),* and *int* CMyConfig::GetPort( ). Likewise, you'll probably want to set up a dialog box that groups the options together using radio buttons and allow users to specify what settings they want, etc. The terminal program that comes with Windows has such a settings screen; take a look at it to give you some ideas.

2. Trap all user keystrokes, and redirect them to a routine that sends them out the chosen port. In this step, note that you will not display the keystrokes on the screen. This operation is the responsibility of your "readcomm( )" function, which allows your server or host to echo the keystrokes back. Thus you don't have to worry about things like typing passwords, etc.; the host will (or will not) echo back the appropriate responses, depending on the user's input.

3. Close the port and perform general housekeeping chores at the end of the communication session.

OPENING A SERIAL PORT

The first topic we'll discuss here is how to open and initialize a serial port. To open a serial port, call the API function:

```
int port_id = OpenComm(LPCSTR lpDevice, UINT nsizeInqueue,
    UINT nsizeOutqueue);
```

This function automatically allocates the memory for the serial port's receive and transmit queues. It returns a negative number if an error occurs. Otherwise, the return value is the numerical value of the selected port. Be aware that a return value of zero (0) is valid, so watch how you trap error conditions and how you use this value.

The argument *lpDevice* is a string specifying the COM port; hence it will be "COM1," "COM2," "COM3," or "COM4." The other two arguments should be the same value, unless you have some unusual reason for wanting to have different queue sizes. We suggest you align these on byte boundaries for the sake of efficiency (e.g.,

128 and 128, 1024 and 1024, etc.). Here is a sample call to OpenComm( ) specifying COM1 and transmit and receive queues of 512 bytes each:

```
int port_id = -1;       // initialize to a "bad" value

if( (port_id = OpenComm("COM1", 512, 512) ) < 0)
    CallSomeErrorFunction(); // error trap if open failed...
```

BUILDING THE DCB

After you've successfully opened the serial port, the next step is to initialize it. Initialization includes setting the preferred baud rate, parity, etc. These values must be installed in a device control block (DCB) structure, defined in *WINDOWS.H*. Two API calls are used for manipulating the DCB: BuildCommDCB( ) and SetCommState( ). You must call them in this order, because BuildCommDCB( ) does not really do anything to the serial port; it just fills in the DCB. It's the job of SetCommState( ) to do the actual modification to the port. Here, in a nutshell, is how you would use these functions after successfully opening a serial port:

```
DCB dcb;            // declare a device control block (windows.h)
COMSTAT ComStat; // declare communications status structure (windows.h)
int err= 0;         // declare an error condition variable
int port_id = -1; // declare & initialize a port identifier

// open the port
if( (port_id = OpenComm("COM1", 512, 512) ) < 0)
    CallSomeErrorFunction();// error trap if open failed...

//
// Fill in parts of the DCB we're interested in...
// We want COM1 at 9600 baud, no parity, 8 data bits, and 1 stop bit.
// In reality, you would probably not hard-code the first argument to
// BuildCommDCB, but instead build a string based on settings
// supplied from the user (via the dialog box mentioned earlier) or WIN.INI
//
int comm_err= BuildCommDCB("COM1:9600,n,8,1", &dcb );
if(comm_err < 0)
{
    CallSomeErrorFunction();// your routine to handle an error
    return 0;               // report error to calling function
}
dcb.fOutX = 1; // set XON/XOFF control
dcb.fInX = 1;
dcb.fNull = 1; // discard null chars

if( SetCommState( &dcb ) < 0)
{
    comm_err= GetCommError(port_id, &ComStat);
    CallSomeErrorFunction(); // your routine to handle an error
}
```

If everything went OK, you are now ready to read and write data using the serial port. This snippet of code also demonstrates a very useful API call, GetCommError( ), which returns the most recent error value (0 if no errors exist).

POLLING VS. INTERRUPTS

The two basic techniques used in serial port communications on the PC are: polling and interrupt-driven checks. In polling, your program will routinely "ask" the serial port if it has received any characters. In interrupt-driven systems, Windows will "tell" you that it has received something through the port. This approach is generally more efficient, since Windows usually has a lot of messages to dispatch and respond to. With an interrupt-driven mechanism, the CPU spends more of its time processing messages than checking the port, which may or may not have anything to report. While both techniques have their place, our emphasis will be on the interrupt-driven paradigm. To those programmers who, for one reason or another, wish to use the polling technique, we suggest that you check the port in a function that responds to the Windows message WM_ENTERIDLE (use ClassWizard and Add Function, etc.). This is a message that Windows uses when no other messages are outstanding—hence, it affords you an ideal time to query the port without worrying about being preempted by a message of higher priority.

For the interrupt method, which, incidentally, is only valid for users of Windows version 3.1, you will trap the message WM_COMMNOTIFY. For some inexplicable reason, perhaps related to the advent of Windows NT, this message will not be supported in future releases of Windows. To use the interrupt method, you must write a function to process WM_COMMNOTIFY messages. In the message map generated by ClassWizard, add an "ON_MESSAGE" clause as in the following example:

```
BEGIN_MESSAGE_MAP(CCommView, CView)
  //{{AFX_MSG_MAP(CCommView)
  ON_WM_CHAR()
  ON_WM_CREATE()
  ON_WM_SIZE()
  ON_WM_SHOWWINDOW()
  //}}AFX_MSG_MAP
  ON_MESSAGE(WM_COMMNOTIFY,OnCommNotify)
END_MESSAGE_MAP()
```

Here, *OnCommNotify* is the name of the function called whenever a WM_COMM-NOTIFY message is generated. This example shows four other messages to respond to: WM_CHAR, WM_CREATE, WM_SIZE, and WM_SHOWWINDOW. These four messages were automatically added from inside ClassWizard. Your CCommView function must also be declared inside your class header file:

```
protected:
  //{{AFX_MSG(CCommView)
  afx_msg void OnChar(UINT nChar, UINT nRepCnt, UINT nFlags);
  afx_msg void OnSize(UINT nType, int cx, int cy);
  afx_msg void OnShowWindow(BOOL bShow, UINT nStatus);
  afx_msg LRESULT OnCommNotify(WPARAM wParam, LPARAM lParam);
  //}}AFX_MSG
  DECLARE_MESSAGE_MAP()
```

Again, this is a manual operation that you must perform—you won't find it inside ClassWizard. Now all that's left to do is to write the member function OnComm-Notify, which will probably look something like this:

```
LRESULT CCommView::OnCommNotify(WPARAM wParam, LPARAM lParam)
{
  WORD notify = 1;         // bit mask for getting type of notification
  int nReadChars; // number of chars received in serial port
  GetCommEventMask(port_id,EV_RXCHAR); //clear event (IMPORTANT !)

  notify = LOWORD(lParam);
  if(notify & CN_RECEIVE)// received characters, not a signal, etc.
  {
    GetCommError(port_id,&ComStat); // check for errors
    nReadChars = ReadComm(port_id,rec_bufr,ComStat.cbInQue);
    if(nReadChars < 0) // error reading from the serial port
    {
     MessageBeep(0);    // alert the user
     comm_err= GetCommError(port_id, &ComStat);
     ); // error reporting function
     return 0;
    }
    rec_bufr[nReadChars]= '\0';// add a NULL terminator
    for(int i; i < nReadChars; i++)
     DisplayChar(rec_bufr[i]);// function that handles
                     // display to screen
  } // end cn_receive
  //
  //Other cases could be checked here, as determined by what was
  //specified in a previous call to SetCommEventMask().
  //
  return 1;
}
```

Because this example was taken out of context, you don't see the declaration of the variables *port_id* or *comm_err*, etc. These were defined elsewhere and declared extern, so that they could be used globally. Also, be aware that it is up to you to write your own error processing routine, such as ReportCommErr( ), to process errors and a routine such as DisplayChar( ) in the preceding example to manage the display of the characters read. The main idea here is to get a feel for the overall structure of the process of using WM_COMMNOTIFY to receive messages. You intercept the message, check to see if it's something you're interested in, and if so, read the port and display the characters (if that's what you want). WM_COMMNOTIFY is closely related to another WINAPI function, SetCommEventMask( ). This function tells Windows what events you wish to trap; you should use it after opening the port and before you call EnableCommNotification( ), which activates the trapping of WM_COMMNOTIFY. You can trap 14 events, defined in the header file *WINDOWS.H;* to trap a combination of events, OR them together in the call to SetCommEventMask( ). In the next example, we wish to be notified when a character is received in the serial port's input queue or a BREAK condition has occurred:

```
SetCommEventMask(port_id, EV_RXCHAR | EV_BREAK);
if( !EnableCommNotification(port_id,m_hWnd,128,128))
{
  int comm_err= GetCommError(port_id, &ComStat);
  ReportCommErr(comm_err); // report the error to the user
}
```

One thing you need to watch out for—every condition specified in SetCommEvent-Mask( ) *must* be cleared by a matching call to GetCommEventMask( ) in the function that you write to respond to WM_COMMNOTIFY. In our previous example, you will see a call to GetCommEventMask( ) at the start of the function. We placed the call here to make sure that GetCommEventMask( ) actually gets called. If we place the call at the end, GetCommEventMask( ) might not be called in certain cases (e.g., should an error occur while reading the port). Failing to clear the event word in this way will cause your program to respond to a WM_COMMNOTIFY message just once (the first time the message is generated), leaving you to wonder why your program stops working after the first WM_COMMNOTIFY message. The debugger won't help you with this one!

WRITING TO THE SERIAL PORT

Writing to the serial port is fairly simple, too. The only tricky part is managing any screen activity. For example, if you are writing a terminal emulator, you will want the user's keystrokes to be echoed back on the screen. In our earlier discussion of responding to Windows messages, that is why WM_CHAR was included and why ClassWizard built the statement

```
afx_msg void OnChar(UINT nChar, UINT nRepCnt, UINT nFlags);
```

in the message map. To write to the serial port as a terminal emulator, just trap the user's keystrokes with the WM_CHAR message and write them to the serial port instead of to DisplayChar( ) or your screen management function.

If you do this, your host (or whatever device you are communicating with) will echo back what it receives. Your function for receiving characters will catch them and be responsible for displaying them on the screen. This facility comes in handy for things like remote logons, where users must enter a password. The host takes care of echoing user input and will not echo back whatever password the user types. This relieves you of the burden of recognizing passwords, etc.

To write to the serial port, use the API call WriteComm( ), prototyped as follows:

```
WriteComm(int port_id, const void FAR * lpOutBuffer, int nSizeBuffer);
```

The arguments that appear in the prototype are:

port_id	The numerical value of the open port (e.g., 0 = COM1, etc.)
lpOutBuffer	A buffer containing the string or character to write
nSizeBuffer	The size of the output buffer, or 1 if it contains just a single character

WriteComm( ) returns 0 if the write was successful; otherwise, it returns a value less than 0. The absolute value of this negative number is a count of the actual number of bytes that did get written. You can use this as an index into *lpOutBuffer* to resend the remaining characters. You must, of course, call GetCommError( ) to determine the cause of the problem and correct it. A likely culprit is something in the handshake or the expiration of a time slice. Bear in mind that WriteComm( ) doesn't really write to the serial port—it writes to the Windows device driver, COMM.DRV, which is the final arbitrator when it comes to sending and receiving characters. You should plan to make considerable use of GetCommError( ), for a variety of reasons. Least among these is the fact that COMM.DRV is known to have bugs. If you experience inexplicable problems, you may rightly suspect that you have encountered one of these bugs. The following example demonstrates how you might respond to the WM_CHAR message (i.e., a keystroke) to send the keystroke out through the serial port. Not all of the variables (e.g., the port identifier, etc.) in this example are defined, since they are assumed to have been defined globally.

```
void CYourView::OnChar(UINT nChar, UINT nRepCnt, UINT nFlags)
{
  // sends a character out the serial port
  int nCharsWrote;

  if((nCharsWrote= WriteComm(nComID,(char)nChar,1)) < 0)
  {
      comm_err= GetCommError(nComID, &ComStat);
      ReportCommErr(comm_err);// show user error, etc.
      return;
  }
  CPoint cur_pos;          // variable for caret position
  cur_pos = GetCaretPos();// get caret position

  caret_location.x = cur_pos.x+nCharsWrote+1;
  caret_location.y = nCurrRow * nYChar;
  SetCaretPos(caret_location);// update caret position
}
```

This example also illustrates some additional programming concepts you need to address, such as tracking the location of the cursor.

READING FROM THE SERIAL PORT

Reading from the serial port is slightly more complicated than writing to it. This complexity is due in part to the type of reading used: polled or interrupt. Regardless of which technique you chose, you will use the API function ReadComm( ), which is prototyped as follows:

```
int ReadComm(int ComPort, void FAR *lpBuf, int nRead);
```

The parameters in the prototype are as follows:

ComPort	The identifier of the communications port (0 = COM1, 1= COM2, etc.)
lpBuf	A pointer to a buffer that stores the characters read
nRead	The number of bytes to be read

The return value from this function is the actual number of bytes read; a value less than zero indicates an error. When reading from the serial port and sending the characters to the video screen, it is best to process each character in *lpBuf* separately. This approach will allow you to manage the screen in a more elegant fashion—you can determine the number of rows and columns available (from TEXTMETRIC) and wrap the text accordingly. For example, if the window you are using is only 40 characters wide and you have just read in 50 characters, you would want to put 40 on one line and 10 on the next. Also, you can more easily coordinate the location of the cursor with the characters being displayed when the characters are processed one at a time, as demonstrated in the previous section. As part of this screen management process, you can use ClassWizard to trap the **WM_SIZE** message. This message allows you to detect any changes made to the size of the output window and adjust your display function accordingly. Here is an example of a message handler that recalculates the number of rows and columns available:

```
void CYourView::OnSize(UINT nType, int cx, int cy)
{
  CView::OnSize(nType, cx, cy);

  // TODO: Add your message handler code here
  TEXTMETRIC tm;
  CClientDC dc(this);    // get Device Context of window
  dc.GetTextMetrics(&tm);// get font size, etc.
  //
  int nRows, nCols;      // make these global
  int nXChar, nYChar;    // font size variables
  nXChar = tm.tmAveCharWidth;// average character width of font
  nYChar = tm.tmHeight + tm.tmExternalLeading; // height of font
  GetClientRect(&rClient); // get size of client area
  nRows = ((rClient.bottom - rClient.top)+1)/nYChar;
  nCols = ((rClient.right - rClient.left)+1)/nXChar;
}
```

As suggested by the comments in this function, you should make some of these variables global so that you don't have to recalculate them every time the user resizes the window. By doing so, you can shrink this function down to just the following statements:

```
void CYourView::OnSize(UINT nType, int cx, int cy)
{
  CView::OnSize(nType, cx, cy);

  // TODO: Add your message handler code here
  //
  GetClientRect(&rClient); // get size of client area
  nRows = ((rClient.bottom - rClient.top)+1)/nYChar;
  nCols = ((rClient.right - rClient.left)+1)/nXChar;
}
```

SPECIAL COMMANDS

A cousin to WriteComm( ) is a function called EscapeCommFunction( ). This API call returns a long, and takes two integers as arguments. The prototype is:

```
long EscapeCommFunction(int port_id, int nFunction)
```

The first argument is the ID of the COM port used, and the second is a flag, or code, that tells the communications device to perform a specific operation. Possible values for this flag are:

CLRDTR	Lowers the DTR signal
CLRRTS	Lowers the RTS signal
SETDTR	Asserts the DTR line
SETRTS	Asserts the RTS line
SETXON	Imitates reception of an XON character
SETXOFF	Imitates reception of an XOFF character
GETMAXLPT	Gets the maximum LPT port identifier
GETMAXCOM	Gets the maximum COM port identifier
RESETDEV	Resets printer if *port_id* indicates an LPT device. It has no effect if it is a COM port (so don't try to reset a modem with this call; use WriteComm( ) instead).

EscapeCommFunction( ) is nice for those times when you want to "force" something to happen. For example, your application may have some reason to interrupt the reception of a file (i.e., using ReadComm( )). In this case, you would want to lower the DTR line and assert the RTS signal, so that you could switch from a receive mode to a transmit mode. A case such as this might also require another API call, FlushComm( ), to clear any characters in either the transmit or receive queue. The prototype for this function is:

```
int FlushComm( int port_id, int nQueue)
```

where *port_id* is the port and *nQueue* indicates which queue to flush. Use 0 for the transmit queue, 1 for the receive queue. This function returns an integer value as follows:

= 0	Indicates success
< 0	Means either *port_id* and/or *nQueue* was invalid
> 0	General error (Call GetCommError( ) to determine the cause.)

Another API call similar to EscapeCommFunction( ) that you can use to "force" or reorder the logical flow of serial port operations is:

```
int TransmitCommChar(int port_id, char cNextchar)
```

This function inserts the character *cNextchar* at the head of the transmit queue. A sample application of this function's usefulness is the case in which the user clicks a Cancel button while a file transfer is in progress between the PC and the host. Rather than make the user wait for the transmit queue to become empty, you could set *cNextchar* to your "end transmission" flag (e.g., ESCape or EOF) and call TransmitCommChar( ).

The receive queue equivalent of TransmitCommChar( ) is UngetCommChar( ). Whereas TransmitCommChar( ) adjusts the transmit queue, UngetCommChar( ) adjusts the receive queue. Its prototype is:

```
int UngetCommChar(int port_id, char cNextchar)
```

In the previous case discussed regarding detection of a Cancel during a file transfer, you could use TransmitCommChar( ) to tell the transmitter to abort the file transfer, and use UngetCommChar( ) to alert the receiver immediately. This approach would simplify the code required upon receipt of a WM_CANCELMODE message by allowing a single routine to handle the duties of ending the file transfer, regardless of whether a Cancel interrupted the transfer or the transfer was completed without interruption. In other words, you could simply set a flag and call UngetCommChar( ) in the event that the user chose to abort the file transfer by clicking a Cancel button. Your program would read the "end-of-file-transmission" character and branch to a housekeeping routine where it would check the flag: If the flag was set, your routine would know that it should not save the file, etc. Otherwise, it would know that the file transfer was completed normally and respond appropriately.

PROCESSING BREAKS

Two ancillary functions useful for synchronizing communications are SetCommBreak( ) and ClearCommBreak( ). Both return integers and take the communications port ID as their sole argument. Use SetCommBreak(int *port_id*) to suspend data transmission and to begin sending a break signal. ClearCommBreak(int *port_id*) does just the opposite—it resumes data transmission (if any characters are waiting in the transmit buffer) after a call to SetCommBreak( ). A return value less than 0 indicates an error. The following example illustrates the tandem use of these functions—transmission is halted for 5 seconds, and then restarted. This example uses a simple loop instead of SetTimer( ) and KillTimer( ) to establish the delay.

```
DWORD dwStart, dwEnd;     // variables for 5-second delay
dwStart = GetTickCount();// get the starting time...

                    . // suspend transmission, send BREAKs
SetCommBreak(port_id);    // assume port_id already open

while(1)                  // begin 5-second delay
{
  dwEnd = GetTickCount();// get end time
  if((dwEnd - dwStart) > 5000)// wait 5 seconds
    break;
}
ClearCommBreak(port_id); // clear the break, resume
                         // transmission
```

CLOSING THE SERIAL PORT

The final API call for Windows communications that we will cover here is CloseComm( ). The prototype of this function is:

```
int CloseComm(int port_id)
```

It is important that you call this function when your application finishes using the port. If the port is left open, other applications cannot use it. Calling FlushComm( ) just prior to calling CloseComm( ) is probably a good idea because the communications driver COMM.DRV will wait for as long as 30 seconds if there is data in the transmit queue and transmission has been halted by a BREAK or by flow control (e.g., XOFF, etc.). A return value of zero indicates that CloseComm( ) has successfully closed the port; a negative value means an error has occurred. In this case, you should call GetCommError( ) and try to resolve the problem so that you can close the port gracefully.

MODIFYING SYSTEM.INI

Before we close the subject of serial port communications, a few points need to be made about the SYSTEM.INI file. You can make some minor adjustments to settings in this file to improve the performance and reliability of your COM port. The first of these is an entry called COMBoostTime, which has a default value of 2. This value represents the number of milliseconds allowed to process a communications interrupt. If your program seems to be losing characters, you might try increasing this value in small increments. Another setting that may improve performance is the COMdrv30 parameter, which is set equal to a Boolean value of On or Off. If this parameter is set to On, it means the Virtual COM Driver (VCD) is using its copy of COMM.DRV's interrupt handler. For Windows 3.0 platforms, you should definitely set this value to On. If you are using Windows 3.1, set this value to Off (which is the default). The last entry to consider is COMxBuffer, where x is 1, 2, 3, or 4. This entry is set to a number indicating the number of characters that will be buffered by the device driver. This value is different from the size of the transmit and receive buffers discussed earlier; they are not related. Recall that you don't really read or write to the serial port—you read or write to the device driver. The driver will buffer characters for you, so that you may read or write to and from this buffer. The value given for COMxBuffer determines the size of this driver buffer (the default is 128). While buffering may slow down communications with a port, it may be required if your program seems to be losing characters when operating at high baud rates. There is only one complicating factor—COMxBuffer relies on another entry in SYS-TEM.INI, a parameter called COMxProtocol. Here again, the value of x indicates which port (1–4) you are using. This entry must either be left blank or given the value XOFF. If your application does text transfers only and you are losing characters at high baud rates, set the value of x in COMxProtocol to XOFF. If you are doing binary data transfers, leave this value blank.

CHAPTER SUMMARY

Serial communications under Windows is tedious and full of perils. There are a lot of areas of programming involved where you can fall through the cracks, so to speak. The Visual C++ documentation virtually ignores the subject, perhaps for good reason. We hope that this chapter has given you some insights into the problems you can expect. One of your main concerns must be synchronizing the video display with the keystrokes pressed by the user. Trapping the WM_CHAR message is the procedure you must use to do so, and it works fine as long as the computer on the other end supports echoing.

A final comment: Bear in mind that you cannot predict when data will arrive at the serial port, nor can you be sure how much data will arrive. Also be sure to take into account the fact that Windows cannot be expected to spend all of its time catering to your needs vis-à-vis managing the serial port. These two problems succinctly summarize the programmer's main concerns with regard to serial port communications.

CHAPTER 13

Drawing Graphics and Text

One of our design goals for this book was to present material in what we considered a logical order for understanding the fundamentals of using Visual C++ for Windows development. Thus far, we've covered a lot of ground and are now ready to take a look at one of the most important and possibly self-complicated issues surrounding Windows programming. The issue of screen I/O can admittedly be somewhat difficult, especially to novice Windows programmers. For starters, the *type* of object being drawn (text or a graphical image) has a lot to do with managing your screen output. Background colors and modes (e.g., TRANSPARENT or OPAQUE), font sizes and characteristics, and so on—in short, the *device context,* which experienced Windows programmers recognize as the oft-used "hDC" data type—all must be taken into consideration when drawing on the screen. For those readers familiar with classical Windows programming, the functionality of an "old-fashioned handle to a device context" remains in the MFC as class CDC. The member functions of this class go a long way toward making the screen I/O operations as painless as possible. One thing that makes screen processing somewhat tedious is the fact that you, the programmer, must ensure that the screen remains in an updated state. For instance, if you are allowing the user to scroll the screen's contents, you have to keep track of both the current screen and the previous one, in case the user wishes to scroll the latter back into view. The performance characteristics of saving each screen as a bitmap are simply unacceptable—you must develop algorithms for "painting" the screen in the most efficient manner possible. Usually, this is not too difficult, regardless of whether the screen contents consist of text, graphics, or both.

GRAPHICS AND THE CDC CLASS

The Microsoft Foundation Classes version 2.0 provides a class for working with a device context such as the display screen or printer. Our discussion will focus primarily on the display screen. The CDC class provides you with a rich set of functions for drawing both text and graphics and includes many tools for working with objects derived from other classes but related to output (e.g., font selection, colors and palettes, etc.). Furthermore, this class makes it a lot easier to work with device contexts, at least when compared to, for example, the SDK and other platforms that are not based on object-oriented languages.

The Device Context

Before we get into the nitty-gritty of drawing on the screen, a quick review of some Windows fundamentals is in order. As Windows evolved, it became clear that hardware capabilities would continue to change, fulfilling the prophecy that hardware changes faster than software. To cope with these changes in a manner that would allow Windows-based programs to run on many different hardware configurations—EGA, VGA, SVGA, etc.—the Windows developers hit upon the idea of separating the hardware from the software via an interface layer. This interface layer is the device context, or DC, a structure maintained by Windows that contains all the information it needs to process output (e.g., number of pixels, colors, etc.). When you draw something on the screen—or the printer, for that matter—you are really drawing on the DC. Windows then sends the information to the screen for you. Windows programmers who grew up on the SDK will be relieved to know that it is generally no longer necessary to call GetDC( ) and ReleaseDC( ) because the Microsoft Foundation Classes take care of all this for you—thanks in no small part to ClassWizard. The programmer may instead concentrate strictly on application-specific tasks such as what to draw and where. However, there are many occasions when it is necessary to have a handle to the device context, especially if you wish to use SDK functions. The next section demonstrates handles and the device context.

Getting a Handle

To retrieve a handle to the current device context, use the CDC member function

```
GetSafeHdc( );
```

This function returns *m_hDC* (of type HDC), the output device context. When you are working with the CDC class, this will generally be your first stop, so that you'll have the handle for use with other functions. To use this function, instantiate an object of class CDC, declare a variable of type HDC, and call GetSafeHdc( ), as in this example:

```
HDC hDC;     // declare HDC variable
CDC cDC;     // instantiate class CDC
hDC = cDC.GetSafeHdc();  // get handle to device context
```

For those readers who are making the gradual transition to C++ and wish to use the Windows API calls, this handle is compatible with those functions.

The MoveTo( ) Function

An important CDC class member function is the MoveTo( ) function. If you think of drawing on the device context (e.g., the screen) as using an electronic sheet of paper, the MoveTo( ) function lets you move your pen to any place you desire. This function is prototyped as follows:

```
CPOINT MoveTo(POINT pt);
```

Alternatively, you may specify an "x, y" argument in logical coordinates. The return value is the previous value of the "cursor," so to speak. This function is quite useful for drawing lines, painting pixels, etc. For example, if you wish to write your own "DrawRectangle" function, use MoveTo( ) to establish a starting point for your drawing operation.

Painting Pixels

One of the things you may need to do from time to time is to change the color of individual pixels. This would have practical applications in, say, a graphics program such as those supplied with Windows. You may use the CDC member function SetPixel( ) for just this purpose. This function is prototyped as follows:

```
COLORREF SetPixel(POINT pt, COLORREF crColor);
```

The first argument, which can actually be either of type POINT or CPOINT, specifies in logical coordinates the pixel that is to be painted. This point must be in the clipping region. The second argument is the color used in painting the pixel. Note that the return value is also of type COLORREF; this is the *actual* RGB value used in painting, and not necessarily the value supplied via the argument "crColor." This discrepancy is due to the fact that not all devices are capable of faithfully rendering the actual color value. Often, an approximation of the color is necessary. Now for some sample code demonstrating how to use SetPixel( ). The following few lines of code paint the pixel at logical coordinates (50, 100) using the color red:

```
POINT pt;        // variable of type POINT
pt.x = 50;              // assign coordinates
pt.y= 100;
CClientDC dc(this);     // get the client area dc
dc.SetPixel(pt.x, pt.y, RGB(255,0,0));// paint the pixel
```

There is also a CDC member function that returns the RGB value most closely matching a given color. This function, GetNearestColor( ), is prototyped as follows:

```
COLORREF GetNearestColor(COLORREF rgbColor);
```

This function comes in handy if the user may specify red, green, and blue numerical values, because it allows you to convert their input to a close approximation. A sister function to SetPixel( ) is GetPixel( ), which returns the RGB color value of a pixel at a specified point. The prototype for GetPixel( ) is:

```
COLORREF GetPixel(POINT pt);
```

As with SetPixel( ), the argument *pt* can be either a POINT or a CPOINT.

Drawing Lines

The CDC function LineTo(POINT p) draws lines, for example, to emphasize the border around control groups. This function takes as a single argument a POINT data type, which is the end point of a line. The starting point is the current cursor position expressed in logical coordinates. A closely related function for drawing lines is MoveTo(POINT p). Lines are always drawn with the currently selected HPEN object. It may thus be necessary to create and select a new pen having the characteristics you require (e.g., color, line weight, and solid or broken line). The following example demonstrates in greater detail how to draw a line using many of the functions described here. First, create a message handler in ClassWizard for the View associated with your application. Visual C++ produces something like this:

```
void CYourView::OnDraw(CDC* pDC)
{
  CDocument* pDoc = GetDocument();
  // TODO: add draw code here
}
```

Your code for drawing goes in after the comment that ClassWizard provides to mark the location at which to insert new code. To draw a line halfway across the screen, regardless of the current size of the window, add the following code to the OnDraw( ) function:

```
RECT rClient;            // size of client area window
GetClientRect(&rClient);// get size of window "now"
hDC.MoveTo(0,20);        // move pen to position over 0, down 20
hDC.LineTo(rClient.right/2,20);// draw half-line
```

To change the visual characteristics of the line, either select a different Windows pen or create your own. Regardless, you simply need to add a call to the appropriate SelectObject function to select a different pen. Create and delete new pens once and only once to avoid decreasing memory availability. The ideal choice is to create pens and other objects in your class constructor and to delete them in its destructor.

Rectangles

Sizing and drawing rectangles is fairly easy in Visual C++. The class CRect provides a wide range of member functions that allow you to use rectangles efficiently. Class CDC also has rectangle functions such as FillRect(LPCRECT lpRectangle, CBrush* pBrush). Any brush you create is ultimately cached. It may therefore be better simply to create and delete the brush only when needed, rather than to use the class constructor and destructor. Since Windows caches objects, you could end up with a brush occupying the space of some other, more valuable resource.

Drawing a Rectangle

To draw a rectangle, use the CDC member function Rectangle( ), which is prototyped as follows:

```
BOOL Rectangle(LPCRECT lpRect);
```

This function returns a nonzero value upon success or zero upon failure. You may also pass the coordinates of the upper left and bottom right corners of the rectangle instead of *lpRect*. These coordinates are given in logical units, and the function is prototyped as follows:

```
BOOL Rectangle(int x1, int y1, int x2, int y2);
```

Rectangle drawing uses the default pen, filled with the current color, and the brush. The rectangle is always drawn such that the width and height are 1 pixel less than the actual coordinates. In other words, if the opposing vertices of the rectangle are (x1,y1) and (x2,y2), then the width is actually x2 − x1, and not (x2 − x1) + 1, which is how you would normally calculate the width (the height is y2 − y1). This means the width and height of a rectangle drawn using this function must be greater than 2 logical units (the maximum size is 32,767).

Drawing a Circle

Drawing a circle is virtually identical to drawing a rectangle. Circles are drawn by describing them by a bounding rectangle. There is no Circle( ) function per se, but there is an Ellipse( ) function. Since a circle is nothing more than a special type of ellipse, this function serves for drawing both circles and ellipses. The function is prototyped as follows:

```
BOOL Ellipse(LPCRECT lpRect);
BOOL Ellipse(int x1, int y1, int x2, int y2);
```

All the rules, return values, etc., used with CDC::Rectangle( ) apply to CDC::Ellipse( ), so refer to the preceding section for more information.

Drawing with Pens

The MFC framework uses the class CPen to encapsulate a pen. A pen is very similar in concept and operation to a brush. For drawing graphical objects, you may wish to change the default appearance (e.g., size, color, style) of a line, rectangle, or some other form. To accomplish this, you'll need to create a pen that has the properties you wish to use. The Microsoft Foundation Class Library supports two techniques—a single-stage constructor and a two-stage constructor. The single-stage technique creates the pen and allocates memory for it in one statement, while the two-stage method constructs the pen first and initializes it in a separate function. The two-stage technique is generally the safer of the two methods, but there are still trade-offs to consider. The single-stage construction offers the advantage of requiring only one line of code; on the downside, the constructor may throw an exception if you don't specify the arguments correctly, or if the memory allocation fails for whatever reason. The two-stage technique has the advantage in that it will not throw an exception, but you must first create the pen in one function (say, the class constructor) and then initialize it in another. Regardless of which technique you use to create a pen, the method for destroying one is the same. Also, all pens share three common properties: style, size, and color. The CPen( ) function for creating a pen is prototyped as follows:

```
CPen(int nStyle, int nSize, COLORREF crColor);
```

The documentation fully describes the styles, and examples include PS_SOLID, PS_DASH, etc. Here is an example using the single-stage technique to create a solid red pen that is 3 pixels wide:

```
CPen myPen( PS_SOLID,3,RGB( 255, 0, 0 ));
```

When the object myPen goes out of scope, its destructor is automatically called. If you used the *new* operator to allocate memory for it, be sure to call *delete* when you exit the class. To create an identical pen using the two-stage technique, follow this example:

```
CPen myPen;                 // instantiate object of type CPen
myPen.CreatePen( PS_SOLID,3, RGB(255, 0, 0 ));
```

This code constructs and initializes the pen. In order to use the pen or any other graphical object you must select it. The following example demonstrates how to select an object. This example is taken out of context (i.e., this belongs in a message handler for WM_PAINT, etc.):

```
CClientDC hDC(this);      // get handle to DC
CPen myPen( PS_SOLID, 3, RGB(255,0,0) );// create red pen
//
// select it into the device context while saving current pen
//
CPen* pOldPen = hDC.SelectObject( &myPen );

// draw a line with the new, red pen
hDC.MoveTo(...);          // go to a starting position
hDC.LineTo(...);          // draw a line...
//
// now restore old pen
hDC.SelectObject( pOldPen );
```

The WM_CTLCOLOR Message

If your application changes the background color—using SetDialogBkColor( ), for example—of a window or dialog box that has controls, you will need to add a message handler that responds to the WM_CTLCOLOR message. This added message takes care of drawing your controls. While this procedure may sound rather straightforward, the issue of color complicates matters. For example, suppose that your default background color is white and you draw a dialog box and set its background color to gray. When you add controls (or static text) to the dialog box, they will appear on a white background, not a gray one. In order to draw the controls on a gray background, you need a message handler for WM_CTLCOLOR that uses a gray brush when "painting" the controls. This gives rise to other issues: the creation, selection, and destruction of the brush. Remember, brushes take up memory (and a slot in the cache table), so you must make sure you create them only once and destroy them when they are no longer needed. You will find sample code demonstrating some of the principles of WM_CTLCOLOR in Chapter 9. Here is a brief overview of how WM_CTLCOLOR affects the various types of controls.

Edit Controls

For edit boxes, WM_CTLCOLOR paints the entire editing box. You will probably want to avoid using WM_CTLCOLOR to process edit controls for this reason.

Buttons and Check Boxes

The WM_CTLCOLOR message paints the area of the screen under the controls. Windows places the text and the shape of the control on top of this area.

List Boxes

The entire listing area is painted with the selected brush.

Group Boxes

The rectangular area behind the title of the group box is painted with the selected brush.

Scroll Bars

The area around the thumb track is painted using the selected brush.

A final word of caution about the WM_CTLCOLOR message when used with Windows 3.0: It is not sent to a combo box window. Thus you cannot draw a combo box with a different color using the procedure illustrated above. Developers striving for backward compatibility should consider other options when using combo boxes that require special drawing considerations.

DRAWING TEXT

In this section, we'll take a look at drawing text on the screen. Windows displays everything with the video configured for graphical output. While this is not a bad idea, it complicates matters for programmers because we are responsible for determining how text will appear to the user—for example, whether it appears proportional or scaled. Fortunately, Windows relieves us of much of this burden by providing data structures that we can use to help us manage our text drawing chores. One of the most important of these is the TEXTMETRIC structure, which maintains data about text characteristics. Since this structure is so important, we will begin with a quick review focusing on those members of immediate interest.

The TextMetric Structure

The TEXTMETRIC structure, defined in *WINDOWS.H*, contains the following members:

```
type def struct tagTEXTMETRIC
```

```
{
    int tmHeight;
    int tmAscent;
    int tmDescent;
    int tmInternalLeading;
    int tmExternalLeading;
    int tmAveCharWidth;
    int tmMaxCharWidth;
    int tmWeight;
    BYTE tmItalic;
    BYTE tmUnderlined;
    BYTE tmStruckOut;
    BYTE tmFirstChar;
    BYTE tmLastChar;
    BYTE tmDefaultChar;
    BYTE tmBreakChar;
    BYTE tmPitchAndFamily;
    BYTE tmCharSet;
    int tmOverhang;
    int tmDigitizedAspectX;
    int tmDigitizedAspectY;
} TEXTMETRIC;
```

This structure contains much of the information necessary for drawing the current font. Users who consult the *Microsoft Windows Software Development Kit: Programmer's Reference* should be warned of an error in Volume 3 on pp. 410–411 of SDK version 3.1 of the documentation regarding the *tmPitchAndFamily* member of TEXTMETRIC. The document states that setting this member to #define TMPF_PITCH displays the font with a fixed pitch. For starters, TMPF_PITCH is not defined in *windows.h;* the value defined is actually TMPF_FIXED_PITCH, and it produces variable rather than fixed pitch. Most of the significance of a member may generally be ascertained simply from its name. Our primary interest here, however, is in those members concerned with font sizes and spacing.

Getting the Text Characteristics

One of the first things you need to do when setting up your application to draw text is to find out what values are in the TEXTMETRIC structure. An ideal place to accomplish this is in an InitDialog function or even in the InitInstance( ) of your program. The following example illustrates a typical call to retrieve the TEXTMET-RIC information:

```
TEXTMETRIC tm;              // the TEXTMETRIC object
CClientDC dc(this);         // get a device context
dc.GetTextMetrics(&tm);     // read TEXTMETRIC's values
```

Now take a look at how you can do some simple math using ClassWizard to derive some useful information about the screen. For example, you might want to know how many "rows" and "columns" you can display based on how the user has sized the window. To determine this, first create a message handler for the WM_SIZE message in ClassWizard. For a fictitious class called "Demo," Visual C++ would create the following prototype:

```
void CDemoView::OnSize(UINT nType, int cx, int cy)
{
  CView::OnSize(nType, cx, cy);

  // TODO: Add your message handler code here
}
```

To this, add the following lines of code after the //TODO: comment, so that the complete function appears as follows:

```
void CDemoView::OnSize(UINT nType, int cx, int cy)
{
  CView::OnSize(nType, cx, cy);

  // TODO: Add your message handler code here
  //
  // *** NOTE— This example assumes TEXTMETRIC 'tm' is global
  // *** and has already been obtained.
  //
  RECT rClient;                        // a RECTangle object
  GetClientRect(&rClient);             // get size of client area "now"
  int nXChar = tm.tmAveCharWidth;      // get size of this font
  int nYChar = tm.tmHeight + tm.tmExternalLeading;
  //
  // Now determine number of columns & rows available in the
  // client are a based on current window size.
  int nRows = ((rClient.bottom - rClient.top)+1)/nYChar;
  int nCols = ((rClient.right - rClient.left)+1)/nXChar;
}
```

Another useful application of the TEXTMETRIC structure is to create a larger text insertion caret. The members *tm.tmAveCharWidth* and *tm.tmHeight* describe the average size of a character from the current font. These values can be passed to CWnd class function CreateSolidCaret( ), as in this example:

```
CreateSolidCaret(tm.tmAveCharWidth, tm.tmHeight);
```

This procedure is useful for creating a larger, more visible text insertion caret than the default "I"-shaped caret.

The ExtTextOut( ) Function

This function is underutilized by most Windows programmers. It is actually very easy to use and faster than its first cousin, TextOut( ). The ExtTextOut( ) function is prototyped as follows:

```
virtual BOOL ExtTextOut( int x, int y, UINT nOptions, LPCRECT lpRect,
LPCSTR lpszString, UINT nCount, LPINT lpDxWidths )
```

If your application will be doing a lot of text display, it will definitely pay you to use this function instead of TextOut( ). TextOut( ) is actually nothing more than a disguised call to ExtTextOut( ) in which the arguments nOptions, lpRect, and lpDxWidth are zero. So you can avoid the time delay incurred from translating TextOut( ) by calling ExtTextOut( ) directly.

The TextOut( ) Function

One of the easiest ways to display a string is to use the TextOut( ) function. This function takes four arguments and is prototyped as follows:

```
TextOut(int x, int y, LPCSTR lpString, int size)
```

The variables x and y are the logical coordinates of the location where *lpString* is to be displayed. The last argument is the number of characters in the string being displayed, *lpString*. Here is an example using TextOut( ):

```
CClientDC hDC(this);        // get handle to DC
hDC.SetBkMode(TRANSPARENT);// set background mode
hDC.SetTextColor(RGB(0,0,0));  // want black text
//
// hide the caret before drawing, then show it when done
//
HideCaret();
char msg[80];               // text buffer
strcpy(msg,"Hello world!");// our sample message
hDC.TextOut(0,0,msg,strlen(msg));// draw the message
ShowCaret();                // show the caret
```

Areas where this code will usually appear include the OnDraw( ) function of your view or in a response to a WM_PAINT message.

The GetTextExtent( ) Function

You can combine the TextOut( ) function with another CDC function, GetTextExtent( ), to create a tool for managing the screen when presenting large amounts of text to the user, as in a document-driven application. If all the text is in the same font size, this function will make it quite simple to track the cursor based on the size of the text. Also, as you'll see later in our example, you should always hide the caret *before* displaying text and show it after the display operation is completed. For times when you want to buffer text for the display—for instance, when scrolling without using class CScrollView—this function is essential for smooth spacing between lines and achieving satisfactory overall appearance of the string. Managing the caret is facilitated by creating a CPoint object in the declaration of your class and making it *public* (usually). For instance, as part of our example, we declare such an object in the header file of a hypothetical class:

```
public:
CPoint caret_location;    // instantiate object of type CPoint
```

Now, in our OnDraw( ) message handler, we could use TextOut( ) to display strings and our CPoint object to keep track of where to put the caret. By making the location of the caret a public data member of our class, we allow other classes that might need to track the caret to access it. This next example pulls together many of the functions and concepts we've covered so far:

```
void CYourView::OnDraw(CDC* pDC)
{
```

```
CDocument* pDoc = GetDocument();
// TODO: add draw code here
//
// NOTE: Putting GetTextMetrics() in OnDraw() not efficient;
//   shown here for illustration ONLY...
//
TEXTMETRIC tm;
CClientDC hDC(this);   // get device context for client area
hDC.GetTextMetrics(&tm);// read TEXTMETRIC's values
int nYChar = tm.tmHeight + tm.tmExternalLeading;

HideCaret();             // remove the cursor prior to drawing
hDC.SetBkMode(TRANSPARENT);// let background color shine in
caret_location.x = 0;  // initialize caret coordinates
caret_location.y = 0;
SetCaretPos(caret_location);// home the cursor
//
char video[80];        // text buffer
strcpy(video,"This is a test, line 1");// dummy text message
hDC.TextOut(0,nYChar,video,strlen(video)); // display dummy msg.
//
//now update the cursor's position
//
CSize len = hDC.GetTextExtent(video,strlen(video));
caret_location.x = len.cx;
caret_location.y = nYChar;
SetCaretPos(caret_location);// Move caret to new location.
ShowCaret();             // Now show the caret at new loc.
}
```

A couple of brief observations about this routine are in order, should you decide to use this technique. The call to TextOut( ) could be placed inside a loop tied to a scrollback buffer and/or to the number of visible lines available in the window based on the window's current size. Keep in mind that any resizing of a window erases its background, so storing the text as an array of pointers makes it easy for your program to draw and scroll the text inside the window. To further stimulate your thinking, try using TextOut( ) in connection with a message handler for WM_ONCHAR. However, don't be lulled into thinking these examples are a panacea, in terms of drawing text and graphics, for all your programs. The show-stopper is the *type* of data being displayed: It must be in the same font and size. Nevertheless, you should expect to find plenty of opportunities where the algorithm and code in these examples apply.

Text Colors

The CDC class has two functions that handle retrieving and setting both foreground and background text colors. To retrieve the current text (foreground) color, use the CDC class member function GetTextColor( ), which is prototyped as follows:

```
COLORREF GetTextColor();
```

This function returns the RGB value of the current text color. To set the text color, use the SetTextColor( ) function, prototyped as:

```
COLORREF SetTextColor(COLORREF crNewColor);
```

Background colors use the member functions GetBkColor( ) and SetBkColor( ). These functions are prototyped as follows:

```
COLORREF GetBkColor();
COLORREF SetBkColor(COLORREF crNewColor);
```

The return values for SetTextColor( ) and SetBkColor( ) are the *previous* color values. You should save these if you plan to restore them after drawing.

Printing a File

This is one of those subjects that doesn't seem to fit into any particular category, so we decided to cover it here, since printing is really nothing more than drawing on the printer's device context instead of the screen. Also, this is one of those topics that you always seem to need, but for which you can't find any sample code. Our discussion centers around those cases where you wish to bypass the CPrintDialog class functions, which use the standard Windows dialog box for printing. The technique we will demonstrate uses the API call SpoolFile( ), which places the file into the spooler queue. The downside to using this function is that the file is *deleted* after it is printed. If you use this technique and need to save the file, copy it to a temporary file with a unique name and print the temporary file. The SpoolFile( ) function is prototyped as follows:

```
HANDLE SpoolFile(lpszPrinter, lpszPort, lpszJobName, lpszFileName);
```

All the arguments are of type LPSTR; the following is an explanation of their purpose:

lpszPrinter	A null-terminated string of the printer name (e.g., "HP LaserJet IID").
lpszPort	The printer port (e.g., "LPT1:").
lpszJobName	A null-terminated string, not more than 32 characters long, that identifies the job. For example, "MyApp_Output".
lpszFile	The file to be printed, including device and directory, for example, "C:\\MSVC\\MYAPP\\foo.txt".

Note the use of the double slashes.

SpoolFile( ) returns a handle that is global in scope and gets passed to the spooler, if the call is successful. Otherwise, Spool File( ) returns one of the following error conditions:

SP_ERROR	General error.
SP_APPABORT	The job was canceled because the application's abort function returned zero.
SP_USERABORT	The user canceled the job through Print Manager.
SP_OUTOFDISK	Not enough disk space was available for spooling, and none will become available.
SP_OUTOFMEMORY	Not enough memory was available for spooling.

The following code demonstrates how to print a file called "TEMPFILE.TMP" using this technique. This is a bare-bones example with no error checking:

```
char szPrinter[64],*szDriver, *szDevice, *szPort;
//
//get information from user's INI file
//
::GetProfileString("Windows","device","",szPrinter,64);
szDevice = strtok(szPrinter,",");  // parse printer
szDriver = strtok(NULL,",");       // parse device driver
szPort = strtok(NULL,",");         // parse port

DOCINFO ReportDoc;                          // instantiate class DOCINFO
ReportDoc.lpszDocName = "TEMPFILE.TMP";
ReportDoc.cbSize = sizeof(ReportDoc);
ReportDoc.lpszOutput = NULL;
CDC cDC;                                     // instantiate class CDC
cDC.CreateDC(szDriver,szDevice,szPort,NULL);
cDC.StartDoc( &ReportDoc );          // start print sequence
::SpoolFile(szDevice,szPort,"MyApp_Output","TEMPFILE.TMP");
cDC.EndDoc();                         // end print sequence
```

As stated earlier, this function deletes the file after printing; any files you wish to print but *not* delete should be copied to a temporary file that gets submitted to the spooler. The C function *mktemp( )* creates a unique filename; the file can then be copied to this unique filename.

CHAPTER SUMMARY

The subject of drawing text and graphics is actually not that intimidating, and it is made even easier by the Microsoft Foundation Classes version 2.0. Close attention to detail must be paid, however, to ensure the proper operation of your program. You must make sure your application tracks the caret and keeps it visible when it is needed. Maintaining the screen will likely be your biggest headache, especially if your program supports scrolling. For things like pop-up dialog boxes, screen repainting of occluded areas is handled automatically by the Windows kernel. For text-intensive programs, you should make use of the ExtTextOut( ) function in order to maximize performance. Likewise, considerable use can be made of the TEXTMETRIC structure because of its flexibility. For example, you may keep it global in scope or encapsulate it in its own class, etc.

Fonts, Colors, and Icons

In this chapter, we'll explore some of the peripheral issues related to design features that can significantly add to or detract from the overall appeal of your program to the user. As this chapter's title clearly suggests, these features include the use of fonts and colors. We will also explore the subject of icons; you'll see how to create and install icons, effectively overriding the Visual C++ defaults. This discussion is not restricted merely to design issues; it also includes sample code to show you exactly how to implement these design features in your Visual C++ applications. The main topics covered are fonts, including a brief discussion of the various types available and the character sets used with Windows, and colors. In addition, this chapter also discusses icons.

CHARACTER SETS

Microsoft Windows supports and uses several character sets; foremost are the ANSI character set and the OEM set. The OEM set consists of all the characters that an IBM PC can recognize and display. Windows *must* use this set from time to time, most notably when performing file access in the File Manager. The ANSI set, used by Windows internally, is more diverse than the OEM set, allowing you to display text using the special diacritical marks found in foreign languages such as Spanish, French, and German. If your applications will be aimed at the international market, you'll need to know about character sets and fonts. Visual C++ includes two member functions for converting between the different character sets: OemToAnsi( ) and AnsiToOem( ), both of which are members of the class CString. Examples of their usage are given in the *Class Library Reference*.

FONTS

Fonts determine the appearance of text in your Windows program. You may use the fonts provided with Windows, those of a third-party vendor, or even fonts you create on your own. For the sake of efficiency, load only a minimum number of fonts from the WIN.INI file, as font loading is a fairly time-consuming operation. Fonts are indicated in the [fonts] section of the .INI file by name and extension, as in this example:

```
[fonts]
Arial (TrueType)=ARIAL.FOT
```

Raster Fonts

The first type of Windows font is the raster font. Raster fonts are simply bitmaps showing how to draw each character and are most widely used in output devices of a specific resolution, such as CRT screens. For this reason, they do not always produce the most pleasing results. Because bitmapped fonts are so easy to build, raster fonts are widely used (or at least presented) with many software packages. These fonts cannot be rotated but they may be scaled by even multiples of their supplied size. Raster fonts shipped with Windows include MS Serif, Courier, MS Sans Serif, System, and Terminal.

Windows version 3.1 introduced a new set of raster fonts called Small Fonts for use at resolutions of less than 8 points. While TrueType fonts (see below) can also support this small a size, the images they produce may not be suitable for some applications. Since images this small do not have much detail or "sharpness," it is better to use raster fonts than TrueType fonts in situations where clarity is a factor.

Vector Fonts

Vector fonts are a collection of Graphics Device Interface (GDI) calls. Since vector fonts must be calculated as a series of lines, they tend to be time-consuming to load but useful for devices where raster fonts cannot be used. Because vector fonts are represented as a series of lines, they are ideally suited for use with plotters but also tend to be the least visually appealing of all the font types. Vector fonts may be scaled to any size or aspect ratio. The Windows fonts Roman, Modern, and Script are classified as vector fonts. Although these fonts use the ANSI character set, they are marked by Windows as part of the OEM character set.

TrueType Fonts

TrueType fonts, which first appeared in Windows 3.1, are fonts that can be scaled to any size and look the same when printed as they do onscreen. Thus one advantage of using TrueType fonts is that your document will appear the same when printed on different printers from different machines as long as the same print resolution is used. In contrast with the other fonts it offers, Windows uses TrueType for both screen and printer display. Thus, "what you see *is* what you get" with TrueType. The TrueType fonts shipped with Windows include Arial, Courier New, Symbol, and Times New Roman. These fonts are identified by the "TT" logo beside their font name in the Fonts dialog box. TrueType fonts are stored as collections of points and *hints* that describe the general shape of each character. Hints are algorithms used to improve character display at certain resolutions. When an application requests a TrueType font, the TrueType rasterizer uses the outline and the hints to produce a bitmap of the font at the size requested by the application—this is what makes TrueType fonts scalable. The first time the user selects a TrueType font, a bitmap must be created for all of the characters. For this reason, font generation is likely to be slower for TrueType fonts than for raster fonts. On the plus side, TrueType fonts are cached, so any subsequent call for the TrueType font will be just as fast as a call for a raster font. From a performance perspective, it is more efficient to cache fonts than to recreate their bitmaps, even at the expense of disk swapping. The maximum number of TrueType fonts that can exist simultaneously on a PC is 1,170 for Windows version 3.1.

The System Font

The System font, a proportionally spaced raster font used to draw the Windows character set, is the default for any given device context. This is the font that Windows uses to display menus, dialog box controls, and other text.

The LOGFONT Structure

The LOGFONT structure describes the attributes of a font; you will override this structure when you create new fonts or change the properties of an existing font. Here is a summary of the LOGFONT structure and its members:

```
typedef struct tagLOGFONT
{
    int    lfHeight;
    int    lfWidth;
    int    lfEscapement;
    int    lfOrientation;
    int    lfWeight;
    BYTE   lfItalic;
    BYTE   lfUnderline;
    BYTE   lfStrikeOut;
    BYTE   lfCharSet;
    BYTE   lfOutPrecision;
    BYTE   lfClipPrecision;
    BYTE   lfQuality;
    BYTE   lfPitchAndFamily;
    BYTE   lfFaceName[LF_FACESIZE];
} LOGFONT;
```

The remainder of this section describes in greater detail the signifance of each member of the LOGFONT structure.

lfHeight   This value specifies, in logical units, the desired height of the font. If this value is greater than zero, it specifies the cell height of the font. If it is less than zero, it specifies the *character* height of the font (the cell height minus the internal leading). (Refer to the TEXTMETRIC structure for additional information on text and cell attributes. Applications that specify the font height in points usually use a negative number for *lfHeight*.) If the value of *lfHeight* is zero, a default height is selected by the font mapper, which chooses the largest physical font less than the requested size (or the smallest font, if all the fonts exceed the requested size). The *lfHeight* member must not exceed 16,384 after it is converted to device units.

lfWidth	This parameter is the average width of the font's characters in logical units. When creating a font, setting this member to zero causes the font mapper to determine the width by correlating the aspect ratio of the output device to similar installed fonts. For TrueType fonts, this value is scaled, using the ratio of *lfWidth* divided by the value of TEXTMETRIC.tmAveCharWidth.
lfEscapement	This is the value of the angle between the baseline of a font character and the x-axis, measured in tenths of degrees.
lfOrientation	This value, which indicates the orientation of the characters, is ignored.
lfWeight	This member specifies the font weight (i.e., how "thick" the font characters appear) and can be one of the following values, found in the file *WINDOWS.H*:

CONSTANT	VALUE
FW_DONTCARE	0
FW_THIN	100
FW_EXTRALIGHT	200
FW_ULTRALIGHT	200
FW_LIGHT	300
FW_NORMAL	400
FW_REGULAR	400
FW_MEDIUM	500
FW_SEMIBOLD	600
FW_DEMIBOLD	600
FW_BOLD	700
FW_EXTRABOLD	800
FW_ULTRABOLD	800
FW_BLACK	900
FW_HEAVY	900

The visual clarity of the font depends on the typeface. Some fonts have only FW_NORMAL, FW_REGULAR, and FW_BOLD weights. If FW_DONTCARE is specified, the font mapper uses a default weight.

lfItalic	This value specifies an italic font when set to nonzero.
lfUnderline	Set this value to nonzero to create an underlined font.
lfStrikeOut	Setting this parameter to nonzero indicates a strikeout font.
lfCharSet	The value indicates the character set of the font (ANSI, etc.); the following constants are allowed:

CONSTANT	VALUE
ANSI_CHARSET	0
DEFAULT_CHARSET	1
SYMBOL_CHARSET	2
SHIFTJIS_CHARSET	128
OEM_CHARSET	255

An application can use DEFAULT_CHARSET to allow the name and size of a font to describe the logical font. If the specified font does not exist, a font from any character set can be substituted for the specified font, and this fact can sometimes lead to unexpected results.

lfOutPrecision This value specifies the desired output precision—that is, how precisely the output should match the height, width, character orientation, escapement, and pitch of the requested font. This member of LOGFONT can be any of the following:

CONSTANT	VALUE
OUT_DEFAULT_PRECIS	0
OUT_STRING_PRECIS	1
OUT_CHARACTER_PRECIS	2
OUT_STROKE_PRECIS	3
OUT_TT_PRECIS	4
OUT_DEVICE_PRECIS	5
OUT_RASTER_PRECIS	6
OUT_TT_ONLY_PRECIS	7

An application can specify TrueType fonts exclusively by indicating OUT_TT_ONLY_ PRECIS. When this value is used, the system chooses a TrueType font even when the name specified in the lfFaceName member matches a non-TrueType font, so exercise caution in making this choice.

lfClipPrecision This parameter specifies the desired clipping precision.

lfQuality This value specifies the output quality of the font, in a relative sort of way. Basically, it defines how closely the graphics device interface (GDI) must match the logical font attributes to those of an actual physical font. This member can be any of the following values:

CONSTANT	MEANING
DEFAULT_QUALITY	Appearance of the font does not matter.
DRAFT_QUALITY	Appearance of the font is less important than when the PROOF_QUALITY is specified. For GDI raster fonts, scaling is enabled. Bold, italic, underline, and strikeout fonts are synthesized when necessary.
PROOF_QUALITY	Character quality of the font is more important than exact matching of the logical font attributes. For GDI raster fonts, scaling is disabled and the font closest in size is chosen. Bold, italic, underline, and strikeout fonts are synthesized if necessary.

lfPitchAndFamily This member specifies the pitch and family of the font. The two low-order bits, which specify the pitch of the font, can be either DEFAULT_PITCH or FIXED_PITCH VARIABLE_PITCH.

The four high-order bits of the member specify the font family and can be any of the following values:

VALUE	MEANING
FF_DECORATIVE	Novelty fonts. Old English is an example.
FF_DONTCARE	Don't care or don't know.
FF_MODERN	Fonts with constant stroke width, with or without serifs.
FF_ROMAN	Fonts with variable stroke width and with serifs.
FF_SCRIPT	Fonts that look like handwriting, such as Script.
FF_SWISS	Fonts with variable stroke width and without serifs.

This member can be formed by ORing a pitch value with a family value.

lfFaceName   This value specifies the typeface name of the font. The length of this string must not exceed LF_FACESIZE – 1. Use the EnumFontFamilies function to enumerate the typeface names of all currently available fonts. If lfFaceName is NULL, GDI uses a device-dependent typeface.

LOGFONT Summary

Your program can use the default settings for most of these members when creating a logical font. The members that should *always* be specified are lfHeight and lfFaceName. If lfHeight and lfFaceName are not set by the application, the logical font that is created as a result becomes device-dependent.

The SetFont( ) Function

The following example shows how you can create a new font and assign it to an edit box. As presented here, this font will be unique to an edit box—when the user leaves the box, the font "goes away." In order to use SetFont( ), you must edit the dialog box constructor and use ClassWizard to create a function to initialize the dialog box. In the constructor found in the header file (the .H file) for the class, declare a member variable called *m_newfont*, as in the following example:

```
class CMyclass : public CDialog
{
// Construction
   CFont m_newfont;          //declare new member variable for new font
public:
   CMyclass(CWnd* pParent = NULL);// standard constructor
     (Visual C++ adds more code here, but we're done...)
}
```

In this example, the header file is called "myclass.h," and the class is derived from CDialog, which is what we want. We now have a member variable of type CFont that we can use. Now, in the file "myclass.cpp," which is where ClassWizard installed the handler for the WM_INITDIALOG message, we create our new font using SetFont( ):

```
BOOL CMyclass::OnInitDialog()
{
    CDialog::OnInitDialog();
    // TODO: Add extra initialization here
    CenterWindow();        // center the dialog box for visual appeal
    //
    // begin code to create & set new font
    //
    LOGFONT lf;            // need the LOGFONT structure
    memset(&lf,0,sizeof(LOGFONT));// initialize the LOGFONT structure
    lf.lfHeight = 20;      // make our new font 20 pixels tall
    lf.lfWeight = FW_BOLD;// ...and give it a BOLD typeface
    _fstrcpy(lf.lfFaceName,"Aquarius");// call our new font Aquarius
    m_newfont.CreateFontIndirect(&lf);// first, create the font..
    GetDlgItem(IDC_MY_EDIT)->SetFont(&m_newfont); // then, set it...
    return TRUE; // return TRUE unless you set the focus to a control
}
```

Now, whatever the user types into the edit box we defined as "IDC_MY_EDIT" in App Studio will be displayed in our new font, Aquarius. The preceding example also illustrates the use of the function CreateFontIndirect, which takes a pointer to the LOGFONT structure as an argument. Alternatively, you can use the CFont member function CreateFont( ), which essentially does the same thing but takes the individual members of the LOGFONT structure as arguments.

The CFontDialog Class

If your Windows program must include the feature of allowing the user to select a font, you'll be happy to learn that all the work has been done for you. Among the Microsoft Foundation Classes is a class called CFontDialog, which allows you to include a font selection dialog box in your program. CFontDialog is a modal dialog box that displays a standard dialog box with a list of all the fonts installed on the system in the WIN.INI file. This class makes use of the COMMDLG structure CHOOSEFONT as well as the API ChooseFont( ) function. To use a CFontDialog class object, instantiate an object using the CFontDialog constructor. The arguments to the CFontDialog constructor are as follows (observe that several have default values):

lplfInitial   The initial settings of the dialog box (defaults to NULL).
dwFlags   These are flags that you can use to customize the dialog. See the CHOOSEFONT structure reference for more information on possible values (the defaults are CF_EFFECTS | CF_SCREENFONTS).
hdcPrinter   A CDC for a printer for which fonts are to be selected (defaults to NULL).
pParentWnd   Pointer to a parent window. This parameter is used only when dispatching customized help messages (defaults to NULL).

After the object has been instantiated, you can modify the CHOOSEFONT structure, *m_cf*, to customize the dialog box as desired. After any further customization, call the DoModal member function, which returns IDOK or IDCANCEL. When using CFontDialog, be sure to test the return value. If it is IDCANCEL, the user clicked the CANCEL button, or an initialization error occurred in the dialog. Use the

CommDlgExtendedError( ) function to check for the initialization error. If IDOK is returned, no errors were detected. The CFontDialog class includes quite a few member functions for extracting information from the dialog regarding the user's choice. These are:

GetFaceName	Returns the face name of the font.
GetStyleName	Returns the style name of the font.
GetSize	Returns the point size in 1/10ths of a point.
GetColor	Returns the color of the selected font as an RGB value.
GetWeight	Returns the weight of the font.
IsStrikeout	Returns TRUE if the strikeout effect was selected.
IsUnderline	Returns TRUE if the underline effect was selected.
IsBold	Returns TRUE if the weight is equal to FW_BOLD.
IsItalic	Returns TRUE if the font chosen is italic.

In addition, the member variable *m_lf,* the LOGFONT descriptor of the font, can be used in a CreateFontIndirect call as demonstrated earlier in this chapter.

The following example illustrates the basics of invoking a CFontDialog box. The sample function, CDemoApp::OnFont( ), is the result of responding to a COMMAND message in ClassWizard for a menu option. Visual C++ builds the handler; we must supply the code. In this example, all that we have done is instantiate an object of type CFontDialog and wait for the user to click the OK or Cancel button. Here we only test for a click of the OK button, since a Cancel means the user did not select a font. After the user has selected a font with specific characteristics (e.g., bold, point size, name, etc.) and clicked the OK button, we can review the parameters of the selection. In our example, we've demonstrated the member functions GetFaceName( ), which returns the name of the font (e.g., Courier, Times New Roman, Arial, etc.), and GetSize( ), which returns the point size. Remember that GetSize( ) returns the point size as the number of *tenths* of the actual point size. Hence, if the user selected a 12-point font, GetSize( ) would return the number 120.

```
void CDemoApp::OnFont()
{
  // TODO: Add your command handler code here
  //
  int ret_val=0;                     // the return value; which button clicked
  CFontDialog dlg;                   // instantiate CFontDialog class
  ret_val= dlg.DoModal();             // fire up a font dialog box, get response
  //
  // now retrieve some of user's selections
  //
  CString font_name;                 // name of font user selected
  int font_size= 0;                  // size of font user selected
  //
  if(ret_val == IDOK)                // user picked a font
  {
    font_name = dlg.GetFaceName();  // Courier, System, etc.
    font_size = dlg.GetSize();      // divide by ten
  }
}
```

COLOR

The use of color can go a long way toward improving the user interface of your program, but it must be properly managed. There is a tendency toward excess once the programmer sees how to manipulate the colors. Likewise, it is easy to fall victim to the desire to "color-code" objects and other features. This approach is all well and good so long as you do *not* make color the single distinguishing factor in the interface—after all, some of your users may be colorblind. A few common-sense guidelines regarding the judicious use of color are presented here for your consideration:

1. Stick to a few primary colors. Bright, flashy, "neon" colors are generally perceived to be unprofessional.

2. Use the same colors and color combinations *consistently* throughout your application.

3. For text presentation, use dark type on a light background, and not vice versa, to reduce eyestrain.

Changing the Window Color

If you decide to change the background color of a window in your application, the easiest way to do so is to create a member function that responds to a WM_ERASEBKGND (Erase Background) message in ClassWizard for the associated VIEW. Recall that the *view* relates to the visual aspect of your program. Should you change the color, don't forget that you'll have to change the text drawing characteristics, too. The following example illustrates what changes you must implement in order to change the background color:

```
BOOL CCMyView::OnEraseBkgnd(CDC* pDC)
{
    // TODO: Add your message handler code here and/or call default
    //
    CBrush backBrush(RGB(255,255,0));     // Set brush to desired
                                          // background color (yellow)
    //
    // Note:      SelectObject's return value is a pointer to the
    //   object it replaced; hence you can save the old
    //   brush while selecting a new one..
    //
    CBrush* pOldBrush = pDC->SelectObject(&backBrush); // save old
                                                       // brush
    CRect rect;                           // need window rectangle
    pDC->GetClipBox(&rect);               // erase the area needed
    pDC->PatBlt(rect.left, rect.top, rect.Width(), rect.Height(),
                PATCOPY);                 // paint it
    pDC->SelectObject(pOldBrush);         // restore the original brush

    return TRUE;
}
```

This example paints the background window yellow. The macro RGB is used to specify the amount of red, green, and blue we want our object to have. Each value is an integer in the range 0–255. It helps to know a little bit about the color wheel in order to use this macro effectively. In our example, we mixed equal portions of red and green and turned off the blue; the result is yellow. Setting all values to 0 results in black; setting all values to 255 sets the color to white. The value RGB(0,255,255) mixes green and blue and sets the color to cyan. All in all, there are over 16 million possible combinations, but you should make do with a mere 16.

Changing the Color of Text

If you change the color of a window, you'll have to change the color of the text that is displayed in it. Where you do this depends largely on the nature of your program, but usually it will be in an OnDraw( ) function created by Visual C++ or anywhere else you do your own text output. To change the color of text, you'll need a handle to the window's client area, a new color definition, and the background *mode.* The mode is set using the SetBkMode( ) function, which is passed an argument defined as either TRANSPARENT or OPAQUE. Setting this argument to TRANSPARENT allows the background color to "shine through." If you've changed the background color elsewhere, you'll definitely want to set the mode to TRANSPARENT; otherwise, a "halo" in your system's default color will appear around each text character drawn. The following example shows how to set the background mode and text color:

```
CClientDC hDC(this);                // get the handle to the DC
hDC.SetBkMode(TRANSPARENT);         // set the background mode
hDC.SetTextColor(RGB(0,255,0));     // set text color to green
```

Changing a Dialog Box's Color

Changing the color of a dialog box is something you can do but probably shouldn't. Several ways of accomplishing this change exist, the most dangerous of which is changing the default system colors using the API call to SetSysColors(COLOR_WINDOW). You can make this change when your program first starts by placing the call in your InitInstance( ) function. Sample code for doing so can be found in the online help file for the SDK. The problem with this approach isn't one of complicated code, as you'll see when you examine the help file; the problem is that *all* dialog and message boxes are affected, including those in Windows applications other than the one(s) created in Visual C++. Here's what happens to users when you adopt this method. In one window, they start up App1, which uses, for example, a gray background for dialog boxes. In another window, they start up App2, where you have changed the dialog box background color. When the users return to App1, its dialog boxes now have the background color used by App2. Such changes can be confusing and lead a novice user to believe that something has gone wrong with the system.

Using SetDialogBkColor( )

This function changes the background color for all dialog boxes in your program when it is placed in your InitInstance( ) function. For example, suppose that you want all your dialog boxes to display black text on a cyan background. Here is what the call looks like:

```
CWinApp::SetDialogBkColor(RGB(0,255,255), RGB(0,0,0));
```

That's all there is to it; the first argument sets the background color to cyan, and the second one sets the text color to black.

Using CWnd::OnCtlColor( )

This is the "safe" way to change the background color of a dialog box. The change only affects the dialog box(es) for which a handler was written to process the message WM_CTLCOLOR. The basic, overall steps we'll demonstrate later follow this logical order:

1. Declare a brush to be used for painting the background and controls.

2. Create the brush in your dialog box's constructor function.

3. Select the brush in the handler for WM_CTLCOLOR.

4. Delete the brush in the dialog box's destructor.

The last step is very important, because the create function locks memory resources and doesn't give them back until the end of the current Windows session. Failure to release the memory occupied by the brush has a significant impact on your program's performance and can ultimately lead to an error condition if free memory is exhausted. During development of painting routines like these, you would be well advised to start up the *Stress* application that comes with Visual C++. Before you test your program, run STRESS.EXE and note the values it reports, especially the GDI memory parameter. Then run your program and exercise the video/painting commands a couple of times. Upon terminating your program, check Stress again. The GDI numbers should be the same. If not, your application is slowly stealing memory. By the way, to get an accurate reading from Stress, run it under the same conditions (i.e., all other windows minimized, etc.), or load, for lack of a better word, both before and after your program runs.

Now, let's take a look at some sample code that implements the logical steps described earlier in this section. This example is based on a hypothetical class, CSomeCls, derived from CDialog; we will paint this dialog box yellow. The following listing contains the comments written by Visual C++ to provide you with a clearer frame of reference as to how these changes are made:

```
// ------------------------------------------------------------------
// NAME = CSOMECLS.CPP
// This is the .CPP file Visual C++ would have created for us.
// We declare a "global" paintbrush.
//
#include "stdafx.h"
#include "ourapp.h"                    // name of your AppWizard application
#include "csomecls.h"                  // our include file, created by VC++

#ifdef _DEBUG
#undef THIS_FILE
static char BASED_CODE THIS_FILE[] = __FILE__;
#endif
```

```
HBRUSH brushnew;                          // declare a new brush here, before the
                                          // implementation of the constructor
//////////////////////////////////////////////////////////////////////////////
// CSomeCls dialog
//
// ****** HERE IS THE CONSTRUCTOR ***********
//
CSomeCls::CSomeCls(CWnd* pParent /*=NULL*/)
   : CDialog(CSomeCls::IDD, pParent)
{
   //{{AFX_DATA_INIT(CSomeCls)
   //}}AFX_DATA_INIT
   brushnew = CreateSolidBrush(RGB(255,255,0));// create brush
}
```

This is all the code we need to create (but not to select or use) a yellow brush. To select the brush, we'll use a message handler for WM_CTLCOLOR. Since we're painting a dialog box and its controls, we also need to set the background mode so that text is displayed on a yellow background, and not the background color defined on the user's machine. There are a few other useful options you should check out in the Help file on this message; we'll use some here.

The following function would be created for you in ClassWizard; we have modified it to demonstrate the preceding principles:

```
HBRUSH CSomeCls::OnCtlColor(CDC* pDC, CWnd* pWnd, UINT nCtlColor)
{
    // TODO: Add your message handler code here and/or call default
    //
    // ** BEGIN NEW CODE **
    // This if statement causes just the dialog box and the static
    // text to be drawn with the yellow paintbrush...
    //
    if((nCtlColor == CTLCOLOR_DLG) || (nCtlColor == CTLCOLOR_STATIC))
    {
        pDC->SetBkMode(TRANSPARENT); // let the yellow shine thru!
        return brushnew;             // select the yellow brush
    }
    else    // see Help file for other "filters"...
        return CDialog::OnCtlColor(pDC, pWnd, nCtlColor); // default
}
```

A couple of quick observations about this example: The only things that get changed are the actual background color of the dialog box *and* the way text is displayed. Without the statement

```
pDC->SetBkMode(TRANSPARENT);
```

in the code, the text would have been drawn in the default screen color. Secondly, it is *crucial* that you always return a handle to a brush when using this function. Failure to do so can cause the application to crash, forcing the user to reboot. The last thing we need to do is delete the paintbrush when the user closes the dialog box. This is handled in the destructor for our hypothetical class, which is placed in the file "csomecls.cpp":

```
CSomeCls::~CSomeCls()      // standard destructor
{
```

```
        DeleteObject(brushnew);// delete the yellow brush
    }
```

That's the whole process, from womb to tomb. To give you more information on color, the following section explores another convenient utility of the Microsoft Foundation Classes, the CColorDialog( ) class.

A Color Selection Dialog Box

A class that is identical in functionality to CFontDialog (except that it allows the user to select a color or create a custom color) is available via the MFC. This class is a modal dialog box that uses the COMMDLG structure CHOOSECOLOR and the Windows API call ChooseColor( ). The COMMDLG structure used for customizing the dialog is CHOOSECOLOR, which can be modified after instantiation of the object and before DoModal is called. The arguments to the constructor are:

clrInit	A COLORREF that is the initial color selection; the default is black, or RGB(0,0,0).
dwFlags	Flags that can be ORed to customize the function and appearance of the dialog. See the CHOOSECOLOR structure reference for more information on possible values (defaults to 0). This information may be accessed by searching for CHOOSECOLOR after starting the Windows SDK Help file under Visual C++'s Help option.
pParentWnd	A pointer to a parent window. This parameter is used only when routing customized help messages (default is NULL).

CColorDialog( ) allows the user to define up to 16 custom colors. CColorDialog saves these custom colors between invocations of the dialog in the static member variable *clrSavedCustom*. In order to save these colors between executions of your program, you must provide appropriate code. After the dialog has been constructed and called, check the value returned. If it is IDOK, you can use the GetColor( ) member function to retrieve the color the user selected, and this color can subsequently be saved. As with all of the standard dialog classes, you can define a message map in your derived CColorDialog class to customize the dialog box's behavior to suit your needs. For example, you can use the member function SetCurrentColor( ) to force the currently selected color to a certain value. The following example illustrates the use of the CColorDialog class; the dialog box is invoked when the user selects an option from the main menu bar. When the user clicks the OK button in this dialog box, the following code determines which color the user selected by calling the GetColor( ) member function:

```
    void CDemoApp::OnColor()
    {
      // TODO: Add your command handler code here
      //
      CColorDialog dlg;        // instantiate a CColorDialog object
      //
      COLORREF color_picked; // variable to hold user's selection
      //
      if(key_clicked == IDOK)// user has clicked the OK button
```

```
        color_picked = dlg.GetColor();// get selection
    }
```

ICONS

We generally think of an icon as the little picture we see when a Windows application is minimized. While this perception is true, icons can also be used *inside* a program, in the guise of a bitmap. A familiar example is the "About..." box option on most help menu lines. Visual C++ will build you one of these, too. However, you can replace the standard "Afx" icon that appears in the dialog box when this option is exercised with one of your own, as will be demonstrated. The size of the icon can be used in other dialog boxes as is or enlarged to give your application a custom touch. It should be mentioned here that whenever your program opens a Help file, its window can be minimized to a custom icon that you have created for that *specific* Help file (remember that you can have several Help files open at once for the same application). This custom icon is specified by using the "ICON = newicon.ico" in the [OPTIONS] section of your application's Help Project File (discussed in Chapter 15).

Changing the Default Icon

When you create a Windows application using AppWizard, Visual C++ gives you a stock icon (a gray-scale icon with the "AFX" logo from Microsoft). To give your program a more custom look and feel, you can easily replace this icon with one of your own. To do so, first run App Studio and create a new icon by selecting "New..." under the menu option "Resource" and then choosing "Icon" from the list of different resources (bitmaps, dialog boxes, etc.). Next, edit your application's .RC file and replace the call to "yourapp.ico" with the name (and path) of this new icon file. (By the way, this would be a great time to create any icon such as a company logo that you plan to ship with the products you create with Visual C++.) This procedure will replace the default icon from Microsoft with your icon and display it in the "About..." box under the Help menu item on the main menu bar and in the main window whenever your application is minimized.

CHAPTER SUMMARY

Modifying fonts, colors, and to a lesser extent, icons can dramatically change the way your program looks. However, doing so presents the danger of deviating from established standards for Windows. You should fully weigh this consideration prior to implementing any font or color changes.Nonetheless, the Microsoft Foundation Classes version 2.0 provide you with a potent arsenal of weapons for accessing and using these objects; the standard dialog box for fonts, files, and colors makes it quite easy for the programmer to exploit these features fully. Special attention must be paid to ensuring that any changes made in these areas are supported on the target platform. Therefore, any special fonts you use must be added to your Install program and shipped with your product. The danger of target platform incompatibility is less acute with colors, as Windows will select an alternative should you specify an unsupported color. For more information on producing a professional Setup/Install program to deal with these details, refer to Chapter 19.

CHAPTER 15

Using the Win Help Engine

Most contemporary Windows-based applications include access to online Help. Visual C++ is no exception. Including online Help can dramatically improve the user community's acceptance of your programs. With online Help, first-time users reduce their learning curve and gain confidence in their ability to navigate your product. Even users more adept at using Windows gain an increased level of comfort simply by knowing they can quickly obtain assistance should they forget a needed piece of information. In this chapter, we'll explore many of the issues surrounding the Windows Help system. We hope you'll come away with a better understanding of how all the pieces fit together and what you can do to optimize your Help files. As a prelude, you don't need to use Microsoft Word in order to write Help files, as is widely believed. Although this product does make it easier to create Help files, any ASCII editor will suffice, as we'll demonstrate later. We'll begin with a discussion of Help in relation to Visual C++ and Windows. Using Visual C++, you can construct three flavors of Help:

1. General Help, usually from the main menu bar. This kind of help usually includes basic information about what Help is available and the presentation of the table of contents or index for Help.

2. Context-sensitive Help, or Help related to the immediate screen or task at hand. Activation begins by pressing the F1 function key or by clicking on a button labeled Help. Enable this feature by checking the Context-Sensitive Help box in AppWizard when you initially define your application. This feature permits you to include brief Help messages inside the status bar as the mouse cursor moves through the menu choices.

3. Discrete Help, or Help related to an on-screen item, such as a control. Pressing the Shift+F1 keys simultaneously invokes this feature. In this mode, the cursor changes to an arrow and a question mark. If the user clicks on a dialog box, or a menu, window, or button, the function OnContextHelp( ) retrieves the Help text for the selected object.

It is always a good idea to use "Help on Using Help," as new users may not be familiar with what the Windows Help engine is all about. See the CWinApp member function OnHelpUsing( ) for more information.

In this chapter, you will learn how to include these features in your application. You'll get a fairly moderate introduction to writing your own Help files (which have the extension .HLP) used by the Windows Help engine, which is called WINHELP.EXE. Incidentally, these HLP files use a proprietary format called RTF (Rich Text Format), supported by Microsoft Word, the suggested tool for creating Help files. Again, it is not necessary to use Word—any ASCII text editor will suffice. But you will need the Windows Help Compiler, HC31.EXE for Windows version 3.1. The Professional Edition of Visual C++ (and most contemporary development packages such as the SDK) includes the Help Compiler, so you should have everything you need to write Help files. A word of caution: The Help format changed between Windows version 3.0 and 3.1; this book covers version 3.1, and everything *should* work the same.

You call WINHELP simply by calling it and passing it parameters that specify where to take the user. For example, for general Help, you'll most likely want to display the list of topics (i.e., an index) that have Help; the user may then click on any item. For context-sensitive Help, you usually don't jump to the index; instead, you take the user directly to the subject matter pertinent to the position within your program. The generic call to invoke WINHELP is:

```
YourApp.WinHelp(id_your_resource,HELP_CONTEXT);
```

where YourApp is your application's primary class, derived from CWinApp. The string *id_your_resource* could be the identifier assigned by the App Studio to a button on a dialog box labeled Help. The string HELP_CONTEXT is a reserved token that instructs WINHELP to jump to the topic identified by *id_your_resource* in the Help file.

Suppose you had a class derived from CDialog that allowed the user to add a new employee to a database or file, and you called this class CAddNewEmp. Also, you've added a button marked Help to the dialog box. In ClassWizard, you add a function to respond to a mouse click on this button. You'd get something that looked like this:

```
void CAddNewEmp::OnClickAddNewEmpHelp(UINT, int, CWnd*, LPVOID)
{
    YourApp.WinHelp(ID_ADD_NEW_EMP_HELP,HELP_CONTEXT);
}
```

(Here, we assume you assigned ID_ADD_NEW_EMP_HELP as the ID of the Help button when you created the dialog box, and that YourApp is an instantiation of CWinApp.)

The call to use if you want to take the user to the Help file's index or table of contents is very similar:

```
YourApp.WinHelp(0L,HELP_CONTENTS);
```

Note carefully: The second argument is HELP_CONTENTS, *not* HELP_CONTEXT.

Make the first argument a long zero, and you'll jump to the main index. You'll next see how to construct the Help file from its project file and topic files.

THE HELP PROJECT FILE

You create a Help file using a minimum of two files; however, you will generally use three:

1. A project file, which has the extension .HPJ.

2. A topics file, which has the extension .RTF.

3. A header file that contains the definitions of your topic "jump labels." This usually has the extension ".H".

A project file consists of up to nine sections, although not all of these are mandatory. The [OPTIONS], [FILES], [BITMAPS], and [MAP] sections are the ones to which we will devote the most attention. Specify these tokens by enclosing them in square brackets on a separate line in the project file. Every project file should have an [OPTIONS] section, even though it is optional. If you use it, it *must* be the first entry in the project file. We recommend that you include the entries in Table 15.1 in the [OPTIONS] section.

Another command token, in some senses, is FORCEFONT. This option instructs the Help Compiler to *always* use a specified font and to disregard any instructions to the contrary. You'll probably not use this feature very often, as it defeats a visually appealing Help file, for example, when you use certain fonts consistently for specific purposes.

The next major section of the Help file is the [MAP]. This section defines the Help topics and gives them their unique numerical value. It is best to place these sections in a header file and include it both in the [MAP] section *and* in the source code for your Windows application. This double inclusion facilitates maintenance by allowing one file to service both the Help portion and the application side of your project.

If you wish to include graphics in your Help file, you'll need a [BITMAPS] section. The graphic images you can include are, as you might guess, bitmaps.

TABLE 15.1
Recommended entries in the [OPTIONS] section.

TITLE	A brief description of the application for which the Help file is being built. This entry is for your own configuration management.
COMPRESS	This option creates a Help file in a compressed format. While developing, you'll want to set this flag to FALSE to save time. (No need to waste time crunching and uncrunching the file until you're happy with it.) Once ready to ship your application, set this flag to TRUE, do a final build, and ship the resulting Help file.
WARNING	This option determines the degree of error reporting, from 1 (least serious) to 3 (most serious). Set it to 3 during development so you'll catch all levels of warning.
CONTENTS	This option is the string token for the Help file's table of contents; its use is *highly recommended.* If you omit this file, Win Help assumes that the first topic found in the topics file is the start of the "Help table of contents."

Windows can recognize bitmap images. They have the extension .BMP. There are many ways to create the image files and many conversion utilities for converting graphics files from one format to another. Here's a slick trick for having your Help file display pictures of what users will see when they run your program:

1. Run your program and get the image that you wish to have in your Help file on screen. Press PRINT SCREEN twice, which saves whatever is on the screen to the Clipboard.

2. While still in Windows, get into a graphics program capable of reading from the Clipboard (e.g., PaintBrush). Paste the contents of the Clipboard into the graphics program, and edit it if you want to. Save the image in a .BMP format. See the next section on topic files for information on how to include the graphics in your Help.

3. Include the path and name of this file in the [BITMAPS] section of your Help project file. This procedure lets you create a great learning aid as your user can see what a screen looks like before even getting to it. You can build complete tutorials in this way just by using WINHELP.

The last section is the [FILES]. Here is where you direct the Help compiler to find the actual Help material, the topic file. For a relatively small Help file, you can easily get away with having just one topic file. For large projects, or when several programmers might be producing their own Help files, here is where you specify multiple topic files. Note that the maximum length of a path-filename specification in the [FILES] section is 259 characters. The Help compiler returns an error if you exceed this limit.

Another fact about the Help Project File—you can use comments. Indicate them by a semicolon (e.g., ; here is a comment).

THE RTF FILE

This is where the real work of creating a useful Help file begins. The RTF file also consists of several sections, although they are not so clearly evident or formalized as those in the Help Project File. Most of the content of the topic files consists of the actual text of your Help. This text will be "richly formatted"—allowing you to select fonts and their colors and sizes; to underline; to use bold or italic type; and to use other utilitarian functions. Like the Help Project File, the RTF topic file consists of logical units:

1. A font table. This table describes which fonts are available. Unless you are writing for a specific target, stick to the fonts shipped with Windows. However, there is a way to specify a "substitute font" should you try to use one not found on the target platform (see the *\rtf1* token description in the next paragraph).

2. A color table, which defines the colors that are available for use in the Help file.

3. The text associated with each Help topic defined in the [MAP] section of the project file or in the header file.

Enclose the entire topic file in the traditional C curly braces ({ }). The first token in the file *must* be "\rtf1", followed by the name of the character set to use and the *default font*. The default font should *always* be one of the stock fonts shipped with Windows. If you specify a font not found on the target platform, Windows can make a graceful substitution. Generally, this default font is the ANSI character set. So, the first line of the topic file is almost always:

```
{\rtf1\ansi\deff0
```

where f0 is defined in the font table. Basically, you define a font as follows:

```
{\fontnumber \fontsize font name}
```

Hence, to define "font zero," an entry would look like this:

```
{\f0\fs12 Courier}
```

This declares f0 to be 12-point Courier.

The color table follows the font table. Color is useful for establishing a pattern. Your application should be consistent in its use of color (as well as font names, font sizes, etc.).

For example, if some words in the Help file have a hypertext connection, indicate the connection by displaying those words in the same color everywhere in the file. Delimit the color table by curly braces, and declare it with the token:

```
\colortbl;
```

The Windows macro RGB (Red, Green, Blue) defines each color value. This definition allows you to assign each primary color a value from 0 to 255. Each color value uses a backslash as a delimiter. Terminate each color definition in the table with a semicolon. Table 15.2 provides some examples of typical color values. So, if you wanted a color table with just the colors of say, black and red, your topics file entry for the color table would look like this:

```
{\colortbl;\red0\green0\blue0;
 \red255\green0\blue0;}
```

Referencing the colors is similar to indexing an array, with one exception. The Help compiler assigns the first color in the table the number 1, *not* 0, with which most C

TABLE 15.2
Typical color values for Windows Help.

COLOR	COLOR TABLE DEFINITION
Black	\red0\green0\blue0;
White	\red255\green255\blue255;
Red	\red255\green0\blue0;
Green	\red0\green255\blue0;
Blue	\red0\green0\blue255;
Yellow	\red255\green255\blue0;
Cyan	\red0\green255\blue255;

programmers are familiar. The next example illustrates the process of selecting a color for display. Consider the following statement:

```
{\f0\fs22\cf2 Write this line in RED.}
```

WINHELP would display "Write this line in RED.", using the font and color tables defined previously. That is, 22-point Courier font, in red. The key here is the "\cf2" token. As a mnemonic, it may be helpful to think of "\cf" as meaning "*C*olor the *F*ont." Remember, you can define over 16 million colors (mathematically speaking) in your color table—the problem is whether you have a video card and monitor capable of such discrete output. Colors are a numerical combination of Red, Green, and Blue; each color has a value from 0 to 255. Thus, you can specify some unique colors, should the need arise. However, you should stick to the basics when using color in a Help file, making it easier for you to manage as well as providing a consistent presentation for your user.

The last key ingredients of the RTF file are the tokens for declaring the content topics and the content text. The "#" concatenated with whatever string you assigned in the [MAP] section defines the label of a context string. This is how WINHELP does a "go to" when you select a topic or click on a hypertext word from inside HELP. A topic begins with a "\footnote" token and ends with a "\page" token. All the text and tokens between these tokens comprise the topic, including the caption (i.e., title), browse sequences, and search keywords. When you are inside WINHELP, there is a button labeled "Search." When clicked, it brings up a dialog box that allows you to search for topics. The letter "K" in the \footnote token identifies these topics. Note the special case for when the search word itself begins with the letter "K"—you must insert an extra space between the "\footnote" and the search word.

Also note that the RTF file can only have a maximum of 32,767 topics. If you have more, you'll need to split your topics into two (or more) topic files. Specify these files in the [FILES] section of your project file. Should you find you have to do this, it is a good idea to check the amount of file handles you have in your CONFIG.SYS file. Also, context strings have a limit of 255 characters, and they are resolved by a hashing algorithm. Sometimes two context strings will collide; the Help compiler reports this error.

Another special case is how to display reserved tokens inside the content of a Help message. Since these tokens are reserved by the Help compiler, you must place a backslash in front of them in order to display them. For example:

```
\{   or   \}
```

The major reserved tokens are the curly braces, the square brackets ([ ]), and the backslash (\ ). If you need to display these tokens on-screen when the user accesses your Help file (a likely occurrence when presenting C or C++ code), place a backslash in front of the token for display purposes. These reserved tokens don't have to be enclosed in curly braces; for example, a typical line from a Help file that demonstrates, say, a typical C language construct might look like this:

```
\par for(k= 0; k < 100; k++)
\par \{
\par\tab somearray\[k\] = k;
\par \}
```

When this is displayed on the Help screen, it appears as:

```
for(k=0; k < 100; k++)
{
   somearray[k] = k;
}
```

which is what you want the user to see. A fuller explanation of the reserved tokens like "\par" appears in greater detail in Table 15.3.

The text associated with a topic is delimited with the "\footnote" statement and the

```
"\page"
```

token. You can also create hypertext links inside your topic text. Use the "\uldb" token to indicate hypertext links. Hypertext links usually follow some descriptive text like "See also:", etc. Also, the cursor changes to a pointing finger when moved over a hypertext link.

A closing word about formatting the text itself. You have quite a few tokens that you can use to control text formatting. Table 15.3 summarizes most of the more frequently used tokens for use with WINHELP.

To include a graphics image, specify the token *bmc* inside curly braces, followed by the name of the image file, also in curly braces. You can include a path descriptor, too, if the image file is not in the current, working directory. If you include a path descriptor, don't forget that you must precede each backslash in the path name by

TABLE 15.3
Tokens frequently used with WINHELP.

TOKEN	MEANING
\par	Inserts a blank line.
\tab	Inserts a tab character.
\b	Turns bold display on.
\b0	Turns bold display off. Use the zero ("0") with a token to turn it off, in general.
\footnote	Identifies and begins a topic; see the \page token entry.
\plain	Restores default display characteristics.
\page	Ends a topic, begins a new group; see the \footnote token entry.
\pard	Sets default paragraph properties. Formatting properties carry over from one paragraph or topic to another, unless reset. Use \pard to "clear and reset" text formatting properties.
#	Indicates a context string (case-insensitive). Can include letters and numbers, but no spaces.
$	Declare the title for the topic; this specifies what the user sees in the Search and History dialog boxes. Can include spaces.
K	Specifies a Keyword, which allows the user to search for topics. If the first character of the topic *also* begins with "K," you must insert a space or a semicolon in front of the topic.
+	Specifies a browse-sequence identifier, if the browse button has been enabled (by using the BrowseButtons macro). These identifiers allow the user to page through related topics in sequential order.

another backslash. The following example would load the image file *myfile.bmp* from directory C:\HLP\MYDIR:

```
\pard {\par\cf2\f6 A Sample:}{ \{}{bmc C:\\hlp\\myfile.bmp}{ \}}
```

Also, note that the entire specification for a bitmap *must* be inside curly braces, as we have done here.

CREATING THE .HLP FILE

When you set up an application in AppWizard, it creates a file called MAKEHELP.BAT, which automates the creation of your project's Help file. Normally, you'll just run this procedure to get an .HLP file. To create an .HLP file using your own project and topic files, simply enter this command from the DOS prompt:

```
HC31 yourapp.hpj
```

where yourapp.hpj is the name of the Help project file. Of course, your PATH must be able to find the Help compiler, HC31.EXE, and any additional files specified in the [FILES] section of your Help project file must also be in your PATH. Be very careful when working within your own RTF file—it is easy to include an extra curly brace or to omit one. Should this happen, the Help compiler will return an error that specifies some byte offset at a hex address, such as:

```
Error 4639: Error in file "yourapp.rtf" at byte offset 0xF27A
```

HELP COMPILER ERRORS

The Help Compiler generates errors that are number-coded into eight categories, as shown in Table 15.4.

The best way to grasp writing Help files is probably by example. The sample program on the source code disk that accompanies this book includes online Help; take a few minutes to study both the .HPJ and the .RTF files to get a feel for how things work. You might also want to make some copies of these files under another

TABLE 15.4
Categories and numbers of Help Compiler errors.

NUMERICAL PREFIX	MEANING
1	There is a problem with the files used to build the .HLP file.
2	There is a problem with the project file (.HPJ file).
5	Other.
30–31	There is a problem with a build-tag or build-tag expression.
35–36	There is a problem with the Help macros.
40–41	There is a problem with a context string.
42–45	There is a problem with a topic footnote.
46–47	There is a problem with the .RTF file.

name and practice trying different formatting techniques. After you create an .HLP file, you can easily test it by running WINHELP from the Program Manager in Windows. Select Run from the File menu, and type WINHELP followed by the path and name of your .HLP file.

WINHELP MACROS

The Windows Help engine, WINHELP.EXE, comes with a rich set of macros that you can combine to create custom features for your Help file. These macros let you modify the way WINHELP.EXE works. They can be used in a wide variety of ways. For example, you can:

- Modify the Help menu bar by adding new buttons.

- Change the location of the primary and secondary Help windows.

- Build conditional jumps to previously saved text markers inside a Help file.

- Run other Windows programs like Clock, Calculator, etc., from inside Help.

- Assign accelerator keys to a Help macro.

Executing Help Macros

After you have decided which macro features you wish to add to your program, the next topic is how, and when, to execute the macros. Macros can (and sometimes *must*) be placed in the .HPJ file (Help project file). When the Help file opens, these macros execute, if only partially (e.g., create menu options). Another way to use macros is to connect them to the Help toolbar; clicking the button could start the macro. Macros can also be placed in the .RTF file; when the user selects Help for a certain topic, the macro would execute. Similarly, you can add hot spots to a topic that start the macro when selected. One word of caution—some macros will not execute from a pop-up or secondary window.

There are a lot of things you can do with the Help macros to spice up your application for both "show" and "go." Consider, for example, creating a new button, but try making the button a bitmapped image. You might assign a special Windows program to this button; say, one that does a disk directory of all your .HLP files. Create a bitmap in App Studio of a question mark with a file-folder (for example), and make this your new button face. You should find enough material in the upcoming sections to at least get you started with the fundamentals of working with macros.

Creating a New WINHELP Button

Whenever you open a Help file, you get six buttons automatically across the toolbar: Contents, Search, Back, History, <<, and >>. Your application can add an additional sixteen buttons; when the user clicks one of your new buttons, a WINHELP macro executes. This is a great way to incorporate some feature of your program with the Help system. To create buttons, you just need to add a couple of lines to your .HPJ file and create the topic or macro associated with your new button. These lines are:

```
[CONFIG]
CreateButton("button-id", "name", "macro")
```

If the [CONFIG] section is already identified in "yourapp.HPJ," then obviously you won't have to add it.

The second line is where the button is created. The first argument is a unique ID string that you assign to the button—WINHELP will use this internally. It must be enclosed in double quotes. It is also the name you'll use in any calls to the DisableButton( ) or DestroyButton( ) macros. The second argument is the text you wish to appear on your new button—you can include the ampersand to indicate a keyboard accelerator, too. This string can have up to 29 characters (anything beyond that gets truncated) and is case-sensitive. The last argument specifies the Help macro or macro string executed when the user clicks the new button. It is valid to specify more than one macro, but you must delimit them by semicolons.

Let's take a look at an example. When you add the following line to the .HPJ file created by Visual C++, you'll get a new button in your Help file that reads "<u>D</u>irectory" and that jumps to a topic defined as "direct" in your .RTF file:

```
CreateButton("new_butt","&Directory","JumpId('yourapp.hlp','direct')")
```

Other macros may refer to our new button as just described by using the reference "new_butt." Don't forget to substitute the name of your application's .HLP file in the call to "JumpId( )."

Keyboard Accelerators

As discussed earlier, there are Help macros for assigning and deassigning keyboard accelerators. These accelerators execute another Help macro when pressed. We'll examine two calls: the AddAccelerator( ) and RemoveAccelerator( ) macros. The prototype for the first is AddAccelerator(key, key-state, "macro"). The first argument, key, is the key pressed by the user to start the macro. The second, key-state, indicates if any modifier keys (e.g., Ctrl, Alt, etc.) are required. The key-state must be in the range of 0–7, as described in Table 15.5.

The last argument is the name of the macro, which must be in quotation marks. In the upcoming example, AddAccelerator( ) displays the Help contents of "YOURAPP.HLP" whenever the user presses Alt+Shift+F12:

```
AddAccelerator(0x7b, 5, "JumpID('yourapp.hlp', 'your_idx')")
```

The argument key is 0x7b, which is the hex value for the F12 button (see *WINDOWS.H* for all the values). The key-state is 5, or Alt+Shift. The arguments for JumpID( ) are dummy ones—we've assumed you have defined "your_idx" as the context string for your application's Table of Contents in its Help file. Now, to deassign this accelerator, you must make a call to RemoveAccelerator( ). This macro has only two

TABLE 15.5
Ranges for key-states in keyboard accelerator macros.

MODIFIER KEYS	VALUE
None	0
Shift	1
Ctrl	2
Shift+Ctrl	3
Alt	4
Alt+Shift	5
Alt+Ctrl	6
Alt+Shift+Ctrl	7

arguments, the key and key-state, which behave as described for AddAccelerator( ). Thus, to remove our Alt+Shift+F12 shortcut key example, the call is:

```
RemoveAccelerator(0x7B, 5)
```

Windows Help does not display an error message if you try to remove an unassigned accelerator key, so take care that you deassign the correct key.

Running a Windows Program from Help

One of the things you can do from inside Help is associate a Windows program to a button you've added to the toolbar. For example, suppose you wanted to add the Windows Calculator program, CALC.EXE, to a Windows Help file. You do this by using the ExecProgram( ) macro, which invokes the appropriate executable when the button is clicked. You can, of course, make this macro an argument to CreateButton( ) to create, and associate, an executable with a button, as in this example:

```
CreateButton("&Calculator", "ExecProgram(`calc.exe', 0)")
```

Note carefully the delimiters for *calc.exe*; because embedded quotation marks are not allowed, these are somewhat unique. The first delimiter is the "apostrophe" on the tilde (`) key, and the second is a single quotation mark. In this example, we start up the Windows calculator, "CALC.EXE"; the second argument, 0, indicates we wish to display the Calculator at normal size. (To display the application minimized, change this to 1. To maximize, change it to 2.) The efficacy of this macro may not be readily apparent, but it can really extend the power of an application—you could even use it to force WINHELP to act as a sort of traffic cop for an application that might execute serially. For example, you could break your program up into smaller tasks (e.g., CheckInventory->FillOrder->UpdateInventory) and make each one a button in Help. Buttons could easily be disabled and enabled as the user moves along a logical path. Similarly, you could incorporate this feature so as to allow the user to run your application without leaving Help. As a stimulus in your thinking as to where and how you might use ExecProgram( ), think of it this way: This is the same as using the Run command in Program Manager. Just one caveat—the Windows programs you wish to execute must reside in your PATH or in the same directory as your .HPJ (*not* .HLP) file.

Conditionally Activating a Button in Windows Help

Just as it is possible to add your own special command buttons to WINHELP's toolbar, so you can selectively enable and disable these buttons based on some condition. For example, suppose you're writing an application that allows the user to install and view graphic images. If you had a command button labeled, say, "Images," this button would be enabled if the images have been installed; otherwise, it would be dimmed. You can create this button following the example given in the previous section. The next fragment of code demonstrates enabling and disabling buttons using the macro facility of the Windows Help engine, version 3.1:

```
char szMacro[255];        // string to hold Help Macro
//
/* This example assumes that a button has been*/
/* defined with an ID of IMAGE_BUTTON, and that */
/* a Boolean flag (bInstalled) has been set */
/* elsewhere if the images have been installed. */

if (bInstalled)           // Images have been installed
 lstrcpy(szMacro,"EnableButton('IMAGE_BUTTON')");
else
 lstrcpy(szMacro,"DisableButton('IMAGE_BUTTON')");

/* Run macro for your application's Help file */

CWinApp::WinHelp(hWnd,lpHelpFile, HELP_COMMAND, (LONG)szMacro);
```

CHANGING HELP-ON-HELP

Visual C++ automatically gives your application information on using the Windows Help system. Should you wish to override the default "Help-on-Help" file and replace it with one of your own, you can use the JumpHelpOn( ) macro in conjunction with the SetHelpOnFile( ) macro to change what the user gets. To do this, first create your new .HLP file containing what you want the users to get when they request Help on Help. Then add the macro SetHelpOnFile( ) to the [CONFIG] section of your program's .HPJ file, specifying as its sole argument the name of your new file, as in this example:

```
[CONFIG]
SetHelpOnFile("NEW_HELP.HLP>main")
JumpHelpOn()
```

The macros in this example would now direct all requests for Help on Help to the file "NEW_HELP.HLP." Another way of saying this is that SetHelpOnFile( ) replaces the file WINHELP.HLP. Note carefully our use of the redirection operator and the string "main" in the example. This displays the Help file "NEW_HELP.HLP" in the main Help window. Incidentally, a macro placed in the project file can be up to 254 characters long.

The JumpContents( ) Macro

Another useful macro is the JumpContents( ) call. This macro jumps to the contents topic, declared in the CONTENTS entry of [OPTIONS] in your project file, of the specified Help file. Here's how this macro appears:

```
JumpContents("spechelp.hlp")
```

The name of the file to which you wish to jump must be in quotation marks. This call is really useful for things like connecting buttons or icons to special Help files. As an example, a Windows program for, say, a home builder might want Help on strictly electrical items, or plumbing items. This call would take them to the table of contents of the designated file.

By the way, don't forget to check out the material later in this chapter concerning performance trade-offs. While the macros demonstrated here will get the job done for you, it behooves you to assess additional issues relative to the optimum usage of your applications. In some situations, there may be better alternatives than using macros like JumpContents( ). For now, it is enough to know that the WINHELP engine includes a lot of horsepower; the challenge is knowing what's there and how to get at it.

The Browse Buttons and Macros

Because WINHELP version 3.1 does *not* provide the Browse buttons (i.e., >> for forward and << for backward), you must use the BrowseButtons( ) macro if any of your Help files have browse sequences. This macro adds these buttons to the toolbar when you run WINHELP.EXE. You define a browse sequence by assigning a plus sign (+) to each topic in the browse sequence. If you are using Microsoft Word to create your Help files, a browse sequence is just a footnote that is formatted as a name, and corresponding number, separated by a colon. The name identifies the browse sequence to which the topic belongs; the number specifies the position in the sequence at which the topic is displayed to the user. If your Help file has only one browse sequence, you don't need the name, just the sequence number. As a result, WINHELP displays the browse topics based on their sequential order. When assigning the sequence number, be sure to leave "room" between them, so that you can add new topics later, if necessary. You don't need to leave room if your Help file will use multiple browse sequences, however. Here, the name, not the number, is the critical factor.

Sizing and Moving a Help Window

A useful Help macro is PositionWindow( ). This macro specifies the size and sets the x and y coordinates of a Help window. The window can be shown maximized, minimized, active, or inactive, etc.—the same "range of motion" that you may exercise in a regular Windows program, as a matter of fact. The macro takes six arguments:

```
PositionWindow(x, y, width, height, state, "name")
```

The arguments x and y are the upper left-hand corner coordinates of the Help window you want to show. These values are ignored if the argument *state* indicates the window is to be maximized. Don't forget that WINHELP has its own peculiar coordinate system, whereby the screen is a 1024×1024 grid. Thus, coordinates 512,512 place the upper left-hand corner of the Help window squarely in the center of the display, regardless of the pixel resolution of the system's video board. The *width* and *height* arguments also use this system, so make sure you do your math right if you decide to use PositionWindow( ). The last argument, *name*, is the string name for the Window; it cannot be "main," which is reserved for the main window. Secondary window names are defined in the [WINDOWS] section of your application's Help Project File. This name must be enclosed in quotation marks in the call to PositionWindow( ).

Menu Bar Macros

As we mentioned in Chapter 5, some macros are useful for manipulating the menu inside a Help file. This discussion will briefly highlight only those macros necessary to add or change a menu item. These should suffice to cover most of your special needs regarding menu bar macros. The first is InsertMenu( ), which is used to insert a new menu choice on the Help menu. As a general rule, you should not use this macro to place a choice as the first or second items, as these positions are occupied by the standard items of "File" and "Edit." The following example inserts the menu option "Tools" between the options "Edit" and "Bookmark" on the Help menu bar:

```
InsertMenu("menu_tools", "&Tools", 2)
```

The first argument is a unique name you give to your menu option; you will use this name later to reference the menu when adding more choices (e.g., our custom "tools"). This identifier must *always* be in double quotes. The second argument is the string we wish to display for the option, along with its keyboard accelerator, if any. This too must be in double quotes. The last argument is the position (with 0 as the first item) where the new option is to appear. This macro should appear in the [CONFIG] section of your application's .HPJ file.

The next thing to do is to add some items under this option, using either AppendItem( ) or InsertItem( ). Here are their prototypes:

```
AppendItem("menu-id", "item-id", "item-name", "macro")
InsertItem("menu-id", "item-id", "item-name", "macro", position)
```

The only difference between the two is that the position is required for InsertItem( ). Using our previous example of a menu for "Tools," we'll now demonstrate each of these macros. The first will use AppendItem to select an option called "Clock":

```
AppendItem("menu_tools","ID_Clk","&Clock","ExecProgram(`clock.exe',0)")
```

This macro places an item uniquely identified to WINHELP as "ID_Clk," with the text "Clock," under the "Tools" option. The macro to run is the Windows Clock program (`clock.exe'), which is displayed in normal size (indicated by the 0 argument).

Now to do the same thing for the Windows Calculator program, we'll use InsertItem:

```
InsertItem("menu_tools","ID_CAL","Calc","ExecProgram(`calc.exe',2),1)
```

This inserts "Calc" as the second choice (position = 1) under "Tools"; note the absence of a keyboard accelerator in the string "Calc" as compared to "&Clock." When the Calculator program runs, it is shown maximized (indicated by the 2 argument).

The functions to enable and disable an option are pretty straightforward—just supply the "item-id" argument you assigned when the menu was created. For example:

```
EnableItem("ID_Clk")
DisableItem("ID_Clk")
```

The first call would enable the Clock program in our example; the second would dim the string and disable the Clock option.

Similar macros exist should you wish to place a check mark beside an item—CheckItem( ) and UnCheckItem( ):

```
CheckItem("ID_Clk")
UnCheckItem("ID_Clk")
```

Both take the same argument, which is the identifier assigned when the menu item was created (regardless of whether AppendItem or InsertItem was used).

HELP AND THE STATUS BAR

An extra bonus with Visual C++ is the ability to display brief Help messages in the status bar that appears at the bottom of the screen (if you included this option in AppWizard when you created the project). When you create a new menu resource in App Studio, you supply an ID, CAPTION, and PROMPT. The field called PROMPT is where you can supply "mini-Help"; when the mouse passes over this menu option, whatever was typed into PROMPT when the menu was created shows up in the status bar. This is a good place to add some "memory joggers" for infrequently used options. As a performance consideration, this reminder might be just enough information to keep your user from needing to consult your application's Help file, which can involve a lot of overhead.

VISUAL C++ HELP TOOLS

To develop Help files for your application, you'll use three primary tools: AppWizard, MAKEHM, and the Windows Help Compiler. The Help Compiler comes with the Professional Edition of Visual C++. If you have another Windows development package such as the SDK or Turbo C for Windows, you probably already have the Help Compiler. Be sure it is the version for Windows 3.1; the file is called HC31.EXE. Also, if you plan to include any bitmapped graphics, you'll need a graphics tool capable of creating a .BMP file compatible with Windows.

AppWizard

When you first create your application in AppWizard, you must check the Context-Sensitive Help option in the Options dialog box. Visual C++ will automatically set up the message entries to support the Help feature. Likewise, it will create a subdirectory in your project's directory called \HLP. It is here that the RTF files and bitmaps are installed. In your project's directory you will find three additional files for Help support: a *project* file, a MAKEHELP.BAT file, and a MAKEHM.BAT file. The .HPJ file is the project file used by MAKEHELP.BAT to create a unique Help file for your program. The batch file MAKEHELP takes care of mapping all the IDs and running the Help Compiler.

Note that when AppWizard creates your application's .RTF file in the HLP directory, you need to edit this file and replace all occurrences of double angle brackets (<< and >>) with the name of your program. This is AppWizard's way of marking what needs to be changed.

MAKEHM.BAT

This batch file called by MAKEHELP.BAT is used to convert the IDs specified in your project's RESOURCE.H file to a map file. This map file eventually gets inserted in the [MAP] section of the Help Project File. Recall that the [MAP] section acts like some sort of giant "GOTO" statement—it gives each context string (or alias) a unique number that allows each Help topic to be uniquely identified. The IDs assigned to each object are not random, and it is very important that you use the prefixes assigned by App Studio when naming resources. Table 15.6 summarizes the relationship between prefixes and resources.

These prefixes tell MAKEHM.BAT what kind of resource it is dealing with and govern the rules for assigning the unique numbers. For string resources, use the IDS_ prefix, but don't write Help topics for them. For string resources inside message boxes, use the IDP_ prefix and *do* write Help topics for them. The user will get a Help message when pressing F1 from inside a message box.

THE HELPWININFO STRUCTURE

When the user starts WINHELP.EXE and opens a Help file, Windows opens a second window and displays the Help in it. It is the job of the HELPWININFO structure to manage the size and position of this window. Your application can modify the size and position by calling the Win Help function with the HELP_SETWINPOS value

TABLE 15.6
The App Studio prefixes for naming resources.

PREFIX ID	OBJECT
IDP_	Message-box prompt
IDD_	Dialog-box ID
ID_ or IDM_	Toolbar or menu command
IDR_	Frame-related resources
IDW_	Control bar

and by adjusting the members of the HELPWININFO structure. This structure is defined as follows:

```
typedef struct {
int wStructSize;
int x;
int y;
int dx;
int dy;
int wMax;
char rgchMember[2];
} HELPWININFO;
```

The following list explains this structure's members:

wStructSize	The size of the HELPWININFO structure.
x	The initial horizontal position of the Help window.
y	The initial vertical position of the Help window.
dx	The width of the Help window.
dy	The height of the Help window.
wMax	A flag indicating if the window should be maximized (in which case, use 1), or set to the x,y positions given.
rgchMember	The name of the Help window.

WINHELP.EXE divides the display screen into 1024 units in both the horizontal and vertical directions. To create a Help window that uses the entire upper half of the display, for example, your application would modify HELPWININFO's members as follows:

```
HELPWININFO.x = 0;        // start at 0,0
HELPWININFO.y = 0;
HELPWININFO.dx = 1024;    // go completely across....
HELPWININFO.dy = 512;     //...and halfway down
```

WIN.INI FILE CONSIDERATIONS

An easy-to-overlook item concerning Help is the WIN.INI file used by Windows. Remember to make use of the Help "settings" found therein. Of the several entries in the section marked "[Windows Help]," these are the four most important:

- M_WindowPosition = *x, y, width, height, ifMaximized*

- H_WindowPosition = *x, y, width, height, ifMaximized*

- A_WindowPosition = *x, y, width, height, ifMaximized*

- C_WindowPosition = *x, y, width, height, ifMaximized*

These entries define the default characteristics of the Main Help window (item 1), the History dialog box (2), the Annotate dialog box (3), and the Copy dialog box (4). The x,y values are the coordinates of the upper left-hand corner of each window or dialog box. The next values are the default width and height. The last parameter is a flag that, if set to 1, causes the Help file window to be maximized on-screen. If this flag is set to 0, the values of *width* and *height* are used to size the Help file window. This flag has no effect on the History, Annotate, and Copy values, since these are dialog boxes and thus cannot be maximized.

The following WIN.INI entries relating to Help all refer to color selections and have the same parameters—a red value, a green value, and a blue value:

`IFJumpColor =` `red, green, blue`	This entry determines the color used for indicating that a word has a hypertext link to another topic. Edit WIN.INI to change this entry.
`JumpColor =` `red, green, blue`	This entry is the same as IFJumpColor. It specifies the text color to be used when making a hypertext jump to another topic. For example, JumpColor = 0,0,0 displays the jump topic in black letters against a white background. Edit WIN.INI to change this entry.
`IFPopupColor =` `red, green, blue`	This entry changes the color of the text used to indicate a pop-up term definition. To see the effects, first click on Help in Program Manager, and then select "Arranging Windows and Icons." The first pop-up term in this file is *"title bar"*; observe its color. Then, quit Windows and add the line IFPopupColor = 0,255,255 to the [Windows Help] section of your WIN.INI file. Restart Windows, and go back into "Arranging Windows and Icons." The term *"title bar"* will now be displayed using a cyan color. Edit WIN.INI file to change the entry.
`PopupColor =` `red, green, blue`	Same as IFPopupColor. Like the JumpColor entry, this entry changes the appearance of the pop-up window for terms. A entry of PopupColor = 255,255,0 results in yellow text on a white background.
`MacroColor =` `red, green, blue`	If your Help file includes any macros, changing this entry changes the color used to indicate them. Edit WIN.INI to change the entry.

PERFORMANCE TIPS FOR WRITING HELP FILES

We'll start to wrap things up for this chapter by giving you a few suggestions for optimizing the Help files used by your application. These suggestions are based on Windows Help version 3.06+; check your version (or that of your target platform) before you rely on these tips.

Project File (.HPJ) Improvements

In this section, we'll examine some ways you can modify your .HPJ file to increase the overall performance of the Help system. First of all, set the COMPRESS option in your .HPJ file when you do your final build for your application's Help file. Also, study the contents of your Help file, and see if you can spot categories. For example, if your program is, say, home-building software, you should put all the material about electrical items in one file, all plumbing in another, and so on. This "clumping" spreads out the load by dedicating certain topics to certain files; besides, a user who wants Help on a topic is likely to want to see *related* Help that can be fetched from the current file. However, you'll have to consider some trade-offs when you increase the number of referenced files, as you'll see later.

CD-ROM, Small Bitmaps, and Large Help Files

Large Help files, and Help files intended to be hosted on a CD-ROM device, should include the command OPTCDROM=1 in the [OPTIONS] section. This option aligns files on 2K boundaries; hence, this command is not recommended for small, multiple files. But for large files and CD-ROM, this option can significantly decrease your access time, especially for CD-ROM.

Bitmaps that are small or rarely used should be included directly in the Help file, not loaded on demand from a dedicated file. The disk I/O penalty just isn't worth it, especially if your Help file will be on CD-ROM. Also, every time you open a file, you lose a DOS file handle, so it makes sense to keep the bitmaps with the Help file.

Likewise, keep large bitmaps *out* of the Help file, as their inclusion will degrade performance. As a guideline, 12K of compressed Help text is buffered in memory; so as long as the combined size of your bitmaps and Help text don't exceed this value, you can "piggyback" your images and allow them to take advantage of buffering. As a bonus, Help topics under 12K compressed do not need to be reread whenever the window changes size or is redrawn. But beware! It is *crucial* that you keep the size under the magic number of 12K. You pay a performance penalty in "bundling" a bitmap with the Help text when the bitmap is used more than once in the Help file. If a bitmap is often used, placing it in its own file might be more appropriate, especially for a large bitmap.

Large Bitmaps

Large bitmaps rate a different perspective from the small ones. All large or frequently used files *should* be stored in their own file. WINHELP caches the 50 most recently accessed bitmap files, so they generally require only one disk read should two or more Help topics make reference to them. These cached files only require rereading when they are "scrolled" out of the cache by other file accesses, low memory, or other reasons. You pay a penalty (in the form of an additional disk seek) when cached bitmaps are not stored with the Help file text, especially if the user only accesses the file once in the session. This penalty is acceptable, however, when dealing with large bitmaps. The same holds true if the bitmap file will be accessed frequently (as when different Help topics all use the same bitmap); observe that a file referenced many times enjoys the advantages of being cached without increasing the 50-file limit.

Using Segmented Hypergraphics

Using segmented hypergraphics can influence Help file performance, especially for CD-ROM–hosted platforms. Segmented hypergraphics allow a single bitmap to define multiple regions as hot spots on the bitmap. By using a single bitmap, you avoid all the disk seeks to fetch all the files that would be needed to draw the final bitmap. You'll need to use the Hot Spot Editor, available with Visual C++, to define the hot spots inside the bitmap.

On closing the subject of performance, you might want to try coming up with a general purpose, knowledge-based algorithm for profiling a Help file; you would supply data such as number of Help files, sizes, access frequency, and so on, and the algorithm would return recommendations for configuring the system. As of this writing (circa 1994), there is a noticeable paucity of information about Windows Help files, and any dissemination of data about them should improve the quality of our craft. In view of the growing demand for Windows-based applications (which includes OS/2 platforms as well), the role of useful Help files, and the tools to create them, will become increasingly important.

Using Help Authoring Tools

If you plan to develop a lot of Help files, you should take a hard look at purchasing a Help Authoring Tool. There are several in the mainstream current of commercial software, and some excellent cost-effective alternatives are available through shareware. Each of these tools has its credits and debits, in terms of price-performance, etc. Broadly speaking, these tools use Microsoft Word, so be sure to budget for this item if you don't already own it. Microsoft provides an unsupported Help Authoring Tool that includes the Help Compiler. You can download it from the Microsoft library on CompuServe. From a performance enhancement viewpoint, using an authoring tool allows you to sharply cut your development time; dramatic savings become apparent as you use the tool on several projects. Likewise, using an authoring tool lets you easily make changes to Help files for applications during the development and testing phases. Also, nonprogrammers can be quickly trained in these tools, so more programming resources can concentrate on writing the application. An authoring tool is really a necessity, not a luxury, for serious Windows developers.

Really adventurous readers may want to take a shot at writing their own tools, based on the information provided in this chapter. After all, the Microsoft Foundation Classes version 2.0 gives you such things as dialog boxes for selecting fonts, sizes, and colors. You could use these from a floating tool palette, allow for data entry, compilation, and testing, and you'd have a pretty snappy little tool.

CHAPTER SUMMARY

The inclusion of an informative Help file is becoming a de facto standard by which all contemporary Windows-based programs are being judged. These files are so easy to build that omitting them is gross negligence for all but the most elementary applications. Online Help is a vital bridge for helping the first-time user overcome the learning curve of your program; seasoned users will likewise appreciate the quick availability of reference material when dealing with those aspects of your application that are used infrequently. Where possible, you should retain a technical writer to develop the Help files, even more so when a product must be delivered under a compressed schedule. Regardless of who writes them, you need to remember to keep the contents of your Help files accurate, complete, and up to date. During beta testing, try having someone who is completely unfamiliar with your program see whether he or she can navigate the program using just your Help file as a guide. Also, add graphics to your Help file to enhance clarity for descriptions of visual objects in your program, like custom controls, icons, and toolbars. Furthermore, bear in mind that your program *might* benefit by adding some of the other features discussed in this chapter, such as the ability to run other Windows programs. The Help engine is nothing less than a fully functional Windows program for which you have been provided some powerful hooks. The more complex your application, the more useful it will be to your users if you exploit these hooks to the greatest extent.

CHAPTER
16

Debugging

This chapter covers the various errors that can befall a programmer and shows how the Visual Workbench can come to the rescue. We will cover the debugger integrated with the Visual Workbench. The Professional Edition of MSVC also contains the full-fledged CodeView Debugger, with which you can also debug MS-DOS programs. The integrated debugger handles Windows executables, both .EXEs and .DLLs.

You will find that the integrated debugger provides several ways to access commands, via menu choices, keyboard accelerators, and the toolbar. We will list each option's keyboard accelerator beside the menu choice in parentheses and mention those choices that have no toolbar equivalents.

This chapter discusses syntax errors, run-time errors, and logic errors. The workbench can help you correct most syntax errors during the compilation process and provide some help on what the errors mean. Microsoft integrates the workbench and the Visual Editor to provide these services. For run-time errors, the application framework provides an exception-handling process that allows you to recover from run-time errors or exit gracefully. Not least, this chapter will show you how to use the integrated debugger to catch those pesky logic errors.

SYNTAX ERRORS

No one would argue that some programmers code better than they spell, and one of the most common mistakes is to mistype a keyword or identifier while coding. If you use the built-in editor, you can use the color syntax feature to help spot that kind of error. If such an error does slip by, the workbench will report syntax errors in the output window, as illustrated in Figure 16.1.

The workbench allows you to place the cursor on the error in the output box and, by double-clicking on the line, jump directly to the offending line in the appropriate source file. (See Chapter 1 for more information on the workbench.)

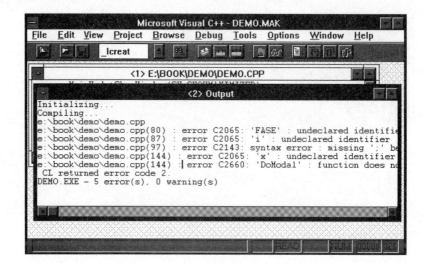

Figure 16.1
Output window
displaying
error messages.

RUN-TIME ERRORS

As we all know, a clean compile does not make for an error-free program. Some items are beyond the developer's control, such as system resources. Common run-time errors include such problems as exhausting memory or trying to open a nonexistent file. In C, a programmer usually checks a function's return value for an error condition. The C++ standard provides a better system, called exception handling. The Microsoft Foundation Classes (MFC) do not implement exception handling as defined by the standard, but it does provide emulation for the system. The framework accomplishes this emulation with a series of macros called TRY and CATCH. Table 16.1 lists the various exception-handling macros and the purpose for each.

Chapter 11 provided some examples of the TRY/CATCH process dealing with file errors. The framework implements these macros with the C RTL functions setjump( ) and longjump( ) and can cause problems if misused. The biggest problem deals with

TABLE 16.1
Exception handling macros.

MACRO	DESCRIPTION
TRY	The entry point for the MFC exception-handling process.
CATCH	Begins the block of code, catching the first thrown exception of the type specified in the CATCH macro.
AND_CATCH	Begins subsequent blocks, catching additional types of exceptions.
END_CATCH	Delimits the final block of code in a series of TRY/CATCH [AND_CATCH] blocks.
CATCH_ALL	Can be used to replace the final CATCH/AND_CATCH/END_CATCH macros in a series. Detailed in Tech Note #32.
END_CATCH_ALL	Delimits the CATCH_ALL block of code.
THROW	Allows you to throw an exception from your routines, thus providing exception-handling capabilities to your functions.
THROW_LAST	Passes the exception on to other handlers for processing.

how C++ allocates and frees memory. If a routine passes control to a far-off exception handler, some clean-up might be left undone, thus leaving memory leaks in your program and jeopardizing system integrity.

THE EXCEPTION CLASS

Each of these macros expects as its first parameter the type of exception class it is processing. MFC derives this class from the CException Class, as described in the *Class Library Reference for the Microsoft Foundation Class Library*. This class is an abstract base class, which means you can't use a variable of type CException. Instead, you must derive and use a new class from CException. MFC provides for the seven derived exception classes listed in Table 16.2.

The classes in Table 16.2 are documented in the *Reference volume 1 of The Class Library Reference* mentioned above, and the online help files.

EXAMPLES

The following examples illustrate several situations you can encounter with exception handling. The usual structure is to enclose a possible exception-throwing statement with a TRY block, followed by one or more CATCH blocks.

```
TRY
{
```

TABLE 16.2
CException-derived classes.

CLASSES	DESCRIPTIONS
CArchiveException	Exceptions relating to CArchive objects. The data member m_cause will contain the reason for the exception.
CFileException	Exceptions relating to CFile objects. The data member m_cause will contain the reason for the exception. Chapter 13 details the various values of m_cause.
CMemoryException	Exceptions relating to failure to allocate requested memory. This object represents only an Out of Memory condition and thus has no other associated causes. Its only function is its constructor, which you never call. Use the function AfxThrowMemory-Exception to generate an object of this class.
CNotSupportedException	Exception indicating that the requested service is not supported under the current framework. Use the AfxThrowNotSupported function to create an object of this class.
COleException	Exceptions relating to Object Linking and Embedding. The data member m_status will indicate the reason for the exception. Use the AfxThrowOleException to create an object of this class.
CResourceException	Exception indicating that the requested resource could not be found or created. Use the AfxThrowResourceException to create an object of this class.
CUserException	Exception allowing you to handle a program-specific exception, usually to stop an end user operation.

```
    char *ptr = new char[32768];
}
CATCH( CMemoryException, e)
{
    AfxMessageBox("Unable to allocate enough memory!");
}
END_CATCH
```

The second parameter to the CATCH macros are pointers to the associated exception objects. The macros will supply this for you. For example, you would not declare a CMemoryException object named *e* because the documentation explicitly states you should *not* do this. If the exception object contained a data member specifying the cause, like CFileException or CArchiveException, then you could access this data member through the pointer.

```
UINT retv(TRUE); // C++ variable initialization
TRY
{
    CStdioFile infile("temp.txt",CFile::modeRead);
}
CATCH( CFileException, e)
{
    if ( e->m_cause == CFileException::fileNotFound)
        AfxMessageBox( "File Not Found");
    retv = FALSE;
}
END_CATCH
return retv;
```

Sometimes, an operation may throw several exceptions, in which case you can use the AND_CATCH macros like so:

```
TRY
{
    // operation that could really mess up the application
}
CATCH( CArchiveException, e)
{
    //handle the archive exception
}
AND_CATCH( CFileException, e)
{
    // handle the CFileException
}
CATCH_ALL( e )
{
    // you could use AND_CATCH again, but the CATCH_ALL macro
    // will save on the code size
}
END_CATCH_ALL
```

THROWING EXCEPTIONS

Sometimes you may develop server-like functions for others to use. If these functions can generate exceptions, such as failure to allocate enough memory, then you

TABLE 16.3
Afx exception-throwing functions.

FUNCTIONS	DESCRIPTIONS
`AfxThrowArchiveException(int cause)`	Sets the m_cause data member to the value of the passed parameter.
`AfxThrowFileException( int cause, LONG lOsError = -1)`	Sets the m_cause to the passed value. If a value for the operating system error is not passed, the exception will use the default value of –1. This is the DOS (or other OS) error code.
`AfxThrowMemoryException()`	Has no parameters. Note that the default operator *new* will throw this exception automatically.
`AfxThrowNotSupportedException()`	Has no parameters.
`AfxThrowOleException( OLESTATUS status)`	Sets the m_status variable to the passed value.
`AfxThrowResourceException()`	Has no parameters.
`AfxThrowUserException()`	Indicates that the user has already been alerted to the error. Thus with this function you can handle the clean-up differently than for system exceptions. The Microsoft documentation suggests you throw this exception after alerting the user via a MessageBox.

should throw an exception. Table 16.3 shows the MFC framework functions that throw an exception to others.

ALERTING THE USER (AND THE DEVELOPER)

Letting the user's machine lock up to indicate an error leaves much to be desired. If possible, you should alert the user to what has happened and why. Also, let the user try to recover if possible. The exception-handling process described in the previous section provides the recovery functionality, but to alert the user you will need to use some type of message box. MFC provides a wrapper for the SDK MessageBox function called AfxMessageBox. The CWnd class also provides a MessageBox function. These functions supply many default parameters that allow you to merely pass a string to the function. If you pass a string, you will get a MessageBox displaying your string and a default OK button. Figure 16.2 illustrates the results of the following sample code:

```
AfxMessageBox("Hello World");
```

You can use sprintf( ) or wsprintf( ) to format a string, but the framework also supplies two functions, AfxFormatString1 and AfxFormatString2, to accomplish the same task. The format of these functions is AfxFormatString1(CString& *rString,* UINT *nIDS,* LPCSTR *lpsz1*), where *rString* is the resultant string you pass to the

Figure 16.2
MessageBox displaying
Hello World.

message box and *nIDS* is the ID for a string in the String table containing the special format character %1. Here's an example:

```
String table entry:
IDS_FMT1 "Unable to Open File %1.".
function call:
CString msg;
AfxFormatString1(msg, IDS_FMT1, "temp.000");
AfxMessageBox( msg );
```

The function would replace the %1 with the string passed in LPCSTR *lpsz1*.

AFXMESSAGEBOX

This function packs a lot of functionality with its various parameters, which each have default values, so all you really have to do is pass it a string to display. The function's two prototypes are:

> int AfxMessageBox(LPCSTR *lpszMsg*,
> UINT *nType* = MB_OK, UINT *bIDHelp* = 0);

> int AFXAPI AfxMessageBox(UINT *nIDPrompt*, UINT *nType* = MB_OK,
> UINT *nIDHelp* = (UINT)–1);

> *lpszMsg* – a CString or null-terminated string to be displayed.

In the first line, *nType* refers to the style of the message box. It can describe the buttons that appear, the modality of the MessageBox, and the icons displayed. You can OR these values together for greater functionality. Table 16.4 lists the possible values.

Debuggers are heavy-duty tools that require time to set up and use. So over the years developers have used the old standby printf (or its language equivalent) to pinpoint the module, or area, where things are going wrong. By using AfxMessageBox, you can get the same functionality. Later, you will find an even better way to display diagnostic messages.

THE INTEGRATED DEBUGGER

The Visual C++ integrated debugger will be familiar to QuickC for Windows programmers. This section will cover how to prepare your program for debugging and then how to use the various tools.

TABLE 16.4
Message box button types.

VALUES	DESCRIPTIONS
MB_ABORTRETRYIGNORE	Displays the three buttons Abort, Retry, Ignore. AfxMessageBox will return IDABORT, IDRETRY, or IDIGNORE, depending on which button the user selects.
MB_OK	The default button. AfxMessageBox will return IDOK.
MB_OKCANCEL	Displays the two buttons OK and CANCEL. The function will return IDOK or IDCANCEL, depending on which button the user selects Also, if the user presses the escape key, the routine will return IDCANCEL.
MB_RETRYCANCEL	Displays a RETRY and a CANCEL button. The function will return IDRETRY or IDCANCEL, depending on the button selected. IDCANCEL will be returned if the user presses the escape key.
MB_YESNO	Displays a YES and a NO button and will return IDYES or IDNO, depending on which button is selected.
MB_YESNOCANCEL	Displays the YES, NO, and CANCEL buttons. The function will return IDYES, IDNO, or IDCANCEL, depending on the button selected. IDCANCEL will be returned if the user presses the escape key.
MESSAGE BOX MODALITY	
MB_APPMODAL	Indicates the user must respond to this message before continuing with the application, but the user can switch to another application and work. This modality is the default.
MB_SYSTEMMODAL	Indicates the user must respond to the message before doing anything else in Windows.
MB_TASKMODAL	Used in routines that have no available Windows handle (like a DLL). This modality has no use in an MFC program.
ICONS	
MB_ICONEXCLAMATION	Displays an exclamation point in the message box.
MB_ICONINFORMATION	Displays the "i" or information icon.
MB_ICONQUESTION	Displays the question mark or Help icon.
MB_ICONSTOP	Displays the stop sign or warning icon.
DEFAULT BUTTONS	
MB_DEFBUTTON1	Indicates that the first button is the default button. This style is the default.
MB_DEFBUTTON2	Indicates that the second button is the default button.
MB_DEFBUTTON3	Indicates that the third button is the default button.

The first step is to include the necessary debug information in your program. The framework will do this automatically by choosing the Debug Build mode from the Options/Project dialog box, shown in Figure 16.3.

Choosing this option will provide debugging information, but it will increase the size of your executables tremendously! When you tell the preprocessor to define the _DEBUG macro, the framework will generate lots of conditionally compiled debug

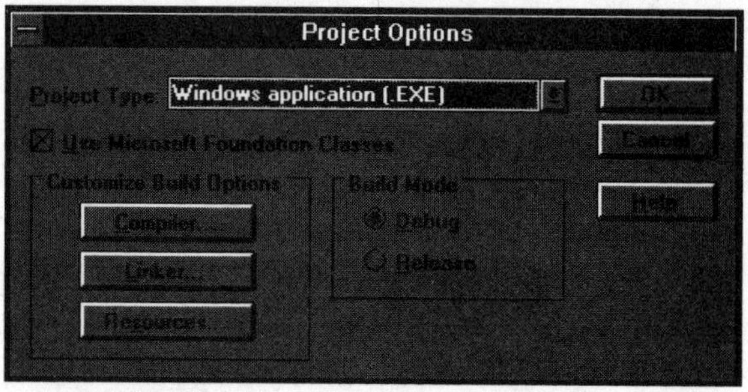

Figure 16.3
Debug Build options.

code. (The framework will not generate this code in a release mode build.) The following sample code demonstrates conditional compilation:

```
#ifdef _DEBUG
    UINT x = TRUE;
#else
    UINT x = FALSE;
#endif
```

As Table 16.5 shows, MFC provides several macros you can use for run-time validation. Note that once you recompile in release mode, these macros have no effect.

The ASSERT( ) macro is the familiar C macro. If the expression evaluates to FALSE, or 0, the program will print out a message and abort. The MFC source files are riddled with this macro. For example:

```
char *ptr = theApp.GetPtr();
ASSERT( NULL == ptr );
```

If ptr is equal to NULL, the program will display a MessageBox like the one illustrated in Figure 16.4. If ptr is not equal to NULL, the macro will do nothing.

The ASSERT_VALID(*pObject*) macro takes a pointer to an object and will check to make sure the pointer is not NULL. The macro will also call the object's AssertValid member function so the object can check itself. If either test fails, the macro aborts the program with a diagnostic message. You should supply the AssertValid member function for any classes you derive and then call the base CObject member function before performing your own checks. For example:

TABLE 16.5
Macros defined by _DEBUG.

MACROS	DESCRIPTION
ASSERT	Boolean expression
ASSERT_VALID	*pObject*
VERIFY	Boolean expression
DEBUG_NEW	
TRACE	
TRACE0, TRACE1, TRACE2, TRACE3	

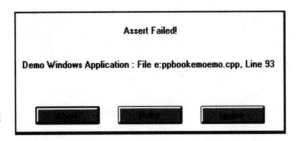

Figure 16.4
Assertion Failed in FILE
in line LINE.

Inside the figure:

Assert Failed!

Demo Windows Application : File e:ppbookemoemo.cpp, Line 93

```
// example for CObject::AssertValid derived functions
void CMyObject::AssertValid() const
{
CObject::AssertValid(); // call the base class first
ASSERT( m_mass > 0 );
ASSERT( m_gravity <= 1 );
.... // test the other data members here
}
```

The VERIFY( ) macro is similar to the ASSERT macro in that if the express evaluates to false, the macro will print the same error message and halt the program. The difference is that the macro will still evaluate the expression when compiled in release mode, but it will not halt the program. Thus you could embed a function call in the macro and still have the program execute the function in release mode.

If the framework detects the DEBUG_NEW macro, it will use a debugging version of the new operator. This version will keep track of the file and line number of where the allocation took place. To see this list, you use the CMemoryState::DumpAllObjects-Since member function. This function will dump the list of every allocation since the last time you called the function. To use this macro, include the following define in your source files:

```
#define new DEBUG_NEW
```

When you compile in release mode, this macro will expand to the original "new" operator.

The framework relies on the THIS_FILE array macro for the information it keeps while in debug mode. AppWizard usually places this macro, shown next, at the beginning of the implementation files it generates.

```
#ifdef _DEBUG
#undef THIS_FILE
static char BASED_CODE THIS_FILE[] = __FILE__;
#endif
```

This macro will place the current file information into the application's base code segment and will share this information with the rest of the program. This arrangement prevents the compiler from littering many copies of the same filename throughout the program's scarce data segments.

Earlier in this chapter, you saw how to print out simple debug messages with the AfxMessageBox, but the TRACE( ) macro will provide that functionality plus a whole lot more. This function will take a format string, just like the printf family of functions, plus a variable number of arguments. The TRACE macro will print its output to AfxDump (more on this later) in Debug mode and will do nothing in release mode. Here are a few examples:

```
TRACE("Beginning test\n");
int x(0), y(4), z(3); // declare 3 ints and initialize them.
TRACE( "x=%d, y=%d,z=%d\n",x,y,z);
BOOL flag(FALSE);
flag = theApp.GetFlag();
x = (flag) ? y : z;
TRACE("X= %d\n");
CString str = (flag) ? "TRUE" : "FALSE";
int len = str.GetLength();
TRACE( "x = %d, the string = %s, and y,z = %d,%d\n",
  x,str.GetBuffer(len),y,z);
str.GetBuffer(-1);
TRACE("END TEST\n");
```

The TRACE0, TRACE1, TRACE2, and TRACE3 macros are similar to the TRACE macro, except they take a fixed number of arguments, as indicated by the number. Thus TRACE0 will print out only a string. TRACE1 will print out a single value, like so:

```
TRACE0("The test begins\n");
TRACE1("The value of X is %d\n",x);
```

WHERE, OH WHERE, DID MY OUTPUT GO?

The TRACE macros afford you the power of printf( ) statements in a non-Windows environment. But unlike printf( ), whose output goes to the display, the TRACE macros' output goes to the workbench's output window. If a debugger is operating, the output will go to the debugger's output window. If neither window is available, the output will go to your system's AUX port. This last can be a major problem, especially if your AUX port is your serial port and you're developing an application that depends on the serial port.

Microsoft provides a debug window that will display all the output from the TRACE macros and the AfxDump calls. This program, called DBWIN, resides in the \mfc\bin directory. Figure 16.5 shows the DBWIN program. You can use this window to receive the messages from the MFC libraries, and you can also use DBWIN to catch the messages generated by the debug version of the Windows DLLs.

The setup program installed the source for this program and its associated DLL in the \mfc\samples\dbwin directory. Thus you can modify the program (e.g., remove the calls to MessageBeep( ) that occur when the message queue overflows) and install the .EXE in the tools menu of the Visual Workbench.

One interesting note is that if your program saturates the Windows message queue so that it starts to lose messages, DBWIN will beep, incessantly. You can comment out the MessageBeep(0)'s from the source code and save some wear and tear on your ears and those of your colleagues.

```
┌─────────────────────────────────────────────────┬───┬───┐
│  ─          Debug Messages                        │ ▼ │ ▲ │
├─────────────────────────────────────────────────┴───┴───┤
│  File   Edit   Options   Help                             │
├────────────────────────────────────────────────────┬────┤
│ err PAINTSHO 06DF:1A2E: Invalid HWND: 0000           │  ▲ │
│ err PAINTSHO 06DF:1A2E: Invalid HWND: 0000           │    │
│ err PAINTSHO 06DF:1A2E: Invalid HWND: 0000           │    │
│ err PAINTSHO 06DF:1A2E: Invalid HWND: 0000           │    │
│ err PAINTSHO 06DF:1A2E: Invalid HWND: 0000           │    │
│ err PAINTSHO 06DF:1A2E: Invalid HWND: 0000           │    │
│ err PAINTSHO 06DF:1A2E: Invalid HWND: 0000           │    │
│ err PAINTSHO 06DF:1A2E: Invalid HWND: 0000           │    │
│ err PAINTSHO 06DF:1A2E: Invalid HWND: 0000           │    │
│                                                      │  ▼ │
├─┬────────────────────────────────────────────────┬─┴────┤
│←│                                                  │  →   │
└─┴──────────────────────────────────────────────────┴────┘
```

Figure 16.5
DBWIN.

The global variable, AfxTraceEnabled, controls whether the macros will print information. You can set this variable to TRUE in your source code, or you can set it to 1 in the AFX.INI file, as shown here:

```
[Diagnostics]
TraceEnabled=1
TraceFlags=31
```

Microsoft provides a utility, called TRACER.EXE, that can control how the framework reports debug messages (see Figure 16.6). The utility modifies the AFX.INI file and the AfxTraceFlags. See Tech Note #7 for a discussion of the various trace flags. Microsoft provides the source for this utility in the \msvc\mfc\samples directory.

ON WITH THE SHOW . . .

Once you have chosen a debug build rather than a release build, you must recompile your program. After rebuilding your application, you can now run the program under the debugger. Well, almost.

At this point you have included the proper macros in your source code, you've run the TRACER.EXE utility to set the trace flags, and you have DBWIN up and running to catch all those messages that you and the framework send. You can run the debugger with the retail version of Windows. But with the SDK and Visual C++ Professional Edition you get a copy of the Windows debug kernel. If possible, you should run *this* version of Windows during development. You will probably see more errors and warnings than you will care to admit, but they will help you create a more stable product. Microsoft usually provides batch files to swap the debug and retail

Figure 16.6
The Tracer utility.

versions of the various .DLLs. They are called N2D.BAT and D2N.BAT. N2D will replace the Normal Windows program files with the Debug versions. D2N will reverse this operation. Both call a batch file called SWITCH.BAT, usually located in the mfc\bin subdirectory, which copies the system files from one subdirectory to the other. These debug files contain a lot of debugging code so your Windows system will respond more slowly than a regular Windows system. Also, you must have a window available to receive debug messages, like DBWIN, or Windows will hang.

THE DEBUGGER

Figure 16.7 shows you the debugger's menu options. Some of these options have counterparts on the toolbar shown in Figure 16.8. Most also have function key accelerators.

GO (F5)

This menu command will execute the program from its current point. Execution will continue until the program encounters a breakpoint, a watch expression becomes TRUE, or the program terminates (normally or abnormally). This command corresponds to the Run button on the toolbar.

Restart (SHIFT F5)

This menu item has no toolbar equivalent. This option will reset the system (excluding watches and breakpoints) by reloading the program and symbols into memory. It will then restart the program and halt at the WinMain function.

Stop Debugging (ALT F5)

This menu item also has no toolbar equivalent. It will stop your debugging session and return you to a normal edit mode. The system will notify and, based on your response, stop the debugging session if you try to recompile a file or exit the workbench.

Step Into (F8)

You can use this menu item, and its equivalent toolbar button, to step into a function call, including all the code inside that function. If the function resides in another

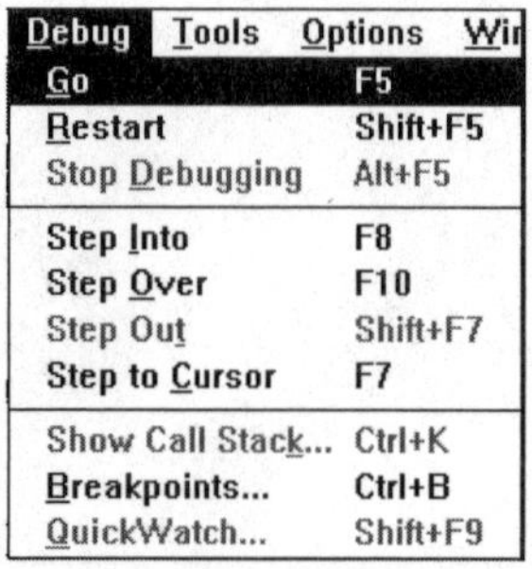

Figure 16.7
The Debug
menu items.

Debug	Tools	Options	Wir
Go		F5	
Restart		Shift+F5	
Stop Debugging		Alt+F5	
Step Into		F8	
Step Over		F10	
Step Out		Shift+F7	
Step to Cursor		F7	
Show Call Stack...		Ctrl+K	
Breakpoints...		Ctrl+B	
QuickWatch...		Shift+F9	

Figure 16.8
Relevant toolbar buttons
and descriptions for the
debugger.

source file, the workbench will load that file and continue from the function's entry point. If the function is part of the MFC library, then you will step into that function, providing the framework knows where you stored the source files. You can set this path in the Options/Directories dialog box (Figure 16.9), or the debugger will ask you for the base path.

This feature is a great way to explore the foundation classes. It can also be a pain if you inadvertently step into an AFX routine. If you do inadvertently step into any function, you can leave with the Step Out menu/toolbar option.

Step Over (F10)

You can use this menu option/toolbar button to prevent stepping into a function, while still single-stepping through the application and executing the function. It will allow you to see the return codes of the function, but it will also leave you vulnerable to any problems with the function in question.

Step Out (SHIFT F7)

As described in the section on Step Into F8, this menu/toolbar option allows you to leave a function you've stepped into and return to the instruction following the function call.

Step to Cursor (F7)

This function unfortunately has no toolbar equivalent. Step to Cursor will allow you to place your cursor on any point in a program and execute the program to that point. The debugger will alert you if that point has no executable code.

Show Call Stack (CTRL K)

This menu option allows you to see the call stack of the functions you have stepped into but have not returned from yet. This option displays the dialog box shown in Figure 16.10.

Figure 16.9
Directories Options
box showing MFC
source files.

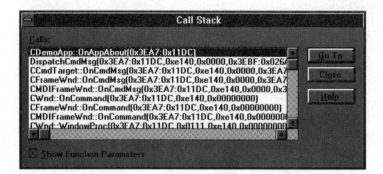

Figure 16.10
The Show Call Stack
dialog box.

This item lists the calls in LIFO order (last-in, first-out), and each function will list its parameters, if you enable the Show Function Parameters check box. If you highlight a function in the list box and click the Go To button, the workbench will open an editor box containing the appropriate source files and display the line containing that function call.

Breakpoints (CTRL B)

Breakpoints allow you to control where in a source file a program will halt execution while running under a debugger. While stopped at that point you can observe the call stack, variable values, or register values. While at a breakpoint, or between steps while stepping through a program, you can also modify a variable's or register's value.

It is up to you to decide where to place a breakpoint in your source code. The output from a TRACE/AfxMessageBox can help you pinpoint where your logic or run-time problems are occurring. You can also use the Breakpoints dialog box shown in Figure 16.11 to set a breakpoint.

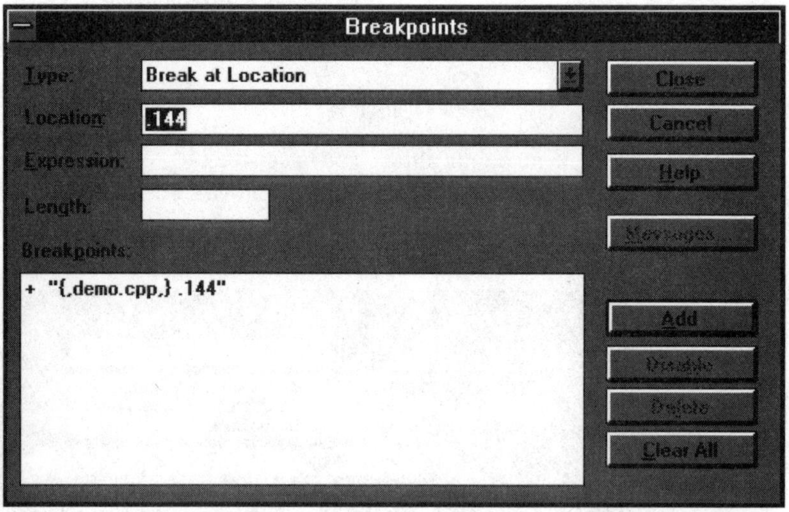

Figure 16.11
The Breakpoint
dialog box.

An easier way is to move to a source line and click the "hand" button on the toolbar, or press the F9 function key. You can't double-click on the source line to set a breakpoint.

The dialog box will show you a list of all the breakpoints located in your project. The workbench saves these breakpoints in the project file, so if you wish to delete them from session to session, use the Clear All button. Note that if you are sharing files in a multiperson development team and one person saves several breakpoints in a project file and then gives you that project file, you now have those breakpoints set in your version of the program. This can be disconcerting if you don't realize they are there and if the two versions of the source file differ. The debugger will alert you to this fact, but it can still be annoying. The debugger will alert you if the chosen line does not contain corresponding executable code. To avoid this situation, simply clear all breakpoints before you begin your debugging session, and create new ones relative to your immediate needs.

Setting Breakpoints on Various Conditions

Setting a single breakpoint on a line of code is but only way, although it is the simplest. From the Types list box shown in Figure 16.12, you can also choose to break at any of these occasions:

If an expression is TRUE.

If an expression has changed.

When the expression becomes TRUE.

When the expression changes.

If the program receives a message.

The Breakpoints dialog will allow you to enter expressions to evaluate before deciding if the debugger should break. You first enter a location (line) for a breakpoint and then the expression in the Expression edit box.

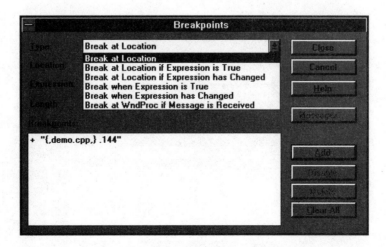

Figure 16.12
The Types list box.

You can enter locations by line number, address in hex, or location relative to the CS register. Use a period in front of a decimal number to indicate a line number. To specify a source file, you must precede the period with the name of the source file and an exclamation point, like so:

```
.100 indicates a breakpoint at line number 100 in the current source file.
Demo.cpp!.100 -indicates a break location at line number 100 in demo.cpp.
```

You can also supply locations as absolute segment:offsets (0x1145:0x1023) as offsets relative to the Code Segment (CS:1023), or as an Instruction Pointer offset from the code segment.

After specifying the breakpoint location, you must enter the expression, which must contain a valid memory address (i.e., the address of a variable; you can use the variable's name). If the variable is a pointer, the debugger will only check its location. If you wish to break on the value the pointer points to, then you must dereference the pointer with the normal C/C++ dereference operator (*). The length field should be set to 1 for most nonpointer values. For pointer values (especially arrays), you must enter the number of bytes in the length edit box that you wish to check to see if a change has occurred. You can enter the ranges by setting the starting location in the Expression box (the beginning of an array, for example) and then the number of bytes in the array you wish to check in the Length edit box. See Figures 16.13a and 16.13b for examples.

One tip you can use is to define a variable to hold the value of the expression and then set a breakpoint based on this variable's value. This way you can also track the

Figure 16.13a
Example of specifying
a breakpoint involving
an array.

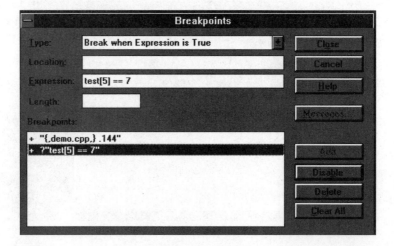

Figure 16.13b
Example result
from encountering
a breakpoint
on an array value.

value and set the value by hand while the program is running (more on modifying variables later in the chapter).

Breaking on Messages

Another good diagnostic technique is to break only on certain messages. MSVC provides the SDK tool Spy, which can help you see which messages your application is generating, receiving, or not receiving. More on Spy later. The Breakpoint dialog will allow you to stop program execution at any Windows callback function. The Dialog box will present you with a list of all available callback functions exported from your application. From the Type box choose the "Break at WndProc..." item and then chose the appropriate Windows callback function. Next choose the message button in the Breakpoint dialog box to display the Messages dialog box shown in Figure 16.14.

You can choose a single message or a group of messages as your breakpoint trigger, depending on which choice you enable in the Message Type group box. When your program receives the selected messages, the debugger will halt at the entry to the WndProc you selected.

QuickWatch (SHIFT F9)

You can display a variable's current value by highlighting the variable in the source code and clicking either the QuickWatch menu item or the eyeglass button on the toolbar. The debugger will display the value in the QuickWatch dialog illustrated in Figure 16.15, but only if the current file contains the variable's definition. If you instantiated the variable in a different source file, the debugger will alert you to that fact.

If the variable is a structure or an array, the ZOOM button will act as a toggle to display each data member in descending order or to collapse the variable back to a single value, usually an address.

You can modify a variable's value while stopped at a breakpoint or while waiting idle between steps. Use the MODIFY button on the QuickWatch dialog box. When you click the button, the Modify Variable dialog box appears and lets you set the variable's value before continuing with the program. If the variable is a structure or an

Figure 16.14
The Messages
dialog box.

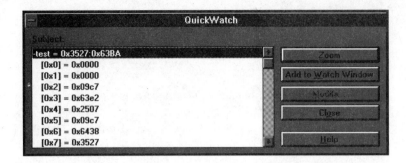

array, you will have to modify each field or data member since you can't modify an entire structure or array at once. Figure 16.16 displays the Modify Variable dialog box.

The Add to Watch Window button will allow you to place the variable into the Watch Window (discussed next). Doing this allows you to track the variable's value as you step through the program, since you must close the QuickWatch dialog to continue debugging.

The Debugger's Windows

The Watch window is another one of the debugger windows accessible to the developer. You will find four others under the Windows menu item on the workbench's main menu, listed between the Close All menu choice and the MRU window choices, as shown in Figure 16.17. The debugger uses these windows to display and receive information about variables as you step through the program. The first window you will encounter during development will be the output window, the last choice in the list.

The workbench displays this window during the make process. The window will report warnings and errors encountered during your project's build process. As we stated earlier, you can click on the line containing the error or warning and receive context-sensitive help, or you can have the workbench place you at the offending line in the appropriate source file. The output window can also receive any debug messages sent by your application via the OutDebugString function, the AfxDump architecture, or the TRACE macros.

Watch

Watch is the next window you will encounter most often in a typical debugging session. This window is similar to the QuickWatch dialog box in that you can view and modify variables while debugging your program. One difference lies in the fact that your choices stay available, even if you close the window, whereas in the

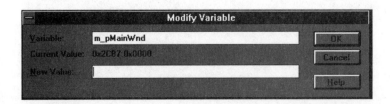

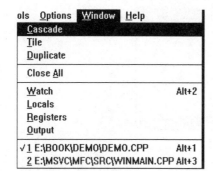

Figure 16.17
The Windows menu
choices.

QuickWatch window, the workbench will delete your selection when you close the dialog box. You can also keep track of multiple items with the Watch window, instead of single items with the QuickWatch dialog box.

As you step through the program, you can add variables to the Watch window and track their values as your program executes. The workbench will display each variable you add along with its current value. You can add variables and any valid C/C++ expression and have its value displayed. You can enter these items into the window at any time, but they are only valid while running the debugger; otherwise you will get an error indication next to the item. You will also get this indication if the variable is currently not in scope. Figure 16.18 illustrates several items added to the Watch window.

To add a variable into the Watch window, you can use the Add to Watch Window button in the QuickWatch dialog box, manually type the item in, or copy and paste it. The item will remain in the window until you explicitly delete it. You delete a variable by highlighting the item and pressing the delete key.

When you add an item to the window, a "+" sign precedes it if it is a structure or an array. This symbol indicates that more information is hidden inside the structure. To display this information you can place the cursor on the item and press the Enter key. Or simply double-click on the item to expand its contents to reveal the values of the various fields or members. Repeating the process collapses this information, thus freeing some space in the window. The workbench will also allow you to collapse an item preceded by a "−" sign.

To modify the item's value, you simply erase the old value and type in a new one.

The Locals window is similar to the Watch window in that it displays a series of variables and their values. The difference is that you do not add or delete items because it only contains the current function's local variables. The workbench will display every item local to the currently executing function along with its value. This

```
┌─────────────────────────── <2> Watch ───────────────────────────┐
│ -test = 0x3527:0x63BA                                            │
│    [0x0] = 0x0000                                                │
│    [0x1] = 0x0000                                                │
│    [0x2] = 0x09c7                                                │
│    [0x3] = 0x63e2                                                │
│    [0x4] = 0x2507                                                │
│    [0x5] = 0x09c7                                                │
│    [0x6] = 0x6438                                                │
│    [0x7] = 0x3527                                                │
│    [0x8] = 0x0000                                                │
│    [0x9] = 0x000c                                                │
└─────────────────────────────────────────────────────────────────┘
```

Figure 16.18
The Watch window.

Figure 16.19
The Registers window.

window will let you modify the value just like the Watch window. A good technique to use if you're tracking a certain data member in an array or structure is to assign the value to a local variable. This value will then appear in the Locals window and you can add it to the Watch window. You will also have easier access to the item's value for evaluating breakpoints.

The last window will display the name and current state of the CPU's registers. Figure 16.19 illustrates an example. This window will allow you to change the value of any register or flag while you are stepping through the program.

Be careful because you can alter the program's execution path by changing the registers! The flags you have access to, and their set and clear values, are Overflow(OV/NV), Direction(DN/UP), Interrupt(EI/DI), Sign(NG/PL), Zero(ZR/NZ), Auxiliary carry(AC/NA), Parity(PE/PO), and Carry(CY/NC). The Registers window will display these flags on the last line of the window.

The Debugger Options Dialog Box

You can locate the last options box to use with the debugger under the workbench's Options/Debug menu item, as displayed in Figure 16.20. This dialog box will allow you to set some parameters for your debugging session.

The first parameter is the Hexadecimal check box. The debugger will display all values in the various debug windows in hex when you enable this check box; otherwise the debugger displays all numbers as base 10 numbers.

The next option deals with what Microsoft calls the Hard/Soft debug mode. In hard mode, your application and the debugger are the only applications executing. You cannot switch to another task, not even to get help. By default, the integrated debugger runs in soft mode, but during system-critical tasks the debugger will automatically switch to hard mode, and then switch back to soft mode. You can force the integrated debugger to run exclusively in hard mode by enabling the appropriate radio button in the Debugger Options dialog box.

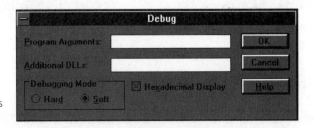

Figure 16.20
The Debugger Options dialog box.

The first edit box in this dialog box allows you to specify command-line arguments passed to the application at run time. You can process these arguments in the application's InitInstance member function, as follows:

```
if (m_lpCmdLine[0] != '\0')
{
    // TODO: add command line processing here
}
```

The additional .DLLs edit box will allow you to enter any .DLLs your application calls so that you can step into the .DLL and trace its execution. If you do not supply the path to the .DLL, the framework will prompt you for the library.

Debugging .DLLs

Debugging DLLs can be tricky, and although it's perhaps best to leave it for the heavy-duty CodeView debugger, you can debug .DLLs in the integrated debugger. The first requirement is a program that calls the .DLL. This can be an actual program or a shell application that merely calls the .DLL. You must enter any programs you use as a wrapper around the .DLL in the first edit box, and then enter the .DLL in the second. The shell program does not need debug information compiled in it. The .DLL, obviously, *must* have debug information, unless you feel like stepping through assembler code. If you do feel like stepping through assembler code, then the framework will also let you intermix source code and assembler code via the Mixed Source/ASM menu choice under the workbench's View menu item (Ctrl+F7).

Other Useful Tools

Earlier in the chapter we mentioned the Spy utility, which is shown in Figure 16.21. Spy will let you pick a window, or all windows on the desktop, from the Windows menu option and then "spy" on the Windows messages they are receiving. Spy also lets you choose, via the Options dialog box (shown in Figure 16.22), the groups of messages that it will display.

You should also know that if your application sends a Windows message to itself via the SendMessage API call while stopped in the debugger, your application will not receive that message. You will have to rely on another debugging technique, such

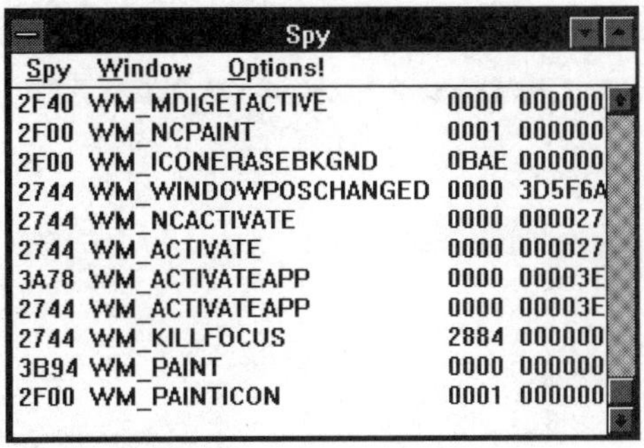

Figure 16.21
The Spy utility.

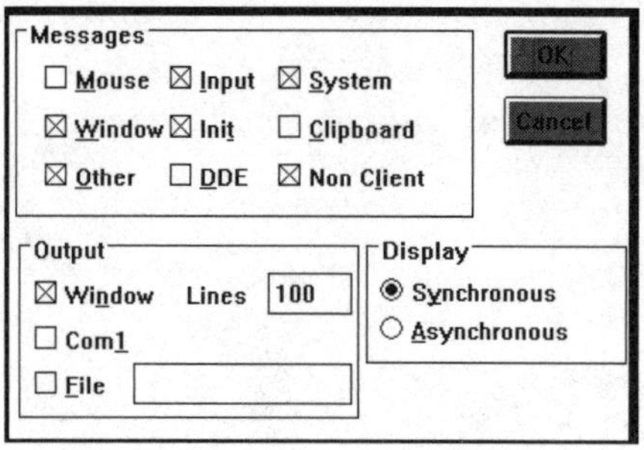

Figure 16.22
Spy's Options dialog box.

as a TRACE macro printout, to see if you received that message, or you could change the SendMessage to a PostMessage.

Several other tools supplied with the professional version of MSVC can make debugging a Windows program a heck of a lot easier. Heap Walker, shown in Figure 16.23, is another tool that allows you to display all currently allocated and free memory in your Windows system. You can use this tool to locate memory blocks that your program has leaked.

A memory leak occurs when your program allocates memory, or a resource, and then forgets to release that memory or resource when it terminates. These resources will then become unavailable to other Windows tasks until you reboot the system. The framework will report memory leaks while terminating if you have an output window available, like DBWIN, and Heap Walker will help you piece together the amount of memory your application acquired but failed to release.

You can use the Stress Application, shown in Figure 16.24, to test how your application reacts in a low memory situation. The Stress Application will allow you to gobble up plenty of resources to see how your application reacts in a low resource situation.

Finally, Microsoft also sells an application called Microsoft Test in which you can write a script to test various parts of your program. The program can operate unattended for hours, logging the results of each test for later analysis.

CHAPTER SUMMARY

This chapter gave you a brief overview of the integrated debugger included in the Visual Workbench. The chapter covered various exception-handling macros and

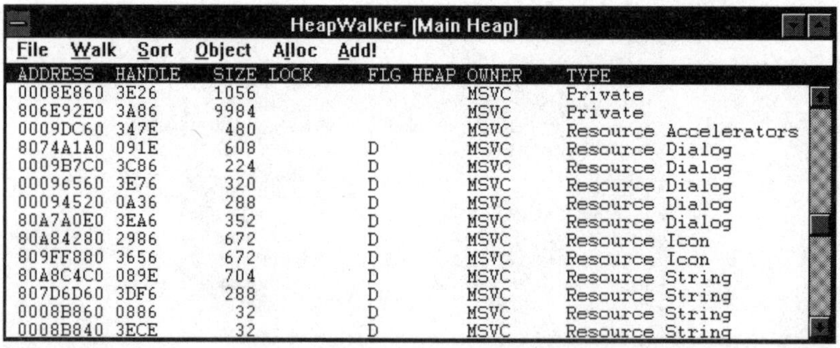

Figure 16.23
Heap Walker.

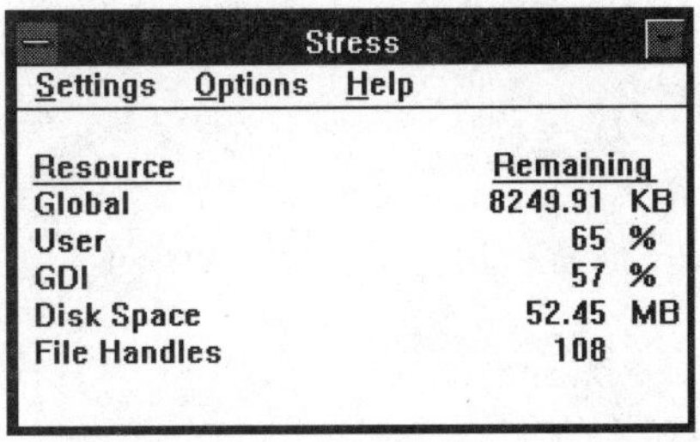

Figure 16.24
The Stress Application.

techniques and showed several substitutes for the programmer's trusted print statement. MSVC also provides several tools to help you track down logic errors. These
include several Spy programs and the Heap Walker program. No question about it:
Windows programming is hard, so developers need all the help they can get while
debugging in such a hostile environment.

CHAPTER
17

Help for
the Developer

Developing applications for the Windows environment is not easy. We hope this book will make that task easier. But ours is not the only source of help, and we would be remiss not to point you toward other resources. You will not find sample code in this chapter. Rather, you will find a wealth of information on where to find more help. (Please note that this chapter does not indicate an endorsement on our part, or that of our publisher, for any of the products or services mentioned. Nor should you construe a lack of endorsement if we've left any product out.)

The world of software and documentation holds a great number of other resources for the Windows developer. We provide this information as a starting point in your search for answers, a starting point that begins with the developer of Windows itself. Microsoft leads the industry with help for developers, so most of this chapter will focus on the services Microsoft offers. Note that you can also find most of this information under the Workbench's Help menu under Obtaining Technical Support.

MICROSOFT'S PHONE SUPPORT

As Microsoft is the developer of Windows, you would expect them to offer myriad services to the developer, and they do. You should also expect that most of these services will cost you money, in one way or another. Microsoft does offer free support through the telephone or on CompuServe. I (Jack Tackett, Jr.) have used the phone service several times, and it can be frustrating. I had to wait a long period to get through, usually to be told to download the needed file from CompuServe or Microsoft's online BBS. You will probably be better off seeking help elsewhere, but phone support is available. Check your documentation for the phone numbers, or check your Help files. Call (206) 635-7007 for help on MSVC++.

MICROSOFT'S RECORDED PHONE SUPPORT

Microsoft also provides automated support for several language products through recorded messages and fax tips. Unfortunately, MSVC++ is not currently one of those products, although they do support MS C 7.0 and MASM. To check out this resource, dial (206) 635-4694 on your touch-tone phone and follow the prompts.

MICROSOFT'S CONSULTING

If you prefer face to face, rather than voice or text, interaction, then Microsoft's consulting services might interest you. The company can provide you, through their Consultant Referral Service, with the names of consultants in your area to help you with your problems. Call (800) 227-4679, ext. 56042, for information. If an independent consultant just won't do, then you can hire Microsoft itself. Microsoft Consulting Services can provide off-site as well as on-site consultants to your project for any length of time. You can contact Microsoft at (415) 905-0235 for more information on this service.

MICROSOFT UNIVERSITY

If you simply cannot afford this type of heavy-duty help, you can consider Microsoft University. This division of Microsoft Corporation provides training in most of Microsoft's products, including their development tools. You can use these classes to train your own consultants. Microsoft holds the classes at Microsoft University's main campus in Washington state, as well as in major cities around the country. Video and self-study courses are also available. You can contact Microsoft University at (206) 828-1507 for more information about their current course offerings.

MICROSOFT AND OTHER SEMINARS

Microsoft also holds seminars across the country on various topics, including development tools. To find out about events in your area, call Microsoft's Developer Services Team at (800) 227-4679. If you attend one of these events, don't be shy! You may get a prize if the presenter asks a question and you answer quickly. The Developer Services Team can also provide information on beta programs.

Please note that Microsoft is not the only game in town when it comes to consulting or training. You can find other sources in most major computing magazines and news weeklies like *PC Week,* so feel free to shop around. Most contracting agencies also have a list of "hired guns" to provide a needed skill on demand.

MICROSOFT BBS

Microsoft does maintain an electronic bulletin board that houses various software files like drivers and utilities. You can access this system with any communications program at (206) 936-6735. But first, set your parameters to eight data bits, one stop bit, no parity, and any of the following baud rates: 1200, 2400, or 9600.

Most of the information is available elsewhere, however, perhaps in a more convenient format. One format supported by Microsoft is CD-ROMs. Compact disks can hold over 600 megabytes of information and programs. We will discuss this format in greater detail later. Other sources of electronic help are online services, like the CompuServe Information Service (CIS). Microsoft provides most of its support through CIS forums.

COMPUSERVE

CompuServe resembles the Microsoft BBS slightly, except it offers many more services and allows multiple users online at once. There are other online services, like Prodigy, America Online, and Genie, but Microsoft hangs out en masse on CompuServe.

FORUMS

CompuServe forums allow you to read and post questions to Microsoft Developer Support Engineers as well as other developers. Each forum also maintains a library of files that you can download. You can interactively communicate with others logged into the same forum. You can direct a question to Microsoft, to a single person, or to the entire community, and you will usually get a response from someone. It may be an answer to your question or a pointer to where you might find the answer.

Each forum also maintains a library. The libraries contain source code examples as well as a myriad of other items, from articles to shareware programs that you can download to your PC. (Be aware that large files can take quite some time to download.)

HOW TO ACCESS COMPUSERVE

You can access all this material through your favorite communications program, although CompuServe does offer its own copyrighted program (WinCim) that eases your trek through the maze of services and as you download files. Although they charge a fee for the program, CompuServe gives you a usage credit toward many online time charges.

You reach most CIS areas with the GO command. For example, if you wish to get information on CIS billing, you can type GO BILLING. If you are using a navigator program like WinCim, instead of typing an area name, you simply double-click an icon or make a choice from a list box.

MICROSOFT SUPPORT AREAS (FORUMS)

Table 17.1 lists the Microsoft support forums available on CompuServe. Microsoft has Developer Support Engineers on duty in each forum whose job it is to help you solve your problems.

TECHNICAL NOTES

When looking for help, don't forget that you loaded several resources when you installed MSVC++. Microsoft provides several resources in the Windows Help format.

TABLE 17.1
The Microsoft developer services areas available on CompuServe.

AREAS	GO COMMANDS
Microsoft Windows Development	(GO WINDSK)
Microsoft Extensions	(GO WINEXT)
Microsoft Win32 Development	(GO MSWIN32)
Microsoft Languages, including MSVC++	(GO MSLANG)
Several forums are dedicated to Visual C++: Visual C++, Setup, MS C/C++, VBX, Visual Workbench, Foundation Classes, App Studio, and Wizard/DDV/DDX.	
Microsoft Basic Languages	(GO BASIC)
Microsoft Access	(GO ACCESS)
Microsoft FoxPro	(GO FOXFORUM)
Microsoft SQL Server	(GO MSSQL)
Microsoft Programming Apps	(GO PROGMSA)
Microsoft Developer Relations	(GO MSDR)
Microsoft Client-Server Computing	(GO MSNET)
Microsoft Developer Network Forum	(GO MSDNLIB)
Microsoft Developer Knowledge Base	(GO MDKB)

One is the Technical Notes that cover various aspects of programming with MSVC and the Foundation Classes. (We've referred to them several times in this book.) Microsoft provides these technical notes for features or problems they deemed inappropriate for the printed documentation. You can find these Help files in the \msvc\hlp subdirectory in the mfcnotes.hlp file. You will also find an icon for the technical notes in your MSVC group. Double-clicking this icon will provide you with access to the Help file.

Technical Notes cover all versions of the Foundation Classes. Notes 1 through 17 cover MFC 1.0, and Notes 18 and 19 apply to migrating MFC 1.0 applications to MFC 2.0. Technical Notes numbered 20 and above are specific to MFC 2.0. Use this list to find the Technical Notes of interest to you:

Tech Note 1. *Window Class Registration.* How the framework registers window classes (not C++ classes).

Tech Note 2. *Persistent Object Data Format.* How the framework stores objects through the CArchive and serialization process. See Chapters 3 and 4 for more on storing objects.

Tech Note 3. *Mapping Windows Handles to Objects.* How to get a valid C++ object that wraps a Windows handle, like HWND and HPEN; also, how to get a valid handle from an object.

Tech Note 4. *C++ Template Tool.* How to create your own collection classes. (Unfortunately, MSVC++ does not support true C++ templates or exception handling.)

Tech Note 6. *Message Maps.* How MFC replaces the switch statement found in SDK programs with macros. These macros simulate C++ virtual member functions, mapping Windows messages to your class member functions.

Tech Note 7. *Debugging Trace Options*. How to use the TRACE macro for debugging applications. See Chapter 16, too.

Tech Note 8. *MFC OLE Support*. More information on MFC 2.0's support for OLE 1.0. (MFC 2.0 supports Object Linking and Embedding 1.0 but currently does not support OLE 2.0. You should also check Technical Note 18 when trying to move MFC 1.0 OLE applications to MFC 2.0. MFC version 2.5 should include support for OLE 2.0 objects.)

Tech Note 11. *Using MFC as Part of a .DLL*. How to use MFC routines in a Windows .DLL.

Tech Note 12. *Using Windows 3.1 Robustness Features*. How to use the STRICT identifier and the debug kernels that help you develop robust Windows 3.1 applications. Also see Chapter 16 for more tips on making your applications crash-proof.

Tech Note 14. *Custom Controls*. How MFC supports self-drawing and custom controls. Also check out the CTRLTEST sample program in the \MSVC\MFC\SAMPLES\CTRLTEST directory.

Tech Note 15. *Windows for Pen*. How the C++ interface into the Windows for Pen environment is supported by the Visual C++ Professional Edition.

Tech Note 16. *Using C++ Multiple Inheritance with MFC*. How the framework restricts using multiple inheritance. It also describes how to use MI when it is viable.

Tech Note 17. *Destroying Window Objects*. Explains the cardinal rule: Thou shalt *not* use the "delete" operator to destroy a C++ Windows object. Instead, thou shalt use DestroyWindow. This note describes how to use CWnd::PostNcDestroy for deleting C++ Windows objects.

Tech Note 18. *Migrating OLE Applications from MFC 1.0 to MFC 2.0*. The Note's title says it all.

Tech Note 19. *Migrating MFC 1.0 Applications to MFC 2.0*. What areas to look out for, like the use of the STRICT identifier in version 2.0 that the framework did not use in version 1.0. It also gives procedures for doing a "minimal" migration and a "full" migration.

Tech Note 20. *ID Naming and Numbering Conventions*. The convention, names, and value ranges used by the various system and application resources.

Tech Note 21. *Command and Message Routing*. This technical note provides details on advanced topics in window message routines. It describes the command routing and dispatch architecture used by the framework. Also, how the framework links the items through the ON_COMMAND macros and some discussion of the ON_COMMAND_UI macros.

Tech Note 22. *Standard Commands Implementation*. The various command IDs, like ID_FILE_SAVE, the purpose of each, and which classes implement each. *NOTE:* This Tech Note has an error: The CWinApp::DoPromptFile function should be called CWinApp::DoPromptFileName.

Tech Note 23. *Standard MFC Resources.* The standard resources, both "clip-art" and standard framework resources, needed by the MFC framework.

Tech Note 24. *MFC-Defined Messages and Resources.* Implementation information for MFC 2.0. You may use this information for advanced applications, but Microsoft warns that they do not support these internal messages and resources. The documentation also warns that these items may change in future versions of MFC. This note gives information such as VBX support, RT_DLGINT resource layout (the only internal resource format specific to MFC 2.0), and MFC Private Windows Messages used to replace C++ virtual functions.

Tech Note 25. *Document, View, and Frame Creation.* How these items interrelate. See Chapter 3 for more information.

Tech Note 26. *DDX and DDV Routines.* How you can write your own DDX or DDV procedure and how to extend ClassWizard, through the .CLW file, to use your routines.

Tech Note 27. *Emulation Support for Visual Basic Custom Controls.* Hypertext jumps to Help on Reporting Problems with VBX Controls; Standard VBX Events; Standard VBX Properties; Grid Control; CVBControl::m_nError_Values; VBX Event-Handling Function Parameters; How to Manage VBX Picture Properties in MFC; and the Differences Between Visual Basic VBX and MFC VBX Support. See Chapter 12 for more VBX information.

Tech Note 28. *Context-Sensitive Help Support.* Rules and other issues involved with context-sensitive Help within the MFC 2.0 framework. See Chapter 17 for help on Help.

Tech Note 29. *Splitter Windows.* How to use the CSplitterWnd class to manage window splits.

Tech Note 30. *Print Preview.* Possibly one of the greatest time-savers afforded by MFC 2.0! This note discusses how to customize your application's printing and print preview functionality.

Tech Note 31. *Control Bars.* Describes the following classes and their uses: CControlBar, CStatusBar, CToolBar, and CDialogBar. See Chapter 8 for more information on control bars.

Tech Note 32. *MFC Exception Mechanism.* Describes the exception mechanism, some undocumented exception macros, and CATCH_ALL and END_CATCH_ALL. The note also gives some sample code for an auto-cleanup class that might get caught in an exception and thus not call the normal C++ destructors. See Chapter 16 for more information on exception handling.

Tech Note 33. *DLL Version of MFC.* How you can use the MFC200[D].DLLs with your MFC application and how to create small applications that can share common library code, rather than statically linking the entire MFC library into each .EXE. This note also details the restrictions you face when using the .DLLs.

Tech Note 34. *Writing a Windows 3.0 Compatible MFC Application.* By default, MSVC builds applications for Windows 3.1. You can create a MFC 2.0 application that can run under Windows 3.0 by using the techniques outlined in this tech note. (You cannot create MFC applications that will run under pre-3.0 versions of Windows.)

Tech Note 35. *Using Multiple Resource Files and Header Files with App Studio.* How to support multiple resource files across a project development. This ability is especially important in a project with multiple developers.

NOTE: The missing Tech Note numbers represent either obsolete topics or topics now documented in the printed manuals.

OTHER HELP TOPICS

The MSVC installation program also installed several other items in your Program group. Although some of these items deal more with the Windows 3.X SDK, you can still get some useful tidbits here and there. The TIPS.HLP file, for instance, contains most of this type of information for the User, Kernel, and GDI DLLs, along with some miscellaneous items. You will also see two Viewer files: one gives you access to the Tech Note tips and one to the documentation files in Readme. Readme contains information too late to make it into the documentation and offers a form for you to use when reporting MSVC and MFC bugs to Microsoft.

THE SAMPLE CODE

Why should you reinvent the wheel? We have often found that the quickest way to learn something is to see how someone else did it. (We hope you find this book, and its sample codes, helpful in this regard.) Besides Technical Notes, Microsoft also provides several sample programs, complete with full source code. We will list some of them here and point out their interesting features. For more information, compile the samples, run them, and then look at their code. You may find it interesting to step through the code with the integrated debugger. The couple of hours this will take will pay off with a better understanding of just what the heck is going on under the hood. You will find the samples in the \msvc\mfc\samples\<sample name> subdirectory. You will also find sample C/SDK code in the \msvc\samples subdirectory. Some of the code was ported from the C 7.0 sample programs. Microsoft did include support for the document and view architecture, but not via separate files like the AppWizard would generate. Finally, you will find information on each sample program in the MFCSAMP.HLP file. Table 17.2 lists the sample programs.

Be aware that if you build these programs in debug mode, you can quickly eat up a lot of disk space! The included make files usually have a "clean" option to delete the unnecessary files.

TABLE 17.2
Sample applications.

PROGRAMS	DESCRIPTIONS
HELLOAPP	Demonstrates a very basic MFC application.
SUPERPAD	Shows several techniques, including an introductory "splash screen" dialog box. Also, how to implement an enhanced About box and how to use the CEditView class as a minieditor.
VBCHART	Demonstrates the use of the grid.vbx control shipped with MSVC++.
VBCIRCLE	Shows how to use VBX controls in dialogs and frame windows.
CHKBOOK	Shows several dialog-box derived views, record-based file processing, and page breaks on printing. Also illustrates the use of a custom DDX/DDV routine.
CTRLTEST	Illustrates custom controls, a bitmap button, and an owner-draw list box.
CTRLBARS	Shows how to use toolbars, status bars, and floating tool pallets.
VIEWEX	Illustrates splitter windows and scroll views.
SCRIBBLE	Gives the sample application illustrated in the *Class Library User's Guide*.
APSTUDIO	Contains the .rc files for system resources like the common dialogs, the indicator strings, and prompts for the standard menu items.
SPEAKEN	Illustrates Pen for Windows and multimedia extensions. You must have Pen for Windows to run this application. Also illustrates handwriting edit controls.
DIBLOOK	Shows you how to read and save device-independent bitmaps (.DIBs).
HIERSVR	Illustrates a full OLE 1.0 server that works with both linked and embedded objects. Also, how to open and save files, how to register document types with File Manager, and how to copy data to the Clipboard.
OCLIENT	Provides a simple OLE 1.0 client and shows how to support the common interfaces that MFC does not directly support. You can use this code to flesh out your own OLE clients.
TEMPLEDEF	A DOS-based application that comes precompiled in the msvc\bin subdirectory, it illustrates how to expand special MSVC macros into C++ template-like entities for the MFC container classes.
DLLHUSK	Shows how to dynamically link to the MFC .DLL, instead of statically linking the MFC library at compile time. Shows how to export routines with a C interface as well as a C++ decorated (mangled) interface.
MAKEHM	A DOS application included in your \msvc\bin subdirectory, it takes the #defined resource IDs in your resource.h file and creates context IDs for your Help file. See Chapter 15 for more information on implementing Windows Help.
MDI	Based on the MFC 1.0 Multiple Document Interface, this sample does not take advantage of MFC 2.0's new document and view architecture.
MINSVR	A simple OLE 1.0 server that supports only embedded objects.

(continued)

TABLE 17.2 *(continued)*

PROGRAMS	DESCRIPTIONS
MULTIPAD	A much better MDI example than the MDI sample program. This sample is based on the Windows SDK MULTIPAD example, ported to MFC 2.0 and its document/view architecture. Also see the SUPERPAD example.
TRACER	Included in your msvc\bin subdirectory, this sample allows you to set debug trace options. This a good example of an application that uses a dialog box as its main window. See Chapter 16 for more information on Tracer's use for debugging.

Your distribution diskettes are not your only source of sample code. The libraries in Microsoft's CompuServe forums contain thousands of lines of code, too. And even more sources are available worldwide, as we'll describe in the next sections.

THE INTERNET

Look, up in the sky, spanning the globe, across all seven continents, touching almost every country, providing seemingly limitless access to information, lies the global Internet. Here you will find plenty of sample code, if you're willing to spend some time looking. The Internet grew out of research in packet-switching networks of the late sixties and early seventies and received much of its funding from the U.S. government. Its popularity may soon be its downfall, as it quickly exhausts its address supply. Commercial networks also vie to take its place, including the so-called Information Superhighway proposed by President Clinton's administration.

Unlike CompuServe and other online services, access to the Internet sometimes appears to be free. Most major corporations and universities provide access as a part of their overhead, with the costs hidden from the typical user. The U.S. backbone still receives most of its funding from the U.S. government, although there are several commercial providers. Unfortunately, how to acquire access to the Internet is beyond the scope of this book, but to those of you who can gain access, you'll find a plethora of resources there.

The Internet allows developers access to worldwide news groups and archives on a myriad of topics, not just Windows programming. News groups provide the CompuServe equivalent of forum message areas, while archives provide the equivalent of forum libraries. CompuServe and other services provide access at baud rates less than 14.4k, whereas access to the Internet typically occurs at speeds between 4 and 10 megabits per second and beyond.

Online facilities do provide a service not usually found on the Internet: formal technical support. You will usually find it easier and quicker to get a direct response from a vendor through an online service than via an Internet news group or an e-mail message. Most vendors would probably like to provide support through the net, but its academic and research nature places restrictions on its commercial use. Thus you will find only a few vendors providing technical support via the Internet. Some major companies do have net access with domain names like microsoft.com and borland.com.

Microsoft does provide an Internet archive site for the Microsoft Support Network. This service became available October 1, 1993. Here are the name and IP address:

```
ftp.microsoft.com 131.101.1.11.
```

The server has this directory structure:

```
\product cluster\product
\docs
\kb (knowledge base articles and index)
\mrktg (marketing information)
\sup-ed (supported drivers, patches, utilities)
\unsup-ed (unsupported drivers, patches, and utilities)
```

News Groups

In news groups, you post questions and read responses just like on CompuServe. Most systems connected to the Internet provide software to read news, file postings, and reply to questions. Many news groups have a moderator (a "sysop"), but many are unmoderated and thus self-policed. Most moderators provide a monthly list of frequently asked questions, or "FAQ." You could consider the FAQ as a mini-knowledge-base article providing answers to common questions and solutions to common problems. Try to obtain and *read* this list before posting a question. You'll save yourself from asking inappropriate or redundant questions that can result in a barrage of messages that politely (or more likely, impolitely) suggest that you read the FAQ. FAQs also provide references to other resources on the Internet, such as software archives.

Archives

Archives hold vast collections of software, much like forum libraries. If you are directly connected to the net, you can download files at great speed; otherwise, you might be able to get the files to your host system quickly, but then you'll suffer the long transfer rate of a 14.4k modem. Most archives maintain an archive-wide index list, as well as an index for each area in the archive. Most archives usually call this area index "00-index.txt." Because most machines connected to the net run the UNIX operating system, you can use file transfer protocol programs like ftp. Most magazines also upload each month's copy of source code to various archives. Unfortunately, there's no single place to get everything, so you have to go hunting for what you need (which can be fun in itself).

We list here the information needed to access the most popular sites, as well as the names of the important news groups for Windows developers. As we stated in the beginning of this section, we cannot provide a great deal of information about the Internet; instead, we suggest you read one or more of these books:

The Whole Internet User's Guide and Catalog. Ed Krol. O'Reilly & Associates. 1993. ISBN 0-56592-025-2.

Zen and the Art of the Internet: A Beginner's Guide. Brendan P. Kehoe. 2nd ed. Prentice-Hall, Inc. 1993. ISBN 0-13-010778-6.

TABLE 17.3
Archives at ftp sites.

NAMES	IP NUMBERS
FTP.microsoft.com	131.101.1.11.
ftp.hawaii.edu	128.171.44.2
grape.ecs.clarkson.edu	128.153.28.129
milton.u.washington.edu	128.95.136.1
serv1.cl.msu.edu	35.8.2.41
msdos.umich.edu	141.211.164.153
wuarchive.wustl.edu	128.252.135.4
bode.ee.ualberta.ca	129.128.16.96
ftp.uni-erlangen.de	131.188.1.43
forwiss.uni-passau.de	132.231.20.10
garbo.uwasa.fi	128.214.12.3
lut.fi	128.214.25.8
methan.chemie.fu-berlin.de	130.133.2.81
ftp.uni-kl.de	131.246.9.95
archie.au	139.130.4.6

Internet Archive Sites

Probably the best known site for Windows 3.X-related files is ftp.cica.indiana.edu. To reach an archive, at the operating system prompt, type ftp <address>. The address can be a string like ftp.cica.indiana.edu or the IP number associated with that string. For example, to access the ftp.cica.indiana.edu archive, you could type "ftp ftp.cica.indiana.edu," or "ftp 129.79.20.17." Type "anonymous" as the login name, and then enter the user name you use on your system, e.g., "tackett@wg.com."

Table 17.3 lists other ftp sites containing Windows files.

Most systems connected to the Internet will allow you to read news from usenet news groups. It is also possible to receive and read news on your PC. The news groups available for MS-Windows are listed in Table 17.4. These groups are specifically for MS-Windows, while other groups with "windows" in their titles deal with other GUI environments like MIT's X.

TABLE 17.4
MS Windows-related news groups.

```
comp.binaries.ms-windows
comp.os.ms-windows:
comp.os.ms-windows.advocacy
comp.os.ms-windows.announce
comp.os.ms-windows.apps
comp.os.ms-windows.misc
comp.os.ms-windows.programmer.misc
comp.os.ms-windows.programmer.tools
comp.os.ms-windows.programmer.win32
comp.os.ms-windows.setup
comp.os.ms-windows.nt.misc
comp.os.ms-windows.nt.setup
```

CD-ROMS

CDs provide an easier way to access the Internet archives. Several companies sell CDs containing most of the files found in an archive, although they often lack a good indexing mechanism to search for the file you might need. But what they lack in search software, most make up in price, with prices ranging from $25 to $50 for over 600 megabytes of software. Walnut Creek CDROM is probably the largest supplier of CD-ROMs. You can reach Walnut Creek at (800) 786-9907 for more information. For more money, you can get the mother of all Windows developers' CDs: from where else but Microsoft?

MSDN

The Microsoft Developer's Network is much more than a CD-ROM. It's an entire program started by Microsoft to assist developers. Some forums on CompuServe are tailored to MSDN subscribers, and there are quarterly newsletters. A year's subscription (currently $195 US) entitles you to quarterly newsletters, quarterly updates to the CD (i.e., you receive four CDs per year), six bimonthly issues of the *Developer Network News* newsletter, and discounts on Microsoft Press books. However, the prize for joining is the CD.

What's Available?

The MSDN CD provides massive quantities of publications, like the Windows 3.1 SDK. It also provides a special edition of CompuServe's WinCim modified to whisk you through Microsoft's Developers' forums. There are tons of sample programs, too, like all the sample code published in the Microsoft Systems Journal, not to mention the article text. The brass ring, however, is the Developer's Knowledge Base. This is the same database available on CompuServe, and the same one that Microsoft support personnel use to answer your questions, except you have it available right at your fingertips! Included are some of the screens available via the CD.

The sample applications found in the software libraries included with the CD-ROM, and available on CompuServe, are tied to articles in the Knowledge Base for easy cross-referencing. To get more information on The Microsoft Developers' Network, call (800) 759-5474.

MAGAZINES

Table 17.5 contains a partial list of magazines that either cater exclusively to or occasionally provide articles on Windows development.

TABLE 17.5
MS Windows-related magazines.

Microsoft Systems Journal	*Byte*
Windows Tech Journal	*PC Magazine*
Windows/DOS Developers Journal	*The Computer Shopper*
Dr. Dobb's Journal	*MFCJournal (by subscription only*
The C User's Journal	*(408) 253-2765)*

CHAPTER SUMMARY

This chapter has given you a mere start to finding help on Windows development. Unfortunately, no single oracle can answer all your questions. The answers are scattered across myriad media, but by using this chapter as a starting point, we feel sure you will find the answer.

CHAPTER 18

The Version Resource

VERSION INFORMATION

Beginning with Windows 3.1, Microsoft provided version information for resource files. This information provides the developer with a way to detect newer, or older, versions of application and library files (like .DLLs and .VBXs). This resource also allows the developer to display information to the user, such as your company name and application copyright information. The version resource contains items useful to the program, such as the version number of the file, operating-system-specific information, information pertaining to how and why the developer created the file, and what languages and character sets the file supports. This chapter will tell you a lot about the Windows version information and then show you how to add this information to your application's About Box.

THE RC FILE

AppWizard writes version information into your application's .RC2 file instead of into its own .RC file because the Wizard does not directly edit this file. You must edit the file yourself to include version information. The framework will then include this file in your application's .RC resource file through a #include statement. The next sample illustrates what our sample program's version information looks like:

```
//
// DEMO.RC2 - resources App Studio does not edit directly
//

#ifdef APSTUDIO_INVOKED
    #error this file is not editable by App Studio
#endif //APSTUDIO_INVOKED

/////////////////////////////////////////////////////////////////////////////
// Version stamp for this .EXE
```

```
#include "ver.h"

VS_VERSION_INFO     VERSIONINFO
  FILEVERSION           1,0,0,1
  PRODUCTVERSION        1,0,0,1
  FILEFLAGSMASK       VS_FFI_FILEFLAGSMASK
#ifdef _DEBUG
  FILEFLAGS           VS_FF_DEBUG|VS_FF_PRIVATEBUILD|VS_FF_PRERELEASE
#else
  FILEFLAGS           0 // final version
#endif
  FILEOS                VOS_DOS_WINDOWS16
  FILETYPE            VFT_APP
  FILESUBTYPE         0   // not used
BEGIN
  BLOCK "StringFileInfo"
  BEGIN
    BLOCK "040904E4"       // Lang=US English, CharSet=Windows // Multilingual
    BEGIN
      VALUE "CompanyName","TriStar Systems\0"
      VALUE "FileDescription", "DEMO MFC Application\0"
      VALUE "FileVersion",      "1.0.001\0"
      VALUE "InternalName",     "DEMO\0"
      VALUE "LegalCopyright",   "1993 TriStar Systems\0"
      VALUE "LegalTrademarks", "All trademarks\0"
      VALUE "OriginalFilename","DEMO.EXE\0"
      VALUE "ProductName",      "DEMO\0"
      VALUE "ProductVersion",   "1.0.001\0"
    END
  END
  BLOCK "VarFileInfo"
  BEGIN
    VALUE "Translation", 0x409, 1252
    // English language (0x409) and the Windows ANSI codepage
    // 1252
  END
END
```

App Studio does not support this information, which is why the framework places it in a separate file. You could combine this file with your .RC as a version info resource, but App Studio only supports a hex editor for this type of information. You are better off using the Visual Workbench's editor to edit the .RC2 file and then running the resource compiler. The resource compiler will add this information into your application's resources. You can then access this information with Windows SDK calls.

STRUCTURE

This section of the resource file, from the FILEVERSION to the FILESUBTYPE, makes up a fixed binary record once it is compiled by the resource compiler. VER.H defines the structure of the fixed-length portion of the version resource information as:

```
typedef struct tagVS_FIXEDFILEINFO
{
    DWORD    dwSignature;
    DWORD    dwStrucVersion;
    DWORD    dwFileVersionMS;
```

```
    DWORD    dwFileVersionLS;
    DWORD    dwProductVersionMS;
    DWORD    dwProductVersionLS;
    DWORD    dwFileFlagsMask;
    DWORD    dwFileFlags;
    DWORD    dwFileOS;
    DWORD    dwFileType;
    DWORD    dwFileSubtype;
    DWORD    dwFileDateMS;
    DWORD    dwFileDateLS;
} VS_FIXEDFILEINFO;
```

VERSION INFORMATION STATEMENTS

The FILEVERSION resource statement specifies the version of this file. MS Windows represents this item with two 32-bit ints, defined as four 16-bit ints. In our sample application, we have it defined to be 1,0,0,1. The resource compiler will translate this number into (a)0x00010000 and (b)0x00000001. The fields in the structure VS_FIXEDFILEINFO corresponding to these values are (a)dwFileVersionMS and (b)dwFileVersionLS. The rest of the version resource file statements correspond to VS_FIXEDFILEINFO fields in a similar way.

The PRODUCTVERSION field is similar in structure to the FILEVERSION entry. This statement specifies the binary version number for the parent product that requires this file. An example might be a utility that you ship with your main application; the version number of your main application would appear here. This relationship corresponds to the dwProductVersionMS and dwProductVersionLS fields of the VS_FIXEDFILEINFO structure.

The structure requires you to list the corresponding VS_FIXEDFILEINFO in parentheses after the description of the resource statement. For more information on possible values for each statement item, see the Help topic VERSIONINFO(3.1) in the SDK Help file win31wh.hlp. Also check out the VER.H header file.

The FILESFLAGMASK statement specifies which bits in the FILEFLAGS field are valid. If a bit is set, then the corresponding bit in the FILEFLAGS is valid. This field is currently set to VS_FFI_FILEFLAGSMASK (dwFileFlagsMask) by default.

The FILEFLAGS statement specifies the ORed Boolean attributes of the file. Table 18.1 lists the possible values (dwFileFlags).

The FILEOS statement specifies the file's target operating system. Table 18.2 lists the possible values (dwFileOS).

The FILETYPE statement specifies the general type of file, as listed in Table 18.3 (dwFileType).

TABLE 18.1
FILEFLAGS field values.

```
VS_FF_DEBUG
VS_FF_INFOINFERRED
VS_FF_PATCHED
VS_FF_PRERELEASE
VS_PRIVATEBUILD
VS_FF_SPECIALBUILD
```

TABLE 18.2
Operating system values.

VOS_UNKNOWN
VOS_DOS
VOS_NT
VOS_WINDOWS16
VOS_WINDOWS32
VOS_DOS_WINDOWS16
VOS_DOS_WINDOWS32
VOS_NT_WINDOWS32

The FILESUBTYPE statement specifies the function of the file. The value is zero, unless the FILETYPE statement is one of: VFT_DRV, VFT_FONT, or VFT_VXD. If the FILETYPE is VFT_VXD, then the value is that of the virtual-device identifier included in the virtual-device control block (dwFileSubType). The other possible combinations are:

VFT_DRV:
VFT2_UNKNOWN, VFT2_DRV_COMM, VFT2_DRV_PRINTER,
VFT2_DRV_KEYBOARD, VFT2_DRV_LANGUAGE, VFT2_DRV_DISPLAY,
VFT2_DRV_DISPLAY, VFT2_DRV_MOUSE, VFT2_DRV_NETWORK, VFT2_DRV_SYSTEM,
VFT2_DRV_INSTALLABLE, and VFT2_DRV_SOUND
FONT:
VFT2_UNKNOWN, VFT2_FONT_RASTER, VFT2_FONT_VECTOR, and VFT2_FONT_TRUETYPE

MISCELLANEOUS FIELDS IN THE STRUCTURE, NOT IN THE STATEMENTS

This covers the layout of the fixed version information, except for a few fields. The resource compiler sets the first two and the last two fields. These fields have no corresponding statements in the resource source (.RC) file. The resource compiler currently sets dwFileDateMS and dwFileDateLS to 0. The first field, dwSignature, tells the functions they are working with version information, and dwStructVersion allow the SDK functions to support different VS_FIXEDFILEINFO structures that may occur over time.

VARIABLE PORTION OF THE VERSION INFORMATION

The other version information blocks follow the fixed-portion. A block can contain variable information or string information. Translation information is currently the

TABLE 18.3
FILETYPE values.

VFT_UNKNOWN
VFT_APP
     3. VFT_DLL
     4. VFT_DRV(dwFileType)
VFT_FONT
     6. VFT_VXD
VFT_STATIC_LIB

TABLE 18.4
Microsoft language and character set information.

ULANG ID	LANGUAGE STRING
0x0401	Arabic
0x0402	Bulgarian
0x0403	Catalan
0x0404	Traditional Chinese
0x0405	Czech
0x0406	Danish
0x0407	German
0x0408	Greek
0x0409	U.S. English
0x040A	Castilian Spanish
0x040B	Finnish
0x040C	French
0x040D	Hebrew
0x040E	Hungarian
0x040F	Icelandic
0x0410	Italian
0x0411	Japanese
0x0412	Korean
0x0413	Dutch
0x0414	Norwegian—Bokmål
0x0415	Polish
0x0416	Brazilian Portuguese
0x0417	Rhaeto-Romanic
0x0418	Romanian
0x0419	Russian
0x041A	Croato-Serbian (Latin)
0x041B	Slovak
0x041C	Albanian
0x041D	Swedish
0x041E	Thai
0x041F	Turkish
0x0420	Urdu
0x0421	Bahasa
0x0804	Simplified Chinese
0x0807	Swiss German
0x0809	U.K. English
0x080A	Mexican Spanish
0x080C	Belgian French
0x0810	Swiss Italian
0x0813	Belgian Dutch
0x0814	Norwegian—Nynorsk
0x0816	Portuguese
0x081A	Serbo-Croatian (Cyrillic)
0x0C0C	Canadian French
0x100C	Swiss French

(continued)

TABLE 18.4 *(continued)*

CHARACTER SET:

VALUES	CHARACTER SET:
0	7-bit ASCII
932	Windows, Japan (Shift—JIS X-0208)
949	Windows, Korea (Shift—KSC 5601)
950	Windows, Taiwan (GB5)
1200	Unicode (not supported by MSVC++ 1.0)
1250	Windows, Latin-2 (Eastern European)
1251	Windows, Cyrillic
1252	Windows, Multilingual
1253	Windows, Greek
1254	Windows, Turkish
1255	Windows, Hebrew
1256	Windows, Arabic

only type of variable resource information stored here. The version file stores this information in pairs. The pairs of numbers indicate which languages and character sets the application supports. The first number is a hex value corresponding to a language given in the first part of Table 18.4. The next number corresponds to a character set given in the second part of Table 18.4.

ADDING VER.LIB TO YOUR PROGRAM

You must make sure that you link with the version library. The framework does not automatically include this library in your project. To include the library in the framework, open your options menu, then the project menu, and then choose linker options. From that dialog box, you will choose Windows libraries in the category box and then the ver library in the import libraries and DLLs list box. By including this library, you will gain access to the functions in Figure 18.1.

THE SDK APIs

Currently, MSVC++ does not support access to this type of resource information. To access the information, you will have to use these SDK functions:

```
DWORD GetFileVersionInfoSize(LPCSTR   lpszFileName, DWORD FAR *dwHandle);
```

This function returns the size in bytes required to hold the VERSIONINFO resource contained in lpszFileName. If successful, the function will return, in lpdwHandle, a pointer to a handle to the information. The function returns NULL if an error occurs, but no other error information.

```
BOOL GetFileVersionInfo(LPCSTR lpszFileName, DWORD dwHandle, DWORD cbBuf,
   void FAR *lpvData);
```

This function retrieves into the supplied buffer lpvData the VERSIONINFO structure found in lpszFileName. The function cbBuf holds the size of this buffer, which should be the value returned by a call to GetFileVersionInfoSize. Using the lpdwHandle returned by GetFileVersionInfoSize will also speed up the function, but you can pass a NULL in the dwHandle parameter. This will result in the GetFileVersionInfo( ) function searching the entire file for the information. If the buffer is not big enough, then GetFileVersionInfo will truncate the data. A nonzero return value indicates success. A zero value indicates either an invalid handle or a nonexistent file.

Here's an example of these two functions:

```
char fname[16] = "demo.exe";
DWORD infosize;
DWORD FAR *lpVerData;
DWORD infohandle;

infosize = ::GetFileVersionInfoSize( fname, &infohandle);
if (NULL == infosize)
{
    AfxMessageBox("ERROR getting size of version information block");
    return FALSE;
}

lpVerData = ::new char [ infosize]    // allocate an array
BOOL retv = ::GetFileVersionInfo(fname,infohandle,infosize,lpVerData);

if( !retv )
{
  AfxMessageBox("ERROR loading version information");
  ::delete [] lpVerData;   // delete the array
}

// lpVerData now contains the version information, which you can access
// with the VerQueryValue, explained next.


WORD GetSystemDirectory( LPSTR lbPath, WORD nNum);
```

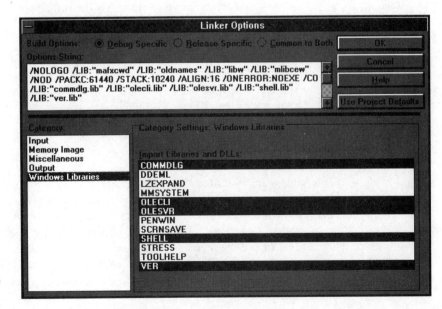

Figure 18.1
Adding VER.LIB to the project file.

This function will return, in *lbPath*, the path where the user installed the Windows system subdirectory. This subdirectory contains most of Windows' system files like .DLLs and .VBXs. The function will copy up to *nNum* characters into *lbBuffer* and return the number of characters written. Use this function to find out where to find files like .DLLs and .VBXs. Installation programs usually place these files in the system directory. If you are using an MS-DOS program, then you can use the function GetSystemDir( ), detailed in the SDK documentation.

```
WORD GetWindowsDirectory( LPSTR lbPath, WORD nNum);
```

This function will return, in *lbPath*, the path where the user installed Windows. The function will copy up to *nNum* characters into the buffer and will return the actual number written. If you are using an MS-DOS program and need to know the location of the Windows directory, then you can use the function GetWindowsDir( ). The SDK documentation explains this function. Remember to link your MS-DOS program with the appropriate library!

Here's an example of the two functions we've just discussed:

```
char sysPath[64];
char winPath[64];
char message[132];

WORD size = 64;

WORD sysnum = ::GetSystemDirectory( sysPath, size);    // note the global
scope operators
WORD dirnum  = ::GetWindowsDirtector( winPath,size);

if ( (dirnume == NULL) || (sysnum == NULL) )
   sprintf(message,"ERROR");
else
{
    sprintf( message,"Your windows dir = %s\n Your system dir is =
%s",winPath,sysPath);
}

AfxMessageBox(message);
```

The next function provides you with the ability to query the various VERSIONINFO fields located in lpvInfoBlock.

```
BOOL VerQueryValue( const void FAR *lpvInfoBlock, LPCSTR lpszRequest, VOID
FAR * FAR * lplpInfoLoc, UINT FAR * lpsize);
```

This is the memory buffer retrieved via GetFileVersionInfo. The second parameter, a null-terminated string, tells the function what kind of information to search for. It takes one of three forms: a single backslash "\\"; the string "\\VarFileInfo\\Translation"; or the pattern "\\StringFileInfo\\" + the hex values of the character set and system language + one of the predefined string names you are seeking (more on this topic later). The third parameter is a pointer to a void pointer. This will point to the data requested, if found, in the memory block lpvInfoBlock. You can use this pointer to retrieve the data. Normally you will have to cast your variable to FAR *. The last parameter will contain the size, in bytes, of the data pointed to by lplpInfoLoc, including the terminating nulll("\0").

FIRST TYPE OF INFORMATION TO SEEK

If you pass a single backslash "\"" as the second parameter, the function will return the position (i.e., address) of the fixed-length portion of the version resource contained in the lpvInfoBlock. Earlier in the chapter we described the structure of the fixed-length portion of the version resource information:

```
VS_FIXEDFILEINFO FAR * lpVSFixedInfo;
UINT uLen;
BOOL result = VerQueryValue( lpVerData, "\\",(FAR * FAR*)lpVSFixedInfo,
            &uLen);
if ( !result)
{
   AfxMessageBox("Error in call to verqueryvalue");
   return ;
}
```

You can now query any field in the structure through normal pointer dereferencing, via the *lplpInfoLoc*. Thus, if you want to know if this file was a prerelease version of the program, you could do this:

```
BOOL fIsPreRelease = lpVSFixedInfo->dwFileFlags & VS_FF_PRERELEASE;
```

VARFILEINFO—TRANSLATION

If you pass the string "\\VarFileInfo\\Translation" as the second parameter, the function will return the location of the Translation section within the VarFileInfo block of the resource. The VarFileInfo block indicates the beginning of the variable-length part of the VersionInfo resource. Translation information is currently the only type of variable resource information stored here. The resource file stores this information in pairs and indicates which languages and character sets the application supports. The first number is a hex value corresponding to a language given in the first part of Table 18.4, earlier in the chapter. The next number corresponds to a character set given in the second part of Table 18.4.

RETRIEVING TRANSLATION INFORMATION

To get the value of the language ID and the character set, you would:

```
UINT uLangID, uCharSet;
DWORD FAR * lpTranslateData;
BOOL result = VerQueryValue( lpVerData, "\\VarFileInfo\\Translation",
            (FAR * FAR *) lpTranslateData, &uLen);
if ( !result)
{
   AfxMessageBox("Error in call to verqueryvalue");
   return ;
}
```

```
uLanId = LOWORD( *lpTranslateData );
uCharSet = HIWORD( *lpTranslateData );
```

This code will give you the numeric values, but if you wish to show this information to the user as a string, you can use the VerLanguageName function:

```
UINT VerLanguageName( UINT uLang, LPSTR lpszLang, UINT cbLen);
```

This function retrieves the language information in the version resource as a string. The *uLang* parameter specifies the language ID as defined by Microsoft. (See Table 18.4 for a list of IDs). The second parameter will hold the returned string. The *cbLen* parameter contains the size of *lpszLang*. The function returns the number of bytes in the language string, without the null-terminator. If it is greater than *cbLen*, then the string was truncated to *cbLen*. The function will return a zero on error. The function does not consider an unknown string ID an error. Instead, the string in *lpszLang* will contain a default value of "Unknown language."

```
char lszLanguage[80];

UINT len = VerLanguageName( uLangId, lszLanguage, 80);

if ( 0 == len )
{
  AfxMessageBox("Error in VerLangName");
  return ;
}

if ( strstr( lszLanguage, "Unknown" ) )   // unknown language
{
  AfxMessageBox(" Encountered an Unknown Language");
  return;
}

char DisplayBuff[132];
wsprintf(DisplayBuf,"Language is %s and %d chars long.",
                    lszLanguage,len);
AfxMessageBox( DisplayBuff);
```

STRINGFILEINFO

The resource compiler will combine these two numbers to create the string in the StringFileInfo block. Here, the two numbers will both be hex values. Following this block will be a block of string information that describes this program. This section in the resource file has the following format:

```
BEGIN
  BLOCK "VarFileInfo"
  BEGIN
    VALUE "Translation", 0x409, 1252
    // English language (0x409) and the Windows ANSI codepage (1252)
  END
BEGIN
```

```
BLOCK "StringFileInfo"
BEGIN
  BLOCK "040904E4" // Lang=US English, CharSet=Windows
  BEGIN
    VALUE "CompanyName", "Tri Star Systems, Inc." "\0"
```

You must add the terminating null character, "\0", because the resource compiler will not do that automatically.

RETRIEVING STRINGFILEINFO

Within StringFileInfo appear various VALUEs to which null-terminated strings are assigned. These fields are themselves given strings as identifiers, like "CompanyName," rather than relying on a static structure. You can retrieve these values by calling VerQueryValue with the third form.

```
char fmtstr[80];
LPBYTE lszSearchData[80];
char SearchString[32];

strcpy(SearchString,"CompanyName"); // or FileVersion, etc.
wsprintf( fmstr,"\\StringFileInfo\\%04x%04x\\%s", uLangId, uCharSet,
        SearchString);

result = VerQuerValue( lpVerData,fmstr,&lszSearchData, &uLen);

// test for error condition, then use the data
wsprintf(DisplayBuf,"%s is %s.", SearchString,lszSearchData);
AfxMessageBox( DisplayBuf);
```

Microsoft currently supports the twelve fields listed in Table 18.5.

The Comments string provides additional information that you can use to display diagnostic messages. The resource compiler does not require a value, but you could use the value to store information about the program.The CompanyName field contains your company's name. The resource compiler requires a value to create the resource. In Chapter 19 we will show you how to let your users enter a value for their company name at install time. The FileDescription field describes the file to the user, and the resource compiler requires this string. The FileVersion string contains this file's version number. The resource compiler requires a value for this string. The InternalName string contains the internal name of the file, if one exists. This should be the original filename without the extension, and the resource compiler requires you to supply a value. The LegalCopyright field contains all the copyright notices for the file. You do not need to supply a value for this string. You also do not need to enter a value for the LegalTrademarks field. This field contains all the trademarks that apply to this file. The OriginalFileName field contains the file's original filename, as installed. This allows the application to tell if the user has renamed the file; you must supply a value for this field. The PrivateBuild string describes why this is a private build. The resource compiler only requires a value for this string if you set the VS_FF_PRIVATEBUILD flag in the dwFileFlags field of the fixed-information structure, VS_FIXEDFILEINFO. The ProductName string specifies the name of the parent product that requires this file. You must supply a

TABLE 18.5
StringFileInfo fields.

```
Comments
CompanyName
FileDescription
FileVersion
InternalName
LegalCopyright
LegalTrademarks
OriginalFileName
PrivateBuild
ProductName
ProductVersion
SpecialBuild
```

value. The ProductVersion string specifies the version of the product and requires a value. Finally, the SpecialBuild string states why this is a special build. This string is required only if the VS_FF_SPECIALBUILD flag has been set in the dwFileFlags field of the fixed-information structure, VS_FIXEDFILEINFO.

THE ABOUT BOX

Version information is invaluable at installation time, where you can use the version API functions in a home-grown installation program to determine which files to copy to your user's system. (Fortunately, Microsoft has made available a toolkit to automate a program's installation, as detailed in Chapter 19.) Yet version information is also important at run time, to display to your users. One appropriate place to display such information is in your application's About Box, as shown in Figure 18.2.

MFC will provide your application with a very basic About Box, as illustrated. This section will show you how to add version and resource information to your application's About Box to give the user data about your application.

The first steps are to decide what information to give the user and how to arrange the information in the About Box. You should include the application's icon, the amount of free resources available, the copyright notice, and, if available, the registered user's name and company. (Chapter 19 will show you how to include this type of information.) Figure 18.3 shows the demo's enhanced About Box. For this example, most of the text displayed in the About Box dialog box will be static text. App Studio usually gives these strings the ID of IDC_STATIC, as shown in the properties box in Figure 18.4.

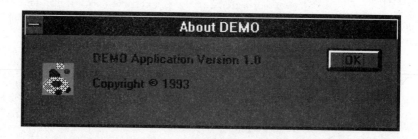

Figure 18.2
Demo application's default About Box.

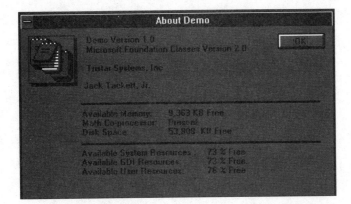

Figure 18.3
Demo application's
enhanced About Box.

The information that can change, such as free memory available, will also be static text, but each string will have a unique string identifier. You give each a unique identifier to use to change its text during the About Box dialog's OnInitDialog member function. You will use the SetDlgTextItem member function to change the default string hardcoded into the dialog resource with the new string containing the appropriate information. SetDlgItemText has the following prototype:

```
void SetDlgItemText( int nID, LPCSTR lpszString);
```

where *nID* identifies the control ID in the dialog resource whose text you will set, and *lpszString* points to either a CString variable or a null-terminated string containing the text you will copy to the control. The following code illustrates how to calculate the memory available resource string and how to format and copy the text to the dialog control for display:

```
CString str, strFmt;
strFmt.LoadString(IDS_AVAIL_MEM);
sprintf(str.GetBuffer(80), strFmt, GetFreeSpace(0) / 1024L);
str.ReleaseBuffer();
SetDlgItemText(IDC_AVAIL_MEM, str);
```

As you can tell from the code, the function uses a format string that is itself a string resource, with the ID of IDS_AVAIL_MEM, instead of using a hardcoded format string, in the sprintf function call. For the version information, you can simply use the functions illustrated in the beginning of this chapter to retrieve the version strings and then call SetDlgTextItem to place the strings in the dialog box at the designated place. The next snippet of code illustrates placing the copyright information into the About Box.

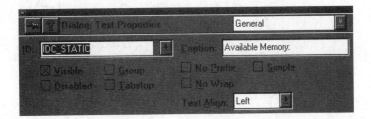

Figure 18.4
Properties box
of a static string
in App Studio.

```
// Fill in the copyright information

BYTE abData[512];
DWORD  handle;
DWORD  dwSize;
LPBYTE lpBuffer;
char szName[512];
UINT FAR dsz;
DWORD FAR *lpdwTranslationInfo;
UINT uLen, uLangID, uCharSetID;
char szStringFileInfo[50];
LPCSTR szCopyRight;

dwSize = GetFileVersionInfoSize("demo.exe", &handle);

GetFileVersionInfo("demo.exe", handle, dwSize, abData);

VerQueryValue(abData, "\\VarFileInfo\\Translation",
    (void __far *__far *)&lpdwTranslationInfo, &uLen);
uLangID = LOWORD( *lpdwTranslationInfo);
uCharSetID = HIWORD(*lpdwTranslationInfo);

if (dwSize!=0)
{
  sprintf(szName,"\\StringFileInfo\\%04x%04x\\CopyRight",
      uLangID,uCharSetID);
  VerQueryValue(abData, szName, (void __far *__far *)&szCopyRight, &uLen);
}
SetDlgItemText(IDC_COPYRIGHT, szCopyRight );
```

You may also wish to display in your application's About Box the percentage of free Windows resource currently available. You would need to add such a report line to your About Box dialog and give the data item a unique ID. Then you call the Windows 3.1 specific SDK function ::GetFreeSystemResources. This function takes the parameters listed in Table 18.6 and returns an unsigned integer indicating the percentage of free system resources.

You should use this function only for information display, not to determine if an application has enough resources to run. This function was not available in Windows 3.0, so if you use it in a 3.0 environment, you will need to explicately load the routine.

```
CString  format;
UINT pcent_all = ::GetFreeSystemResources( GFSR_SYSTEMRESOURCES );
UINT pcent_gdi = ::GetFreeSystemResources( GFSR_GDIRESOURCES );
UINT pcent_usr = ::GetFreeSystemResources( GFSR_USERRESOURCES );
char str[80];

sprintf(str,"Free system resources = %d%%",pcent_all);
SetDlgItemText(IDC_FREE_SYSRES, str );

sprintf(str,"Free GDI resources = %d%%",pcent_gdi);
SetDlgItemText(IDC_FREE_GDIRES, str );

sprintf(str,"Free USER resources = %d%%",pcent_usr);
SetDlgItemText(IDC_FREE_USRRES, str );
```

TABLE 18.6
GetFreeSystemResources parameter values.

PARAMETERS	DESCRIPTIONS
GFSR_SYSTEMRESOURCES	Returns the percentage of free space for system resources.
GFSR_GDIRESOURCES	Returns the percentage of free space for GDI resources.
GFSR_USERRESOURCES	Returns the percentage of free space for USER resources.

FORMATTING

The code in the previous section that displays the amount of memory available will display a single (preferably) large number with no separators between the thousands. In the United States, this separator is the comma, but in other parts of the world, this separator can be other characters like the period. To make Windows portable to other cultures, Microsoft provided developers with the ability to query the value of various separators by placing them and their current values in the [intl] section of the WIN.INI file. The ID thousandths corresponds to the thousandths separator used in numeric quantities, as illustrated here:

```
[intl]
sLanguage=enu
sCountry=United States
sThousands=,
```

The following function will format a number with the appropriate separator and will pass back a string that you can display to the user:

```
void FmtThousandths( DWORD Value, char *buffer )
{
char temp[80];   // temp string
char thsep;  // the character to use as the thousands separator.
int ip = 0, op = 0;  // string indices
int len;  // length of printed string, before separator added

// first get the thousands separator from the win.ini file
// use a comma as the default separator.
::GetProfileString("intl","sthousands", "," temp,sizeof (temp) );
thsep = temp[0];

sprintf(temp, "%.0Lf",Value);
len = strlen(temp);

do
{
    buffer[op++] = temp[ip++];
    —len;
    if ( (len > 0) && (0 == ( len % 3 ) ) )
      buffer[op++] = thsep;
  }
```

```
        while( len >= 0 );

        while ( 0 != temp[ip] )
            buffer[op++] = temp[ip++];
        buffer[op] = '\0';

    }
```

You can then add a call to this function for each numeric quantity in your application to provide a string that is easy for your users to decipher at a glance, rather than mentally adding commas. You can also enhance the function in several ways, such as overloading a function to format a financial value with the currency symbol and with negative value symbols. Another change you could make is to overload the first parameter so that you can use any numeric data type. You could also pass the separator character to the function rather than rereading the .INI file each time you call the function. To do this you could query the .INI file at start-up, save the various international delimiters as data members in your application object, and then merely retrieve the values and send them to the function.

CHAPTER SUMMARY

This chapter described the version resource information available in Windows versions 3.1 and higher. We showed you how to access this information to adapt your program at run time. You also learned how to display version information to your users, such as in your application's About Box, complete with some special numeric formatting tips. Please note that you can also use these techniques to display information in an application's start-up splash screen. See the sample code, or the MFC SUPERPAD example program, for an example of a splash screen.

Setup

First impressions are important, and your users' first impressions will originate with how well your application installs. So you want your program to put its best foot forward at installation, allowing the user to get up and running with as few distractions as possible. Fortunately, Microsoft provides the Setup Toolkit with which you can create a professional-looking, Windows-based installation program. This Setup Toolkit is part of the C7.0 SDK, although, if you purchased Visual C++, the toolkit was not included. You can download the files from CompuServe, from the Microsoft Languages library (GO MSLANG). Search the library for the files setupd.zip (the documentation) and setup.zip (the example files). Most of the material in this chapter is based on Microsoft's Setup Toolkit for Windows manual and the sample files included with the toolkit.

This chapter will give you a broad overview of the Setup Toolkit, but it is not a replacement for its documentation. You will also find the sample files invaluable when creating your own installation programs.

You also have several other alternatives for setup support. Commercial products have automated installation, both in an MS-DOS or MS Windows environment. Microsoft's Visual Basic probably has the easiest example setup program, which you can modify for prototypes. The Visual Basic example is not very robust, however, but it is an excellent way to prototype an application's installation program for demonstrations to your upper management or customers.

VERSION INFORMATION

Chapter 18 demonstrated the version resource information. This information is useful because Microsoft places a great deal of Windows functionality in .DLLs. Thus you only need to distribute the new .DLL, not the entire system, for updates. Table 19.1 lists the files you, as a developer, can distribute with your application.

TABLE 19.1
Files developers may distribute.

FILE	DESCRIPTION
COMMDLG.DLL	Contains the Common Dialog box library.
DDEML.DLL	The Dynamic Data Exchange library.
LZEXPAND.DLL	Lemple-Zev file (de)compression library.
MFC200.DLL	MFC application support via a .DLL, instead of statically linked libraries. This allows for smaller application .EXE files.
OLECLI.DLL	Object Linking and Embedding client library.
OLESVR.DLL	OLE server library. Note: At presstime, MFC 2.0 supports only OLE 1.0.
PENWIN.DLL	Pen for Windows library.
SHELL.DLL	The Shell application library.
STRESS.DLL	Stress-testing library.
TOOLHELP.DLL	Developer tools library.
VER.DLL	Contains the version-checking library.
WINMEM32.DLL	32-bit memory support library.
GRAPH.VBX	Visual Basic Graph control.
GRID.VBX	Visual Basic Grid control. Most, if not all, VBX suppliers license you to ship the .VBX file with your application.

Why check version information? Simple: What if you have a new and improved .DLL that the user needs to run your application? You would like to detect this and copy the file to the user's system. If the files were the same version, however, then you would not want to waste the time to copy the file. If your file is older, you probably don't want to copy the file either. See Chapter 18 for more information on the version resource.

SETUP

The Setup Toolkit uses a script language and dialog boxes that you design. A run-time version of Microsoft Test interprets this language. Microsoft provides this program with the toolkit (_MSTEST.EXE). The following paragraphs describe the basic toolkit components.

SETUP.EXE is the bootstrap program that copies needed files to a temporary directory on the user's hard drive. SETUP.EXE performs the actual installation. After installing the system, the program will delete all temporary files. The installation kit requires that this file be on the first disk, and you must not compress it.

_MSTEST.EXE is a run-time version of Microsoft's Microsoft Test product. This program, which is required, interprets your supplied script file to install your product. This file should be on your first installation script.

SETUP.LST is a sample file that contains the files that SETUP.EXE will copy to the temporary directory. You should create your script file first and then modify the SETUP.LST file to match your .MST file. SETUP.LST will have two sections: [Params] and [Files]. The *Params* section lets you specify various items, including the amount of disk space that SETUP will need for the temporary files; the title of the window that displays while the program initializes; and the command line with which you will invoke _MSTEST. (This command line will be the name of your *script file.MST* and some parameters.) You must *not* change the last line in the *Params* section that sets the DrvModName to DSHELL, but you should change the other values to reflect your installation requirements.

The *Files* section is a list of the files that SETUP.EXE will copy to the temporary directory: your script file (.MST), your .INF file, SETUPAPI.INC, all .DLLs, and _MSTEST.EXE. These files must be on the first disk. You can compress all the files except SETUP.EXE and SETUP.LST.

SETUP INCLUDE FILES

.INC files contain variables and function declarations needed by your setup script. Any files you include in your script must be on your first installation disk. The SETUPAPI.INC file is required; it contains the most commonly used declarations. MSDETEC.INC is also required if you use any of the functions in MSDETSTF.DLL. MSREGDB.INC is required if you intend to use the registration database routines. If you include both this file and the MSSHARED.INC file, then you must include the MSREGDB.INC file first. The MSSHARED.INC file contains the declarations for the functions used to update shared system files. You must include this file if you use the functions in the MSSHLSTF.DLL library.

SAMPLE SCRIPT FILES

The toolkit includes three sample script files that illustrate various setup scenarios you may encounter. You can modify these samples to create your own script files. Your .MST file must be on the first disk. The .MST file and all the .INC files must be listed in your SETUP.LST file.

SETUP'S .DLLs

The toolkit includes sample dialogs via their resource files and their .C implementation files. The kit also provides six .DLLs, containing useful routines for items like detecting the user's current environment, copying files, and modifying .INI files. These six files are required. The MSUILSTF.DLL contains the user interface library responsible for displaying and manipulating dialog boxes. MSSHLSTF.DLL contains the shell library that manages the frame window. The MSINSSTF.DLL contains the install library that handles installing files to the user's hard disk. MSDETSTF.DLL contains the detection library that supplies Setup with information about the user's system. You must create the MSCUISTF.DDL. This library will provide the routines to manipulate the dialogs you create for your installation program. The next .DLL file, MSCOMSTF.DLL, contains the supporting routines for the common dialog boxes. The final .DLL is VER.DLL, which is required if you want the user to be able to install the application on a Windows 3.0 system.

You can create a set of customized routines not included in MSCUISTF.DLL and place them in a custom DLL. You will need to include this file in your SETUP.LST list. Then you will need to declare the functions in your script file (.MST) in this format: DECLARE FUNCTION function-name LIB "dllname.dll" (arg1%, arg2%) AS VALUE. For example:

```
DECLARE FUNCTION DelDir LIB "filefunc.dll" (arg1%, arg2%) AS INTEGER
```

The DSKLAYT.EXE and DSKLAYT2.EXE programs help you create the installation disks you ship to your customers.

The MS-DOS program _MSSETUP.EXE allows you to update Window system files that may be in use when a user tries to install your program. This file reads an MS-DOS batch file, MSSETUP.BAT, that updates the necessary files. The Setup function calls ExitExecRestart to exit Windows, run MSSETUP.BAT, and then restart Windows. Note that this function is only available for Windows version 3.1 or higher. If you are installing to Windows 3.0, then you will need to tell the user, via a message box, to shut down Windows and manually execute MSSETUP.BAT to update the system files. If you use it, _MSSETUP.EXE must be on your first installation disk.

TESTDRVR.HLP

This Windows Help file for the developer explains the various MSTEST functions demonstrated in the sample setup scripts.

STEPS FOR CREATING A SETUP SCRIPT

Step One

To create a setup program, you must first identify the files your application will need. Then for each file you must decide if it is unique or will be shared among a family of applications. Is the file a system file or a shared file? Then you will wish to check for prior versions before blindly copying the file to the user's hard disk. If the file is currently in use, you may have to use the _MSSETUP.EXE program to complete the installation.

You must decide if the user can choose not to install the file. Perhaps you have sample files that consume large amounts of disk space; you could allow the user the choice whether to load this group of files now or later.

Step Two

The next step is to design the directory structure of your application. You must decide if all the files will reside in one subdirectory, or if some will reside in a main subdirectory and others in subordinate directories. An example would be the library, include, and sample subdirectories found in the MSVC directory. You will need to place some files, like an application's .INI file, or system files like .VBXs, in the Windows or Windows\System directories.

Step Three

The third step is to identify the possible responses you will require from the user, including, as mentioned earlier, whether the user is allowed to decide which files to install. Will you allow the user to enter a company name and user name that you stamp into an application's version resource? Will the user be able to decide in which directory to install your application? All these choices will require a dialog box to display information and choices and then to retrieve the responses. You may also wish to include message boxes along the way. You can use the boxes to suggest that your users send in their registration cards or to alert them that a file is being deleted. These items too will require dialog boxes. This step will give you an idea of which sample script to modify in later steps.

Step Four

Once you have identified the resources needed, you must then identify the controls you will need. This step will help you pick which dialog templates to modify. Table 19.2 provides a list of dialogs provided in the dialog.rc.

Each dialog usually displays your application's icon. Some templates will have from one to four command buttons that allow the user to continue, exit the process, go back to the previous dialog, or request Help.

Using App Studio

You can use App Studio to lay out your dialogs, but the Setup Toolkit is an SDK-based product, so you will have to make some changes. First, the toolkit splits the resources into two files: DIALOGS.DLG and DIALOGS.RC. The .RC file contains the version information. It includes the dialogs.dlg file as part of the include section. To use App Studio you will need to combine the .DLG and .RC files. Then merge the DIALOGS.H files supplied by the toolkit and created by App Studio. You will need to modify the supplied dialog procedures, too, since you will not be able to use ClassWizard to modify the various dialogs' actions. To modify the procedures, you will have to modify the DLGPROCS.C file. Chapter 2 of the Setup Toolkit for Windows documentation describes the available functions supplied. You can also investigate these functions in the sample source code files. The toolkit does not limit you to these routines, because you can add functions as needed to this file for inclusion into the user interface library (.DLL). Finally, you will have to modify the supplied makefile to reflect the changes made to the various files. This makefile will create a customized user interface library called MSCUISTF.DLL. You can also create your own .DLLs.

Step Five

Next, you will write your setup script file. To help with this process, Microsoft provides three sample script files and their associated .INF files. (More on .INF files later.) You can modify these files to create your own setup script.

The first sample script file, SAMPLE1.MST, shows how to set up a simple installation. SAMPLE2.MST illustrates how to set up an application with various options. The final sample, SAMPLE3.MST, details how to set up programs that contain shared files that may require the user to shut down Windows and use _MSSETUP to finish the installation process.

TABLE 19.2
List of dialogs provided with the Setup Toolkit.

APPHELP	A sample dialog to display a Help message.
ASKQUIT	Warns the user that the installation is incomplete.
BADPATH	Tells the user the response is invalid.
CDALREADYUSED	Warning that this product has been previously installed. This template has two edit fields to place data from the version resource into the dialog.
CDBADFILE	Same as CDALREADYUSED without the edit fields.
CDBADNAME	Tells the user that a response is required.
CDBADORG	Tells the user that a company name is required.
CDCONFIRMINFO	Displays the company or user name information entered by the user and asks if the data is correct.
CDGETNAME	Contains an edit field for the user's name.
CDGETNAMEORG	A dialog to collect both the user's name and organization.
CDGETORG	Contains an edit field for the user's company name.
CHECK	A simple dialog with three check boxes.
CUSTINST	A complicated dialog that lets the user customize their installation.
DESTPATH	Contains an edit field for the user's destination path choice.
EXITFAILURE	Alerts the user that something bad happened and that the install failed. This is one screen you hope your user never sees!
EXITQUIT	Similiar to EXITFAILURE, but this dialog is displayed in response to the user's wish to exit, instead of a catastrophic failure.
EXITSUCCESS	A dialog you hope your users always see.
EXTENDEDLIST	A dialog that contains a simple multilist box.
MODELESS	A sample modeless dialog for use with the FModelessDlgProc Setup script command. Use these dialogs to display messages, like "Now would be a good time to Register." while the program is copying files.
MULTILIST	A sample dialog using a multiple selection list box.
OPTIONS	A simple radio button dialog.
SINGLELIST	Selecting a single item from a list.
TOOBIG	Tells the user the selected files are too big for the selected drive. You should remind the user to check for adequate disk space for attempting to install any program.
WELCOME	A dialog to welcome the user to your installation program.

Once you've modified the appropriate script file, you will need to modify the SETUP.LST file to include your .MST file. SETUP.EXE will read this file to figure out which files to copy to the user's hard disk.

The Disk Layout Utilities create the .INF files. Microsoft suggests that you let these utilities modify the .INF files, rather than your doing the modifications. The format of the file is very strict, and it may not recover from syntax errors. These files state the properties each file will have when copied to the user's system.

Step Six

Now copy all your files into the directory structure you created. The Disk Layout Utilities will then allow you to define each file's special properties. These utilities will also create the images you will place on your installation disks. This process will also create the .INF file. These utilities will help you specify which files to place on which distribution disk and which files you can compress to save space.

Step Seven

Finally, you should test your setup installation by installing the application on a variety of systems under various situations. You can create your distribution disks once you are satisfied with the setup program.

CREATING THE SETUP SCRIPT FILE

Designing a trouble-free installation process is your primary concern. Next to the packaging, installation is the first impression your users will get of your application. So, before you start modifying one of the sample script files, you should ask yourself some questions and identify the various parts of the installation process and their associated risks. You can group items of concern into two areas: hardware related and software related.

Areas of concern include: Does the user have enough disk space to install your product? Will you give the user a choice of which parts to install? Does the user need a specific piece of hardware to run your application? Will you warn the user or abort the installation if a needed hardware item is missing? Other items you should be aware of include installing sharable files; installing system files that may require special exit procedures; and modifying the user's .INI files.

SETUP SCRIPT SECTIONS

Once you have a general idea of what your installation program requires, you can write your setup script. You can do it from scratch, but you'll be better off modifying one of the sample scripts included with the toolkit. Answering the questions in the previous section will give you a general idea of which sample to modify. The next few paragraphs describe each section of a setup script you can modify.

INCLUDE FILES

The beginning of each sample contains an include section. Here you list the .INC files your setup script will need. The Microsoft Test command to include a file is:

```
'$INCLUDE 'setupapi.inc'
```

Note the single quotation mark around commands. To mark a line as a comment, you would precede it by two single quotation marks, as follows:

```
'' this is a comment, rather than a command
```

You must enclose string variables in double quotation marks.

DIALOG BOX CONSTANTS

This section declares the resource IDs of each dialog box you intend to use in your program. They have the form of CONST *DIALOG* = ID VALUE. For example:

```
CONST WELCOME = 100
```

INITIALIZATION AND THE SYMBOL TABLE

In the initialization section, you will set the title that appears in the installation window's caption. You can set the bitmap logo for your program. You will initialize any variables you will need here, such as strings and integers. To store these variables, the setup program creates a temporary storage area called a Symbol Table. Setup will automatically create and initialize three variables when it begins. They are STF_SRCDIR, STF_CWDDIR, and STF_SRCINFPATH. STF_SRCDIR is a string that holds the source directory. STF_CWDDIR holds either the current working directory or the temporary setup directory. STF_SRCINFPATH holds the path for the .INF file. Microsoft recommends you clear all the String Table entries after you use them, to conserve memory. The initialization code will also read the .INF file to set various variables, as we described earlier. The code will also tell the program which files to copy and whether they need decompressing. The code will then set the needed files' attributes. You will also prototype your .DLL functions in this section.

SUBROUTINES

After the initialization section of the file, you will find the subroutines to execute your dialog box functions. This section will remind you of a BASIC program. You must preface each procedure with a name followed by a colon (e.g., WELCOME:).

THE INSTALL SUBROUTINE

The install subroutine, declared in the declaration section as a SUB, is the heart of the install process. In this subroutine you call the various setup script procedures to perform your application's installation. Chapter 5 in the Setup Toolkit manual details all the setup procedures available to the developer. The samples will show you how to add items to the WIN.INI file and how to add groups to Program Manager. You will also see how to add items to program groups. SAMPLE3.MST will show you how to install shared and system files, which can be tricky. Also make sure you read the supplied Readme files because they contain important information left out of the documentation. Especially look over the README.WRI file that contains updates to the manual detailing the various setup procedures and their parameters.

CUSTOM INFORMATION

One item the samples don't illustrate is how to stamp a program with custom information, like company name and user name (see Figure 19.1). In Chapter 18 we described how to retrieve version resource information and display it to the user.

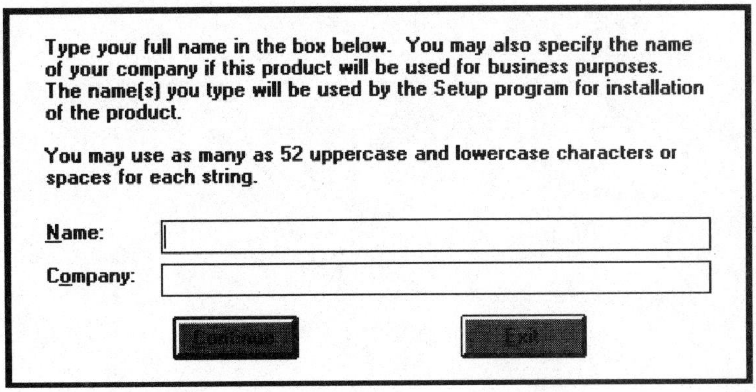

Figure 19.1
User name and
company request
dialog.

Now we will show you how to collect information from the user and use it to overwrite information already in a resource. The Knowledge Base article Q92525—"Using the Setup Toolkit Function StampResource( )" contains most of this information. Also see Chapter 17 for information on how to access Microsoft's Knowledge Base.

The first step is to include enough empty bytes in your program's resources to hold the strings you plan to add at install time. The size is up to you, but you must make sure your dialog limits the users to fewer than the allowed number of characters! Once you have the information, you will call the StampResource setup script procedure. Here's the syntax of this command:

```
StampResource szSection$,szKey$,szDst$,wResType%,wResId%,szData$,cbData%
```

PARAMETERS

The szSection$ specifies the section in the .INF file that contains the description line of the file to be modified, usually your application .EXE file. As we stated earlier, you use the disk layout tools to create the .INF file. The file will contain various sections identified by names located between "[ ]," just like a typical Windows .INI file.

The szKey$ string specifies the reference key to the description line of the file being modified. This string is the first item on a line describing the file to be installed. This name will be enclosed in quotes. You will learn more about the .INF file later in this chapter. The szDst$ contains the destination directory where the file is currently located, (i.e., where it has been installed). The wResType% specifies the resource identification type. This example uses strings, or type 6. Table 19.3 lists the possible type values.

wResId% specifies the resource identification number and, in the case of string resources, identifies the beginning string table segment. szData% contains the data you wish to stamp into the resource, and cbData% is the size of that data, in bytes. If cdData% is less than or equal to the original size of the resource segment, StampResource will overwrite the data. If cbData is greater than the original size, then the function will fail.

STRINGS

To make life easier, your resource strings, type 6, should be consecutive in the resource string table. The reason is that StampResouce copies bytes, not resources

TABLE 19.3
Resource identification types.

TYPE NUMBER	TYPES
1	CURSOR
2	BITMAP
3	ICON
4	MENU
5	DIALOG
6	STRING
7	FONTDIR
8	FONT
9	ACCELERATOR
10	RCDATA
12	GROUP_CURSOR
14	GROUP_ICON
16	VERSION

(i.e., it does not overwrite a string ID; it overwrites bytes). Also, the resource compiler stores string tables in segments, each containing exactly 16 strings. The resource compiler will group strings with the same upper 12 bits into the same segment. The resource compiler also stores strings with a size value in the first byte followed by the rest of the characters in the string, up to 255 characters.

Not only should your strings be consecutive, but the first string resource ID should be a value for which the first nibble equals 0x00. This assures us that it and the following IDs are in the same segment. You usually declare these values in the resource.h file, but you can also use the App Studio resource editor to place the "modifiable" strings in their own segment. Never place read-only strings in the same segment with "modifiable" strings. You could do this by specifying a string ID = 0x4500 in the string table, as shown in Figure 19.2.

STAMP THE RESOURCE

To write the new strings over the old strings in that segment, fill in szData$ with the length of each string, followed by the string entered by the user. Make sure to concatenate the strings in the order of their associated IDs. The resulting length of szData, to be placed in cbData%, should *not* exceed the size of the original segment. A piece of sample code is worth a thousand muddled words, so take a look at this:

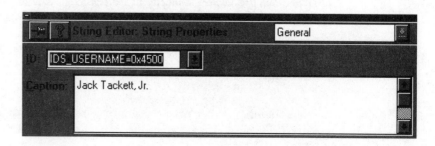

Figure 19.2
String table editor.

```
// bound to your application by the resource compiler
// contents of resource.h
IDS_COMPANY_NAME          0x4500    //1st nibble should be 0
IDS_USER_NAME             0x4501    // strings must be consecutive

// contents of .RC file
STRINGTABLE DISCARDABLE
BEGIN
  IDS_COMPANY_NAME        "                               " // padding! 52
  IDS_USER_NAME           "                          "
END

// section of SETUP.MST, collect strings from user for company and name
DEST$ = '' the path to the application's .exe.
szUser$ = "Jack Tackett, Jr." ''normally a value from a dialog box.
szCo$ = "TriStar Systems, Inc." ''usually from a dialog, too.
'' now build the buffer to overwrite the data. remember to place the
'' size of string first.
szBuffer$ = CHR$(LEN(szUser$))+szUser$+CHR$(LEN(szCo$))+szCo$

'' now stamp the resource
''szSection = "Files", szKey = "gen", szDst = DEST$, wResType = 6,
'' wResId% = &H451
'' H=hex, 45 = 1st 12 bits plus a 1, szData = szbuffer$, cbData=
LEN(szbuffer$)

StampResource "Files", "gen", DEST$, 6, &H451, szbuffer$, LEN(szbuffer)
```

LAYOUT TOOLS

You've heard a lot of talk about the .INF file and the layout tools that create it. This file describes the files on your installation disks. The format of this file is very rigid, so let the tools create it for you. They will also maintain the .INF file throughout your development cycle. Thus you do not have to create one from scratch every time you add a file or modify a file's attributes. An .INF file will have a minimum of three sections: Source Media Descriptions, File Descriptions, and Default File Settings.

The Source Media Descriptions section describes each of the disks in your installation set, with one line per disk. The File Descriptions section describes each of your files, giving such information as a reference key (the value of the szKey$ parameter to StampResource), file attributes, and whether Setup compressed the file on the disk. If you do not provide default values, then the Default File Settings section will describe the defaults that Setup will use to install a file. Appendix A of the Setup Toolkit manual describes the layout of the .INF file.

THE DSKLAYT PROGRAM

You should never have to directly edit this file. You will use the Windows program DskLayt. This program allows you to list the files needed to install your product. The tool also lets you set layout time options, such as where the program can place the file and the file's attributes. You can specify the section and reference key at layout time, too.

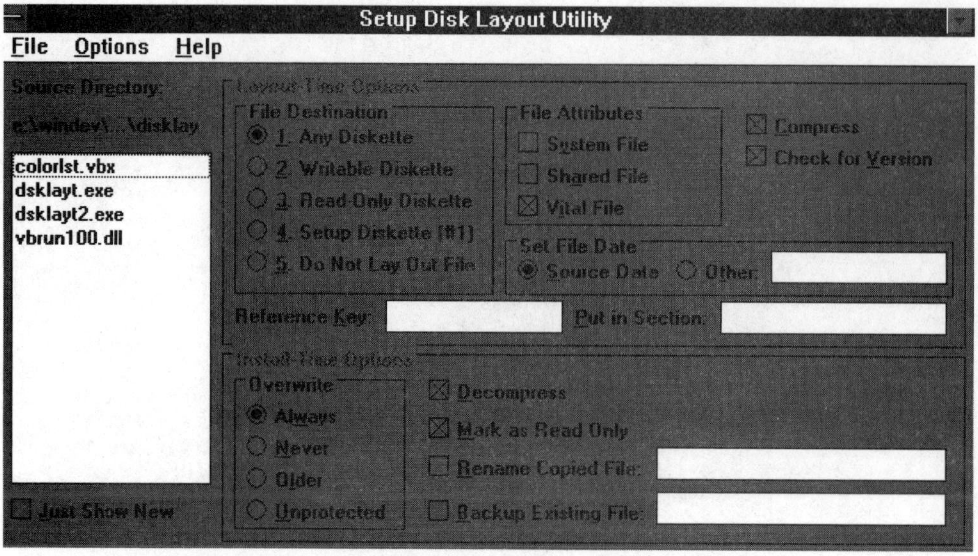

Figure 19.3
The DlkLayt
tool.

The tool will also let you set install time options. This setting includes such parameters as indicating whether to back up an existing file before overwriting that file.

Once you've created a layout file, you can modify it later without creating a new one. This allows you to add, delete, or change settings on your installation files. Once you have the files and their properties set, you will need to create disk images to copy to diskettes, and an .INF file for your setup program. Figure 19.3 gives you an illustration of this tool.

THE DSKLAYT2 TOOL

Microsoft provides a second program to accomplish the tasks discussed in the previous section. This program is an MS-DOS–based application that reads the file created by DskLayt and creates an image of each disk that you can copy to floppies for shipment.

CHAPTER SUMMARY

Projecting a professional image, whether for in-house developed software or commercial applications, will instill confidence in your users. Microsoft's toolkit helps developers produce a robust and professional-looking installation program. By following the demo application's setup program and the samples provided with the toolkit, you can give your users a fantastic first impression.

Index